W9-CHB-996

The ECONOMICS of *Comparable Worth*

Mark R. Killingsworth
Rutgers University

1990

W.E. UPJOHN INSTITUTE for Employment Research
Kalamazoo, Michigan

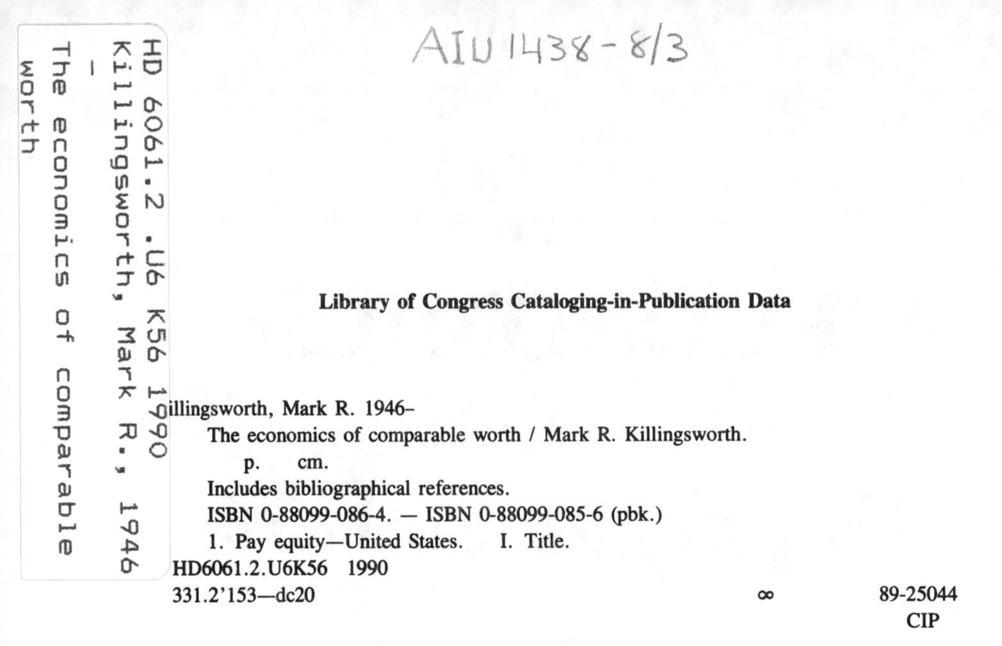

Library of Congress Cataloging-in-Publication Data

Killingsworth, Mark R. 1946–
The economics of comparable worth / Mark R. Killingsworth.
p. cm.
Includes bibliographical references.
ISBN 0-88099-086-4. — ISBN 0-88099-085-6 (pbk.)
1. Pay equity—United States. I. Title.
HD6061.2.U6K56 1990
331.2'153—dc20 ∞ 89-25044
CIP

THE INSTITUTE, a nonprofit research organization, was established on July 1, 1945. It is an activity of the W. E. Upjohn Unemployment Trustee Corporation, which was formed in 1932 to administer a fund set aside by the late Dr. W. E. Upjohn for the purpose of carrying on "research into the causes and effects of unemployment and measures for the alleviation of unemployment."

The facts presented in this study and the observations and viewpoints expressed are the sole responsibility of the author. They do not necessarily represent positions of the W. E. Upjohn Institute for Employment Research.

To Katherine and Siân

THE AUTHOR

Mark R. Killingsworth is professor of economics at Rutgers University and research economist at the National Bureau of Economic Research. His research interests include employment discrimination, labor supply, wage differentials and immigration. He has served as a consultant to parties involved in litigation under Title VII of the Civil Rights Act, including the Equal Employment Opportunity Commission, the Department of Labor and the Department of Justice. He has testified on immigration issues before the U.S. Senate Committee on the Judiciary and on comparable worth before the Joint Economic Committee of the U.S. Congress. He has a B.A. from the University of Michigan and M.Phil. and D.Phil. degrees from the University of Oxford, where he was a Rhodes Scholar.

PREFACE

This study was supported by a grant from the W.E. Upjohn Institute for Employment Research. I am deeply grateful to the Upjohn Institute; to Saul Blaustein, who was originally responsible for overseeing my work under the Institute's grant; and to Robert Spiegelman, executive director of the Institute, who saw things through to completion after Mr. Blaustein's retirement and provided me with invaluable comments, assistance, advice and well-deserved nagging. Funds for travel to Australia (in connection with the analyses presented in chapter 5) were provided by the Sloan Foundation; it is a pleasure to thank Al Rees and Michael Teitelbaum of the Sloan Foundation for its support in this connection. As indicated at the beginning of each chapter, I have received numerous suggestions from many individuals.

CONTENTS

LIST OF TABLES

LIST OF FIGURES

1

Introduction

Comparable worth was one of the most hotly debated employment issues of the 1980s, and seems certain to provoke controversy into the 1990s. Its supporters range from the National Organization for Women to the Association of Junior Leagues, from the AFL-CIO to the staunchly conservative Republican mayor of Colorado Springs, Colorado. Opponents have called it "socialism in drag"; one Federal judge has contended that it is "pregnant with the possibility of disrupting the entire economic system of the United States of America." Several bills before Congress have called for studies of the federal civil service pay structure along comparable worth lines. The 1988 Democratic platform endorsed comparable worth; the Republican platform rejected it.

The basic notion underlying comparable worth is simple: jobs of the same worth should receive the same pay. (An obvious corollary is that jobs of different worth can legitimately receive different pay.) In a sense, the concept is long established: since the late nineteenth century, the "worth" of different jobs has been a concern of personnel managers, industrial psychologists, industrial engineers and others responsible for developing pay systems.

In a different sense, however, comparable worth is a relatively recent development stemming from concerns about the labor market status of women. Present day advocates of comparable worth (or "pay equity," as it is sometimes called)[1] readily agree that predominantly female jobs such as nursing, teaching or library work differ from predominantly male jobs such as plumbing, tree trimming or truck driving. However, they argue that predominantly female jobs are all too often paid considerably less than predominantly male jobs that, although dissimilar in

I thank Cordelia W. Reimers and M. Anne Hill for comments and suggestions on previous drafts of this introduction.

terms of their functions and duties, are nevertheless comparable in terms of a composite of factors such as skill, effort, responsibility and working conditions, and that such underpayment of women's jobs is discriminatory.[2] Nor is this problem likely to be alleviated by other means, say the proponents: the average earnings of full time, year round female workers have remained at about two-thirds of the figure for similar male workers—essentially unchanged for the past 20 or 25 years—and other kinds of antidiscrimination measures (e.g., Title VII of the Civil Rights Act, the Equal Pay Act, Executive Order 11246) can be expected to work slowly if at all in alleviating labor market discrimination. Hence the case for a new antidiscrimination remedy: comparable worth.

Comparable worth received a degree of official recognition when, at the end of the Carter administration, the National Research Council's Committee on Occupational Classification and Analysis issued a report, commissioned by the Equal Employment Opportunity Commission, which endorsed the concept in measured but unequivocal terms (Treiman and Hartmann, eds., 1981, pp. 66–7):

> The committee is convinced by the evidence, taken together, that women are systematically underpaid. Policies designed to promote equal access to all employment opportunities will affect the underpayment of women workers only slowly. Equal access to employment opportunities may be expected to be more effective for new entrants than for established workers and more effective for those who have invested less in skills than for those who have invested more. Since many women currently in the labor force have invested years of training time in their particular skills (e.g., nursing, teaching, librarianship, and secretarial work), access to other jobs (e.g., physicianship, plumbing, engineering, or sales) may not be preferred. For these reasons the committee believes that the strategy of "comparable worth," that is, equal pay for jobs of equal worth, merits consideration as an alternative policy of intervention in the pay-setting process wherever women are systematically underpaid.

Both before and after the NRC report, proponents of comparable worth attempted to advance the concept—primarily focusing on state and local government employment – both by litigation under Title VII of the Civil Rights Act and by lobbying (e.g., legislation, changes in union contracts, administrative revision of pay scales). The latter route has produced considerably more success for comparable worth advocates than the former.

Most court cases alleging discrimination against women on the grounds that predominantly female jobs were paid less than comparable male jobs have gone against female plaintiffs. In general, the federal courts have been unwilling to declare such situations to be discriminatory, even when the plaintiffs could present evidence, based on job evaluations,[3] that the predominantly female and predominantly male jobs in question were indeed "comparable."

A relatively early example is *Christensen v. Iowa* (563 F.2d 353 (8th Cir. 1977)), in which predominantly female clerical workers at the University of Northern Iowa argued that they had been discriminated against because their jobs received lower pay than predominantly male physical plant jobs even though the university's job evaluation system put the two job categories in the same labor grade and assigned equal point values to both. The university argued that the wage difference simply reflected different wage rates prevailing in the external labor market, and the Eighth Circuit Court of Appeals apparently agreed, saying, "We do not interpret Title VII as requiring an employer to ignore the market in setting wage rates for genuinely different work classifications." Similar cases (e.g., *Lemons v. City and County of Denver*,[4] in which nurses employed by the City of Denver argued that their jobs were paid less than predominantly male jobs – tree trimmers, sign painters, real estate appraisers – that required less training and skill) have met with the same fate. In 1983, a federal district judge ruled in *AFSCME v. State of Washington* (578 F.Supp. 846 (1983); 770 F.2d 1401 (9th Cir. 1985), *reh'g den.*, 813 F.2d 1034 (1987)) that the state had discriminated against its women employees by paying predominantly female jobs less than comparable predominantly male jobs, but in 1985 the Ninth Circuit Court of Appeals reversed the district court's ruling on all counts, echoing its prior decision, which also rejected comparable worth claims, in *Spaulding v. University of Washington* (740 F.2d 686 (1984), *cert. denied*, 105 S.Ct. 511 (1984)).[5] More recently, the federal courts have rejected comparable worth claims in lawsuits brought by state government employees in Michigan (*International Union, UAW, v. State of Michigan*, 673 F.Supp. 893 (ED Mich. 1987), *aff'd sub nom., International Union, UAW, v. State of Michigan*, no. 87-2228 (6th Cir. Sept. 28, 1989)) and in California (*California State Employees' Association v. State of California*, no. C-84-7275, U.S. District Court (ND Calif. October 3, 1989)).

Developments on the lobbying front have generally been more successful for proponents of comparable worth. No entirely comprehensive survey exists. It appears, however,[6] that about 30 state governments have at least begun to undertake formal job evaluation studies to determine whether compensation does reflect the "worth" of predominantly female as well as predominantly male jobs, and that over a dozen states have adopted changes to bring about a greater correspondence between jobs' pay and their assessed worth. Comparable worth wage adjustments have also been implemented at the local government level, either by negotiation (Colorado Springs, Colorado), as the result of a strike (San José, California), by administrative decision (Los Angeles), or adoption and implementation of a charter amendment (San Francisco). The Ninth Circuit's appellate decision notwithstanding, Washington State and the American Federation of State, County, and Municipal Employees (AFSCME) agreed in January 1986 to settle *AFSCME v. State of Washington* out of court. The settlement provided for pay adjustments for predominantly female jobs costing an estimated $482 million, and was hailed by the governor and the chief negotiator for the largest state employee union as a victory for comparable worth (*New York Times* 1986).

Finally, comparable worth studies of federal employment are also a real possibility. On several occasions since 1984, the Congress has considered legislation calling for a study of the pay system in the federal civil service aimed (among other things) at determining whether the worth of predominantly female job classifications was reflected in pay rates; in each case, the legislation has passed the House of Representatives but has died in the Senate.[7]

In contrast, developments bearing on comparable worth in the private sector have been negligible (*Wall Street Journal* 1985a). Recent years have seen no comparable worth litigation in which private firms were defendants. Some firms, including telephone companies and other employers of electrical workers, are reported to have made some pay adjustments along comparable worth lines; these firms have not, however, publicly disclosed the cost of these adjustments (*New York Times* 1989b). Advocacy groups have purchased stock in several companies (including Aetna, Cigna, Kimberly-Clark and J. P. Morgan) and have then introduced resolutions for the firms' shareholders' meetings calling for the companies to pay their employees on the basis of comparable worth. None of these resolutions has been approved, however (*IRRC News for Investors* 1988, p. 125; 1989a, p. 38; 1989b, p. 118). In Wisconsin, employer groups played a leading role in defeating legislation that would have required state government employee pay to be set along comparable worth lines; in neighboring Minnesota, employer groups said little about a 1982 law (discussed at length in chapter 4) requiring comparable worth for state government employees but have since mobilized against application of comparable worth to the private sector (*Washington Post* 1985). In 1988, the Province of Ontario, Canada, adopted a law requiring comparable worth in both the public and the private sectors. Reaction of business groups has been mixed: organizations representing small employers have remained stoutly opposed, but groups representing large employers have professed willingness to wait a year before judging the law (*Wall Street Journal* 1988a,b). (For further discussion of developments in Canada, see *New York Times* 1989a, Hutner 1986, pp. 41–58, and Gunderson and Riddell 1988, pp. 458–467. Willborn 1989 discusses developments in Great Britain.)

At the national level, the Reagan administration actively opposed comparable worth, particularly during its second term (1985–89). During the 1984 presidential campaign, the ranking member of the President's Council of Economic Advisers criticized comparable worth as "a truly crazy idea" and a "medieval concept," and the President's press spokesman—saying he was expressing President Reagan's views—said the concept was "nebulous" and would represent "an unprecedented intrusion into our private affairs" (*New York Times* 1984). In 1984, the U. S. Department of Justice filed an *amicus curiae* brief in support of the State of Illinois, which was being sued by the American Nurses' Association on comparable worth grounds;[8] and in 1988 it filed an *amicus* brief in support of the State of Michigan, which was being sued on similar grounds by the United Auto Workers.[9]

Perhaps the most vociferous opposition to comparable worth within the Reagan administration came from the U. S. Commission on Civil Rights, whose former staff director, Linda Chavez, often criticized the concept and whose then chairman, Clarence M. Pendleton, Jr., called it "the looniest idea since Loony Tunes came on the screen." In June 1984 the Commission held extensive hearings on the issue (U. S. Commission on Civil Rights, 1984); in April 1985, the Commission voted by a 5–2 margin to urge Congress and government agencies to reject the doctrine of equal pay for jobs of comparable worth (*New York Times* 1985a; U. S. Commission on Civil Rights 1985). The U. S. Equal Employment Opportunity Commission followed suit in June 1985; its five commissioners voted unanimously that federal law does not require employers to give equal pay for different jobs of comparable worth (*New York Times* 1985b).

The Bush administration is unlikely to change the attitude of the federal government and its civil rights policy and enforcement agencies towards comparable worth: as noted earlier, the 1988 Republican platform rejected the concept, and the then Vice-President's campaign speeches on employment discrimination were limited to expressions of support for equal pay for *equal* work, presumably as embodied in the Equal Pay Act of 1963.[10]

The volume of debate on comparable worth – in the courts, Congress, government agencies, the news media, public forums and even scholarly journals – has been considerable. On the whole, however, the quality of the debate has been sadly deficient. Two features of the public debate seem particularly unfortunate. First, in much of the controversy, both proponents and opponents have failed to define terms and concepts clearly – even the concept of comparable worth itself.[11] Relatively little effort has been devoted to describing, in concrete terms, what would be involved in implementing and enforcing a policy of equal pay for jobs of comparable worth. Still less attention has been devoted to the ways in which such a policy would resemble or differ from existing antidiscrimination policies (e.g., under the Civil Rights Act).

A second problem with the public debate on comparable worth is that the protagonists have often been preoccupied with essentially ideological and normative issues, to the almost total exclusion of important conceptual and empirical questions.[12] (Indeed, some of the protagonists seem to be concerned more with questions about how labor markets operate, e.g., whether labor markets are better described by neoclassical or institutional models, than with questions about the merits of requiring "equal pay for jobs of comparable worth.") Both sides in the debate seem to agree that comparable worth is intended to serve as a means of redressing some of the economic effects of discrimination against (or labor market segregation of) women. The likely effects, however, of actual or potential comparable worth policies on labor market outcomes for women—on wages, employment, etc.—have received relatively little attention. Even less thought has been devoted to comparing the likely impacts of comparable worth measures with the effects of other antidiscrimination measures (e.g., enforcement of Title VII of the Civil Rights Act).

The basic objective of this monograph is to contribute to the debate about comparable worth in two ways. First, I want to provide a clear statement of the definitional and conceptual issues surrounding comparable worth: although policy decisions are ultimately a matter of ideology and normative judgments, such choices can be shaped and informed in important ways by careful dissection of definitional and conceptual questions. Second, I want to analyze the actual or potential effects of comparable worth. One of the most important criteria in the evaluation of any proposed policy is the question of its actual (as opposed to its intended) impact on key "outcome" measures. By analyzing economic models of how comparable worth might work in alternative labor market settings, and by performing empirical studies of the effects of comparable worth measures that have actually been implemented, I hope to contribute significantly to understanding how comparable worth (or comparable worth-like measures) would actually work in practice.

One general remark seems appropriate at the outset: since I am an economist, my discussion focuses on *economic* aspects of comparable worth. Other aspects of comparable worth (e.g., legal questions) have been discussed elsewhere (see, e.g., Becker 1984, 1986; Blumrosen 1979, 1986; Clauss 1986; Dean, Roberts and Boone 1984; Fischel and Lazar 1986a-b; Freed and Polsby 1984; Gold 1983; Heen 1984; Holzhauer 1986; Nelson et al. 1980; Stone 1985; Stone, ed. 1987; Weiler 1986; and *Yale Law Journal* 1981), and I have no special expertise in fields other than economics. Accordingly, it seems appropriate to exploit the principle of comparative advantage, and to focus on economic rather than other aspects of comparable worth.

The plan of this work is as follows. Chapter 2 discusses definitions, concepts and analytical issues: the basic premises underlying comparable worth and practical details of implementing it; the nature of labor market discrimination and the question of whether equal pay for jobs of comparable worth is nondiscriminatory; analysis of how adoption of comparable worth might affect wages and employment of men and women. Chapter 3 is concerned with empirical questions: conventional economic and comparable worth studies of the actual magnitude of the female/male pay gap, and methodologies for analyzing the actual effects on wages and employment of adoption of comparable worth policies. Chapters 4–6 describe the adoption of comparable worth or comparable worth-like policies in three different settings—San José, California; Minnesota; and Australia—and present analyses of the effects of these policies on wages and employment. Chapter 7 summarizes the work and presents the main conclusions.

NOTES

[1] Some writers appear to use "comparable worth" and "pay equity" interchangeably; others appear to regard "pay equity" as synonymous with nondiscrimination in pay and "comparable worth" as one means (among others) to that end.

[2] In principle, there is no reason why comparable worth is not as pertinent to minorities as it is

to women. However, proponents of comparable worth appear, for the most part, to regard the problem of unequal pay for jobs of comparable worth as affecting women more than minority men (see, e.g., Treiman and Hartmann, eds., 1981, esp. pp. 9, 28). The Rev. Jesse Jackson's speech to the 1988 Democratic National Convention referred to "working women seek[ing] comparable worth" (*New York Times*, 1988a); the Democratic platform referred to "pay equity for working women" (*New York Times*, 1988b).

[3] See chapter 2 for a discussion of job evaluation methods. In brief, such evaluations assign "points" to jobs on the basis of characteristics (skill, effort, responsibility, working conditions, and the like), with jobs receiving many points (i.e., requiring much effort, involving onerous working conditions, etc.) being deemed to have a greater "worth" than jobs receiving few points.

[4] 17 FEP Cases 906 (D. Col. 1978), 620 F.2d 228 (10th Cir., 1980), *cert. denied*, 449 U. S. 888 (1980).

[5] As noted below, the parties ultimately agreed to settle out of court, rendering moot a request made by the plaintiffs for a rehearing *en banc* by the Ninth Circuit. For detailed discussions of the case, see Remick (1988) and Willborn (1989).

[6] See Bureau of National Affairs (1981), Cook (1984), and (quoting a survey conducted by the National Committee on Pay Equity) *The New York Times* (1987).

[7] For a summary of developments in Congress through 1988, see U. S. Congress, House (1988).

[8] The ANA contended that nurses in state government employment were paid less than persons in predominantly male jobs that, according to Illinois' job evaluation results, were comparable in terms of skill, effort, responsibility and working conditions. The federal district court decision (606 F.Supp. 1313 (1985)) dismissed the ANA's suit on the basis of arguments similar to those used in *Christensen*. On appeal, the Seventh Circuit (783 F.2d 716 (7th Cir., 1986)) reversed the district court and remanded the case for further proceedings on the grounds that although the ANA had alleged intentional sex discrimination, the state had answered only on the theory that plaintiff's entire claim was based on comparable worth. The appellate court made clear, however, that it also rejected the ANA's complaint to the extent that it raised comparable worth issues, and intimated that the complaint might not survive a future motion for summary judgment if plaintiffs failed to produce evidence that went beyond comparable worth.

[9] See *International Union, UAW*, mentioned earlier in this chapter. In the interest of full disclosure, I should note that I served as a consultant and expert labor economist for the defendant (the State of Michigan) in this litigation.

[10] For example, see the then Vice-President's July 24, 1988, address to a convention of business and professional women's clubs (The Vice President, Office of the Press Secretary, 1988), which expresses support for "equal pay for equal work" but does not mention "comparable worth" or "pay equity."

[11] The same comment applies even to discussions of the issue by neutrals interested primarily in reporting, rather than debating, the issue. For example, the Bureau of National Affairs (1981, p. 1) discusses "several interpretations of the 'comparable worth' doctrine," including (a) "the 'pure' comparable worth doctrine," according to which "discrimination exists when workers of one sex . . . in one job category are paid less than workers in a totally different job category . . . when the two groups are . . . , *in some sense*, of 'comparable worth' to their employer" (emphasis added); and (b) "the 'common' comparable worth doctrine," according to which "discrimination exists when workers of one sex in one job category are paid less than workers of the other sex in the same

general job classification...when the two groups are performing work that is not the same in content but that is *of comparable worth* to the employer in terms of requirements" (emphasis added). The circularity of both of these definitions is evident.

[12] An exception is a 1986 symposium on comparable worth in the *University of Chicago Law Review* (Fischel and Lazear 1986a-b, Holzhauer 1986 and Becker 1986).

2

Comparable Worth: Definitions, Concepts and Analytical Issues

This chapter is concerned with definitional, conceptual, and analytical issues about comparable worth. What *is* "comparable worth"? How could (or should) the "worth" of jobs be measured? Is it discriminatory for employers to pay different wages for jobs of comparable worth? How would adoption of comparable worth – i.e., requiring equal pay for jobs of comparable worth – affect wages and employment of men and women?

2.1 *What Is Comparable Worth?*

Any labor market transaction involves both a buyer and a seller: for example, the wage paid by an employer is also the wage received by the employee. Likewise, the "worth" of jobs can be viewed from the perspective of either employers (the demand side of the labor market) or workers (the supply side of the market).[1] Thus, in principle, the worth of a particular job can be defined in either of two ways: as "value to the employer," or as "desirability to the employee." I will refer to the first of these definitions as the "marginal productivity" or MP definition of comparable worth, and to the second as the "compensating wage differentials" or CD definition.

To understand the meaning of the MP definition, suppose that an

I thank Lawrence Kahn, Marlene Kim, David Neumark, Cordelia Reimers, Lawrence Summers, and participants in seminars at the Australian National University, Indiana University, the U. S. Bureau of Labor Statistics, the University of California at Berkeley, the University of Maryland, the University of Melbourne, the University of New South Wales, the University of Western Australia, and Rutgers University for many helpful comments on previous versions of this chapter.

employer has 100 workers who are all alike (have the same schooling, work experience, etc.) and can be placed into one of two jobs, A or B. If the increase in output that the employer would derive by assigning these workers to job A is equal to the increase that would result from placing them in job B, then the two jobs would be called "comparable" in this sense. In economic jargon, jobs of comparable worth under this definition are jobs in which the marginal product of a given type of labor is the same.[2]

Although comparable worth has sometimes been defined in this way (see, for example, Bureau of National Affairs 1981, p. 1), and although proponents of comparable worth not infrequently use the terms "jobs of comparable worth" and "jobs of equal value to the employer" as if they were equivalent, most discussions of comparable worth explicitly define comparable worth differently. Two jobs are said to be of comparable worth if they are comparable in terms of a composite of four kinds of factors: skill (e.g., education and training requirements), effort, responsibility and working conditions. (For example, see Treiman and Hartmann, eds. 1981, p. 1.) Thus, whereas the MP definition in effect defines comparable worth from the standpoint of *employers* (i.e., the "worth" of jobs measured in terms of their contribution to the employer's *output*), the second definition in effect defines comparable worth from the standpoint of *employees* (i.e., the "worth" of jobs measured in terms of the requirements that workers must satisfy in order to hold them, the conditions experienced by workers who perform them, etc.).[3]

At least in general, the two definitions are different. For example, although working conditions may not usually have much to do with productivity, they will usually play an important part in workers' views of different jobs.[4] Moreover, the two definitions have quite different implications. To determine whether two jobs are comparable in the MP sense, one would need to measure the contribution each makes to the employer's output; whereas an assessment of the comparability of two jobs in the CD sense requires an evaluation of the jobs in terms of skill, effort, responsibility and working conditions, or what the jobs ask of workers.

In almost all cases, proponents of comparable worth have either implicitly or explicitly used the second (CD) definition, so that is the focus of this monograph. I now consider several subsidiary (but still quite important) issues: coverage, compliance and determination of job comparability under a standard of payment based on job worth.

Coverage

Virtually all proponents of comparable worth specify that comparable worth requirements would cover *individual employers*, and that job evaluations would be performed for particular employers rather than on any more general basis (e.g., labor market- or economy wide). Thus, comparable worth would entail an assessment of the comparability of the jobs of, say, tool mechanic and secretary at a given employer, and would require pay changes if the two jobs were found to be comparable but paid differently. Virtually all proponents agree, however, that comparable worth would *not* entail evaluations of these jobs *across firms*, would not set a uniform national wage for either job, and would not even necessarily require that any other employer adjust the pay of tool mechanics and secretaries. That would depend on whether, at any other such firm, the two jobs were found to be comparable.

Thus, determinations of job comparability would be conducted *within* individual firms. Other questions about coverage, however, have largely been neglected. For example, would coverage be limited to employers with at least some specified number of employees, as under provisions of fair labor standards laws? Would the same comparable worth standard be applied to all establishments of a given employer, regardless of geographic location or industrial classification? Such details have not yet been discussed systematically.

Compliance

Most discussions of comparable worth say little about compliance, i.e., about how wages would be adjusted if two jobs covered by comparable worth and deemed to be comparable nevertheless pay different wages. The possible compliance procedures are numerous: the wage of the low-paying job could be raised to equal that of the high-paying job; or the wage of the high-paying job could be reduced to equal that of the low-paying job; or one could split the difference, raising the wage of the low-paying job and reducing the wage of the high-paying job until they were equal; and so on. In practice, however, most proponents of comparable worth who address this question opt for wage increases for the low-paying job as either the only, or else the preferred, method of compliance. For example, laws proposed in state legislatures frequently specify that compliance with the standard of equal pay for jobs of comparable worth shall in no event result in a reduction in the pay of any job (see Perrin 1985, esp. pp. 27–28). Similarly, comparable worth plans actually adopted by state and local governments have generally prohibited cuts in pay for employees or job categories (for example, see Orazem and Mattila 1989, p. 180).

Determining Comparability

The most important question confronting any attempt to develop a comparable worth policy concerns the determination of job comparability. Virtually all proponents of comparable worth advocate the use of *job evaluation* in assessing the "worth" of jobs. Job evaluations are often (though not always) conducted in the following stages. First, the evaluators describe the characteristics, requirements, duties, working conditions, etc., of the jobs to be evaluated and identify the specific "compensable factors" on which the different jobs are to be evaluated. Second, the evaluators assign scores or "evaluation points" to each compensable factor for each job. Third, the evaluators determine weights to be assigned to the different factors (e.g., whether skill is to be given greater or lesser weight than working conditions). Finally, the evaluators determine the total point score (or "worth") of each job by computing the appropriately weighted sum of the points awarded to each of the factors for that job. Jobs with the same (or very similar) total scores are then said to be "comparable."

Although there seems to be general agreement on these broad outlines, there is, perhaps not surprisingly, less uniformity on questions of detail. First, different job evaluation systems categorize the four basic compensable factors (skill, effort, responsibility and working conditions) in different ways. For example, the evaluation of government jobs in the State of Washington by Norman D. Willis and Associates (1974, 1976) assigned points for "knowledge and skills," "mental demands," "accountability," and "working conditions." Hay Associates assigned points to municipal government jobs in San José, California, on the basis of the "know-how," "problem-solving," "accountability" and "working conditions" involved in each job (U.S. Congress, House 1983, p. 340). The U.S. Office of Personnel Management's Factor Evaluation System of Position Classification (FES) considers nine factors: "knowledge required by the position," "supervisory controls," "guidelines," "complexity," "scope and effect," "personal contacts," "purpose of contacts," "physical demands" and "work environment" (U.S. Civil Service Commission 1977, pp. 13–31; Werwie 1987). Industry groups such as the National Metal Trades Association, the National Electrical Manufacturers Association and the American Association of Industrial Management have developed systems with 11 factors.

A second source of variation among different evaluation procedures concerns whether the same job evaluation, with the same set of compensable factors, is used to evaluate all jobs at a given firm. Not infrequently, different job evaluations are applied to different job "families." For example, the Cooperative Wage Study (CWS), initiated in 1944 by 12 of the largest steel corporations at the direction of the War Labor Board, uses 12 compensable factors in evaluating hourly jobs, and 7 in evaluating nonexempt office and technical positions. For a considerable period of time, the Westinghouse Electric Corporation maintained separate scales for its predominantly male and predominantly female jobs. As explained in its 1939 *Industrial Relations Manual*[5]:

> The occupations or jobs filled by women are point rated on the same basis of point values for Requirements of the Job and Responsibility, with the same allowance for Job Conditions, as are the jobs commonly filled by men. . . .
>
> The gradient of the women's wage curve, however, is not the same for women as for men [*sic*] because of the more transient character

> of the service of the former, the relative shortness of their activity in industry, the differences in environment required, the extra services that must be provided, overtime conditions, extra help needed for the occasional heavy work, and the general sociological factors not requiring discussion herein.
>
> The rate or range for Labor Grades do not coincide with the values on the men's scale. Basically, then, we have another wage curve or Key Sheet for women below and not parallel with the men's curve.

Finally, job evaluations differ in the extent to which they incorporate information about labor markets, both internal and external to the enterprise at which the jobs are being evaluated. Most commercial job evaluation systems rely, at least to some degree, on such labor market information. In contrast, many comparable worth proponents advocate "bias-free" job evaluations, which explicitly avoid using such information on the grounds that the labor markets that generate it are distorted by discriminatory behavior.

Commercial job evaluations. Although it is difficult to be certain, it appears that job evaluation has been in use since at least the late nineteenth century[6] and has been extensively developed and implemented since the 1930s and, in particular, 1940s (Schwab 1985, p. 37). Evaluation methods may be grouped under two main headings: "whole job" methods, and "compensable factor" methods. As their names imply, the former approach considers individual jobs "as a whole," whereas the latter is concerned with identifying attributes or characteristics of work that different jobs possess in different degrees.[7]

The simplest (and probably oldest) form of whole job evaluation is commonly known as "job ranking": one simply compares all jobs at an enterprise with each other and ranks them from most to least important, with pay rates revised as necessary to reflect the ranking. A variant, known as "market pricing," entails several steps: (1) match the jobs under review with similar jobs in the relevant external labor market(s); (2) determine the wages paid to these reference jobs in the relevant external labor market(s), and (3) when necessary, adjust pay rates for the jobs under review so as to match the rates paid externally. Finally, under the "market pricing guideline method," the jobs to be evaluated and their rates of pay are initially linked to external labor market "reference" jobs, but pay rates for the reference jobs are only a guideline: the evaluators may change the rank of the jobs to be evaluated, and further change pay rates, within specified limits if it is decided that the initial ranking of the enterprise's jobs and/or the initial matching of these jobs with external reference jobs was inappropriate.

Compensable factor job evaluations identify qualities or features common to many (ideally, all) jobs in an organization, and quantify the degree to which each job possesses those. The first step under this approach is to identify all qualities or features – "factors" – to be compensated, by examining job descriptions, administering questionnaires to workers and supervisors, etc. Some evaluations of this kind simply describe, in qualitative and narrative terms, how an enterprise's jobs differ in terms of such factors,[8] but most compensable factor evaluations are quantitative: evaluators assign points for each factor to each job, based on the extent to which each each job entails each factor. (For example, jobs requiring much skill or training might receive 10 points for the "skill" factor, whereas jobs requiring minimal skill might receive 1 or 2.) In awarding points to jobs, some quantitative plans[9] use jobs identified as "benchmark" or "key" jobs as a reference point. These are jobs judged to be especially sensitive to external labor market conditions, to be "standardized (employed by many organizations) and [to possess] stable content" (Schwab 1980, p. 55). The number of such key jobs should be "sufficient . . . to cover the entire range of difficulty or importance of each [compensable] factor" (Henderson and Clarke 1981, p. 17).

One of the most popular quantitative procedures is the "Factor Guide Chart Method" or, more simply, "Hay Plan," named after its chief progenitor, Edward N. Hay. This plan considers three basic factors, "know-how," "problem solving," and "accountability," although a fourth, "working conditions," can be included if desired, and each basic factor is divided into various subfactors (Hay and Purves 1951, 1954). Charts are used to determine points to be awarded for different combinations of the factors and subfactors. A hallmark of the Hay method is its capacity for substantial modification so as to be applicable to different organizations. Although the Hay approach is not tied explicitly to particular "key jobs" (unlike some other methods), it appears to be intended primarily for evaluation of a given job family (or set of related job families) within an organization, rather than of the entire set of jobs at an organization. In principle, then, an enterprise would use not one Hay plan but several to evaluate its entire range of jobs.[10]

Once evaluators have assigned points to factors under methods such as those just discussed, the next task is to combine them for each job to arrive at a total point score, i.e., a measure of the total "worth" of each job. In general, job evaluations compute total worth as a weighted sum of the points awarded to each of the different factors; differences among evaluation methods in this regard have to do with how the weights are determined. In the main, commercial job evaluations derive weights using the so-called "policy-capturing" approach (Treiman and Hartmann, eds. 1981, p. 74). Under this approach, weights are constructed to reflect the *existing relationship* (as determined by statistical procedures such as regression analysis), *at the enterprise in question*, between each individual compensable factor and pay.

To see what this means in practice, consider the following simple hypothetical example. An employer evaluates jobs on the basis of two compensable factors, physical demands and mental demands. Points are awarded to all jobs reflecting the extent of each of these two factors possessed by each job. The employer then analyzes the relation between actual current compensation and the points awarded for these two factors, and finds the following: (1) among jobs with the same evaluation points for physical demands, each extra evaluation point for mental demands is associated, on average and other things being equal, with $3 per hour in extra pay; and (2) among jobs with the same evaluation points for mental demands, each extra evaluation point for physical demands is associated, on average and other things being equal, with $4 per hour in extra pay. Then the weight given to mental demands evaluation points would be 0.75 (=3/4) the weight given to physical demands. Thus, a job with 1 mental demand point and 2 physical demand points might have a composite score or total "worth" of $(3\times1)+(4\times2)=11$ points, whereas a job with 2 mental demand points and 1 physical demand points might have a worth of $(3\times2)+(4\times1)=10$ points.[11]

Bias-free job evaluations. Although most proponents of comparable worth accept – indeed, advocate – the general concept of job evaluation as a means of determining job worth, they are often critical of the way in which commercial job evaluations are carried out.[12] According to these comparable worth proponents, bias against predominantly female jobs can (and, all too often, actually does) creep into each stage of the evaluation process.

The first problem is that the compensable factors chosen to be included in the evaluations may tend to be those prevalent in predominantly male jobs and/or that factors typical of predominantly female jobs may be excluded or deemphasized: "for example, physical effort/exertion is often [included in commercial job evaluations], while fine motor skill usually is not" (Beatty and Beatty 1984, pp. 73–4).

A second set of problems involves the assessment of each factor. One difficulty is that existing evaluation procedures may not fully elicit the degree to which predominantly female jobs do in fact possess relevant characteristics. For example, one questionnaire administered to incumbents to gather information about compensable factors asked, "How important is setting up or adjusting equipment (setting up a lathe or drill press, adjusting an engine carburetor, etc.)?" As those responsible for analyzing data generated by this questionnaire (Pierson, Koziara and Johannesson 1984, p. 123) note:

> A person in a female job might not respond to [this question], because the examples relate only to traditionally male-held jobs. This item was changed by adding behaviorally similar examples that were less sex-biased and became: "How important is setting up or adjusting equipment (attaching devices to patients, setting up a lathe or drill press, adjusting office equipment)?"

Even if the questions asked about jobs are neutral, the responses may not be:

> Male tree trimmers for the city of Denver, interviewed for a television report on the efforts of nurses in that city to raise their wages [via *Lemons v. City and County of Denver*], repeatedly said that they thought tree trimmers deserved a higher salary because their work was more "difficult," "dangerous," and "dirty." . . . It would seem fair to conclude that the tree trimmers are referring to the physical difficulty of climbing trees and ladders, the danger of physical labor at heights and with certain machinery, and the dirt of outdoors work. They, and many others, do not see the difficulty of work in intensive care units, the danger of dealing with disease and psychotic patients, or the dirt of vomit. . . . Many nurses I have talked to see their job as clean, in part because of the constant effort to make the environment sterile, in spite of their exposure to vomit, urine, feces, blood, pus, dead people, disease and so on. Garbage collectors do dirty work, while food service workers, producing the garbage, do clean work. (Remick 1984, p. 114.)

Thus, assessments of the skill requirements, difficulty or working conditions of jobs may be a function of general cultural perceptions and, in particular, of the sex composition of the jobs' incumbents, regardless of whether those performing the assessments are outside evaluators, supervisors or even the incumbents themselves – a notion that has received some confirmation in the research literature (McArthur 1985).

A final problem with commercial job evaluation, in the view of many comparable worth proponents, concerns the way in which evaluation points are combined into a total point score and then converted into pay rates. The main concern here stems from the belief that the existing wage structure is contaminated by discriminatory employment practices. Thus, reliance on it in commercial job evaluations is highly undesirable.

Comparable worth proponents are especially critical of the practice, commonly followed in commercial evaluations, of conducting different evaluations for different groups or families of jobs within the same enterprise. For example, as noted above, many evaluation systems evaluate clerical and production worker jobs separately. Since the separate job families considered tend to be demarcated along sexual and/or racial lines, comparable worth proponents are critical of this approach. At best, the resulting final evaluation will be incomplete (since it will not evaluate all jobs, in all families, on the same basis). At worst, it may be biased against predominantly female job families (to the extent that it sanctions, or does not prohibit, pay differences between predominantly female and predominantly male job families that might have been found comparable had they been evaluated on the same basis).

Not infrequently, commercial evaluations not only reflect the existing distribution of the workforce by sex and occupation, but also rely on information about the existing wage distribution. As noted earlier, some evaluations use information on wages paid for "key" or "benchmark" jobs (ones deemed to be especially sensitive to external market forces), or (more generally) surveys of local area labor market wage rates, to convert evaluation points into pay for all jobs. Others use "policy-capturing" analyses of the association between evaluation points and the *existing* structure of wage rates within the firm in question to derive the weights that will be applied to the points awarded to individual compensable factors in determining the total "worth" of individual jobs. Either way, advocates of comparable worth point out, the resulting relation between total evaluation points and proposed pay levels generated by the evaluation procedure will "necessarily reflect in turn any biases that exist in market wages."[13]

Thus, most comparable worth proponents are, at best, skeptical about the merits of such methodology as a means of adequately assessing the worth of different jobs, in particular predominantly female vs. predominantly male jobs. Accordingly, they prefer the use of "bias-free" job evaluation methodology in determining the worth of different jobs. "A bias-free evaluation system probably does not yet exist" (Remick 1984, p. 100), so operational details of bias-free evaluations are necessarily somewhat vague. Most comparable worth proponents who have addressed this question (e.g., Remick 1984; Treiman and Hartmann, eds. 1981), however, appear to agree that a bias–free procedure would have most if not all of the following features.

(1). Determination of the compensable factors, and of the points awarded for each such factor for any given job, on scrupulously sex-neutral grounds.

(2). Application of a single uniform evaluation methodology to the entire set of jobs (rather than of different procedures for different job families) at the enterprise under evaluation.

(3). Deemphasis, or even complete avoidance, of information on the existing structure (external and/or internal) of wage rates by combining points awarded to individual compensable factors using weights derived on *a priori* grounds without reference to market wage rates[14] rather than via policy-capturing techniques (Treiman and Hartmann, eds. 1981, pp. 72, 80).

It seems clear, then, that bias-free job evaluations of the kind proposed by comparable worth advocates would differ at least to some extent from the commercial job evaluations currently in use in most enterprises in the private or public sectors. In terms of underlying philosophy, however, both comparable worth and commercial evaluation methodologies have one essential point in common: both take the compensating differentials or CD approach described earlier, since the basic objective of each is to assess jobs in terms of skill, effort, responsibility and working conditions. As Schwab (1980, p. 64; emphasis original[15]), speaking of commercial job evaluations, remarks:

> These factors appear to conform rather closely to the components articulated in *net-advantage* discussions going back to Adam Smith's *Wealth of Nations* [footnote omitted]. That is, they represent requirements that the employee must bring to the job (e.g., skill), or characteristics of the job (e.g., working conditions) that may make the job onerous or attractive.

Adam Smith's discussion of these factors[16] is, at least to economists, one of the best-known and most celebrated passages in *The Wealth of Nations*:

> The five following are the principal circumstances which, so far as I have been able to observe, make up for a small pecuniary gain in some employments, and counter-balance a great one in others: first, the agreeableness or disagreeableness of the employments them-

> selves; secondly, the easiness and cheapness, or the difficulty and expence of learning them; thirdly, the constancy or inconstancy of employment in them; fourthly, the small or great trust which must be reposed in those who exercise them; and fifthly, the probability or improbability of success in them.

Smith laid the foundations for what economists now call the theory of "compensating wage differentials." In its simplest version, the theory implies that, other things being equal *and in the absence of artificial constraints*, jobs that ask much of workers in terms of requirements or working conditions will typically have to pay a premium or "compensating differential" in order to attract enough workers to them (see chapter 3 for further discussion).

There is a seeming irony here. Economists who have discussed comparable worth (e.g., Lindsay 1980; O'Neill 1984b; Raisian, Ward, and Welch 1985) usually react negatively to it because they perceive it as antithetical to the concept of wage determination by market supplies and demands; and comparable worth proponents are not infrequently skeptical about the outcome of wage determination by supply and demand. Yet in an important sense one can trace the rationale for comparable worth directly back to Adam Smith, whose language is strikingly similar to that used by present day comparable worth advocates. In economic jargon, comparable worth would appear to amount simply to an insistence that the theory of compensating wage differentials be taken seriously. If two jobs are indeed comparable in terms of skill ("the easiness and cheapness, or the difficulty and expence of learning them"), responsibility ("the small or great trust which must be reposed..."), effort and working conditions ("agreeableness or disagreeableness," etc.) but pay very different wages, can the wage differential really be said to be simply "compensating," i.e., justifiable? If, in addition, the wage differential is related to sex, can an inference of sex discrimination reasonably be ignored? Comparable worth advocates emphatically answer both questions in the negative; in the remainder of this chapter, I consider these issues in detail.

2.2 *Economic Analysis of Labor Market Discrimination*

Much of the motivation for comparable worth is related to women's disadvantage in the labor market. For example, advocates frequently cite the sizeable pay gap—the fact that, on average, year-round full time women workers make less than 70 percent of what men make—and note that, as shown in table 2.1, it has changed relatively little in the past 30 years or so, despite adoption of major antidiscrimination laws and programs.[17]

Beyond the relative stability of the pay gap, some of the most striking stylized facts about women's disadvantage in the labor market are the following:

(1) *Unequal pay for equal work.* Women typically earn less than men in the same job or occupational category (e.g., teacher), even when other things (education, years of work experience, etc.) are the same. (See, for example, Ashenfelter and Pencavel 1976.)

(2) *Unequal access to better work.* Relative to men, women are more likely to work in lower paid jobs or occupations (e.g., clerical as opposed to managerial), even when other things are the same. (See, for example, Malkiel and Malkiel 1973.)

(3) *"Femaleness" associated with low pay.* On average and other things remaining the same, "overrepresentation" of women in a job or occupational category—the more "female" it is—is associated with lower pay in that occupation, on average, for all employees (men and women) taken together. (See, for example, Treiman and Hartmann, eds. 1981, esp. chapter 2.)

(4) *"Femaleness" more strongly associated with low pay for men than for women.* On average and other things remaining the same, "overrepresentation" of women in a job or occupational category appears to be associated with greater wage differentials among men than among women: pay is lower in predominantly female jobs than in predominantly male jobs for both women and men; but the negative effect on pay of being in such jobs is greater for men than it is for women. (See, for example, Roos 1981; Johnson and Solon 1986.)

Table 2.1 The Female/Male "Pay Gap," 1956–1987

Year	Women's Median Earnings ($)	Men's Median Earnings ($)	Median Earnings Ratio: Women/Men
1956	2,827	4,466	0.633
1957	3,008	4,713	0.638
1958	3,102	4,927	0.630
1959	3,193	5,209	0.613
1960	3,293	5,417	0.608
1961	3,351	5,644	0.594
1962	3,446	5,794	0.595
1963	3,561	5,978	0.596
1964	3,690	6,195	0.596
1965	3,823	6,375	0.600
1966	3,973	6,848	0.580
1967	4,150	7,182	0.578
1968	4,457	7,664	0.582
1969	4,977	8,227	0.605
1970	5,323	8,966	0.594
1971	5,593	9,399	0.595
1972	5,903	10,202	0.579
1973	6,335	11,186	0.566
1974	6,772	11,835	0.572
1975	7,504	12,758	0.588
1976	8,099	13,455	0.602
1977	8,618	14,626	0.589
1978	9,350	15,730	0.594
1979	10,169	17,045	0.597
1980	11,197	18,612	0.602
1981	12,001	20,260	0.592
1982	13,014	21,077	0.617
1983	13,915	21,881	0.635
1984	14,780	23,218	0.637
1985	15,624	24,195	0.646
1986	16,232	25,256	0.642
1987	16,909	26,008	0.650

Source: U.S. Department of Commerce, Bureau of the Census, *Current Population Reports*, Series P-60 (money income of families and persons in the United States), various issues. All figures refer to median earnings of year-round full-time workers. For 1956–66, "earnings" includes wage and salary earnings only; for 1967–87, "earnings" is "total money earnings," including earnings from self-employment as well as wage and salary earnings. For 1956–78, figures refer to persons age 14 and older; for 1979–87, figures refer to persons age 15 and older.

Figure 2.1 Discrimination

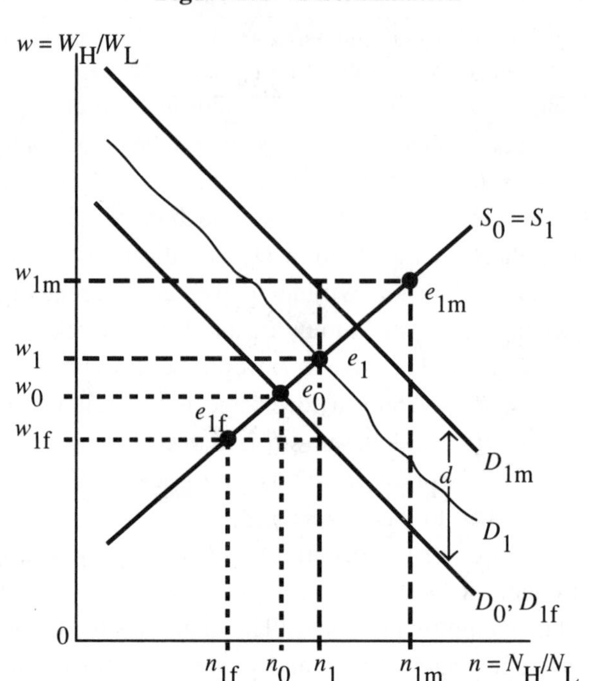

Advocates of comparable worth usually argue that such patterns are caused by labor market discrimination, and that comparable worth can offset them.

Can labor market discrimination account for the stylized facts just noted? Are patterns of this kind due *exclusively* to labor market discrimination? To address these and similar issues, it is useful to consider a simple model of an economy with two jobs: a high-wage job, *H*, and a low-wage job, *L*.[18] To focus initially on questions about labor market discrimination, suppose to begin with that, *on average*, men and women are equally productive at, and equally interested in doing, either kind of job.[19] In the absence of labor market discrimination, relative demands and supplies for these jobs will appear as shown in figure 2.1.

In figure 2.1, *W* is the wage paid to workers in a job (either *H* or *L*) and *N* is the number of workers in a job. Thus, W_H/W_L is the *relative* wage (i.e., the wage in *H* relative to that in *L*), with $W_H/W_L > 1$ to reflect the fact that *H* is the high-wage job; and N_H/N_L is *relative* employment (i.e., employment in *H* relative to that in *L*).

Now consider relative supplies and demands in this market. Employer relative demands are downward-sloping: if *H* must be paid a high wage (relative to *L*), less *H* will be employed (relative to *L*).[20] It is equivalent, but, particularly in terms of what follows, much more helpful to think of the aggregate relative demand curve D_0 as indicating the (aggregate) relative wage employers are willing to pay at different (aggregate) relative employment levels: if employment in *H* is high relative to that in *L*, then *productivity* of *H* relative to *L* would be low and so employers would be willing to pay only a low wage for *H* relative to *L*. The aggregate supply curve S_0 slopes upward: to raise the aggregate number of workers wanting to work in *H* (relative to *L*), it would be necessary to raise pay in *H* relative to that in *L*.[21]

In figure 2.1, equilibrium occurs (aggregate supply and aggregate demand are equal) at the aggregate relative wage w_0, at which point aggregate relative employment is n_0. The quantities w_0 and n_0 refer to the *overall* average wage (of men and women combined) and to *total* employment (of men and women combined), respectively. What does this equilibrium imply for men and women, considered separately?

As regards demand, note first that, by assumption, there is no labor market discrimination. Thus, the relative wage will be w_0 not only in the aggregate but also for each sex group: in other words, in the absence of discrimination, the relative wage W_H/W_L that employers are willing to pay to women at a given *aggregate* relative employment level N_H/N_L is the same as the relative wage they are willing to pay men at the same *aggregate* relative employment level. In this "offered wage schedule" sense, D_0 is not only the aggregate relative demand curve but also the relative demand curve for both men and women; note that for both men and women as well as in the aggregate, offered (relative) wages as given by D_0 depend on *aggregate* relative employment.

As regards supply, note that, by assumption, men and women have identical qualifications and interests, on average.[22] At any given relative wage, then, male and female relative supplies would be the same. In this sense, S_0 is not only the *aggregate* relative supply schedule (showing *aggregate* relative supply forthcoming at a given relative wage), but also the relative supply schedule of each sex group (showing relative supply *of that group* forthcoming at a given relative wage).

It follows that, in the nondiscriminatory equilibrium e_0, relative wages will be w_0 and relative employment will be n_0 not only in the aggregate but also for each sex group. Hence, under the conditions depicted in figure 2.1, women and men will receive the same wage within a given job (*H* or *L*); will receive the same *relative* wage $w = W_H / W_L$ and have the same *relative* employment levels; and so will be represented to the same extent in both jobs (e.g., the proportion female will be the same in *H* as it is in *L*).

To determine the effects of labor market discrimination, first consider demand. To introduce discrimination, assume that employers favor men in filling the *high-wage job H* in the sense that, at given wages, employer demand for male workers in *H* exceeds that for female workers. Equivalently, assume that employers are now willing to pay a *higher* wage to men in job *H* than to women in the same job. Then although the (relative) demand curve for women is still $D_0 = D_{1f}$, the demand curve for men is now D_{1m}, where the vertical distance between the two curves, *d*, indicates the relative wage premium employers now are willing to give men in *H*.

It is important to note that, even in the presence of discrimination, employer demand for persons of a given sex still depends only on *aggregate* relative employment (exactly as in the nondiscriminatory labor market just discussed). This is because, in a simple discriminatory two-job labor market of the kind described here, the relative wage a firm is willing to offer a worker depends on only two things: his or her sex, and the relative marginal productivity of the job he or she is doing. The latter depends only on *aggregate* relative employment (of men and women combined) in the two jobs, not on relative employment of persons of either sex. It follows that, at any given *aggregate* relative employment level, employers still are willing to pay relative wages to women as they used to; but that at the same *aggregate* relative employment level, employers are now willing to pay higher relative wages to men. The *aggregate* relative demand (or "wage offer") schedule (for men and women combined) must therefore lie in between the schedules D_{1m} and D_{1f}; it is shown as D_1. Note that the new aggregate relative demand or wage offer schedule D_1, like both the old one D_0 and the new sex-specific ones D_{1s}, s=m or f, shows the relative wages that employers are willing to offer workers (overall, or of a specific sex) at a given *aggregate* relative employment level.

As in the nondiscriminatory case, the aggregate supply schedule (showing the aggregate relative wage necessary to elicit each aggregate relative supply level) is still S_0, and, in the absence of any sex difference in job qualifications or job preferences, the relative supply schedule of each sex (showing the relative wage necessary to elicit each relative supply level *for that sex*) is identical to S_0. Equilibrium occurs where aggregate supply S_1 $(=S_0)$ equals aggregate demand D_1, at the new *aggregate* equilibrium relative wage rate w_1 and *aggregate* relative employment level n_1.

To work out wage and employment levels for men and women in this discriminatory equilibrium, note that, in equilibrium,[23] (1) men in H must receive a relative wage premium of d, and (2) relative supply for each sex group is set by the relative wage received by that sex group, subject to the condition that *aggregate* demand must also equal *aggregate* supply. The discriminatory equilibrium entails aggregate relative employment of n_1; by definition of the wage offer or demand curves for each sex, at this aggregate relative employment level employers are willing to pay relative wages of w_{1f} and w_{1m} to women and men, respectively, with $w_{1m}-w_{1f}=d>0$ (the vertical distance between D_{1m} and D_{1f}), as required for equilibrium. Since the supply schedules of both groups (giving their relative supplies at different relative wages) are given by S_1, it follows that, at these equilibrium wages w_{1f} and w_{1m}, the relative supplies (and, thus, relative employment levels) of women and men are n_{1f} and n_{1m}, respectively. (Note also that, since aggregate demand must equal aggregate supply at the equilibrium aggregate wage, appropriately weighted sums of sex-specific wage rates and employment levels must equal the aggregate wage and the aggregate employment level, respectively.)

Thus, compared with a nondiscriminatory setting, discrimination favoring men in the high-wage job H entails lower (higher) relative wages *and* employment levels for women (men): $w_{1f} < w_0 < w_{1m}$ and $n_{1f} < n_0 < n_{1m}$. Intuitively, employer preference for men in the high-wage job raises the demand for men and reduces the demand for women in that job; this leads to a male/female pay gap within the high-wage job, greater representation of men in that job, and a greater difference in pay for men than for women between the high-wage job and the low-wage job. On the other hand, since women now find it harder to be employed in the high-wage job, they crowd into the low-wage job, reducing the wage there (Bergmann 1971; Edgeworth 1922).

Since $d > 0$ (i.e., employers favor men in the high-wage job), there is unequal pay for equal work: the only way women can get a high-wage job is by working for less in that job than do men. Since $n_{1f} < n_{1m}$, there is unequal access to better work: women are underrepresented (relative to men) in the high-wage job, H; equivalently, the proportion female is smaller among high-wage workers than among low-wage workers. This also means that the higher the proportion female, the lower the (overall) rate of pay in a job: the "femaleness" of jobs is negatively related to wage rates. Finally, since $w_{1f} < w_{1m}$, pay differentials among jobs are smaller among women than among men: the relation between pay and "femaleness" of jobs is stronger for men than it is for women. In sum, the simple model of labor market discrimination illustrated in figure 2.1 can account for all of the "stylized facts" about women's labor market disadvantage discussed earlier in this chapter.

Is such discrimination the *only* source of the pay and employment differences shown in figure 2.1, however? Having examined demand-side causes (i.e., employer discrimination), it is natural to consider supply-side causes (e.g., sex differences in job preferences and/or job qualifications) as well. Figure 2.2 reproduces the original aggregate demand and supply curves (D_0 and S_0, respectively) of the initial nondiscriminatory setting. Now suppose that employers do *not* discriminate (in the sense used in discussing figure 2.1) but that for any of a variety of reasons—differential socialization, sexual role differentiation, unequal access to education—women prefer and/or are better qualified

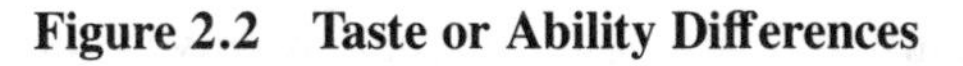
Figure 2.2 Taste or Ability Differences

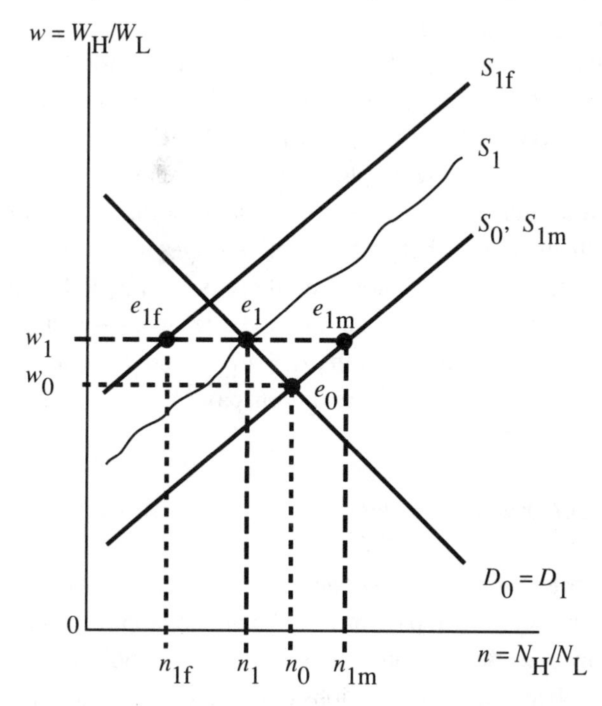

for job L than are men. In this case, the relative supply of women to job H will be lower, at any given relative wage, than that of men. Thus the female relative supply curve now becomes S_{1f}, whereas the male relative supply curve remains at $S_0 = S_{1m}$.

The *overall* or aggregate supply curve S_1 is now a kind of average of the female and male relative supply curves.[24] In the absence of labor market discrimination, the overall or aggregate demand curve is unchanged and is the same for both men and women. As before, equilibrium requires that aggregate demand equal aggregate supply. This occurs at the aggregate relative wage w_1 and aggregate relative employment level n_1. Since employers do not discriminate, equilibrium also requires that both men and women receive the same relative wage, i.e., w_1. Supplies of the two sex groups at this common relative wage may then be determined from their relative supply schedules, S_{1f} and S_{1m}: at

w_1, women supply n_{1f}, less than the male relative supply of n_{1m} at the same relative wage (w_1).[25]

Intuitively, the now-greater preference of women for the low-wage job (or their now-lower qualifications for the high-wage job) reduces aggregate supply to the high-wage job, raising the relative wage (of H to L), w, and reducing relative employment (in H relative to L), n. Thus, in equilibrium, there is "equal pay for equal work" and the pay differential between the two jobs (that is, the relative wage, w_1) is the same for both men and women. Overall, however, there is (1) a male female pay gap, (2) the appearance of unequal access to better work—women are underrepresented in the high-wage job ($n_{1f} < n_{1m}$)—and (3) a negative relation between "femaleness" of jobs and their pay.

2.3 *Pay Differentials for Jobs of Comparable Worth*

The preceding analysis suggests that a negative relation between "femaleness of job" and pay may not be due to labor market discrimination. I now consider a related question: will a nondiscriminatory labor market generate equal pay for jobs of comparable worth? I first present some general analytic results, and then turn to some examples involving specific jobs.

General analytics

To analyze the question of whether there will be equal pay for jobs of comparable worth in the absence of discrimination, it is helpful to analyze the question of market supply to different occupations (e.g., the relative supply schedule S of figures 2.1–2.2) in more detail.

Consider a labor market with two jobs, A and B. As implied earlier (see especially note 21), it would be surprising if literally every worker viewed these two jobs in precisely the same way. Worker preferences for the two jobs may be summarized by a preference distribution such as the one shown in figure 2.3. The height of the preference curve at any given relative wage $w = W_A / W_B$ shows the proportion (more precisely, proba-

Figure 2.3 Taste Distribution

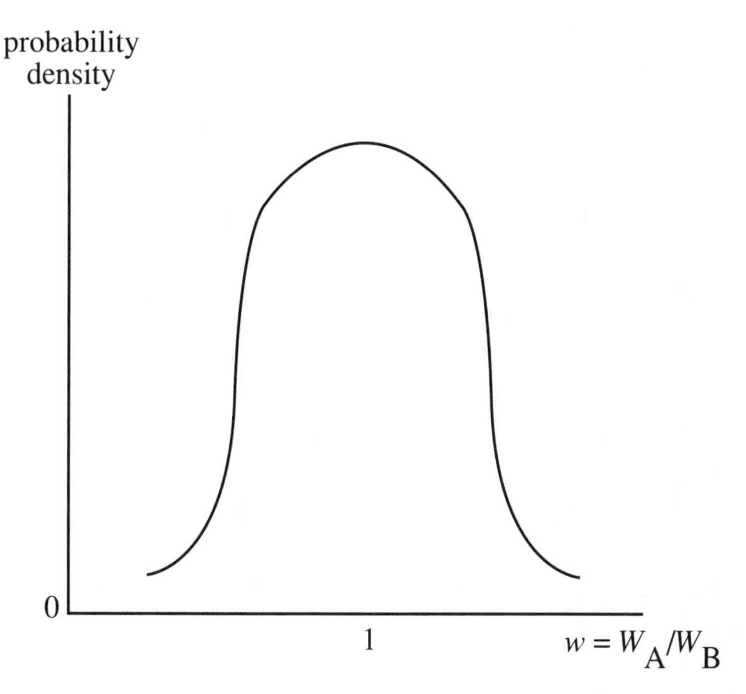

bility density) of workers who are indifferent between *A* and *B* at that relative wage; the area underneath the curve and to the left of any given relative wage *w* shows the proportion who prefer *A* to *B* at that relative wage. Clearly, the higher the relative wage (that is, the higher the wage in *A* relative to that in *B*), the greater the proportion of workers who prefer *A* to *B*; but even at very high relative wages, some workers still prefer the lower-paying job, *B*, to the higher-paying job *A*.

To highlight the nature of comparable worth job analyses, assume that (1) a job evaluation has found that the two jobs, *A* and *B*, are comparable in terms of a composite of skill, effort, responsibility and working conditions; and that (2) this evaluation is in fact congruent with worker preferences, in the sense that if pay were the same in both jobs, the average or "representative" worker would in fact be indifferent between them. This means that the median worker is indifferent between the two jobs at a relative wage of unity; and that at this point, half the workers prefer *A* whereas the other half prefer *B*.

Now consider the relative supply curve under these assumptions. Relative supply (i.e., $n=N_A/N_B$, the number desiring to do *A* relative to those desiring to do *B* at any given relative wage $w=W_A/W_B$) is positive-sloped: the higher the *A* wage is relative to *B*, the larger the number of workers who want to do *A* relative to those preferring *B*. Since the representative (more precisely, median) worker is indifferent between the two jobs at a relative wage of 1, the relative supply curve also passes through the point (1, 1).

Although (by assumption) the jobs are comparable in terms of both the job evaluation and the representative worker's preferences, it is nevertheless not possible to say anything about either relative wages or relative employment in the absence of information about the relative demand curve. In particular, suppose that employers do not discriminate and that technology and product market conditions are such as to entail high demand for *A* relative to *B*, with demand curve D_H as shown in figure 2.4. Then equilibrium will occur at e_H with relative wage w_H and relative employment n_H. On the other hand, if demand for *A* relative to *B* is low, as with demand curve D_L in figure 2.4, then, even in the absence of employer discrimination, equilibrium will occur at e_L with a lower relative wage w_L and a lower relative employment n_L.

In sum, even though (by assumption) the two jobs are comparable, they will not necessarily pay the same wage, even in the absence of employer discrimination. In general, there will be "equal pay for work of equal value" (i.e., for jobs of comparable worth, *A* and *B*) only if the demand curve (whose shape depends on technology, product market conditions, etc.) *as well as* the supply curve passes through the point (1,1).

The one exception to this general rule highlights the key assumption implicit in comparable worth: the case in which all workers have *identical* job preferences. In this case, the preference distribution of figure 2.3 collapses to a vertical straight line and the relative supply function of figure 2.4 collapses to a horizontal straight line. For example, if all workers regard the two jobs as comparable, the preference

Figure 2.4 Supply, Demand and Wages

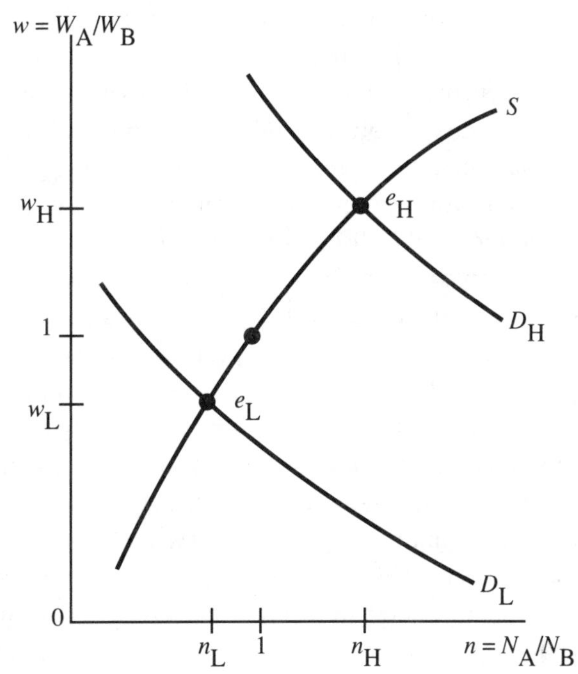

distribution of figure 2.3 would be a vertical straight line intersecting the w axis at $w=1$, and the relative supply schedule would become a horizontal straight line intersecting the w axis of figure 2.3 at $w=1$. Similarly, if all workers would be indifferent between the two jobs if *A* paid 10 percent more than *B*, and would all prefer *A* (*B*) if *A* paid a wage that was more (less) than 10 percent above the *B* wage, then the preference distribution and relative supply schedule would again be straight lines, intersecting the w axis at $w=1.10$.

In cases such as these, in which preferences are homogeneous, the wage differential between the two jobs is purely supply-determined and the position of the relative demand curve (whether demand is as depicted by D_L or D_H in figure 2.4) is irrelevant: the relative supply schedule alone is sufficient to determine equilibrium relative wages. The difficulty with this as a justification for comparable worth is that it is only under the special condition of identical worker preferences that even a nondiscriminatory labor market would generate equal pay for jobs of comparable worth.[26] In the more general case, in which worker preferences are heterogeneous, relative wages are both supply- and demand-determined; the relative supply schedule alone is not sufficient to determine relative wages; and there is no basis for expecting equal pay for jobs of comparable worth, even if employers do not discriminate.

Of course, nothing in this discussion of figures 2.3–4 can explain the "stylized fact" of a negative relation between "femaleness" of jobs and pay. That is, however, merely because figure 2.3 assumes that, although different individuals have different job preferences, there are no *sex-related* differences in job preferences (recall note 22). Allowing for sex-related differences in job preferences would entail not one but rather two preference distributions in figure 2.3, and would lead directly back to the discussion of figure 2.2, i.e., to a negative relation between "femaleness" of jobs and the pay of jobs—*even those of "comparable worth.*" It should be noted that the term "job preferences" has no normative implications here: for present purposes, it does not matter whether sex differences in job preferences are inherent and biological, or culturally imposed. All that matters is that they be independent of *employer* behavior—that, for whatever reasons (sexual role differentiation, cultural stereotyping or anything else) other than employer actions, women are more likely to seek the low-paying job L at a *given* relative wage than are otherwise identical men. In sum, a central analytical difficulty with comparable worth is that it ignores the importance of heterogeneity in job preferences in general, and the importance of *sex-related* differences in job preferences in particular.

Adam Smith's comments on butchers' wages provide an instructive example of the importance of heterogeneous tastes in generating wage differences (and of why equal pay for jobs of comparable worth need not arise, even in the absence of discrimination, when job preferences are heterogeneous). As noted earlier, Smith's discussion of wage differentials includes all of the factors considered in job evaluations, and suggests (*inter alia*) that "dishonourable" or "disagreeable" work will tend to be better paid than other kinds of work, other things (e.g., skill and effort requirements) being equal. As a case in point, Smith remarked that the trade of butcher was a "brutal and odious business," and suggested that the disagreeableness of butchering explained why butchers' pay exceeded that of many other "common trades" (1937, p. 100). As modern writers have pointed out, however, this reasoning tacitly assumes that preferences are homogeneous and, in particular, that all would-be butchers in eighteenth century Britain shared Smith's fastidious tastes. In the more general case of heterogeneous preferences, a wage differential favoring butchers need not arise even if large numbers of persons find the notion of butchering unpleasant. As Rees (1976, p. 340) notes, if enough people have no strong feelings about or actually enjoy butchering, "it would then clearly be possible to fill all positions for butchers without any compensating wage differential."[27]

Another example is provided not by Adam but rather by Sharon Smith (cited in Gold 1983, pp. 43–44). Consider an employer with only two jobs: French-English translator, and Spanish-English translator. *A priori*, it would seem that neither job involves more skill, effort or responsibility than the other; and they would presumably entail the same working conditions. The jobs would therefore be determined to be comparable and, hence, to merit the same pay. If the French translators were predominantly male and better paid than the Spanish translators who, let us suppose, are predominantly female, is this not convincing evidence of discrimination? Perhaps, but now add one more "fact" to this hypothetical example, says Smith: suppose the employer in question is located in Miami. Is there still any reason to suppose that, (even) if the firm does not discriminate, it would necessarily pay the two groups of translators the same wage? Clearly not.

Indeed, it is not even possible to say, *a priori*, which of the two jobs would be better paid. True, many Spanish-speaking persons live in the Miami area, which would presumably raise the relative supply and reduce the relative wage of the Spanish translators; but Miami is also a center of U.S.–Latin American commerce, which would presumably raise both the relative demand for and the relative wage of the Spanish translators. Even under the assumption of no labor market discrimination, there is no obvious basis for saying which one of these two forces will be stronger or, therefore, for determining whether, on balance, the wage of the Spanish translators will exceed or be lower than that of the French translators.[28]

The essential point of the butchers and translators examples is that wage determination need not entail equal pay for jobs of "comparable worth" even in the absence of discrimination. In response, a number of writers have criticized the notion, embodied in figures 2.1–2.4, that supply and demand determine wage rates. For example, Weiler (1986, p. 1723, n. 133) argues that "no simple logic of supply and demand . . . explains the operation of the labor market; rather, the labor market is shaped by a complex, often counterintuitive set of principles. . . ." Similarly, some writers note that real-world labor markets are characterized by such phenomena as implicit or explicit long-term employment contracts, unions, and segmented labor markets.[29] The fact that real-world labor markets are complex, however, is clearly not sufficient to establish that such markets would generate equal pay for jobs of comparable worth in the absence of discrimination.[30] Moreover, if even the simple nondiscriminatory labor market depicted here does not entail equal pay for jobs of comparable worth, that hardly supports the claim that the more complex labor markets of the real world would do so absent discrimination.

A final argument, developed by Aldrich and Buchele (1986, esp. pp. 77–79, 112), amounts to a reformulation of the comparable worth principle. They argue that a nondiscriminatory market ought to entail the same marginal return (in terms of additional pay) to productivity-related characteristics (e.g., education or training) in all jobs, whether predominantly female, predominantly male or "mixed." This reformulation of comparable worth, however, like the original version, is valid only under rather special conditions.[31] As one example, provided by Ronald G. Ehrenberg, note that there is no obvious reason why the marginal return to either education or physical strength should be the same in both secretarial work and stevedoring even in a non-discriminatory labor market.

Some specific examples

Some readers may have little difficulty accepting this section's general analytic discussion of the conceptual flaws inherent in comparable worth. Since tastes are heterogeneous, however, other readers may find some specific examples of interest. For this purpose, the findings of Raisian et al. (1985, esp. pp. 75–88; 1988) are particularly instructive.

Raisian et al. focus on job "scores" developed by the National Research Council's Committee on Occupational Classification and Analysis (Miller et al., eds. 1980, esp. appendix F) for most of the "detailed" or three-digit occupational categories developed by the U.S. Census with respect to four factors: substantive complexity; motor skills; physical demands; and undesirable working conditions.[32] For selected jobs, Raisian et al. tabulated not only these scores but also the average hourly wage and proportion of employment that is female; their results appear in table 2.2.

Since many comparable worth job evaluations consider jobs' total point scores, it is interesting to consider, first, jobs that have the same total number of points under the Committee's methodology. Such jobs are at least arguably "of comparable worth" according to the total point scores generated by the Committee's procedures. Those jobs, however, sometimes make strange bedfellows. For example, the Census occupation categories of Physician (Census three-digit code 065), Athlete (code 180) and Roofer (code 534) each received a total score of 19.6 points, even though their hourly wage rates were between $6.48 and $15.88 as of 1981. Similarly, the following two jobs both received a total point score of 10.9 and, thus, would presumably be deemed "comparably worthy": University teacher (code 140) and Dishwasher (code 913). Gardeners (code 755) and Computer programmers (code 003) both received a total point score of 12.0, and so are presumably also of comparable worth. Likewise, Garbage collectors (code 754) received 0.1 more points than, and so are presumably worth at least as much as, Real estate agents (code 270).

The basic reason why quite different jobs such as these can neverthe-

Table 2.2 Characteristics of Selected Occupations

Census Occupation (Code)	Points: Total	Points: Subst. Complx.	Points: Motor Skills	Points: Phys. Dem.	Points: Wkg. Cond.	Percent Female	Wage Per Hour
Carpenters (415)	20.2	4.7	7.0	8.4	0.1	1.8	8.05
Electricians (430)	20.1	5.9	7.0	7.2	0.0	2.2	11.03
Physicians (065)	19.6	8.9	9.9	0.8	0.0	15.1	15.88
Athletes (180)	19.6	5.4	7.2	6.9	0.1	47.9	6.48
Roofers or slaters (534)	19.6	3.1	6.5	10.0	0.0	1.0	8.12
Aircraft mechanics (471)	17.5	5.1	7.1	5.2	0.1	2.0	10.76
Machinists (461)	15.2	4.9	8.3	2.0	0.0	4.5	9.19
Construction laborers (751)	14.5	1.3	4.6	8.3	0.3	4.2	6.85
Hairdressers and cosmetologists (944)	14.3	5.1	9.2	0.0	0.0	90.9	4.80
Bank tellers (075)	13.8	6.1	6.6	1.0	0.0	89.9	4.98
Secretaries NEC (372)	13.8	5.5	8.3	0.0	0.0	99.3	5.88
Medical secretaries (371)	13.8	5.6	8.2	0.0	0.0	100.0	5.60
Legal secretaries (370)	13.8	5.5	8.3	0.0	0.0	100.0	6.44
Police (964)	13.8	4.1	5.3	4.4	0.0	7.5	9.39
Registered nurses (075)	13.7	6.1	6.6	1.0	0.0	94.9	8.73
Truck drivers (715)	12.8	2.2	5.9	4.7	0.0	2.2	8.34
Carpet installers (420)	12.5	3.4	7.4	1.7	0.0	1.0	6.35
Psychologists (093)	12.5	8.5	3.9	0.0	0.1	52.5	9.67
Lawyers (031)	12.2	10.0	2.2	0.0	0.0	14.0	14.46
Gardeners (755)	12.0	1.2	3.7	7.1	0.0	6.6	5.43
Computer programmers (003)	12.0	7.4	4.3	0.3	0.0	34.6	11.12

University teachers (140)	10.9	7.8	2.9	0.2	0.0	38.5	11.11
Dishwashers (913)	10.9	0.6	3.0	2.7	4.6	31.7	3.55
Elementary school teachers (142)	10.8	6.2	3.6	1.0	0.0	80.1	9.38
Fork lift operators (706)	10.1	1.2	5.4	3.4	0.1	8.1	7.93
Library assistants (330)	9.8	3.5	4.2	2.1	0.0	82.4	4.55
Accountant (001)	9.8	6.9	2.9	0.0	0.0	40.1	10.00
Machine operatives (690)	9.8	3.4	4.6	1.4	0.4	33.3	7.21
Sales managers – non-retail (233)	9.7	7.2	2.5	0.0	0.0	36.1	11.65
Public administrators NEC (222)	9.6	6.8	2.6	0.2	0.0	34.0	11.41
Misc. operatives (694)	9.6	2.0	5.2	1.8	0.6	38.3	6.32
Machine operatives NS (692)	9.6	2.0	5.2	1.8	0.6	38.0	6.85
Operatives NS (695)	9.6	2.0	5.2	1.8	0.6	38.7	7.18
Typists (391)	9.3	2.6	6.7	0.0	0.0	97.9	5.81
Examiners and inspectors – manufacturing (610)	9.0	2.6	5.8	0.5	0.1	57.6	7.26
Garbage collectors (754)	8.7	0.3	3.6	4.6	0.2	2.0	5.95
Real estate agents (270)	8.6	5.3	3.3	0.0	0.0	53.0	9.06
Textile operatives – spinners (672)	8.6	1.2	5.8	1.5	0.1	75.3	4.82
Sales clerks – retail (283)	8.3	3.4	4.7	0.2	0.0	74.8	5.04
Mail superintendents (224)	8.1	5.9	2.2	0.0	0.0	30.0	12.47
Sales representatives – wholesale (282)	7.8	4.6	3.0	0.2	0.0	16.6	10.66
Teacher aides (382)	7.5	4.5	2.9	0.1	0.0	91.9	4.37
Waiters (915)	6.5	2.1	3.3	1.1	0.0	90.7	3.96

Notes: "Points" components are substantive complexity, motor skills, physical demands and undesirable working conditions. NEC = "not elsewhere classified"; NS = "not specified." "Percent female" refers to proportion of workers in the occupation as of 1982 who were female. "Wage per hour" refers to mean, for workers in the occupation, of ratio of 1981 earnings to product of weeks worked in 1981 and usual hours worked per week.

Sources: Raisian et al. (1984, Table 24, pp. 82–83; 1988, Tables 8.3–4, pp. 190–191).

less receive the same total point score is simple: low (or high) scores on some factors, e.g., "substantive complexity," are offset by high (or low) scores on others, e.g., "undesirable working conditions." Many actual attempts to implement "equal pay for work of equal value" (including those in Minnesota and San José, described in chapters 4 and 5, respectively) have been based on this use of total, unweighted point scores. As this review of table 2.2 suggests, however, some rather dubious conclusions follow when "worth" of jobs is defined in this way.

Of course, one might argue—contrary to the approach adopted in several attempts actually to implement comparable worth—that the points awarded for different job attributes should not all be given equal weight: that, say, points awarded for undesirable working conditions should receive only half the weight given to points for substantive complexity. This leaves plenty of room for argument about (and no objective basis for resolving) the question of what the weights should actually be. Indeed, Evans and Nelson (1989, p. 57) note that both male and female workers have criticized some *a priori* evaluation systems for giving insufficient weight to working conditions. Likewise, Orazem and Mattila (1989, p. 180) report that, in conducting its *a priori* evaluation of state government jobs, Iowa changed the factor weights twice after examining the impact on the final results.

Although the "strange bedfellows" problem in the Committee's total point scores is partly a consequence of weighting, the problem persists even when one considers jobs that score the same in terms of *each* of the four factors developed by the Committee.

For example, Bank tellers (Census code 301), Medical secretaries (code 371), Legal secretaries (code 370) and Secretaries NEC (code 372) have nearly identical point scores for all four attributes. Under a comparable worth standard, they would almost certainly be deemed "comparably worthy." Yet Bank tellers (at 89.9 percent female, the "least female" of the four) received an average of $4.98 per hour in 1981, about 23 percent less than pay of Legal secretaries (virtually all of whom are female). Machine operatives (code 692), Miscellaneous operatives (code 694) and Operatives NS (code 695) are all about 38 percent female, and all received identical scores in terms of each of the four factors derived by the Committee. Although they would therefore be deemed comparably worthy, average pay in these jobs in 1981 ranged from $6.32 to $7.18 per hour. Similarly, Sales representatives–wholesale (Census code 282) and Teacher aides (code 382) differ by only 0.1 of a point in terms of substantive complexity, motor skills and physical demands, and are identical in terms of undesirable working conditions. Yet average hourly earnings of Sales representatives are more than twice those of Teacher aides.

A final set of comparisons concerns jobs that–at least in terms of the Committee's evaluation–are unambiguously superior or inferior to others. Carpenters (Census code 415) received more points than Sales representatives–wholesale (code 282) for each of the four factors considered by the Committee. Thus, Carpenters (less than 2 percent of whom are female) are presumably of greater "worth" than Sales representatives (over 16 percent of whom are women), yet the latter are in fact paid 25 percent more than the former. Likewise, Electricians (code 430) receive at least as many points for each of the four factors as do Mail superintendents (code 224), and so are presumably of greater "worth." Yet the average hourly wage of Electricians (less than 3 percent of whom are female) was about 12 percent lower than that of Mail superintendents (30 percent of whom are women).

The somewhat dubious comparisons highlighted in table 2.2 cannot easily be dismissed. The point scores used in these comparisons are not the product of the political infighting and log-rolling that seem to characterize real-world attempts to evaluate jobs, or of the limited expertise of a single researcher. Rather, they came from an extensive and thorough analysis undertaken by a committee of the National Research Council. True, one could argue that "outliers" and anomalies crop up in any study, no matter how sophisticated. This, however, misses a crucial point. The purpose of the National Research Council's study was to measure the "worth" of different jobs. The anomalies and outliers produced by this analysis suggest not only that the "worth" of particular occupations can be seriously mismeasured, but also that the very notion of measuring the "worth" of individual jobs is suspect.

These doubts are reinforced when one asks whether the "job worth" factors identified by the National Research Council's committee (which are similar to those used in actual attempts to implement comparable worth) are related to jobs' pay. This frames the question in a way that is particularly favorable to comparable worth. One now asks not whether the factors accurately reflect the worth of *individual* jobs, but, rather, whether, *on average*, the factors are related to the "worth" of jobs as reflected in their pay. Even the answer to this general question is equivocal at best. In their regression analysis of 499 wage and salary occupations based on 1970 Census data, Hartmann et al. (1980) found that neither "physical demands" nor "undesirable working conditions" were statistically significantly related to pay of jobs at conventional test levels. Similarly, Raisian et al. (1988) performed a regression analysis of 247 occupations using 1982 Current Population Survey data, and found that of the four factors considered by the National Research Council's committee, only one ("substantive complexity") was statistically significantly related to jobs' pay at conventional test levels.[33]

Other studies find a similar (absence of) pattern. For example, Pierson et al. (1984, esp. pp. 130–131) derived scores for nine factors (cognitive judgment, people orientation, complexity, physical demands, machine tending, working conditions, word and paper processing, and reading and listening) and regressed pay of individuals in both predominantly male and predominantly female jobs on their jobs' scores for these factors. Working conditions, word and paper processing, and reading and listening were not statistically significantly related to reported wages in the regression for incumbents of either female or male jobs; in addition, physical demands were not statistically significant in the regression for persons in female jobs.

Similarly, Ehrenberg and Smith (1987b, esp. pp. 256, 260, 264) analyzed pay rates in relation to job evaluation scores for limited sets of jobs in state employment in Minnesota, Washington State and Connecticut. For Minnesota (which awards points to jobs for know-how, problem solving, accountability and working conditions using the Hay system), monthly maximum salary of predominantly male jobs was statistically significantly related only to know-how points, whereas pay of predominantly female jobs was not significantly related to points for either problem solving or accountability. For Washington State (which awards points for knowledge and skill, mental demands, accountability and working conditions using the Willis system), minimum salary of male jobs was not significantly related at conventional test levels to any of the four factors, and minimum salary for female jobs was significantly related at conventional levels only to knowledge and skill points. For Connecticut (which also used the Willis system), annual salary of male jobs was not significantly related to mental demands or accountability, whereas for female jobs pay was significantly related only to knowledge and skill points.

2.4 *Consequences of Adopting Comparable Worth*

The argument thus far may be summed up as follows: Supply-side factors (societal discrimination, sexual role differentiation, etc.) as well as demand-side employer discrimination can lead to a concentration of women in low-paid jobs; jobs of comparable worth would not necessarily receive the same pay even if employers did not discriminate. Thus, concentration of women in low-paid jobs is not necessarily evidence of employer discrimination; and equal pay for jobs of comparable worth is not necessarily an appropriate standard for evaluating pay differences among jobs. Contrary to what some of its proponents assert (see, e.g., note 38 below), equal pay for jobs of comparable worth is not necessarily fair, and unequal pay for jobs of comparable worth is not inherently discriminatory.

Thus, comparable worth does not provide useful information about discrimination. Likewise, neither the bias-free approach (favored by most proponents) nor the policy-capturing approach (favored by Ferber 1986, pp. 273–274) to job evaluation provides meaningful information on what wages would be, or should be, in the absence of discrimination: even if one could be certain that concentration of women in low-wage jobs were a result of discrimination rather than supply-side factors, and even if the low-wage jobs received the same number of evaluation points as higher-paid predominantly male jobs, it would not necessarily follow that the two sets of jobs would receive the same rate of pay in the absence of discrimination, or that rates of pay for the two sets of jobs should be equalized. "Job worth," as measured by a job evaluation, is unlikely to provide a meaningful guide to what jobs would be paid in the absence of discrimination, and may well be seriously misleading.

From an economic standpoint, then, the basic concepts underlying comparable worth are flawed. To some advocates of comparable worth, however, all this is, ultimately, beside the point. The empirical evidence (discussed in chapter 3) suggests clearly that discrimination *by employers* is responsible for a significant part of the male/female pay gap, even though supply-side factors, including societal discrimination, are not unimportant. Moreover, societal discrimination is discrimination too. Thus, even if literal adherence to a policy of equal pay for jobs of comparable worth is unwarranted, increases in pay for low-wage predominantly female jobs—moving pay in such jobs closer to levels prevailing in higher-wage but comparable (and predominantly male) jobs—will complement conventional antidiscrimination measures (e.g., equal opportunity and affirmative action laws), help close the pay gap and help redress some of the effects of societal *as well as* employer discrimination. In this view, the ultimate test of comparable worth is a pragmatic one: can it deliver the goods? Can it raise women's pay and close the male/female pay gap without serious adverse side effects?

The obvious difficulty here is that, precisely to the extent that it raises pay in predominantly female jobs, comparable worth will make it more expensive to employ workers (male or female) in such jobs without, however, creating additional employment opportunities in either those or other occupations. As with increases in the minimum wage, there will be winners from comparable worth wage increases, but there will also be losers.

To work out the effects of comparable worth wage increases in detail, consider the simple two-job model discussed earlier. A wage increase for the low-wage job, *L*, imposed pursuant to comparable worth will reduce the pay differential between it and the high-wage job, *H*. Thus, it reduces total employment (and employment of men and of women, considered separately) in *L*. It does so for two reasons: a substitution effect, and a scale effect. First, since *L* labor is now more expensive, employers have less reason to use it in place of *H* labor in situations where the two can be substituted, so employment of *L* falls for this reason.[34] Second, the rise in labor costs causes the employer's scale of operations to contract, leading to further declines in the demand for *L* labor.[35]

The comparable worth wage increase for *L* will also affect both wages and employment in the high-wage job, *H*, but here the outcomes cannot readily be determined. The substitution effect *increases* demand for *H* to the extent that it is possible to use *H* workers in place of the now more expensive *L* workers (although, as indicated in note 34, this effect may be small or even zero if the *H* and *L* jobs are truly different). On the other hand, since the scale effect causes the entire scale of operations to contract, it reduces demand for *H* as well as *L*. Thus the net effect on *H* employment depends on which of the two effects is stronger. Unless the two jobs can easily be substituted, however, demand for *H* will fall on balance.

This decrease in demand for *H* tends to reduce the wage of *H* labor. On the other hand, some workers will be attracted towards *L* and away from *H* due to the rise in the *L* wage,[36] so supply to *H* is reduced; that tends to raise the wage in *H*. Thus, the net effect on pay in *H* depends on whether the effect of the reduction in supply to *H* exceeds that of the reduced demand for *H*.

In sum, requiring comparable worth wage increases for predominantly female jobs is akin to putting a tax on employment in such jobs: it makes it more expensive to employ predominantly female labor. However, there is a major difference between an employment tax and a comparable worth wage increase: under comparable worth, the "revenues" from the "tax increase" go not to the Treasury but, rather, to those workers in predominantly female jobs who are able to remain employed after the "tax" takes effect.[37]

Thus, there will be both "winners" and "losers" from comparable worth wage increases. Relative to what would prevail in the absence of such increases, some workers in predominantly female jobs will enjoy higher wages, but others will be unemployed. Depending on one's point of view and in the absence of conceptual objections such as the ones discussed above, the merits of comparable worth depend on demand elasticities, i.e., on whether the gains from higher wages are enough to offset the losses from reduced employment.[38]

To some extent, then, the case for or against comparable worth depends on empirical questions: How much of the pay gap is demand-side rather than supply-side in origin? Would comparable worth pay adjustments lead to large employment losses, or would they have only modest effects on employment? I discuss these questions in the next chapter.

NOTES

[1] Since some noneconomists (and, for that matter, some economists) misunderstand the meaning of the terms "supply" and "demand," I want to emphasize at the outset that, at least at the present level of generality, there is not much analytical content, and literally *no* normative significance, in the concept of "wage determination by supply and demand." Employer demand for labor may be affected by many factors (e.g., discriminatory attitudes towards prospective employees, the wage required, collusion with other employers, the likely impact on sales revenues), and so can the supply of labor (which may be affected by, e.g., trade unions, the wage offered, cultural norms, and sexual or other kinds of role differentiation). Thus, at the present level of generality, reference to supply and demand simply summarizes the potentially quite lengthy list of motives underlying the decisions of the two sides of labor market transactions, i.e., firms and workers. (In particular, the notion of wage determination by supply and demand does not entail any assumption that labor market transactions are free from coercion, that both sides of such transactions enjoy complete information, etc.) Hence, the statement that wages are "determined by supply and demand" has literally no normative significance: given the lengthy list of factors (just noted) that could in principle affect supply and demand, it is clear that the process of wage determination by supply and demand may entail outcomes that, at least in the eyes of some, are clearly unjust and inequitable. Indeed, in the most general sense, comparable worth is an attempt to determine whether the result of wage determination by supplies and demands is in fact unjust or inequitable.

[2] This definition focuses on one *particular* motive underlying employers' demand for labor (the effect of employing labor on production, and hence on sales and profits) and ignores others (e.g., discriminatory motives towards potential workers, collusion between employers, etc.); I say more about this below. One technical point about this definition is that it measures the "worth" of jobs in real terms (i.e., in terms of jobs' marginal productivities), and so would entail a comparison between job worth and the *real* wage (i.e., the ratio of the money wage to the product price) paid for that job. An alternative definition with the same substantive meaning would measure the "worth" of jobs in nominal terms (i.e., the *dollar value* of the jobs' contribution to output, or "marginal *revenue* product" in economic jargon), which entails a comparison between job worth and the money ("nominal") wage per se.

[3] Indeed, some discussions *first* define "comparable" to mean, "of equal value to the employer,"

and *then* assert that, as a practical matter, "comparable" would mean "comparable in terms of skill, effort, responsibility and working conditions." (See, e.g., Bureau of National Affairs 1981, p. 1.) Thus, such discussions treat the two definitions as similar or equivalent, although they are at least potentially quite different.

[4] Of course, there may be exceptions to this general rule. For example, the productivity of work performed in extreme heat or cold may be less than the productivity of work performed under normal climatic conditions.

[5] Cited in Heen (1984, p. 214); see also Newman and Vonhof (1981).

[6] Treiman (1979) traces the concept to studies undertaken by the U.S. Civil Service Commission in 1871 and Frederick W. Taylor's "scientific management" studies of 1881.

[7] Part of the following discussion is based on the work of Henderson and Clarke (1981), who provide a useful review of different kinds of commercial job evaluation methodologies.

[8] For example, see the "Time Span of Discretion" method (Jaques 1964) and the "Broadbanding" method (Paterson and Husband 1970).

[9] Early examples include the "Point-Factor Method" (Lott 1926) and the "Factor-Comparison Method" (Benge 1946). These and similar procedures led to numerous methods, sometimes called "point-factor-comparison methods," developed by firms such as the Western Electric Co. and industry groups such as the National Metal Trades Association, the National Electrical Manufacturers Association, and the American Association of Industrial Management.

[10] For detailed discussion of actual implementation of the Hay methodology at an Australian college of education, see Burton et al. (1987). Dr. Alvin O. Bellak, general partner in the Hay Group, described the Hay philosophy as follows (U.S. Congress, House 1983, p. 345):

> . . . scales of job value, which are one of the ways to measure comparable worth and pay equity, are most acceptable in relation to jobs within a single establishment utilizing a limited range of different occupational skills. That is, the scales are most acceptable for establishing pay equity among job classes within related job families. Scales may have one factor or multiple factors, independent factors or redundant factors, emphasis on measurement precision or emphasis on credibility and acceptance of results. Consistently, however, it can be observed that the scales will not be accepted if they are imposed by fiat, without explanation or communication. They must be adopted through widespread organizational consensus. Only through substantial efforts to introduce flexibility in processes of deliberation and judgment is it possible to apply such scales to increasingly broad ranges of job families, of establishments within an organization, or of organizations within an industry or an economy.

The Hay Group has, however, been willing to consider various approaches to job evaluation. For example, as discussed in chapter 5 of this book, Hay used a single scale to evaluate different "job families" in municipal employment in San José, California, and contended in a "Client Briefing" (Hay Associates 1981, p. 2) that the Hay Guide Chart-Profile Method of job measurement is "the appropriate methodology" for use in implementing comparable worth. As some astute observers have noted, Hay has thus expressed "strong agreement on every side of the question" (Aldrich and Buchele 1986, p. 72, n. 2; see in particular the statements cited therein).

[11] In actual applications, this approach can become considerably more complex than the simple hypothetical example outlined here. One version begins with a "structured job analysis questionnaire" (in some variants, a Position Analysis Questionnaire or PAQ) that analyzes jobs in terms of a total of 187 job elements (e.g., "operates keyboard devices," "works under high-temperature

conditions"). Factor analysis and stepwise regression analysis are then used to reduce these 187 elements to a much smaller number, which are then used in a regression analysis of the association between job elements and pay. (See Treiman and Hartmann, eds. 1981, esp. pp. 119–26; McCormick 1979, pp. 147–9; and McCormick, Jeanneret, and Meacham 1972.)

[12] The discussion in the text focuses on problems with commercial job analyses with a direct bearing on assessments of predominantly female vs. predominantly male jobs. Brief mention should also be made of more general problems with commercial (or for that matter any) job evaluation. One is inter-rater reliability: different evaluators using the same evaluation system often may not produce similar evaluations of the same set of jobs. Another is inter-system reliability: different job evaluation systems may not yield similar rankings of the same set of jobs. For further discussion of these issues, see Beatty and Beatty (1984), McArthur (1985) and Schwab (1985). A final problem concerns the information content of the separate elements used in job evaluations; several writers (e.g., Ehrenberg and Smith 1987b; Aaron and Lougy 1986, esp. p. 33, quoting Remick) have noted that the correlation among the scores on each pair of job attributes considered in such evaluations (e.g., between "skill" and "working conditions") is very high–sometimes in excess of 0.9. This raises questions about the extent to which the measures of the different attributes actually incorporate genuinely different information about the jobs being evaluated.

[13] Treiman and Hartmann, eds. (1981, p. 76); see also p. 72 and Remick (1984, p. 100). The comment cited in the text refers to the use of policy-capturing methods to derive weights for individual compensable factors, but it applies equally to the use of key or benchmark jobs and area wage surveys.

[14] For example, such *a priori* weights could be derived by union-management negotiation, committees consisting of employees and/or outside consultants, etc. As Evans and Nelson (1989, p. 56) note, "most comparable worth supporters" favor an *a priori* approach that does not refer to market wage rates; and numerous comparable worth job evaluations conducted for state and local governments have explicitly avoided using external labor market wage data. (For example, see Orazem and Mattila 1989, p. 179, on Iowa; Willis and associates 1974, p. 1, on Washington State; Chapter 4, on Minnesota; and Chapter 5, on San José.)

[15] The footnote refers to Kerr and Fisher (1950), who make the same point.

[16] Smith (1937, p. 100); see Rees (1976) for a bicentennial appreciation of Smith's analysis in light of subsequent economic analysis.

[17] Changes (or lack of change) in the pay gap (or in the ratio of female to male earnings) may be due to changes in discrimination, in enforcement of antidiscrimination measures, and in workers' characteristics. These changes may be mutually reinforcing or offsetting. For example, Smith and Ward (1984) argue that the decline in the ratio of female to male *average* earnings during the 1960s and constancy in the 1970s is attributable to an influx of relatively unskilled women (some of whom were returning to the workforce after a spell of childbirth and childrearing) that more than offset improvements in wages of women (relative to men) with given characteristics. Similarly, other researchers–some of whose work is surveyed by Brown (1982)–argue that, abstracting from effects such as those described by Smith and Ward, enforcement of antidiscrimination measures tended to raise the ratio of female to male earnings for workers with given characteristics. The relative importance, however, of each of these factors–e.g., antidiscrimination efforts vs. changes in worker characteristics and/or in the extent of discrimination–in explaining the behavior of the pay gap remains controversial.

[18] The following discussion is based on Killingsworth (1987), which provides further details.

[19] Note the "on average" here: this means that, although some women may be more interested in

and/or better qualified for one job rather than another relative to some men (and relative to other women), there is no systematic difference related to sex in either job interests or job qualifications.

[20] Equivalently, a higher relative wage for *H* induces lower relative employment for *H*. To some extent, demand for *H* falls when the wage in *H* rises because of a substitution effect: firms may substitute *L* labor for *H* labor when the *H* wage rises. However, even if no such substitution is possible (as in the case of a "fixed-coefficients" or "Leontief" production technology that requires that inputs must be used in fixed proportions, e.g., one secretary per typewriter), demand for *H* falls when the *H* wage rises because of a scale effect: a rise in the *H* wage raises the firm's marginal costs and thus reduces the optimal scale of the firm's operations and its use of all inputs, including *H* labor. (Analogously, a rise in labor costs causes public sector employers to reduce use of labor inputs generally because the same personnel budget can now buy less labor.) Of course, a rise in the *H* wage induces a decline in demand for *H relative to* that for *L* only if the substitution effect is nonzero, as assumed in figures 2.1–2.

[21] Since the relative supply curve has a positive (rather than a zero) slope, I am assuming that some workers would want to work in the "high wage" job *H* even if pay in it were *lower* than in the "low wage" job *L*; and, similarly, that some workers will want to work in the low wage job *L* even though pay in it is less than pay in *H*. The basic reason is that *H* and *L* will have non-wage attributes (e.g., working conditions) that different workers will evaluate differently. For example, *H* might entail outdoor work, which some workers would (would not) want to do even if it were very badly (well) paid.

[22] Note the "on average" here. This model allows for differences among individuals in terms of (e.g.) job interests (see note 19 above); in the absence of such differences, the relative supply schedule would be horizontal. For the time being, however, I also assume that, on average, the distribution of men's job preferences is the same as the distribution of women's job preferences; and that, at given wage levels, the average woman is no more or less likely to prefer job *H* to job *L* (or vice versa) than the average man.

[23] Note that equilibrium does *not* imply (and is not implied by) intersection of S_1 with D_{1s}, s=m *or* f. S_1 shows the relative wage that must be offered to a *given* sex group to elicit specified levels of relative supply *from that sex group*. D_{1s} shows the relative wage that employers are willing to offer to sex group s at specified levels of *aggregate* relative employment.

[24] Note, however, that whereas S_{1s}, s=m or f, shows the relative supply *of sex s* at different relative wages, the aggregate relative supply schedule S_1 shows *aggregate* relative supply (a kind of weighted average of the two sex groups' relative supplies) at different relative wages.

[25] Note that the condition $S_{1s}=D_1$ $(=D_0)$, s=m *or* f, does not imply (and is not implied by) equilibrium. S_{1j} denotes the relative supply of *sex s*, whereas D_1 refers to *aggregate* relative demand (of both sexes combined). Even though they do not lie on D_1, the points e_{1f} and e_{1m} in figure 2.2 are equilibria (exactly as in figure 2.1), since they merely indicate the implications for each sex group of the aggregate equilibrium e_1. On the other hand, equilibrium is impossible except at e_1: w_1 is the only (aggregate) wage rate at which (aggregate) relative supplies equal (aggregate) relative demands.

[26] For example, Bergmann and Gray (1984) and Bergmann (1985) consider a two-job model under the assumption that *all* workers have *identical* tastes and abilities and conclude that, absent discrimination, the two jobs would receive the same pay. This is said to establish the economic case for comparable worth, although Bergmann (1985, p. 81) asserts that "a considerably weaker assumption" would do so also: that "just enough women need to be willing and able to change occupations so that the 'crowding' of labor in the women's occupations would be relieved if employer-enforced segregation were relaxed." However, if "relieving" the effect of "'crowding' of

labor in the women's occupations" simply means making the proportion female the same in the two jobs, this clearly does not establish that *wages* in the two occupations would be equal in the absence of such crowding. And if "relieving" the effect of crowding means equating wages in the two jobs, then the argument is circular.

[27] Smith also remarked (1937, p. 100) that "the most detestable of all employments, that of public executioner, is, in proportion to the quantity of work done, better paid than any common trade whatever." However, my colleague, Michael K. Taussig, reminds me that when the convicted mass murderer Gary Gilmore was to be executed, numerous individuals telephoned the prison in which Gilmore was held in order to volunteer their services gratis. Perhaps state prisons might auction the rights to execute prisoners to the highest bidder! Again, the essential point is that tastes are heterogeneous: what one individual might be unwilling to do even at unimaginably high rates of pay, another individual might be willing to do at very low (or even negative!) rates of pay.

[28] Several writers have questioned this "translators" example, but their arguments are unconvincing. For example, Aaron and Lougy (1986, p. 36, n. 46) contend that excess supply of, say, Spanish translators would ultimately mean that "the jobs of Spanish translator and French translator would cease to be the same" because employers, having less incentive to economize on the time of Spanish translators, would provide them with less advanced equipment and secretarial assistance, require them to perform more menial tasks, etc. However, this possibility reinforces Sharon Smith's original point: if excess supply of Spanish translators led to (among other things) a deterioration in their working conditions relative to those of French translators, as Aaron and Lougy are effectively arguing, then a comparable worth standard would presumably require that Spanish translators' wages be *greater* than French translators' wages. Similarly, Weiler (1986, p. 1762, n. 133), who erroneously infers that "the greater demand for Spanish translation in Miami" would necessarily entail higher pay for Spanish translators than for French translators, asserts that provided there is no difference in training or skill required to become a translator in either language, "one would expect the compensation rates for these two jobs to move together" in the long run. This ignores the possible influence of heterogeneous preferences for geographic location (which might well entail a wage differential between the two jobs even in the very long run) and does not, of course, mean that pay for these two "comparable" jobs must necessarily "move together" all the way to equality.

[29] For example, see Aaron and Lougy (1986, esp. pp. 16–24) and Treiman and Hartmann, eds. (1981, esp. chapter 3).

[30] Indeed, one might even suspect that, precisely because they are complex, real world labor markets would be quite unlikely to entail any simple relation between job worth and job pay even if it were possible to eliminate all vestiges of employer discrimination from the pay structure.

[31] The Aldrich-Buchele proposition is based on an assumption of arbitrage: workers who found that a given skill (e.g., college education) paid a higher return in one occupation rather than another would switch into the occupation in which it was paid more. However, as Aldrich and Buchele themselves note (1986, p. 101, n. 1), equal marginal returns to a characteristic in different jobs requires *constant* returns to the characteristic: for example, if there were "strongly increasing or decreasing returns to training" and if "different groups of workers differed widely in the amount of training they had, nondiscriminatory differences in returns to training between different groups of workers could exist." For more general discussions of this issue, see Heckman and Scheinkman (1987), Rosen (1983), and Welch (1969). One factor that tends to prevent returns to given characteristics (e.g., education) from being the same in different jobs is that workers must usually work in only one job and cannot "unbundle" their characteristics – using their education in one job and their physical strength in another, say – in order to engage in arbitrage across jobs.

[32] The "detailed" or three-digit U.S. Census occupational taxonomy is the most detailed

categorization of occupations available for analysis of national survey data; whereas the Census' "broad" or one-digit classification consists of broad groupings (e.g., professional, clerical, craft), its detailed or three-digit classification refers to much more homogeneous groups of jobs (e.g., lawyer, file clerk, plumber). The Committee's four-factor scores for Census occupations were later used by another analysis undertaken for the National Research Council of the extent of unequal pay for work of equal value (Treiman and Hartmann, eds. 1981, esp. pp. 24–31).

[33] See Hartmann et al. (1980, table 3, "all occupations" regression II) and Raisian et al. (1988, p. 194, table 8.5, specification 2). Hartmann et al. (1980, table 3) also studied "mixed" and male and female "dominated" occupations separately. In these further analyses, undesirable working conditions were never statistically significantly related to pay; physical demands were not significant for male occupations; motor skills were significant only for female occupations; and substantive complexity was not significant for female occupations. Parcel (1989) finds similarly tenuous connections between pay and job content variables in an analysis of 1980 Census data.

[34] Of course, to the extent that the two jobs are "different"—say, if H refers to tree trimmers or zoo keepers and L refers to nurses or file clerks—they are more or less by definition not easily substitutable. If so, the substitution effect may be small or even zero, as in the case of a fixed-coefficients (Leontief) production function.

[35] For-profit employers find that the wage increase raises the marginal cost of production; unless they can pass all of the cost increase on to consumers, this rise in marginal cost induces a decline in production, and hence in demand for inputs. Nonprofit employers (e.g., government) find that the wage increase reduces the purchasing power of their employment budget; unless they can increase their budget (e.g., via higher taxes or spending cuts elsewhere) to offset this fully, this leads to decreases in employment.

[36] Proponents of comparable worth sometimes suggest that, if pay in predominantly female occupations were raised via comparable worth, more men would be attracted to them and they would therefore become more integrated (for examples, see Gold 1983, p. 56; and Steinberg 1986, esp. p. 122). Mary Hatwood-Futrell, secretary-treasurer of the National Education Association, testified at Congressional hearings (U.S. Congress, House 1983, p. 264) that "I think you would see more men coming into the [teaching] profession" if wages were adjusted along comparable worth lines. However, this overlooks the distinction between supply and demand: although comparable worth pay increases may attract more men to predominantly female jobs, such pay increases will also reduce the number of such jobs. Whether the jobs will, on balance, be more or less integrated is therefore unclear.

[37] Thus, a full accounting of the gains and losses from adoption of comparable worth on an economywide basis will require a general equilibrium approach (see Beider et al. 1988, for an example). See Oi (1986) for further discussion of labor market effects of comparable worth.

[38] Hartmann (1986, p. 175, emphasis original) appears to assign zero weight to employment effects: "Once unequal pay [for jobs of comparable worth] is understood as sex-based wage *discrimination*, even arguments that redress would be costly or might lead to some unemployment won't hold up against the basic issue of fairness and the importance of removing discrimination."

3

Comparable Worth: Empirical Issues

This chapter is concerned with empirical issues related to comparable worth. Since comparable worth is usually regarded as a remedy for the male/female pay gap, I first discuss both conventional economic and comparable worth analyses of the empirical magnitude of the pay gap, with special reference to methodological and conceptual differences between these two types of analyses and their likely empirical consequences. I then discuss methodologies for analyzing the empirical effects on wages and employment of adopting the principle of equal pay for jobs of comparable worth.

3.1 *Conventional Economic Analyses of the Pay Gap*

The discussion of chapter 2 may be briefly summarized as follows. Labor market (demand-side) discrimination can lead to concentration of women in low wage jobs, a negative relation between "femaleness" and pay among different jobs, and a male/female pay gap. But various supply-side factors (sex differences in job preferences and/or job qualifications, due to sexual role differentiation, societal discrimination, etc.) can also do so. *Unequal* pay for jobs of comparable worth is not necessarily discriminatory; *equal* pay for jobs of comparable worth is not necessarily nondiscriminatory.

For these reasons, economists usually stress the importance of "other-

I thank Paul Decker, Cordelia W. Reimers, and participants in seminars at Indiana University, Johns Hopkins University, Princeton University, the U. S. Bureau of Labor Statistics, and the University of Maryland for many helpful comments on previous versions of this chapter.

things-being-equal" (*ceteris paribus*) comparisons in empirical analyses of pay, i.e., ones that allow explicitly for the effects on pay and on the overall pay gap of male/female differences in job preferences and job qualifications. Typically, studies of this kind are based on regression analyses of individual workers' pay, controlling for individual workers' characteristics—ones that are related to job preferences and job qualifications (e.g., level of education, college major, years of work experience and the like). Economists are willing to infer the existence of labor market discrimination only if pay is systematically related to sex on an other-things-being-equal basis, i.e., only if pay is related to sex among workers who are the same in terms of these other personal characteristics.

To discuss these issues, it is useful to write down a simple explicit statistical model of pay. Let pay of worker i, Y_i, be given by

$$Y_i = bX_i + dM_i + e_i \qquad (3.1)$$

where X_i refers to measured personal characteristics of worker i (variables denoting i's job qualifications and job preferences);[1] M_i is an indicator or dummy variable equal to 1 if i is male and equal to 0 if i is female; and e_i denotes unobserved or unmeasured characteristics pertinent to i's pay. To simplify exposition with no loss of generality, assume that the coefficients on X, b, are positive, i.e., $b > 0$; this simply means that the X_i are defined as factors that are positively associated with pay (so that factors that are negatively related to pay have all been multiplied by -1). The main object of interest in empirical analysis of (3.1) is, of course, the magnitude of d, the coefficient on the male indicator variable; d measures the adjusted pay gap—i.e., the extent to which, on average and other things (the X) being equal, men receive more (if d is positive) or less (if d is negative) pay than women.[2]

Since they play an important role in the following discussion, several points are worth noting at the outset. First, the overall or "total" or "raw" pay gap—the simple difference in average pay of men vs. average pay of women —may be due *either* to male/female differences in *observed* personal characteristics, the "X" of (3.1); *or* to male/female differences in *unobserved* personal characteristics, the "e" of (3.1); *or* to labor market discrimination, the "d" of (3.1). In turn, a positive d, signifying discrimination favoring men and against women, can arise due to unequal pay for *equal* work (i.e., women receiving less pay than men who have the same X *and* who are doing the *same* job) and/or to unequal access to *better* work (i.e., women having a lower chance of holding a highly paid job than men with the same X).

Finally, a key statistical point: empirical estimates of d, the coefficient on M, will be biased upwards (downwards) if the error term e and the indicator variable M are positively (negatively) correlated at *given* X. For example, the estimate of the adjusted pay gap will overstate the extent of pay discrimination favoring men and adverse to women if men possess "more" unobserved factors, e, than do women who are the same in terms of observed characteristics (X). To see in intuitive terms why this is the case, note that d is supposed to measure the effect on pay of being male, other things being equal, and that being male is measured, whereas unobserved characteristics by definition are not. If men have more of these unobserved characteristics e than do women with the same *measured* characteristics X, then some of the pay difference between men and women with the same X is not really due to the difference in sex but rather to the difference in unobserved characteristics; yet, because the unobserved characteristics that are positively related to being male are unobserved whereas being male is observed, conventional statistical analysis will end up crediting all of the pay difference to being male, i.e., will reflect not only the "true" sex difference in pay for people with the same characteristics, d, but also the effect of unobserved characteristics e, to the extent that e and M are correlated among persons with the same observed characteristics X.

The extent to which the male/female pay gap is in fact attributable to labor market discrimination rather than differences in personal characteristics remains controversial. Most studies find that no more than about two-thirds of the pay gap can be "explained" by (i.e., is associated with) differences in personal characteristics. (See Cain 1986, esp. pp. 743–759, for a methodological overview and summary of results obtained in numerous studies of the pay gap.) In the view of many economists, the rest of the pay gap can reasonably be attributed to labor market discrimination. Economists often call this "unexplained" portion of the pay gap the "adjusted" gap, since it has been adjusted for (and thus does not incorporate) the effects of male/female differences in measured personal characteristics. Since the adjusted gap is one-third (or more) of the total gap, the extent of labor market discrimination would appear to be sizeable.

Numerous economists question this reasoning, however. O'Neill's remarks (1984b, p. 263) are typical of this skeptical view:

> After adjusting for the different proxy variables that social scientists use to measure productivity differences, studies have explained varying proportions of the wage gap. . . . Among those studies that have used broad national samples, perhaps the central finding has been that about half of the gap is accounted for by a few key variables: schooling, years of work experience, years out of the labor force, and job tenure. The unexplained residual, however, cannot be taken as a measure of discrimination. It is more correctly described as a measure of our ignorance. Work experience and qualitative aspects of schooling are usually measured crudely, and variables that may be important are omitted because of lack of data. Chief among these is the intensity and motivation with which a career is pursued. The intangible qualities that affect training, job search, and job advancement are likely to be related to the extent to which one's energies must be shared between home responsibilities and a career.

Similarly, Roback (1986) notes that cross-section analyses of pay have "explained" no more than 40 to 50 percent of the overall variation in wages (i.e., the value of R^2 in such analyses is no more than about 0.50) among *white men*: due to data limitations, it was not possible to include many factors that are relevant to pay among white men and that could account for some or even all of the remaining wage variation among white men. The same "missing variables" problem hampers attempts to estimate the portion of the male-female *pay gap* attributable to discrimination. She argues (1986, p. 29) that

> . . . it seems quite likely that residual earnings disparities are not really an index of discrimination; in fact, the possibility that there is

> no discrimination whatsoever cannot be ruled out. Unmeasurable factors account for some 60 percent of the variation in white male earnings, while unexplained earnings differences between the sexes amount to somewhere between 13 and 34 percent. So it is possible that men and women have widely different amounts of unmeasured characteristics, at least enough so that if they could be measured, there might be no significant wage differential at all.

This "missing variables" argument has dominated discussion of conventional economic analyses of the pay gap. In a nutshell, it asserts that, if it were possible to measure and include variables which have not been included in regression analyses of pay because of data limitations, then the fraction of the overall pay gap attributable to discrimination in such a revised study might be smaller—perhaps substantially smaller—than the figure implied by most current research.

Stated in these carefully qualified terms, the missing variables argument is unexceptionable. In terms of equation (3.1), it is simply saying that if unobserved characteristics (e) are positively related to M (male sex) among persons with the same observed characteristics (X), then the estimate of the adjusted pay gap, d, will be overstated (or upward biased, in statistical terms). It should be noted, however, that precisely because the missing variables in question are not now included, there is no way to be certain what their inclusion would do to the results.[3] In particular, and contrary to what O'Neill and Roback appear to be suggesting, even if women "score" less "well" in terms of such missing variables than do men, inclusion of these variables will not necessarily reduce the remaining pay gap. In other words, in terms of equation (3.1), d need not be biased simply because unobserved factors are positively correlated with M. Rather, for inclusion of unobserved factors to reduce the remaining pay gap, the variable in question must be correlated with sex "at the margin," i.e., be related to sex *among persons who are the same in terms of all of the variables already included in the analysis*: in terms of equation (3.1), e must be correlated with M among persons *with the same X*.

As a simple example, suppose one analyzes pay using a regression analysis that does control for educational attainment but does not control for years of work experience, and obtains a sizable estimate for the adjusted male/female pay gap. Even if women have, on average, fewer years of work experience than men, it does not follow that omission of the experience variable produces an overstatement of the estimated pay gap (or that inclusion of this missing variable will reduce the estimate of the adjusted gap). That will occur only if women *with the same educational attainment as men* nevertheless have less work experience, on average. Indeed, if work experience and education are perfectly correlated, omission of the work experience variable will not affect the estimated pay gap at all: in that case, the work experience variable would add no information not already provided by the education variable.

Likewise, even if women are less "motivated" or "career-oriented" than men, omission of a variable denoting "motivation" or "career commitment" would bias the estimate of the pay gap obtained in the studies O'Neill discusses only if women who are the same as men in terms of all previously included factors (education, years of work experience, etc.) are nevertheless less motivated or career-oriented, on average.[4]

Thus, different economists put different weights on the potential importance of the omitted-variables issue—heterogeneous tastes once again!—and so are not equally willing to accept the results of conventional economic analyses of male/female pay differences as evidence of labor market discrimination. This important difference notwithstanding, there is fairly broad agreement on methodological issues. Conventional economic analyses of labor market discrimination focus on characteristics of *individual workers*, and, provided a suitable set of variables measuring these characteristics could be obtained, economists would treat the "adjusted" pay difference—i.e., the pay difference between men and women who are the same in terms of these characteristics—as a measure of labor market discrimination. How does the methodology of comparable worth pay analyses differ from this approach?

3.2 *Comparable Worth Analyses of the Pay Gap*

Unlike conventional economic analyses, which focus on people, comparable worth analyses of the pay gap focus on *jobs*. Studies taking this approach fall into two categories: first, analyses of specific employers, usually state or local governments; and, second, studies of national survey data.

Most of the studies in the first category were prepared for or by administrative bodies, e.g., state or local government agencies. Perhaps the earliest examples are the studies by Willis and associates (1974, 1976) of state government employees in Washington State. Similar procedures have been used in subsequent studies of state government employment in Connecticut, Illinois, Iowa, Minnesota, and Michigan, and of municipal government employment in New York City and San José, California.[5] Pierson, Koziara and Johannesson (1984) took basically the same approach in studying a private-sector firm, as did Baron and Newman (1989) in studying California state government.

In these studies, the unit of analysis is the job (often called "class" or "job classification"). Generally, an administrative pay construct established for each job (e.g., the maximum of the pay range) is regressed on its evaluation score (e.g., the points assigned to it by a job evaluation) and a variable denoting the sex composition of employment in the job. In some cases, the sex composition variable is the proportion of employment in the job that is female; in others, it is an indicator denoting whether the job is female-dominated (i.e., denoting whether a high proportion—the usual cutoff is 70 percent or more—of those in the job are women).[6]

Thus, as regards the question of analyzing pay at a specific employer, the procedures required for comparable worth studies are much simpler than those necessary for conventional economic analyses. The employer under study may have many employees with quite diverse characteristics (e.g., educational background); data on some potentially important employee characteristics (e.g., education) may not even be available; and analysis of these employees along conventional economic lines can require substantial computer programming and data processing work. In contrast, comparable worth analyses of this kind require data for a much smaller number of objects—jobs, rather than individuals; the necessary variables—e.g., salary maxima, comparable worth evaluation points and "femaleness"—for each job may well be readily available. It is not surprising, then, that many state and local governments, with hard pressed personnel staff who may not have much experience doing conventional economic analyses, opt instead for comparable worth analyses of pay.

Comparable worth studies of national survey data include those by Aldrich and Buchele (1986), Treiman and Hartmann, eds. (1981, pp. 28–31), and Treiman, Hartmann and Roos (1980). Although prepared by academic researchers using national survey data sets—the U.S. Census Public Use Sample (Treiman and Hartmann, eds.; Treiman, Hartmann and Roos) or the National Longitudinal Surveys (Aldrich and Buchele)—they clearly were inspired by the first kind of comparable worth analysis, and appear to some extent to be attempts to apply the same kind of methodology to national survey data. The differences of approach are largely imposed by the differences in data. National survey data sets provide no information on workers' job titles as such, on administrative pay constructs (e.g., the maximum pay rate) or job evaluation points for workers' jobs. Instead, the unit of analysis is the "occupation" (e.g., the "detailed" or three-digit occupations defined by the U. S. Census' occupational taxonomy), and the measure of pay is usually the average (e.g., mean or median) hourly earnings of workers in the occupation. In lieu of a job evaluation point variable, these studies use a set of variables denoting characteristics of the occupation (e.g., measures of its complexity, the extent to which it requires working with machines or making cognitive judgments, etc.), derived from the *Dictionary of Occupational Titles*.[7] The measure of pay is then regressed on the occupation characteristics variables and a variable measuring the sex composition of employment in the occupation.

3.3 *What Do Comparable Worth Analyses Measure?*

It is clear from the foregoing that conventional economic and comparable worth analyses of male/female pay differences use different methodologies and procedures. These differences raise an even more important issue: whether the two kinds of analyses are even addressed to the same set of questions. The basic question considered in conventional economic analyses is reasonably clear: do individual workers with the same characteristics (reflecting, e.g., productivity and job preferences) receive the same pay, on average, regardless of sex? In contrast, and somewhat surprisingly, the nature of the basic issue addressed in comparable worth analyses is less clear.

On the one hand, it could be argued that comparable worth analyses are addressed to essentially the *same* question considered in conventional analyses: whether identical workers receive the same pay regardless of sex. On the other hand, however, it could be argued that, because they focus on jobs rather than individual workers as the unit of analysis, comparable worth analyses are concerned with questions about discrimination that are fundamentally different from those addressed by conventional economic analyses.

Comparable worth analysis as a form of conventional economic analysis

According to some of its proponents, there is nothing particularly novel about comparable worth analysis: like the conventional economic approach, the comparable worth approach is concerned with measuring the extent of discrimination, defined as different treatment (with respect to pay for the same work *or* access to better-paid work) of otherwise identical men and women. In this view, methodological differences among studies embodying the two approaches are relatively unimportant: such differences merely reflect practical problems encountered in different settings (e.g., lack of data on individual worker characteristics or, alternatively, on jobs' assessed "worth") rather than major conceptual differences.[8]

If this view is correct, then comparable worth and conventional economic analyses of pay should yield essentially similar results despite their methodological differences. Is this likely to occur, however? Here I consider the possible consequences of the three major methodological differences between the two kinds of analyses: the nature of the dependent variable (pay); the nature of the independent variables (measures of either individual or job characteristics); and the difference in the unit of analysis (individuals or jobs). As will become clear shortly, the effect of these methodological differences on estimates of the male/female pay gap will depend, in general, on the relative importance of the various phenomena underlying the gap: male/female differences in skills and job preferences; unequal pay for equal work; and unequal access (via differences in *either* assignment at hire *or* rates of promotion) to better-paid work.

Use of an administrative pay construct. The first major difference between conventional economic and comparable worth studies of pay is that, in the former, the dependent variable (pay) is generally the actual rate of pay received by the individual worker, whereas in comparable worth studies it is frequently an administrative pay construct, e.g., the maximum rate of pay in the worker's job classification.[9] Use of such an administrative pay construct instead of an actual rate of pay may generate an errors-in-variables problem that can bias the estimate of the adjusted male/female pay gap.

To see why, let A_i denote the administrative pay construct pertinent to worker *i*'s job, A_i, and consider the effect of using A_i rather than the worker's actual pay, Y_i, when estimating the model (3.1) by ordinary least squares (OLS) while following conventional economic methodology in all *other* respects.[10] The relation between A and Y is simply

$$Y_i = A_i + a_i \qquad (3.2)$$

where a_i is the *difference* between the worker's actual pay and the administrative construct. For example, if A is the minimum (maximum) rate of pay for the worker's job, then a is the amount, if any, by which the worker's actual pay is above the minimum (below the maximum) for his or her job; thus, $a \geq 0$ (≤ 0) always. In econometric parlance, A measures Y with error, where the magnitude of the error is a. Now combine (3.1)–(3.2) and rearrange to get

$$A_i = bX_i + dM_i + e_i^*, \quad \text{where } e_i^* = e_i - a_i. \qquad (3.3)$$

Suppose first that the administrative construct A is the *minimum* rate of pay for the employee's job, so that a is the amount by which his or her pay exceeds the minimum. The coefficient on M, d, will be biased if the composite error term e^* and M are correlated at *given* X. The potential problem introduced by use of A in place of Y is that the presence of a in the composite error term may induce a correlation between it and M, even at given values of X. Under what conditions will this occur? If there is "unequal pay for equal work" favoring men, then, on average, men receive more pay in excess of the minimum for their job than do women with the same characteristics (X): at given X, a (the amount paid above the minimum) will be positively correlated with M. Then, at given X (and even in the absence of any correlation between unobservables e and the male indicator variable M), both the *negative* of the amount paid above the minimum, $-a$, and the composite error term $e^* = e - a$ will be *negatively* correlated with M.

Thus, to the extent that there is unequal pay for equal work, OLS regression that uses the administrative pay construct rather than actual pay will *understate* the extent of discrimination favoring men and disfavoring women. Moreover, it appears unlikely that this would be affected by "unequal access to better-paid work" because of discrimination in initial assignment (i.e., differential treatment of equally qualified men and women with respect to job assignment *at hire*). Such initial assignment discrimination will mean that, relative to women with the same qualifications (X), men will receive higher pay (Y) *and* will hold jobs with higher maximum *and* minimum rates of pay (A). At least to a first approximation, raising *both* Y *and* A (for men relative to women at given X) is unlikely to affect their *difference* (the measurement error $a = Y - A$), or, therefore, the correlation (if any) between the composite error term $e^* = e - a$ and sex (M) at given X.

That is not necessarily the end of the story, however. If there is "unequal access to better work" due to differential rates of *promotion* for equally qualified men and women, then, on average and relative to men with the same X, women are trapped in lower-paid jobs and are "maxed out"—earning the highest rate paid for their low-level job. Conversely, men will move rapidly to successively better-paid jobs, earning less than the highest rate for the jobs they hold (i.e., receiving small "excess payments" a) but occupying jobs with substantially higher salary minima A and thus receiving substantially higher salary levels, Y.[11] In this case, a (the amount paid above the minimum) will be negatively correlated with M at given X; and so at given X (and even in the absence of any correlation between unobservables e and the male indicator variable M), both the *negative* of the amount paid above the minimum, $-a$, and the composite error term $e^*=e-a$ will be *positively* correlated with M. Thus, to the extent that differential treatment of equally qualified men and women with respect to promotion causes unequal access to better-paid work, OLS regression that uses the administrative pay construct rather than actual pay will *overstate* the extent of discrimination favoring men and disfavoring women.

Similar conclusions apply when A is the salary maximum. In this case, a is the amount by which one's actual pay (Y) falls short of the maximum for one's job, and so will be either negative or zero. To the extent that women suffer from unequal pay for equal work, men will be closer to (and more likely to be at) the salary maximum than women with the same X. If so, a will be larger in absolute value ("more negative") for women than for men with the same X; M will be positively correlated with a, and negatively correlated with both $-a$ and the composite error term at given values of X. Hence, to the extent that women suffer from unequal pay for equal work, OLS regression that uses the salary maximum for employees' job classifications rather than their actual pay will understate the extent of discrimination favoring men and disfavoring women. (Again, unequal access due to discrimination in initial assignment appears unlikely to change this conclusion.)

On the other hand, to the extent that women suffer from unequal access to better-paid work due to differential promotion rates, they will "max out" more often than men with the same X; i.e., M will be negatively correlated with a and positively correlated with both $-a$ and the composite error term at given values of X. Hence, to the extent that women suffer unequal access via promotion, use of the salary maximum for employees' job classifications rather than actual pay in OLS regression generates an errors-in-variables bias that overstates the extent of discrimination favoring men and disfavoring women.[12]

In sum, use of an administrative pay construct can induce two different errors-in-variables biases, of opposite signs, in the estimate of discrimination. *A priori* statements about which of the two biases will in fact be stronger, and thus about the net bias, are inevitably speculative. However, to the extent that comparable worth advocates are correct in arguing that concentration of women in low-paid occupations is a serious problem, and to the extent that this can be regarded as unequal access to better paid work due to differential promotion rates, overstatement of the female salary disadvantage in comparable worth analyses of the pay gap is likely to be a serious problem.

Use of job characteristics. A second major difference between conventional economic and comparable worth studies of pay is that, whereas the former control for actual differences in characteristics (e.g., education or years of work experience) of individual *workers*, comparable worth studies control for differences in characteristics of *jobs*. As noted earlier, in some cases a job's characteristics are summarized by a set of variables denoting its skill requirements, complexity, etc., whereas in others, there is a single composite variable, the job's "evaluation point score" (e.g., Hay or Willis job evaluation points), which effectively collapses a set of characteristics pertaining to the job—skill, effort, responsibility and working conditions—into a single number.

On first consideration, this difference between the two kinds of pay studies might appear relatively minor. Could it not be argued that both kinds of studies control for skill—conventional economic analyses, by including measures of individual workers' education, years of work experience, etc.; and comparable worth analyses, by including measures (either explicitly and separately, or else as part of composite point score) of the skills required for the jobs the workers are doing? However, the two kinds of studies do not, in fact, treat skills in a similar way. The skill variable(s) used in comparable worth analyses effectively imputes exactly the same amount of "skill" to all workers in a given job. In contrast, since they use variables that measure skills of individual workers, conventional economic analyses do not suppress the variation in skills typically observed even among workers who are doing the same job. The two kinds of analyses, conventional economic and comparable worth, would be equivalent in this respect only if all workers in each job had the same amount of skill (e.g., education, manual dexterity).

To the extent that comparable worth analyses impute minimum skill levels to all workers and ignore variation in skills, they may induce additional errors-in-variables biases that arise from two distinct phenomena: unequal access to better-paid work; and sex-related "supply-side" differences in actual worker characteristics. To see this, think of X as the actual skill level of the worker; let X^* denote the *minimum* skill level required for one's job; and consider the effect of using X^* rather than actual skill level X when estimating the model (3.1) by OLS while following conventional economic methodology in all *other* respects. (Thus, as in the previous case, one aspect of comparable worth analyses is considered in isolation from the others; see note 10.) The relation between X and X^* may be written as

$$X_i = X_i^* + x_i \qquad (3.4)$$

where x_i (≥ 0) is i's "excess" skill, i.e., the amount of skill he or she has in excess of the minimum level X_i^* required for his or her job. Since X_i^* is used in place of X_i in comparable worth analyses of the pay gap, substitute (3.4) into (3.1) and rearrange terms to obtain

$$Y_i = bX_i^* + dM_i + e_i^*, \quad \text{where } e_i^* = e_i + bx_i. \qquad (3.5)$$

Note that the composite error term, e^*, now consists of unobservables (e) and of "excess" skills, bx.

To assess possible bias in OLS estimates of (3.5), first consider the implications of unequal access to better-paid work. "Unequal access" due to differences in *either* initial assignment *or* rates of promotion typically means that women are less likely to be in better-paid jobs than are men with the same *actual* skill, X. More or less equivalently, it means that, on average, women must have more skill in excess of the minimum (greater x) than men with the same *minimum* skill level (the same X^*). M will therefore be negatively related both to x and to the composite error term, $e^*=e+bx$; and so unequal access will induce a negative bias in the estimate of d, i.e., will result in an understatement of the male salary advantage (female salary disadvantage).

An alternate route to the same conclusion starts with the observation that most comparable worth analyses use one or more variables denoting *job evaluation points* of workers' jobs, P, rather than measures of (minimum or actual) skill levels (X^* or X) as such. To the extent that P amounts to an index of the "level" of workers' jobs (with, e.g., higher values of P denoting higher-paid jobs), analyses of this kind amount to analyses that estimate *only* the extent of unequal pay for *equal* work: that is, they estimate the difference in pay between men and women who are in jobs with essentially the same (overall average) pay. If so, analyses of this kind necessarily understate the overall male salary advantage (female salary disadvantage), which includes not only an unequal pay for equal work component but also a component attributable to unequal access to better paid work.

On the other hand, supply-side differences in worker characteristics (job qualifications and job preferences) may generate sex differences in *actual* "skills" (or, more generally, job skills and/or job preferences), X. In particular, to the extent that men's actual skill levels generally exceed those of women, men will possess "excess" skills to a *greater* extent (their x will be larger, on average) than will women, both overall and within given job categories. To the extent that this is so, M will be positively related both to x and to the composite error term, and so neglecting the greater actual skill levels of the male workers will induce a positive bias in the estimate of d—i.e., will overstate the male salary advantage (female salary disadvantage).

To see why, consider the simple example illustrated in figure 3.1. A sex-blind company has two jobs, A and B. *Minimum* skill requirements, X^*, and pay, Y, are higher in A than in B. All employees have at least

X_B*, the minimum skill level required for *B* (otherwise, they would not have been hired); let X_B* be normalized to zero without loss of generality. Let X_A* be the minimum amount of skill necessary (and sufficient) for an employee to be assigned to the high-wage job, *A*. Next, suppose that the skill distributions of the men and women at this company have the same variance but that, because of supply-side factors noted previously, the *mean* of the skill distribution for men exceeds that for women. Then, as shown in figure 3.1, the mean skill level *and* pay of men will exceed that of women within *both* the low-skill job (*B*) *and* the high-skill job (*A*).[13] Thus, *x* will be positively correlated with *M* at given levels of *X**; and so the OLS *estimate* of *d* will be upward-biased, giving the appearance of a male salary advantage when none in fact exists. In such cases, comparable worth analyses such as (3.5) effectively ignore both (i) the extent to which, because of supply-side reasons, men's actual skill levels exceed those of women and (ii) the fact that these differences in actual skill levels explain some of the pay gap. Thus, such analyses may overstate the extent of the gap that is due to labor market discrimination.

In sum, using minimum instead of actual skill levels can induce two different errors-in-variables biases, of opposite signs, in comparable worth analyses of discrimination. *A priori* statements about the net direction of the two biases are inevitably speculative. To the extent that supply-side differences in skill levels are an important source of the overall pay gap, however, upward bias in the male salary advantage (overstatement of the female salary disadvantage) induced by the use of minimum skill level measures in comparable worth analyses of the pay gap is likely to be a serious problem.

Use of job as the unit of analysis. A third major difference between conventional economic and comparable worth studies of pay is that, whereas the former take the individual worker as the unit of analysis, in the latter the *job* is the unit of analysis. On first consideration, this difference might also appear of relatively minor importance: could one not argue that the job-level regressions used in comparable worth analyses are simply the aggregated or grouped-data equivalents of the

Figure 3.1 Mean Skill Levels by Sex and Job

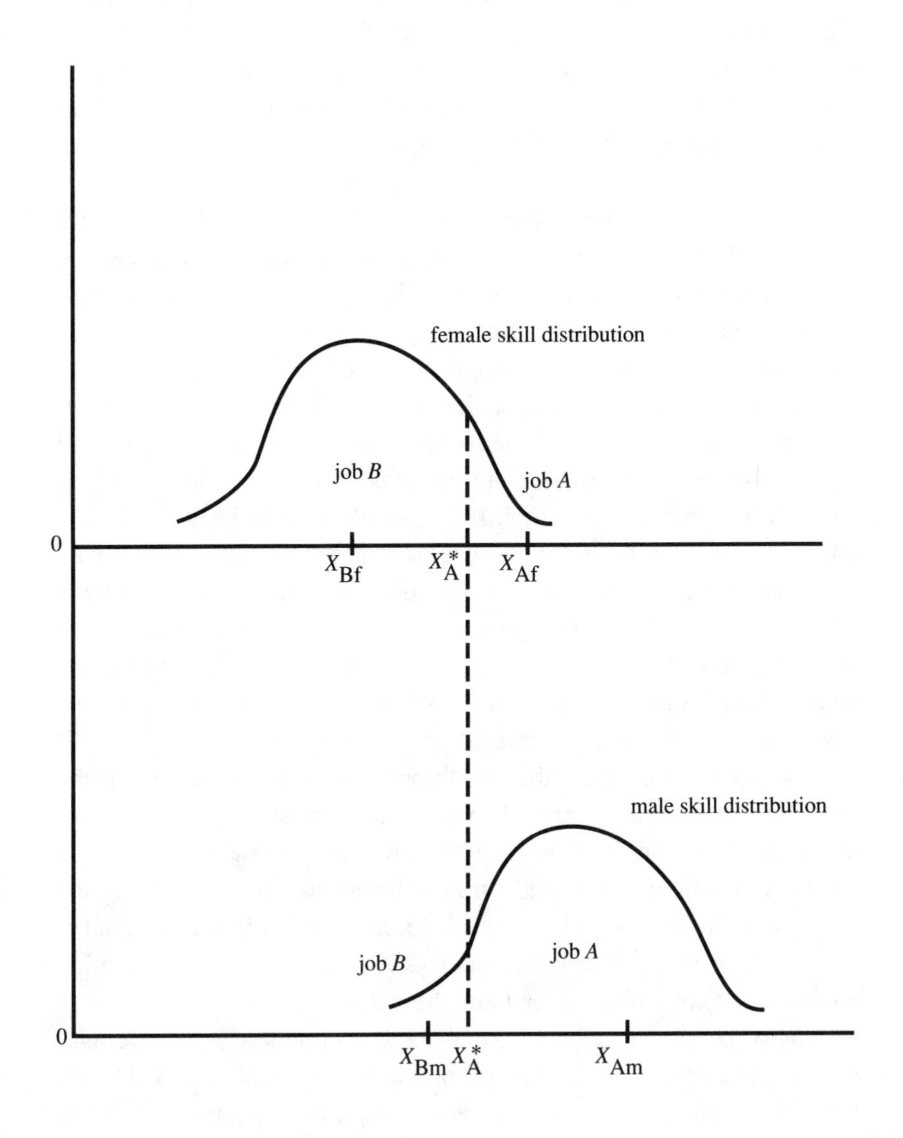

individual-level regressions used in conventional economic analyses?[14] Although grouped-data regression is less desirable in some respects than individual-level regression, standard econometric results (see, e.g., Kmenta 1971, esp. pp. 322–336, or other econometrics textbooks) do suggest that grouping or aggregating does not generate statistical bias under conventional econometric assumptions. Thus, it could be argued, so long as the primary concern is avoiding statistical bias in estimates of discrimination, it makes relatively little difference whether one uses individual-level regression, as in conventional economic analyses, or grouped-data (job-level) regression, as in comparable worth analyses.

The problem with this argument is that standard econometric assumptions on grouped-data estimators do not necessarily hold when jobs define the groups to be considered. In particular, the usual conclusions about the unbiasedness of grouped-data estimators apply only if the variable determining the grouping is independent of the individual-level error term. Here that is unlikely to hold: the individual-level error term—the e of (3.1)—refers to unobservables that affect pay, given observed characteristics; and the variable determining the grouping is the job. Are unobservables that affect one's pay (e.g., motivation) independent of the job one holds, given observed characteristics? If not, application of conventional grouped-data techniques to job-level regressions, as in comparable worth analyses, is inappropriate.

In particular, under plausible conditions, taking the job rather than the individual worker as the unit of analysis, as in most comparable worth analyses of the pay gap, is likely to *overstate* the magnitude of the adjusted male/female pay gap. In intuitive terms, using the job as the unit of analysis induces a form of selection bias in OLS estimates of the relation between pay and (average) skill level. Even in a sex-blind environment, this bias understates the extent to which differences in (average) pay among jobs are attributable to differences in (average) skill levels among jobs. To the extent that men have higher skill levels than women, they will be concentrated in high-paying jobs (for reasons that have nothing to do with discrimination by the employer), so that the understatement of the importance of skill differences will turn into an overstatement of the importance of the proportion male in generating pay differences among jobs, even at given (average) skill levels. Thus, even when the employer's pay practices are sex-neutral, comparable worth analyses will imply that males enjoy a salary advantage at given skill levels—a spurious effect due entirely to selection bias induced by taking job as the unit of analysis.

To see the essential ideas underlying this notion,[15] note that, by (3.1), a regression that uses within-job means (as in a comparable worth analysis) is concerned with estimating

$$Y_j = bX_j + e_j, \quad j = 1, 2, \ldots, J \qquad (3.1')$$

where Y_j, X_j and e_j are the *mean* values of the variables Y, X and e, respectively, for those individuals i who are actually in job j; and where there are J total jobs. (3.1′) is an explicit model of (average) *pay* within jobs; at least implicitly, there is also a process of some kind that determines selection *into* the different jobs. Let u_{ji} denote unobserved characteristics (e.g., "motivation") that affect individual i's probability of being selected into job j. If these unobserved "selection" characteristics u_{ji} are *uncorrelated* with unobserved characteristics that affect individual i's *pay*, e_i, then e_j—the average value of e_i *among those individuals actually in any job j*—will be zero (in expected value). In this case, conventional grouped-data methods raise no problems of bias.

However, what if the u_{ji} are *positively* correlated with the e_i—that is, what if unobservable factors that affect selection *into* any job j are positively related to unobservables that affect *pay*? If so, then, on average, individuals who are in high-paying jobs will enjoy high pay not only because they have high X, but also because they have a high u_j for the job they hold and thus (because of the positive correlation between e and u_j) a high e. In other words, on average, jobs that score high (or low) in terms of X will also do so in terms of e. In this case, (3.1′) will suffer from an omitted variables problem: the nature of the job selection process induces a positive correlation between average within-job measured skill X_j and the within-job error term e_j. Note also that if, for any reason (e.g., supply factors), men have more measured skill X than women, on average, then e_j in (3.1′) will also be positively correlated with M_j, the "maleness" of jobs.

The consequences for comparable worth pay analyses are now apparent. Consider the prototype comparable worth regression equation:

$$Y_j = bX_j + dM_j + q_j, \quad j = A, B \tag{3.6}$$

where q is an error term. If men have a higher average skill level than women, then, for entirely nondiscriminatory reasons, (1) men will be overrepresented in the high-X job and underrepresented in the low-X job; (2) the e_j of (3.1′) will be positively correlated with the "maleness" of jobs; (3) the expression $dM_j + q_j$ in (3.6) is therefore essentially the equivalent of the e_j of (3.1′); and so (4) the estimate of d, the coefficient on M_j in (3.6), will be positive.

A positive estimate of d in the "job aggregate" regression (3.6), in these circumstances, is simply a statistical artifact. It would, however, normally be treated as evidence of discrimination favoring men. Thus, aggregating by job, as in comparable worth analyses, can produce the appearance of discrimination favoring men even at a sex-blind employer.

In sum, because of the three features noted above—use of an administrative pay construct, use of minimum rather than actual skill levels and use of jobs rather than individuals as the unit of analysis—estimates of sex differences in pay obtained in comparable worth analyses are likely to differ from those obtained in conventional economic analyses of pay. It should be noted at once that these results on the potential for bias(es) in comparable worth analyses are not necessarily conclusive. The preceding discussion has considered each of the three major features of comparable worth analyses in isolation from the other two, but of course in actual comparable worth analyses all three features appear simultaneously and may interact with each other. Determining the *net* effect on the statistical results of using all three features together is therefore a much more complicated question to which the preceding discussion provides only tentative answers.

Despite this caveat, however, it seems clear that there is no basis for the notion that estimates yielded by comparable worth analyses are likely to be the same as, or even similar to, those derived using conventional economic methodology. Depending on the relative importance of unequal pay for equal work, unequal access to better work (via both initial assignment and promotions) and male/female differences in skills and job preferences, comparable worth analyses may produce upward- *or* downward-biased measures of the adjusted male/female pay gap, relative to what conventional economic analyses would suggest. In particular, to the extent that job evaluation points simply index workers' actual jobs, comparable worth analyses will measure only the extent of unequal pay for equal work (i.e., work in the same job), and will therefore understate the adjusted pay gap relative to conventional analyses (which reflect not only unequal pay for equal work but also unequal access to better work). On the other hand, comparable worth analyses are likely to overstate the adjusted pay gap relative to conventional economic analyses to the extent that male/female skill or job preference differences and/or unequal access to better work via unequal promotion rates are especially important.

Comparable worth analyses and "systematic underpayment of women's jobs"

To some proponents, comparable worth analyses have essentially the same purpose and ask essentially the same questions as conventional economic analyses. However, to other proponents, the focus of comparable worth analyses on jobs rather than on individuals reflects an outlook on the labor market generally and on discrimination in particular that is fundamentally different from the one underlying the conventional economic approach, providing a "new doctrine of sex discrimination" (England and Norris 1985).

Based on what might be called "institutional analysis," this alternative view emphasizes "the importance of institutional features and their relative inflexibility in determining wages and other conditions of employment," and asserts that this emphasis "offers a more fruitful perspective from which to understand the existence and the persistence of wage differentials between men and women" than does conventional economic analysis (Treiman and Hartmann, eds. 1981, p. 45). Jobs and related concepts (e.g., job families, job ladders, salary ranges for jobs, the distinction between entry-level jobs and jobs filled internally by transfer or promotion, internal labor markets, segmented labor markets) are heavily stressed–indeed, reified. In this view, individuals are of less interest than jobs for analytical (though certainly not normative) purposes, since all that individuals can do is to try to fit into the job structure as best they can: "Workers do not operate as individuals in the labor market, but rather as members of groups defined by their relationship to labor market structures, and labor market structures effectively limit the choices open to them" (Treiman and Hartmann, eds. 1981, p. 52).

A general difficulty with this view is that it does not always distinguish satisfactorily between cases in which jobs and related concepts play an independent role in labor market outcomes, and cases in which such concepts are merely the surface manifestations of underlying processes whose outcomes are actually determined by individual worker characteristics and actions.[16] As regards specific issues related to sex differences in pay, there are further difficulties. Do labor market structures generate such pay differences *independently* of other phenomena, highlighted by conventional economic analysis? If so, how? In particular, apart from unequal pay for equal work and unequal access to better work, which the conventional economic view also identifies as mechanisms for discrimination, are there other mechanisms, resulting from labor market structures *rather than* from causes identified by the conventional economic approach, that may give rise to such pay differences? The institutional literature has generally not provided clear answers to such questions.

In the present context, the best example of these difficulties has to do with one of the stylized facts noted in chapter 2: even with "other things" (e.g., education and years of prior work experience) held constant, workers of *either* sex in predominantly female jobs earn less, on average, than workers of *either* sex in predominantly male jobs. As shown in section 2.2, this stylized fact (and others) can readily be explained in terms of a simple conventional economic model of a two-job labor market with discrimination (in particular, exclusion from, or more generally unequal access to, the high-wage job *H* of figures 2.1–2). In contrast, after citing sex-related differences in job choices and exclusion of women from high-paying jobs as possible explanations, two prominent institutionalists offer a third and presumably distinct explanation "for the lower pay rates of jobs held mainly by women": "women's work is underpaid because women do it—that is, that the same work would be paid more if it were done by men" (Treiman and Hartmann, eds. 1981, p. 56). But this is less an "explanation" than a tautology; moreover, the subsequent discussion of how firms manage "to implement an explicit decision to pay women or minority workers less than men or whites" (p. 57) turns out to rest heavily on exclusion, i.e., unequal access to better work (pp. 58, 62–63). The unanswered questions remain: What mechanisms—in particular, what *institutional* factors—*other than* exclusion make it possible for employers to engage in "systematic underpayment of jobs held mainly by women" (p. 65)? Will such systematic underpayment be overlooked or understated by conventional economic analyses, and yet be accurately measured by comparable worth analyses?

The answers to these questions are somewhat surprising. Systematic underpayment of predominantly female jobs relative to predominantly male jobs need not require exotic job structures (as in the institutionalist view) *or* exclusion (as in the conventional economic view). Although such systematic underpayment will be entirely overlooked by conventional economic analyses of pay, comparable worth analyses of pay are quite unlikely to measure it accurately. The way to avoid mismeasurement of such systematic underpayment is to analyze not compensation, but rather vacancies and shortages.

Two examples help illuminate the basic ideas. First, consider how comparable worth and conventional economic analyses would be used to determine whether a university discriminates against female faculty relative to male faculty. The conventional economic approach would entail regressing individual faculty members' pay on an indicator variable denoting sex and on variables measuring personal characteristics—highest degree, years since highest degree, age, field of academic specialization (social work, sociology, statistics, etc.), years of university service, prior work experience, etc. The unit of analysis would be the individual faculty member. The question to be investigated would be whether men are paid more than women, other things (personal characteristics related to qualifications and preferences) being equal.

In contrast, a comparable worth analysis would take "job" as the unit of analysis, and would start with an evaluation of the worth of each job. In a university setting, "job" might mean academic department, or possibly cells constructed by academic rank and department: that is, sociology faculty would be treated as doing one job and statistics faculty another; alternatively, associate professors in sociology would be treated as being in one job and associate professors in statistics would be treated as being in another. Presumably, all faculty jobs (or, more narrowly, all faculty jobs at the same academic rank), regardless of academic department, would be assessed as requiring the same skill, effort, responsibility and working conditions: in other words, jobs (perhaps at the same academic rank) in social work, statistics, etc., would be assessed as "comparable."[17]

Taking jobs (either departments, or department-rank cells) as the unit of analysis, one would then regress an administrative pay figure (e.g., the maximum or midpoint of a pay range) or a summary statistic for pay (e.g., mean pay) on the *proportion* female in each job. Since all jobs (e.g., departments) would be assessed as comparable, it would be unnecessary to include any measure of job evaluation points, since these would be the same for all departments.[18] Moreover, it would be inappropriate to include any indicators denoting the academic field (statistics, sociology, etc.) of each job, for that would amount to treating interfield pay differences as "legitimate" despite the job evaluation's conclusion that all fields are comparable.[19]

Predicting the likely results of such a comparable worth evaluation of faculty pay is straightforward. Pay of faculty in predominantly male disciplines such as economics or engineering usually exceeds that of faculty in predominantly female (or less heavily male) disciplines such as humanities or nursing. Thus, one would almost certainly obtain a negative relation between pay and "proportion female," even with faculty rank held constant (as a means of allowing for differences across ranks in skill, effort and responsibility).

Clearly, then, an analysis of this kind is different from a conventional economic analysis of discrimination, and is likely to lead to different conclusions. In particular, if women and men with the same personal characteristics (degrees, years of service, fields of academic specialization, etc.) enjoy the same access to better-paid academic ranks (professor, associate professor, etc.) and receive the same pay in the same academic rank, conventional economic analysis would find no difference in pay by sex. In contrast, even if similar individuals enjoy both equal pay in the same rank and equal access to better-paid ranks, a comparable worth evaluation would obtain a negative relation between average pay and "proportion female" in different jobs (e.g., departments or rank-department cells). This would be due entirely to the fact that, relative to men, women who are otherwise similar (in terms of degrees, years of service, etc.) are more likely to be in relatively low-paid academic specialties (e.g., humanities or nursing as opposed to economics or engineering). But would it be correct to infer from this that the *university* being studied discriminates against women?

In terms of conventional economic analyses, such an inference would be warranted only if, relative to male faculty *with the same training*, the university locked female faculty out of high-paid specialties and kept them instead in lower-paid disciplines. Since the notion of "training" encompasses field of academic specialization, that seems very unlikely. It would seem most implausible that anyone with training in engineering, regardless of sex, would be "kept" in any discipline other than engineering; and equally implausible that anyone, regardless of sex, with training in the humanities would be able to gain access to a position on the engineering faculty.[20] A relation between proportion male and average pay among different disciplines would appear, rather, to be a consequence of supply-side differences beyond the university's control, whereunder—because of differential socialization or other prelabor market factors—women seek training in and enter low-paying fields to a greater extent than otherwise identical men.[21] To the extent that these differences exist, a negative relation between proportion female and average pay by discipline will arise even at an entirely sex-blind university, but would be treated as evidence of discriminatory employment practices in a comparable worth analysis.

None of this, however, addresses the question of "systematic underpayment." What if the university is not sex-blind, but rather has decided systematically to underpay predominantly female disciplines (or overpay predominantly male disciplines)? Conventional economic analyses of pay will effectively ignore this possibility, because they would typically include "academic discipline" (e.g., a set of discipline indicators) among the *X* in expressions such as (3.1). The alternative—comparable worth analysis of pay—requires the dubious assumption that, in the absence of discrimination by the university, everyone, regardless of discipline, would receive the same pay (on average and other things, such as years of service, being equal). Thus, neither conventional economic nor comparable worth analysis of pay will provide a suitable basis for estimating the extent of discrimination via such systematic underpayment.

As a second example, suppose that an employer or a group of employers decides to exercise monopsony power over (workers in) a predominantly female job, e.g., nurses or clerical workers.[22] Conventional economic analysis of pay at such a monopsonistic employer would generally include (if possible) one or more indicators for type of skill possessed, e.g., training in nursing or prior experience in clerical work. Thus, the employer's systematic underpayment (via exercise of monopsony power) of its nurses or clerical workers would be subsumed into the coefficient on the relevant skill indicator(s) and would not affect the estimated sex difference in pay (the coefficient *d* in expressions such as (3.1)) in any way. As in the previous example, although conventional economic analysis of pay would clearly be unsatisfactory in a setting of this kind, comparable worth analysis of pay here would be equally unsatisfactory, for it would require the dubious assumption that a job evaluation will accurately measure the wage differential between nurses (or clericals) and other jobs that would prevail in the absence of discrimination.

In sum, neither conventional economic nor comparable worth analyses of *pay* are adequate for assessing the question of systematic underpayment (or overpayment) of jobs based on the sex composition of the persons who do them. Fortunately, however, this question can be addressed by analyzing *other* employment practices using quite conventional concepts, such as vacancies and waiting lists (Fischel and Lazear 1986a). Systematic underpayment of women's jobs—social work or nursing—will inevitably lead to systematic shortages: chronic vacancies, unfilled positions, etc. Systematic overpayment of men's jobs—engineers or tree-trimmers—will inevitably lead to systematic surpluses: a chronic excess of applicants relative to available positions, long waiting lists of qualified persons seeking a small number of vacant jobs, etc.[23]

Development of a methodology for empirical analysis of the presence (and, even more so, the magnitude) of systematic underpayment (or overpayment) of jobs according to sex composition is beyond the scope of this book. For present purposes, it is sufficient to note that although conventional economic analyses of pay are not a satisfactory means for addressing this question, neither are comparable worth analyses of pay.

3.4 *Analyzing the Effects of Comparable Worth Wage Adjustments*

Many discussions of comparable worth focus on conceptual issues of the kind examined in chapter 2, e.g., whether unequal pay for jobs of comparable worth is necessarily discriminatory and whether it is appropriate to require equal pay for jobs of comparable worth. To a lesser extent, analysts have considered technical issues such as the ones discussed in this chapter, e.g., the statistical merits and demerits of comparable worth analyses of pay. To many observers, however, the most important issues regarding comparable worth have to do with its likely effects on wages, employment and other labor market outcomes. In this view, the acid test is not whether the concept of comparable worth is analytically sound or whether comparable worth pay analyses yield statistically unbiased measures of discriminatory pay practices. Rather, the crucial issue is an entirely pragmatic one: whether actual implementation of comparable worth can raise the pay of women workers, reduce the pay gap, etc., without serious adverse side effects.

Prior research

To date, analyzing the empirical consequences of actually adopting comparable worth has been difficult: comparable worth has not yet been adopted on a widespread basis. Consequently, most assessments of the effects of comparable worth have attempted to work out what would be *likely* to occur *if* wage adjustments were made along comparable worth lines. Studies of this kind have focused on the effects on wages and on the male/female pay gap. In most cases,[24] the starting point is a comparable worth wage regression, with jobs as the unit of analysis, that regresses jobs' pay Y_j (e.g., maximum or minimum pay rates) on one or more variables denoting the jobs' characteristics X_j (e.g., Haypoint or other evaluation scores, measures of working conditions, etc.) and a sex composition variable M_j (e.g., the proportion male in the jobs, or whether the jobs are predominantly male or female, etc.). Thus, such analyses start with a relation such as (3.6).

The next step in these analyses is to use the estimate of d, the coefficient on the sex composition variable M, to work out the wage effects of full implementation of a comparable worth standard. For example, if M measures the proportion of incumbents in a job who are male, so that M ranges between zero (for an all-female job) and one (for an all-male job), then the estimate of d in (3.6) is treated as an estimate of the male salary advantage. In order to ensure that (average) pay in all-female jobs equals that in all-male jobs of the same "worth" (that is, the same value of X_j), one would have to raise pay for each all-female job by d. More generally, comparable worth would require raising pay for a job j that is p_j percent female by $0.01p_jd$.[25] The total cost of these pay increases can be then derived by multiplying the pay increase for each job, $0.01p_jd$, times the number of incumbents in that job, N_j, and then summing over all jobs j.

Analyses of this kind are not without interest, but they are inevitably limited. At best, they indicate the maximum potential effect of comparable worth on wages rather than the actual consequences of a politically and budgetarily feasible set of wage adjustments. Indeed, to the extent that comparable worth pay adjustments are adopted through labor management bargaining and/or the exercise of administrative discretion, analyses of this kind do not necessarily indicate even the relative magnitudes of the wage increases given to different jobs. (For example, a given job might receive either more or less than the amount $0.01p_jd$ required under a strict implementation of a comparable worth standard depending on whether the union representing workers in that job was strong or weak.) Also, such analyses usually do not consider the potential effects of comparable worth wage increases on employment.

Analyses for this book: an overview

The alternative, adopted here, is to analyze the empirical effects of adoption of comparable worth in actual settings rather than under hypothetical assumptions. Chapters 4–6 present studies of: the State of Minnesota, which passed legislation requiring equal pay for jobs of comparable worth in state employment; San José, California, which adjusted pay of municipal employees along comparable worth lines; and Australia, which since the early part of this century has had a national wage arbitration system that has several comparable worth features. These analyses of the effects of actual adoption of comparable worth (or comparable worth–like criteria) do not provide information on the maximum potential consequences of completely applying such a standard. They do, however, indicate the consequences of adopting comparable worth subject to constraints imposed by economic and political realities. Moreover, the studies in chapters 4–6 explicitly consider effects on employment, a subject that was generally ignored in most prior work.

The questions to be examined can be stated very simply. Relative to what would have prevailed in the absence of comparable worth, is a labor market outcome of interest—wages, the sex gap in pay, employment, etc.—either higher or lower as a result of the version of comparable worth actually adopted? If so, by how much?

The empirical analyses of these issues in chapters 4–6 proceed sequentially. The first step is to analyze the independent effect of adopting comparable worth on wages; the second, to estimate the *ceteris paribus* relation between employment and wages. The final step uses the results of the previous two steps to derive an estimate of the independent effect of adopting comparable worth on employment. One interesting feature of these analyses is that they use time-series data for periods both before and after adoption of comparable worth. In contrast, the studies of the potential effects of comparable worth described earlier have been confined to analysis of single cross-section "snapshots" as of a single date.

As noted in section 3.3, the results of analyses of pay may be quite sensitive to one's choice of the unit of analysis: either individuals or jobs. In this connection, one important feature of the studies in chapters 4 and 5 is worth emphasizing at the outset. The basic data available for analysis of San José's comparable worth wage adjustments refer to jobs rather than individuals: the necessary individual-level data do not exist for the relevant period. Here, there is no way to avoid using jobs as the unit of analysis. In contrast, the basic data available for analysis of Minnesota's experience with comparable worth refer to individual state employees. This makes it possible to perform both conventional economic analyses (using the data in their original individual-level form) *and* comparable worth analyses (by aggregating the individual-level data up to the level of jobs). Accordingly, I discuss the Minnesota results before the San José results: the information provided by the Minnesota analyses on the consequences of using jobs rather than individuals as the unit of analysis turns out to be very useful in assessing the San José analyses, in which, as just noted, jobs must be used as the unit of analysis. (The data available for Australia are conventional macroeconomic time-series data, so I defer discussion of the framework used in evaluating Australia's experience with comparable worth to chapter 6.)

Wage effects

The first step in the analyses in subsequent chapters is to regress a measure of the wage of observation i at time t, W_{it}, on a set of control variables pertinent to i at t, X_{it}, and a "comparable worth" indicator C_{it} denoting the existence at t of a comparable worth policy with the potential to affect i's wage:

$$W_{it}=bX_{it}+kC_{it}+e_{it}, \quad i=1, 2, \ldots, N; t=1, 2, \ldots, T. \qquad (3.7)$$

The data are longitudinal, consisting of observations for each of N individual units as of each of a total of T dates. Depending on the nature of the available data, the unit of analysis, "i," is either an individual worker (in some of the analyses for Minnesota) or a job (in other analyses for Minnesota, and in all analyses for San José). How is the comparable worth variable C_{it} in (3.7) to be defined? As actually adopted in the "test sites" considered in this work, comparable worth was not applied equally to all jobs or people. Some jobs (and, thus, the people in those jobs) were "targeted" for comparable worth wage increases, but others were not. This suggests at least two ways to define the comparable worth variable C_{it}: as an indicator denoting either (1) whether the observation i was itself "targeted" and eligible for a comparable worth wage increase as of time t; or (2) that the comparable worth policy was in force as of time t.

The distinction is not trivial; rather, it can have important econometric implications. Under the first definition, C_{it} will vary cross-sectionally as well as over time, whereas under the second it will vary only over time.[26] The major objective here, of course, is to obtain unbiased estimates of the "comparable worth effect," k. As the preceding discussion suggests (albeit in rather different contexts), the estimate of k will be biased if, at given values of the X_{it}, the comparable worth variable C_{it} is correlated with the error term e_{it}. The interesting point here is that since the data used to estimate (3.7) are longitudinal, i.e., a cross-section (of individuals or jobs) observed over time, correlation between C_{it} and e_{it} at given X_{it} can arise either cross-sectionally or over time, depending on how C_{it} is defined.

Under the first definition, C_{it} equals one for an observation (a job, or an individual working in a job) targeted for a comparable worth wage increase with the potential to affect wages as of time t. Use of this definition raises two kinds of questions: selection bias issues, and conceptual issues.[27]

The selection bias issue arises if targeting of comparable worth wage increases is based in part on the e_{it} of jobs (or of the persons in those jobs). For example, if jobs (or jobs with workers) that have consistently had low e_{it} over time – "chronically underpaid jobs" – are "targeted" for comparable worth wage increases, then C_{it} defined in this first sense will be negatively correlated with e_{it} (even given X_{it}) for essentially cross-sectional reasons: here the comparable worth wage increases go to jobs (or workers) that have consistently had low or negative values of e_{it} at all dates t. If so, the estimated effect of comparable worth will understate the actual effect due to selection bias. This problem is similar to the one that arises in analyses of wage effects of employment training programs when program administrators go out of their way to select "disadvantaged" trainees, or persons with below-average earnings (i.e., low or negative unobserved components e) even when observed characteristics (X) are taken into account. Various techniques to address the selection bias problem are available (for a review, see Heckman and Robb 1985), but they can be difficult to implement and may require assumptions about the precise form of the relation between e_{it} and (the first definition of) C_{it} that are to some extent arbitrary.

Use of the first definition of the comparable worth variable C_{it} in (3.7) also raises a conceptual issue. Even if an unbiased estimate of k can be derived, under the first definition of C_{it} the magnitude of k indicates only the amount of additional pay received by (persons in) targeted jobs *relative to* (those in) nontargeted jobs. It will not necessarily indicate the amount of additional pay received by *either* (persons in) targeted jobs *or* (those in) nontargeted jobs *relative to what would have been received in the absence of adoption of comparable worth*.[28]

This conceptual distinction is potentially important. Pay increases for individual jobs or workers are not normally made in a vacuum. Comparable worth wage increases do not necessarily amount to pure "add-ons" to the pay of (workers in) targeted jobs, and do not necessarily leave pay of (workers in) nontargeted jobs unaffected (Evans and Nelson 1989, p. 96). Rather, comparable worth wage increases for some jobs may be financed, in whole or in part, by wage *decreases* (or smaller wage increases) for others. (Evans and Nelson 1989, pp. 117–121, report that in Minnesota, 60 percent of state employees expressed concern that that state's comparable worth wage adjustments might mean that some salaries would be "frozen.") Alternatively, comparable worth wage increases for (workers in) some jobs may be accompanied by, or give rise to, wage *increases* for others, even if the latter wage changes are not labelled "comparable worth increases" as such.[29]

Given the potential statistical and (in particular) conceptual problems associated with the first definition of C_{it}, the studies in this work use the second definition: C_{it} is a simple "before or after" indicator variable, equal to unity if the observation pertains to a date on or after the date of a comparable worth wage increase, and zero otherwise. As such, this second version of C_{it} varies over time but not cross-sectionally: for a given job (or individual), it will equal zero for dates prior to the date of a comparable worth wage increase and unity thereafter, but it will have the same value (either zero or unity) for all observations as of the same date. Hence, unlike the first definition, the second has little or no potential for selection bias. The second definition also avoids the conceptual problem to which the first definition may be subject. For example, when (3.7) is estimated for predominantly *male* jobs using this second definition of C_{it}, the coefficient on k will reflect the extent (if any) to which comparable worth wage adjustments were accompanied by wage changes (increases or decreases) for predominantly male jobs, even if such jobs were not explicitly targeted for comparable worth wage increases and were not supposed to "pay for" (or "share in") such wage increases.

Of course, a potential for biased estimates of comparable worth wage effects arises under this second definition, largely because of time-series (as opposed to cross-sectional) reasons. The key problem is to specify correctly the appropriate "counterfactual," i.e., to control for changes in the outcome of interest that would have happened (even) in the absence of comparable worth. For example, suppose that adoption of comparable worth in a given area coincides, purely by chance, with a major contraction (or expansion) of the surrounding economy, decreases (or increases) in the general wage level, etc. Then unless the X_{it} appropriately reflect these changes in the economic environment, C_{it}, as defined in the second sense, will be negatively (or positively) correlated with e_{it} and the comparable worth effect, k, will be downward- (or upward-) biased. Hence, the empirical hurdles here resemble those confronting researchers studying the employment effects of minimum wage increases or the wage effects of affirmative action. For example, since employment grows over time along with (and despite?) increases in the minimum wage, simple before-and-after comparisons may yield the erroneous conclusion that increases in the minimum "caused" *increases* in employment.[30]

For this reason, the control variables X used in estimation of (3.7) include measures not only of characteristics of the unit of analysis as of the relevant date (e.g., years of state government employment, in the Minnesota analyses of individual workers) but also of the general economic environment prevailing as of that date. Specifically, the "environmental variables" consist of measures of prices, private-sector employment and private-sector average earnings as of the same date[31] and time trend terms, thereby abstracting from fluctuations in general economic conditions and secular trends.

A final and more subtle set of issues concerns the technique to be used to estimate (3.7). The data are longitudinal, so that each of the N units of observation (jobs or individuals) appears in the analysis a total of T times. In principle, pooled OLS regression can yield consistent estimates of all of the parameters of the model. To the extent that the error term e_{it} tends to be the same for a given individual unit (person or job) over time, however, the properties of simple pooled OLS estimators will suffer. Rather than rely on pooled OLS, I therefore use fixed-effects estimation. This is equivalent to specifying the error term e_{it} as consisting of an individual- (person- or job-) specific time-invariant component e_i and a purely random component v_{it} that varies both across individuals and over time, i.e.,

$$e_{it} = e_i + v_{it} \tag{3.8}$$

Fixed-effects regression is equivalent to OLS regression on all NT observations using (3.7) with a dummy variable added for *each* cross-section unit i: that is, by (3.7)–(3.8), the e_i in (3.8) is equivalent to the coefficient a_i on the dummy variable D_i in

$$W_{it}=bX_{it}+kC_{it}+fD+v_{it} \tag{3.9}$$

where D is a vector of dummy variables, with the *ith* equalling unity if the observation refers to the *ith* job (or individual) and zero otherwise, and f is the vector of coefficients on the D. The coefficient f_i on the dummy variable D_i for observation (person or job) i is that observation's "fixed effect." Since time-invariant factors for a given observation are collinear with the dummy variable for that observation (and since their combined effect on the dependent variable plus that of any time-invariant unobserved variables is captured by f_i), all time-invariant regressors in X are dropped from the fixed-effects regression itself; only time-varying regressors remain.

The problem of bias may be less severe in fixed-effects regression than in pooled OLS regression: bias induced by correlation between the error term e_{it} and observables X_{it} that is caused by *fixed* effects e_i has, of course, been removed because the e_i itself has effectively been removed. In particular, some of chapter 5's analyses of San José's experience with comparable worth use data on jobs to estimate (3.7) by fixed effects using the first (targeted job) definition of the comparable worth indicator C_{it}. To the extent that jobs are targeted for comparable worth wage increases because they are "chronically underpaid," it seems reasonable to treat the fixed effect e_i in (3.8) as a determinant of "being targeted." Then, although fixed-effects estimation, i.e., estimating (3.9), does not avoid the conceptual issues raised by use of the first definition of C_{it}, it may at least avoid the bias that would arise if (3.7) were estimated by OLS.

Wages and employment

The second step in the analyses performed here is to estimate the relation between wages and employment using a regression model of the form

$$\log N_{it} = bX_{it} + g \log W_{it} + u_{it} \tag{3.10}$$

in which the unit of analysis (i) is the job; N is employment, X is a set of control variables, W is a measure of the wage rate in the job, and u denotes unobservables. As in the wage analyses, the data used here are longitudinal, referring to each of J jobs observed at each of T dates.

This is, of course, a rudimentary labor demand function. As an example of the kind of underlying process that generates such a function, consider a two-level CES-style cost function in which sets of different jobs make up composites or groups, g:

$$C_t = Y_t^s \{\Sigma_g [\Sigma_{i \in g} a_i W_{it}^{r(g)}]^{v/r(g)}\}^{1/v} \tag{3.11}$$

where C=cost, Y=output, W_i=wage rate paid for job i, t subscripts denote time, and s, v, the $r(g)$ and the a_i are parameters. Then, by Shephard's Lemma, a cost-minimizing employer's employment N_i of workers in a job i that belongs to a group j is given by

$$\log N_{it} = \log Z_{it} + [r(j) - 1] \log W_{it}, \quad i \in j \tag{3.12}$$

where Z in (3.12) is given by

$$Z_{it} = C_t^{1-v} Y_t^{-s(1-v)} v [\Sigma_{k \in j} a_k W_{kt}^{r(j)}]^{(v - r(j))/r(j)} a_i, \quad i \in j. \tag{3.13}$$

On the (somewhat heroic) assumption that $\log Z$ in (3.12), as defined in (3.13), can be approximated by a smooth function of time and exogenous variables, (3.10) is equivalent to (3.12).

Several comments about estimation and interpretation of (3.10), particularly in light of (3.12), are appropriate at this point. First, since the right hand side of (3.10) does not include an explicit measure of output or total cost, it might appear that the coefficient on W is an ordinary wage-elasticity, incorporating both the substitution and output (or "scale") effect of wage changes. As (3.12)–(3.13) indicate, however, the X vector in (3.10) may be regarded as a proxy for output Y (and the other factors included within Z, e.g., costs C). Hence the coefficient on the wage variable in (3.10) should be interpreted as an output-constant wage elasticity that does not incorporate output (or "scale") effects. Second, note that the coefficient on $\log W_i$ in (3.12), $r(j) - 1$, is the same for all jobs i belonging to the same group j. In the analyses of chapters 4 and 5, I have put jobs into three groups, according to the sex composition of their employment: predominantly female jobs are in one group, predominantly male jobs are in a second group, and all other jobs are in the third group. Finally, in keeping with the interpretation of (3.10) as a labor demand function, the samples used to estimate (3.10) are limited to jobs with positive employment (N) over the entire period of analysis: jobs with zero employment at some date are inframarginal (at least at that date) and so observations for that date are not on the relevant demand function.

There are two obvious potential bias problems connected with estimation of (3.10). The first is that, in a hierarchical organization, high-paid jobs (e.g., senior clerk, police chief) usually have relatively few incumbents at any given date, whereas low-paid jobs (e.g., file clerk, police officer) usually have relatively many. Thus a negative coefficient on W in (3.10) may indicate only that employment is indeed hierarchical, rather than that wage increases reduce employment in a *given* job. I address this problem by estimating (3.10) using fixed-effects regression; to the extent that a job's position in the employment hierarchy is fixed, this provides a means of abstracting from the hierarchy-induced negative relation as of any given date between jobs' pay rates and their employment levels.[32]

The second problem is that, as noted above, I exclude jobs with zero employment at any point during the period of analysis. It is possible that this generates a form of selection bias. To the extent that a job's having zero employment at some point is a consequence of attributes that are essentially fixed, however, fixed-effects regression provides a means of obtaining consistent estimates of the parameters of (3.10). The alternative, including jobs even when they are not on the demand curve, seems much less appealing.

Employment effects

The final step in the analysis is to use estimates of the comparable worth effect on wages, derived from (3.7), and of the relation between wages and employment, derived from (3.10), to work out the effect of comparable worth on employment. Since the analyses use log-log specifications, the wage effect in (3.7) is expressed as a percentage and the effect of wages on employment in (3.10) is expressed as an elasticity. Thus, the effect of the comparable worth wage adjustments may be derived by multiplying the wage effect times the employment elasticity.

As indicated in subsequent chapters, these employment effects are usually negative. It should therefore be emphasized at the outset that these are *ceteris paribus* effects that abstract from the effects of other factors. That is, to say that the employment effect of comparable worth was negative is *not* to say that adoption of comparable worth actually reduced employment relative to the level that prevailed prior to adoption. Rather, it means that, in the absence of comparable worth, employment *would have been* higher than it *actually was* or, more or less equivalently, that adoption of comparable worth reduced *growth* in employment. Indeed, as documented in the following chapters, adoption of comparable worth in the "test sites" considered here did not cause anyone to lose his or her job.[33] Rather, the employment effects were more subtle: the wage increases resulting from adoption were large enough to reduce employment *growth*, but were not so large as to cause complete stagnation of employment, much less actual declines. Thus, the evidence in the following chapters suggests that, in general, the real losers from the comparable worth wage adjustments were persons who were seeking jobs but were unable to get them (rather than people who already had jobs but lost them) because of adoption of comparable worth.

Appendix to Chapter 3: Selection Bias Induced by Use of Grouped-Data Regression

To see the potential selection bias problem that may be induced by use of grouped-data regression methods, consider the following simple example of a sex-neutral company employing workers in only two jobs, *A* and *B*. Pay of individual *i* depends on his or her observed characteristics, X, and on unobserved characteristics, e, but does *not* depend on sex, M. Thus, in terms of (3.1), $d=0$; equivalently, pay is now given by

$$Y_i = bX_i + e_i. \tag{A3.1}$$

Next, suppose the job actually held by i depends on the index function

$$I_i = hX_i + u_i \tag{A3.2}$$

where u_i denotes unobserved characteristics of i that affect whether he or she is in job A or B, and where individuals for whom I is positive (nonpositive) are selected to hold job A (B).[34] Thus, by (A3.2),

$$u_i > -(hX_i) \quad \leftrightarrow \quad \text{individual } i \text{ is in job } A \tag{A3.3.1}$$

$$u_i \leq -(hX_i) \quad \leftrightarrow \quad \text{individual } i \text{ is in job } B \tag{A3.3.2}$$

By (A3.1)–(A3.2), the *mean* of Y given I is

$$E(Y|I) = E(bX+e|hX+u) = E(w|v) \tag{A3.4}$$

where $w=bX+e$ and $v=hX+u$. To simplify, suppose that the X of (A3.1)–(A3.2) is a single variable, normally distributed, with mean μ_X and variance σ_X^2, and independent of both e and u; and that e and u are jointly normally distributed mean-zero random variables with finite variances σ_e^2 and σ_u^2, respectively, and covariance σ_{eu}. Then w and v are also jointly normally distributed random variables with finite variances σ_w^2 and σ_v^2, respectively, and covariance σ_{wv}.

Now consider estimating (A3.1) by OLS using data aggregated by job, as in comparable worth analyses (instead of data for individual workers, as in conventional economic analyses), while following conventional economic methodology in all *other* respects. (Thus, as in the previous two cases, one aspect of comparable worth analyses is considered in isolation from the others; see note 10 in the text.) Equations (A3.1)–(A3.4) and familiar results on selection bias (e.g., Heckman 1979) yield the following expressions for average pay, skill level, etc., within the high-paid job A:

$$Y_A = E(Y|I>0) = b\mu_X + [\sigma_{wv}/\sigma_v]L_A \tag{A3.5.1}$$

$$e_A = E(e|I>0) = [\sigma_{ev}/\sigma_v]L_A \tag{A3.5.2}$$

$$X_A = E(X|I>0) = \mu_X + [\sigma_{Xv}/\sigma_v]L_A \tag{A3.5.3}$$

$$Y_A = bX_A + e_A \tag{A3.5.4}$$

where $L_A = f(-h\mu_X/\sigma_v)/[1-F(-h\mu_X/\sigma_v)]$, f is the standard normal probability density function and F is the standard normal cumulative density function. Note that L_A is positive-valued and monotonically increasing in its argument (Heckman 1979). Similarly, equations (A3.1) -(A3.4) and conventional selection bias analysis yield the following expressions for average pay, skill level, etc., within the low-paid job B:

$$Y_B = E(Y|I \leq 0) = b\mu_X + [\sigma_{wv}/\sigma_v]L_B \tag{A3.6.1}$$

$$e_B = E(e|I \leq 0) = [\sigma_{ev}/\sigma_v]L_B \tag{A3.6.2}$$

$$X_B = E(X|I \leq 0) = \mu_X + [\sigma_{Xv}/\sigma_v]L_B \tag{A3.6.3}$$

$$Y_B = bX_B + e_B \tag{A3.6.4}$$

where $L_B = -f(-h\mu_X/\sigma_v)/F(-h\mu_X/\sigma_v)$; note that L_B is negative-valued and decreasing in its argument.

If e and u are uncorrelated, then $\sigma_{ev}=0$ and the error term e_j, $j=A$ or B, has zero expectation. In this case, regression of Y_j on X_j where both variables are job averages, as in a comparable worth regression, should yield (1) an unbiased estimate of b and (2) a zero (in statistical terms) coefficient for M_j, the proportion male in job j, unless men are in fact paid more than women with the same X. Here, that is, aggregating over jobs does not induce a selection bias in estimates of the male salary advantage.

On the other hand, if u and e are positively correlated – if unobserved factors (e.g., "motivation") that enhance one's chances of *getting* a high-paid job, u, are positively correlated with unobserved factors that raise pay, e – then aggregating over jobs induces a selection bias that creates the appearance of a male salary advantage even if none exists.

To see this, consider equations (A3.5)–(A3.6). In the "true" salary relation, (A3.1), pay Y depends (only) on skill X and unobserved characteristics e, where average e is assumed to be zero at all levels of skill. In the high-paid job A, the average skill level is X_A. However, by (A3.5.2) and (A3.5.4), average pay *of persons in* A, Y_A, exceeds the average pay *of persons with skill level* X_A by an amount $e_A = E(e|I>0) = [\sigma_{ev}/\sigma_v]L_A > 0$. That is because selection into A depends not only on measured skill X but also on unmeasured attributes, u, that are (by assumption) positively correlated with unmeasured factors that affect pay, e; thus, persons in A enjoy high pay, on average, not only because they have high X but also because they have high e. Similarly, in the low-paid job B, the average skill level is X_B but, by (A3.6.2) and (A3.6.4), average pay *of persons in* B, Y_B, is less than the average pay *of persons with skill level* X_B by an amount $e_B = E(e|I \leq 0) = [\sigma_{ev}/\sigma_v]L_B < 0$. Selection into B also depends on both measured skill X and unmeasured attributes, u, that are (by assumption) positively correlated with unmeasured factors that affect pay, e; thus, persons in B receive low pay because they not only have low X but also, on average, have low e.

What does this imply about regression using within-job means, as in a comparable worth analysis? By (A3.5.4) and (A3.6.4), the relation between pay and skill across jobs is given by

$$Y_j = bX_j + e_j, \qquad j = A, B. \tag{A3.1'}$$

By (A3.5.2)–(A3.5.4) and (A3.6.2)–(A3.6.4), e_j is positively correlated with X_j: on average, jobs that "score high" (or low) in terms of X also do so in terms of e. In effect, (A3.1') suffers from an omitted variables problem: the nature of the job selection process induces a positive correlation between average within-job measured skill X_j and the within-job error term e_j. Note also that if, for any reason (e.g., supply factors), men have more measured skill X than women, on average, then e_j in (A3.1') will also be positively correlated with M_j, the "maleness" of jobs.

The consequences for comparable worth pay analyses are now apparent. Consider the prototype comparable worth regression equation:

$$Y_j = bX_j + dM_j + q_j, \qquad j = A, B. \tag{A3.7}$$

If men have a higher average skill level (μ_X) than women, then, for entirely nondiscriminatory reasons, (1) men will be overrepresented in the high-X job and underrepresented in the low-X job; (2) the e_j of (A3.1′) will be positively correlated with the "maleness" of jobs; and (3) the expression dM_j+q_j in (A3.7) is therefore essentially the equivalent of the e_j of (A3.1′); and so (4) the estimate of d, the coefficient on M_j in (A3.7), will be positive.

NOTES

[1] Note that the X may include a vector of ones, i.e., an intercept. Examples of variables typically included among the X are total years of work experience, tenure (years of service with current employer), age, educational attainment, field of educational attainment, and the like. Both proponents and critics of the conventional economic approach sometimes loosely refer to such variables as "human capital variables" and/or to equations like (3.1) as a "human capital earnings function" (for example, see Smith 1977, pp. 35–40, and Treiman and Hartmann, eds. 1981, pp. 17–24). Such references to human capital may simply be intended to indicate that expressions like (3.1) may have been inspired in part by the seminal work of Becker (1964) and Mincer (1974) on human capital models of earnings. It should be noted, however, that regardless of their original inspiration, (3.1) and similar expressions may well be entirely consistent with other models of earnings, even ones whose underlying assumptions differ radically from those of human capital models. For example, screening models of earnings (surveyed by Riley 1974) reject the "human capital" notion that education affects earnings by affecting productivity; but they nevertheless imply that the "human capital variable" of educational attainment will have a significant independent effect on earnings, and thus that it belongs in expressions such as (3.1).

[2] Following Oaxaca (1973), who first popularized the approach in economics, many investigators estimate separate equations for men and women rather than a single equation (with sex indicator variable M) such as (3.1) for both sexes combined. The single-equation approach embodied in (3.1) in effect assumes that the male and female pay structures differ by a constant amount regardless of other characteristics (the X), whereas the two-equation approach allows for the possibility that the payoffs to individual characteristics (the X) differ by sex; see Cain (1986) for further discussion. However, in my own experience, the two approaches have very similar quantitative implications regarding the overall average sex difference in pay for persons with the same characteristics (which is not surprising, since the single-equation approach provides what amounts to a matrix-weighted average of the effects yielded by the two-equation approach). As a practical matter, the differences between the single- and two-equation approaches are more in the nature of fine tuning rather than important methodological differences with significant implications for estimating sex differences in pay.

[3] Note that *variation* in earnings among men and the male/female *pay gap* are two quite different things: the former refers to *variation about the mean* among men, whereas the latter refers to a *difference in means* between men and women. Comparing the two amounts to comparing apples and oranges. It is therefore inappropriate to infer, as Roback apparently does, that because the fraction of *earnings variation* among men that is "unexplained," 60 percent, is larger than the fraction of the *pay gap* between men and women that is "unexplained," 13 to 34 percent (according to Roback), inclusion of omitted variables might explain all of the latter. As a simple example, due to Fisher (1982), imagine a company in which all employees are identical and at which monthly

salaries are 10 times the figure derived by spinning a roulette wheel plus either $600 (in the case of women) or $1,100 (in the case of men). Among both men and women, much of the variation in earnings would be "unexplained" (that is, R^2 for an earnings regression would be relatively low), but the pay gap of $500 would clearly be discriminatory, and would persist even if a variable measuring each employee's roulette wheel number were added to the analysis, thereby making it possible to explain perfectly all of the variation in pay.

[4] The last sentence in O'Neill's discussion, quoted above, suggests that "intangible qualities"—omitted variables—may well be correlated with variables that are typically included in analyses of the pay gap (e.g., years of work experience, years out of the workforce, schooling). To the extent that this is so, omission of variables denoting the intangible qualities O'Neill mentions will not bias the estimated pay gap at all. For further discussion of the omitted variables issue, see Bloom and Killingsworth (1982).

[5] For example, see Willis and Associates (1980); Young (n.d., esp. Part IV; and 1984); Stackhouse (1980); Council on the Economic Status of Women, State of Minnesota (1982); Commission on the Status of Women, State of Illinois (1983); and Urban Research Center (1987). Several of these studies have not involved the use of formal statistical analysis; for example, Remick (1988, p. 226) writes that the original Willis study for Washington State (1974) was based not on regression but rather on "eyeballing" the relation between pay and evaluation points.

[6] Instead of running a single regression with a sex composition variable, some analysts (e.g., Sorensen 1986) fit two regressions, for predominantly female and predominantly male jobs considered separately. The pay difference disfavoring the "female" jobs is then calculated as the difference between actual mean pay in those jobs and "predicted" pay, calculated using the mean level of job evaluation points among the female jobs and the regression coefficients derived for the "male" jobs. (The pay difference *favoring* predominantly *male* jobs can be derived in a similar manner.) This procedure is analogous to the two-equation approach adopted in many conventional economic analyses of pay (recall note 2). In general, two-equation comparable worth analyses, like their counterparts in conventional economic analyses, yield implications regarding overall sex differences in pay that are quantitatively very similar to those yielded by the single-equation approach.

[7] Since Pierson, Koziara and Johannesson (1984) did not have job evaluation point scores, they took this approach in their study of a single private-sector employer. Lacking "formal ratings of job worth," Baron and Newman (1989, p. 110–111) analyzed jobs in the California civil service using either (1) vectors of dummy variables denoting detailed state civil service job families or (2) variables denoting minimum requirements (education, work experience, etc.) established for jobs.

[8] For example, see Newman (1976) and Newman and Vonhof (1981). Newman was counsel to the plaintiffs in *AFSCME v. State of Washington*, discussed in chapter 1, and has been a leading advocate of the concept of comparable worth. Indeed, Bergmann (1988, p. 186) calls Newman one of the originators of comparable worth. Newman and Vonhof (1981, p. 322) contend that "pay equity, the so-called 'civil rights issue of the 80's,' is nothing more than a simple garden variety wage rate inequity [*sic*] which the industrial relations world has historically wrestled with and resolved." Newman (1976, p. 265) argues that *existing* laws are adequate to address this problem, and presents data for an industrial plant showing unequal rates of pay for jobs with similar evaluation point scores to support his contention that, at the plant in question, women were adversely treated relative to men in terms of unequal access to better-paid work as well as unequal pay for identical work.

[9] This appears to be the case in all of the comparable worth analyses prepared for administrative bodies or legal proceedings, e.g., the Willis (1974, 1976) studies. To simplify, the discussion here assumes that the absolute magnitude of salary "ranges" (i.e., the dollar difference

between the maximum and minimum for different job classifications) does not vary systematically with salary *levels* (e.g., the midpoint of the salary range or the average actual salary). The argument, however, can readily be adapted to an alternative case in which the *proportionate* magnitude of salary ranges does not vary with salary levels (in which case the *absolute* magnitude of salary ranges will be wider at higher salary levels). The former approach amounts to an assumption that the appropriate dependent variable (Y) is the dollar amount of salary; the latter, to an assumption that the appropriate dependent variable is the logarithm of salary.

[10] Thus, consequences of *other* differences between the conventional economic analysis and comparable worth analysis of pay—use of job rather than individual characteristics, use of jobs rather than individuals as the unit of analysis—are temporarily ignored; the discussion here refers *only* to the effect of using an administrative pay construct instead of actual pay.

[11] For example, suppose a firm has two jobs, each with minimum salary rates. If men enjoy favored treatment in hiring and/or promotion into the better-paid job, then, on average and other things (job preferences and qualifications, X) being equal, women will typically be in the lower-paid job and will have been there for a long time, whereas men will typically be in the higher-paid job and will have been there for less time. Thus, particularly when pay in excess of the minimum for one's job depends on "time in job" (e.g., time in rank or time in grade), the amount of pay received in excess of the minimum for one's job, a, will be greater among women than among men. (Of course, this does not mean that the firm favors women: since women are denied equal access to the better-paying job, they will be concentrated in the job with the lower minimum salary and will be earning a lower "total" salary, $Y=A+a$, relative to otherwise similar men.)

[12] The same arguments apply when A is the salary *midpoint* for employees' jobs (so that a can be either positive, i.e., pay in excess of the midpoint, or negative, i.e., pay below the midpoint). Unequal pay for equal work would mean that, at given X, women's a will tend to be negative and men's a will tend to be positive; thus, at given X, unequal pay for equal work entails a positive correlation between M and a, and a negative correlation between M and both $-a$ and e^*, resulting in a downward bias in the estimate of d, i.e., to understatement of the male salary advantage and female salary disadvantage. On the other hand, to the extent that there is unequal access to better work via differential promotion rates, so that women "max out" at lower-paid jobs more often than do men with the same X, women's (men's) a will tend to be positive (negative). This induces an upward bias in the estimate of d.

[13] Because the company is assumed to be sex-blind, the *same* dividing line, X_A^*, separates persons working in jobs A and B regardless of sex. For either sex, average skill *within* job B (A) is simply the mean of the skill distribution to the right (left) of X_A^*. The mean skill levels within job j ($=A$ or B) for sex s ($=m$ or f), X_{js}, are shown in figure 3.1. For each job j, $X_{jm}>X_{jf}$, reflecting the assumption that the skill distribution of men has a higher mean than that of women.

[14] To distinguish between the two concepts, imagine a company with 1,000 employees divided into 100 jobs (with employment in some jobs greater, and in others less, than the overall average of 10 employees per job). A conventional economic analysis would run a regression for individual workers, and would thus have a sample size of 1,000. A grouped-data equivalent would be to compute the mean, *within each of the 100 jobs*, of each of the variables considered in the conventional approach and to run a regression using the within-job mean values of all variables. This grouped-data regression would have a sample size of 100. The jobs in such a regression can be weighted according to employment in each job; this ensures that jobs with many employees receive a greater statistical weight in the calculations than do jobs with only a few employees. Most comparable worth analyses, however, have used unweighted rather than weighted data.

[15] See the appendix to this chapter for a formal demonstration in the context of a simple model of a firm with two jobs.

[16] A simple example may be helpful here. Several years ago, as director of the Rutgers graduate program in economics, I advocated a sizable raise for the graduate program's secretary. Rutgers has a highly bureaucratized civil service-style job structure, complete with job descriptions, salary ranges, etc., so, to support the raise, it was necessary to argue that the secretary's *job* should be reclassified. It was, and the raise duly took effect. Why did she receive the raise? The institutionalist answer might be: because her position in the job structure changed. From a conventional economic perspective, however, that does not answer the question, but merely reformulates it: why did her position in the job structure change? The conventional economic answer to this fundamental question seems natural: because of her productivity, which is a function of both "measured" characteristics X (e.g., education, prior service) and "unmeasured" characteristics e (e.g., motivation, intelligence).

[17] Presumably, working conditions are essentially the same in all departments, as are responsibility and effort. Depending on what enters into the evaluation, "skill" might vary from one department to another, although it would seem likely that individuals at the same academic rank (full professor, associate professor, etc.) would be assessed as having the same "skill" even if they are in different departments. Note the similarity between this hypothetical situation and the translators example discussed in chapter 2.

[18] If "job" were defined as a department-rank combination, it would, however, be necessary to include a variable measuring the difference in assessed worth of the different academic ranks. Alternatively, one could simply include a set of indicator variables that denoted each job's academic rank. The former approach is the equivalent of a bias-free job evaluation, whereas the latter is equivalent to a policy capturing approach to job evaluation (see chapter 2).

[19] One can imagine expanding the regression to include measures of the average characteristics possessed by the individuals in each job (i.e., each department or each department-rank combination). For example, if one were defining "jobs" to be department-rank combinations, one might add variables measuring the proportion of persons in each job who have a Ph.D., the average years of service of persons in each job, etc. Again, however, one would not include an indicator for the field of each job (e.g., social work or statistics) because the jobs would already have been determined to be comparable.

[20] Discrimination by the university against women engineers in *hiring* would certainly contribute to a negative relation between "femaleness" of discipline and pay among faculty *employed* by the university; but neither conventional economic nor comparable worth analysis of *pay* is concerned with discrimination in hiring.

[21] Note that sex discrimination by educational institutions in providing scholarships and research grants, evaluating students, making admissions decisions, etc., may contribute to overrepresentation of women in low paying fields. Thus, the discussion in the text should not be taken to mean that "choice" of academic discipline is entirely voluntary, or that discriminatory behavior on the part of universities is in no way responsible for underrepresentation of women in high-paying fields such as engineering. However, when it comes to employment decisions, even a sex-blind university must take the sex composition of individuals qualified for each discipline as a given.

[22] The nursing labor market is literally a textbook example of a monopsonized labor market (Ehrenberg and Smith 1982, pp. 65–66). Devine (1969, p. 542) and witnesses at congressional hearings (U.S. Congress, House 1983, p. 70) have described collusive wage-fixing agreements adopted by hospital administrators. Other witnesses have described similar arrangements adopted by employers of clerical workers in San Francisco and Boston (U.S. Congress, House 1983, pp. 88, 96).

[23] See Baker and Bresnahan (1985), whose methodology for analyzing whether collusion of

firms affects product prices is clearly applicable to questions about whether employers' collusion affects wage rates. Note that it may be particularly difficult to analyze systematic underpayment of predominantly female (relative to predominantly male) jobs based on shortages and surpluses when the employer—e.g., a state government—pays above-market rates to essentially all jobs, albeit to a greater extent for mostly male than mostly female jobs. In that case, there will be excess applicants for essentially all jobs, albeit to a greater extent for mostly male than mostly female jobs.

[24] For example, see Treiman and Hartmann, eds. (1981, esp. chapter 4) and Sorensen (1986). Ehrenberg (1989) provides a comprehensive review of such studies.

[25] A job that is p_j percent female is already $1-p_j$ percent male, so adding p_jd to its pay is equivalent to making it (for pay purposes, at least!) an all-male job. Although comparable worth need not require *raising* pay of predominantly *female* jobs—an alternative would be to *reduce* pay in predominantly *male* jobs—all discussions of comparable worth that I have seen call for pay increases, not pay decreases (recall the discussion in chapter 2).

[26] For example, suppose that job *A* is targeted for a comparable worth wage increase effective January 1, 1986, and that job *B* is not targeted for any such increase. Under the first definition, C_{it} would equal zero both for job *B* (or persons in job *B*) at all dates *t and* for job *A* (or persons in job *A*) at dates prior to 1986, and would equal unity for job *A* (or persons in job *A*) at all dates on or after 1986. Under the second definition, C_{it} would equal zero for *all* observations (all individuals or jobs) before 1986, and would equal unity for *all* observations on or after 1986.

[27] Similar remarks apply to a related definition: defining C_{it} as the *amount* of the comparable worth wage increase accorded (persons in) the job, and set at zero for all (persons in) jobs not targeted for such increases.

[28] The analogy here is to traditional studies of the union-nonunion pay differential, which estimate the pay *gap* between unionists and nonunionists but do not estimate the *gain* or *loss* in pay for either group relative to what would have prevailed in the absence of unionism.

[29] For example, in Minnesota, most of the state's comparable worth wage adjustments were targeted to jobs held by employees represented by the American Federation of State, County and Municipal Employees (AFSCME). Evans and Nelson (1989, pp. 96–102) note that after these adjustments, a rival union, the Minnesota Association of Professional Employees (MAPE), fought the resulting compression in pay differentials traditionally enjoyed by its members. If successful, MAPE's initiative would effectively have meant comparable worth-induced pay adjustments even for some nontargeted jobs. Ironically, in some of their subsequent discussion, Evans and Nelson (1989, esp. p. 99) treat the state's comparable worth pay adjustments as pure add-ons to existing salary levels. Likewise, Orazem and Mattila (1989, esp. p. 182) analyze the wage effects of proposed comparable worth adjustments in Iowa by simply recomputing each employee's salary as if the adjustments were pure add-ons: salary of any employee in a nontargeted job is kept at the same level; salary of any employee in a targeted job is increased by the amount specified by the proposed comparable worth adjustments.

[30] O'Neill, Brien and Cunningham (1989) analyze the wage effects of Washington State's 1984 and 1986 comparable worth wage adjustments using cross-section regressions for state employees' pay in 1980, 1983 and 1987. They find that the sex differential in pay narrowed during 1983–87. However, they also find that (1) during 1983–87 the sex differential in pay for nonstate workers also narrowed, and (2) the differential for state workers narrowed during 1980–83 as well as 1983–87. Since they do not explicitly control for environmental variables of the kind discussed in the text (indeed, they are precluded from doing so because they have only three years of data), they are therefore unable to quantify the wage effects of the comparable worth adjustments *per se*.

[31] For example, in the case of Minnesota, the environmental variables include (in addition to

current and lagged values of the Consumer Price Index) a set of measures of total employment and average monthly earnings in the private sector in both the Minneapolis-St. Paul Metropolitan Statistical Area and in the state as a whole, derived from the U.S. Bureau of Labor Statistics' ES-202 data file. The ES-202 data file is described in further detail in chapter 4.

[32] Note that fixed-effects estimation can be thought of as roughly equivalent to first-differencing the data, and thus to analyzing whether *changes* in wages are associated with *changes* in employment levels. Although the hierarchical nature of organizations may induce a relation between wage changes and employment changes that has nothing to do with factor demands, this seems much less plausible than the notion that hierarchy induces a relation between wage *levels* and employment *levels*.

[33] Strictly speaking, comparable worth did not lead to net job losses, i.e., net decreases in employment relative to prior levels. It may have led to some gross reductions in employment. However, long-run trends, cyclical factors, etc., induced enough new accessions to offset any such gross reductions in employment. On balance, employment was higher after adoption of comparable worth than it was before adoption.

[34] One could think of I as a "score" whose value is affected by observed characteristics of the individual, X (which in general—though not in the case considered here—might well include sex), and by unobserved characteristics, u, such that a sufficiently high score causes the individual to be placed in job A. See Bloom and Killingsworth (1982) for further discussion.

4

Comparable Worth in Minnesota State Government Employment

In this chapter, I discuss Minnesota's experience with comparable worth. A series of studies and reports on the status of women state government employees ultimately led to a state Pay Equity Act adopted in 1982.[1] Since then, state government employees have received three sets of comparable worth pay adjustments. Minnesota's Commission on the Economic Status of Women (1985, p. 1) has said that the state is

> in the forefront of pay equity efforts in the nation . . . the first [state] to implement pay equity legislation for its employees. . . . Minnesota's experience shows that pay equity can be implemented smoothly and at a reasonable cost.

How has the state's comparable worth legislation affected the female/male differential in pay, and employment of women and men, in state government?

4.1 *Background*

Minnesota employs over 30,000 workers in about 1800 job categories ("classes" or "classifications"). About 90 percent are covered by collective bargaining agreements and are divided into 16 bargaining units, more or less according to occupation, represented by 11 unions, the most important of which is the American Federation of State, County, and Municipal Employees (AFSCME). (The Minnesota State Univer-

I thank Ronald G. Ehrenberg, Cordelia Reimers and participants in seminars at the U.S. Bureau of Labor Statistics, the University of Maryland and Rutgers University for many helpful comments on previous versions of this chapter.

sity System is autonomous in pay and other matters, and is not considered in this chapter.)

The period before adoption of the 1982 comparable worth statute saw considerable discussion of the status of women in state government employment.[2] In 1975, AFSCME and the state agreed to study issues about pay and promotion discrimination against women, but no funds were appropriated for this purpose. In October 1976, the Twin Cities branch of the National Organization for Women published a report on women's status in state government employment. That same year, the state legislature established a Council (later renamed the Commission) on the Economic Status of Women (CESW), consisting of state legislators and public members. The commission promptly held hearings on women in state employment, and, in 1977, published a report on the subject. The next year, the state's Legislative Audit Commission (LAC) reported on its year-long study of the state personnel commission, which included analyses of the relative status of female and male state employees. LAC's report documented sizable sex differences in occupational status and earnings in state government employment, as did a May 1979 report by CESW.

As these studies and discussions took place, the state began a comprehensive Public Employment Study (PES). As part of the PES, the state retained Hay Associates to conduct an evaluation of 762 job classifications, based mainly on job descriptions (most of the jobs not evaluated were either managerial or else had fewer than 10 incumbents; see CESW 1982, p. 19). The evaluations were carried out by three separate committees of state employees, trained by Hay Associates in its factor-point job evaluation methodology.[3] Each committee consisted of a Department of Personnel Representative and seven state employees from other departments.[4] The committees evaluated the state's jobs using the Hay system, which considers "know-how," "problem-solving," "accountability" and working conditions (Minnesota Department of Finance 1979a, p. 18); "market factors" (e.g., wages paid in the private sector) were not considered.[5]

According to Hay Associates, the evaluations showed only a "slight tendency" for predominantly male occupations to receive higher pay than predominantly female occupations (Minnesota Department of Finance, 1979a, p. 72). Furthermore, the PES said, predominantly female office and clerical jobs (in which the great majority of women were employed) were typically "paid about the same as are most other classes [i.e., jobs] at similar levels of complexity" (Minnesota Department of Finance 1979b, p. I–19).

"Although the contract with Hay Associates was not undertaken for the purpose of conducting a comparable worth study, or even as a basis for compensation" (Rothchild 1985, p. 107), and although neither Hay Associates nor the PES suggested much reason to adjust pay for predominantly female job classes, in October 1981 the CESW set up a pay equity task force to analyze pay differences between male and female jobs. Task force members included state legislators, public members, union representatives and representatives from the Department of Employee Relations. The Task Force's report directly contradicted the relatively benign conclusions of Hay Associates (CESW 1982, p. 21; emphasis original):

> In almost every case, the pay for women's jobs is lower than the pay for comparable male jobs. In most cases the pay for women's jobs is lower than the pay for men's jobs with *fewer* [job evaluation] points.

Overall, the Task Force found, the gap in pay between predominantly female and predominantly male jobs was about 20 percent.[6] Accordingly, it recommended that "comparable worth, as measured by skill, effort, responsibility and working conditions, shall be the primary consideration in establishing salaries for those jobs which are at least 70 percent female," and that there be a "pay equity set-aside to target job classes which are at least 70 percent female to be brought up to salaries for other jobs with comparable value" (CESW 1982, p. 25).

The legislature acted quickly in its 1982 session to put the Task Force recommendations into law. The policy statement for the legislation (Minnesota Statutes, chapter 43A.1, subdivision 3) reads:

> It is the policy of this state to attempt to establish equitable compensation relationships between female-dominated, male-dominated,

> and balanced classes of employees in the executive branch. Compensation relationships are equitable within the meaning of this subdivision when the primary consideration in negotiating, establishing, recommending, and approving total compensation is comparability of the value of the work in relationship to other positions in the executive branch.

The law requires the Commissioner of Employee Relations to list, by January 1 of odd numbered years, predominantly female classes that are paid less than other classes with the same number of Hay points, and to estimate the cost of equalizing pay for classes with the same Hay points.[7] The Legislative Commission on Employee Relations must then recommend an amount to be appropriated for special pay comparability adjustments. Funds for such adjustments, appropriated through the usual legislative process, are earmarked for "salary equalization" for the job classes on the Commissioner's list. These funds are allocated to different bargaining units according to their share of the total estimated cost of pay equalization; actual distribution of salary adjustments is determined by collective bargaining (CESW 1985, p. 14).

The first two sets of comparable worth pay adjustments, adopted in 1983, were implemented in July 1983 and July 1984 at a total cost (including fringes and other nonwage items) of $21.7 million. About 8225 employees in 151 job classes received pay adjustments of about $1,600 over the two-year period. A third set of adjustments, costing a total of $11.7 million, was adopted by the 1985 legislature and implemented in July 1985. The cost of the three adjustments represented about 2.4 percent (1983–4) and 1.3 percent (1985) of the state's payroll. By the end of the adjustments, individual annual "pay equity" salary increases averaged about $2,200; all clerical workers and about half of the state's health care workers received some increases; about ten percent of the beneficiaries were men. (See CESW 1985, pp. 14–15; Rothchild n.d., p. 4; and Rothchild 1984, pp. 124–125.)

According to CESW (1985, p. 15), the two waves of salary adjustments enacted under the state's comparable worth law "will allow for full implementation of pay equity for Minnesota state employees by . . . June 30, 1987." Specifically, according to a Commission newsletter (1986, p.

2), effective June 30, 1987, the average maximum monthly salary for female jobs was to be the same as the average maximum monthly salary for male jobs with similar Hay job evaluation point values.

Adoption and implementation of the comparable worth pay adjustments for state employees proceeded quite smoothly (although in 1985 police and firefighter unions in St. Paul broke with other unions and opposed that city's job evaluation, conducted as part of the extension of comparable worth to local government). Private-sector employer groups were largely quiescent, although some expressed fears – which, thus far, have not materialized – that "the next step is the private sector" (*Wall Street Journal* 1985b).

4.2 *Data*

The data used in this chapter's analyses of pay and employment in Minnesota state government both before and after the comparable worth pay adjustments described above are contained in a set of computerized quarterly "slice files." Each of these files has information on each state employee present and active during the relevant quarter from October 1981 to April 1986 inclusive:[8] the employee's sex, ethnicity, birth date, date of entry into state employment, job classification, date of entry into current job classification, handicap status, veteran status and other characteristics. Since each employee has a unique identifying number, the files can be linked over time to form a longitudinal database.[9] A companion "class file," providing the title (e.g., "Engineering Aide") and Haypoint score (e.g., 178) for job classifications, can be merged with the slice files for analyses of relationships among pay, Haypoints and other factors for individual state employees. An obvious advantage of the slice files (especially once they have been merged with the class file) is that they permit analysis at both the level of the job (i.e., class), as in comparable worth studies, and at the level of individuals, as in conventional economic studies of pay.

Table 4.1 lists the variables used in the first set of analyses, of pay, reported below, and also provides descriptive statistics for individual employees. This indicates that as of October 1981 the state's workforce was about 44 percent female, was almost entirely white, had an average age of about 40 years, and had been in state employment for an average of almost nine years.[10] No Haypoint rating (job evaluation score) is available for about 15 percent of the individuals; for the most part, rates of pay for the jobs these individuals held were well above average. Overall (including both Hay-rated and unrated jobs), the average hourly rate of pay (as of October 1981) is about $8.23 (or about $17,122 for a 2,080-hour year), although hourly rates vary from the minimum wage, $3.35, to a maximum of over $26. In the following analyses, pay and some other variables mentioned later are measured in units of natural logarithms (I use "ln," the customary abbreviation, to refer to natural logarithms), so that coefficients on variables measured this way may be interpreted as percentage effects.

As noted in section 3.4, analyses of wage and employment changes over time in the presence of comparable worth may depend critically on one's ability to control for the counterfactual, i.e., for changes that would have occurred (even) in the absence of comparable worth. In the longitudinal analyses discussed in sections 4.4–5 below, I have therefore included regressors pertaining to (1) consumer prices and (2) the private-sector economy in both the Minneapolis–St. Paul Metropolitan Statistical Area (MSA) and in the state of Minnesota as a whole. The basic data for the private-sector economy are contained in the U.S. Bureau of Labor Statistics' ES–202 data file, which is derived from state employment security agency reports on employment and wage payments of employers covered by state unemployment insurance programs (U.S. Bureau of Labor Statistics n.d.). These data provide direct measures of total persons employed for each month and total dollar earnings per quarter (including payments not subject to unemployment insurance tax). Quarterly employment is derived by summing monthly employment figures for the relevant quarter. Monthly wage data—i.e., earnings per employed person per month—are derived by dividing total quarterly earnings by quarterly employment.

Table 4.1 Definitions and Descriptive Statistics for Variables Used in the Pay Analyses

Short Name	Definition	Mean for Employees at 10/81
LOG_HRLY	ln (hourly wage rate)	2.108
Dummies (for sex and ethnicity)		
FEMALE__	indicator: sex is female	0.435
BLACK___	indicator: race is black	0.014
INDIAN__	indicator: race is American Indian	0.008
HISPANIC	indicator: race is Hispanic	0.006
ASIAN___	indicator: race is Asian	0.005
Percent (for sex/ethnic makeup of job class)		
PCTFEMAL	own job class: % female	0.435
PCTBLACK	own job class: % black	0.014
PCTINDIA	own job class: % American Indian	0.008
PCTHISPA	own job class: % Hispanic	0.006
PCTASIAN	own job class: % Asian	0.005
Haypoint Variables		
HAY_MISS	indicator: Haypoint rating is unknown	0.149
HAYPOINT	Haypoint rating (0 if unknown)	182.628
HAYPOISQ	HAYPOINT squared × 0.001	52.643
Standard Regressors		
AGE_____	age at end of quarter	39.739
AGE___SQ	AGE_____ squared × 0.001	1.734
SVC_FRST	service with State from earliest entry date	8.741
SVC_F_SQ	SVC_FRST squared × 0.001	0.139
SVC_MREC	service with State from most recent entry date	8.741*
SVC_M_SQ	SVC_MREC squared × 0.001	0.139*
AGESVC_F	AGE_____ * SVC_FRST	0.402
AGESVC_M	AGE_____ * SVC_MREC	0.402*
HANDICAP	indicator: handicapped	0.054
VET_VIET	indicator: Vietnam-era veteran	0.078
VETOTHER	indicator: other veteran	0.117

* By construction, SVC_MREC = SVC_FRST as of the first date in the panel (October 1981). For later dates, these two variables will differ only if an individual both left and then returned to State employment during the period covered by the panel (October 1981–April 1986).

4.3 *Cross-Section Analyses: Sex Differentials in Hourly Pay, 1981 and 1986*

I begin by presenting cross-section regression analyses of pay using the October 1981 and April 1986 slice files. First, I use individuals as the unit of analysis, as in conventional economic studies of pay; then, I use classes (jobs), as in comparable worth studies of pay. These cross-section analyses provide information on numerous issues discussed in chapter 3, including the following: To what extent do methodological differences between comparable worth and conventional economic analyses of pay lead to different results regarding the sex differential in pay? To what extent did cross-section sex differentials in hourly rates of pay change during 1981–86, when the state's comparable worth pay adjustments were being implemented?

Individual-level results

Table 4.2 summarizes results for conventional ordinary least squares (OLS) cross-section regressions in which the unit of analysis is the individual employee (the full results appear in appendix tables A4.1, for October 1981, and A4.2, for April 1986). There are four specifications: "raw differentials," in which the only regressors are variables denoting employees' sex and ethnicity; "raw differentials with Haypoints," in which the regressors consist of Haypoint variables pertaining to employees' classes (i.e., jobs)[11] as well as sex and ethnicity variables; "standard regressors," in which the regressors are measures of employee characteristics like those conventionally used by economists analyzing pay differentials–e.g., age, years of service and sex/ethnicity; and "standard regressors with Haypoints," i.e., the standard regressors with Haypoint variables added. Table 4.1 lists all variables by type (e.g., Haypoint variables).

For each of these four specifications, I use three different versions of the sex and ethnicity variables: indicators ("dummies"); measures of the proportion female, black, etc., in employees' job classes ("percent"); and both indicators and proportion variables ("dumm & %"). The first

Table 4.2 Summary of Individual-Level Pay Regressions (dep. var. = LOG_HRLY; *t* in parentheses)

	Raw Differentials			Raw Diffs. with Haypoints		
Variable	**Dummies**	**Percent**	**Dumm & %**	**Dummies**	**Percent**	**Dumm & %**
October 1981:						
FEMALE__	−0.2867		−0.0151	−0.1493		−0.0152
	(92.148)		(3.531)	(64.347)		(4.781)
PCTFEMAL		−0.4814	−0.4663		−0.2707	−0.2555
		(131.740)	(82.759)		(88.226)	(57.774)
April 1986:						
FEMALE__	−0.2158		−0.0136	−0.0681		−0.0136
	(67.797)		(3.051)	(33.406)		(4.752)
PCTFEMAL		−0.3796	−0.3659		−0.1217	−0.1081
		(93.720)	(60.565)		(42.468)	(26.687)

	Standard Regressors			Stand. Regs. with Haypoints		
Variable	**Dummies**	**Percent**	**Dumm & %**	**Dummies**	**Percent**	**Dumm & %**
October 1981:						
FEMALE__	−0.2255		−0.0208	−0.1238		−0.0192
	(74.244)		(5.328)	(56.017)		(6.685)
PCTFEMAL		−0.3932	−0.3740		−0.2266	−0.2088
		(109.494)	(73.447)		(78.835)	(53.408)
April 1986:						
FEMALE__	−0.1636		−0.0178	−0.0438		−0.0104
	(51.292)		(4.316)	(22.310)		(4.063)
PCTFEMAL		−0.2974	−0.2814		−0.0812	−0.0719
		(73.989)	(51.419)		(30.193)	(20.309)

(dummies) version is the one typically used by economists. The second (percent) has been popularized by proponents of comparable worth. The third version simply combines the first and second. Although the third may at first seem a rather strange hybrid, the percent variables used here are analogous to the "percent organized" variables sometimes used in studies of union wage effects. In the present setting, coefficients on the percent variables derived using the second (percent) approach indicate the extent to which pay for individuals in all-female jobs differs from that of individuals in all-male jobs, when the other things in the analysis (e.g., Haypoints, age, etc.) are held constant.[12] Likewise, in the third (dumm & %) version, coefficients on the percent variables indicate the extent to which, ceteris paribus, pay for individuals *of the same sex* differs depending on whether they are in (virtually) all-male or (virtually) all-female jobs; whereas coefficients on the dummy variable for sex indicate how much, ceteris paribus, pay for individuals *in classes with the same sex composition* differs depending on whether they are male or female.[13] Accordingly, I refer to the coefficient on the "female sex" indicator, FEMALE__, as the "sex differential," and to the coefficient on the "proportion of the class that is female" variable, PCTFEMAL, as the "class composition differential."

Several patterns are apparent in table 4.2. First, for any given specification (e.g., standard regressors), the *sum* of the sex and class composition differentials in the dumm & % version is usually very close to the class composition differential in the percent version: the dumm & % version (which explicitly takes account of the sex of individual employees) effectively subdivides the class composition effect of the percent version (which ignores individuals' sex) into a class-composition-constant sex effect and a sex-constant class-composition effect. More or less equivalently, for any given specification, the dumm & % version almost exactly partitions the sex differential in the dummies version (which ignores class composition) into a sex effect and a class composition effect (Welch, 1988): interaction between the effects of sex and class composition is minimal in these data.

To see this, note that, in the dummies version, a "change in sex" amounts to a change in both (a) sex per se and (b) the sex composition of one's job. In the dumm & % version, the overall change in (the ln of) pay associated with changing sex from male to female is therefore $d \ln Y = b_F + b_{\%F}(\%F_F - \%F_M)$, where b_F and $b_{\%F}$ are the coefficients on FEMALE__ and PCTFEMAL, respectively, obtained in the dumm & % version, and $\%F_s$ is the mean of PCTFEMAL for sex s (=men or women). In October 1981, $\%F_F - \%F_M$ equals about $0.7648 - 0.1816 = 0.5832$; in April 1986 it equals about $0.7598 - 0.2057 = 0.5531$.

Evaluated at these values for the relevant year, the magnitude of $d \ln Y$ in the dumm & % version is usually very similar to the magnitude of the coefficient on FEMALE__ in the corresponding dummies version of the same specification (e.g., standard regressors) for the same year.[14]

A second feature of the results is that controlling for Haypoints reduces both the sex and class composition differentials considerably. Controlling for the standard regressors also reduces these differentials, but to a lesser extent.[15] To some degree, then, Haypoints do indeed serve as an index of employees' jobs (i.e., classes), as suggested in section 3.3.

The most noteworthy aspect of these tables, however, is the considerable reduction in both the sex differential and, in particular, the class composition differential between October 1981 and April 1986, when the state's comparable worth pay adjustments took place. (In the dumm & % specification, virtually all of the reduction has been in the class-composition differential, i.e., in the coefficient on PCTFEMAL rather than in the coefficient on FEMALE__. Since actual implementation of comparable worth focuses on class-composition differentials rather than on sex differentials per se, the relative magnitude of the changes in these two differentials is about what one would expect.) This suggests that CESW's enthusiasm for Minnesota's comparable worth pay adjustments may not be not misplaced.

Class-level results

As noted in chapter 3 (see particularly the discussion of the prototype comparable worth equation (3.6)), comparable worth proponents usually do not undertake individual-level analyses of the kind summarized in table 4.2. Rather, comparable worth analyses usually (1) take jobs (classes) rather than individual employees as the unit of analysis; (2) use an administrative pay construct (the A of chapter 3), usually either the maximum or the minimum rate of pay within each job, rather than the actual rate of pay as the dependent variable; and (3) use class composition measures and job evaluation scores (e.g., PCTFEMAL and Haypoint variables) rather than individual employee characteristics (e.g., age and years of service) as independent variables. Typically, comparable worth analyses are not weighted to reflect the numbers of persons in each job (although some jobs are often simply excluded from the analyses on the basis of an arbitrary size cutoff, e.g., having fewer than 10 incumbents). In such analyses, the coefficient on the class composition variable (e.g., PCTFEMAL) is taken as *the* sex differential in pay.

Table 4.3 summarizes class-level analyses of the Minnesota data for October 1981 and April 1986. For these analyses, the unit of observation is the class. As the dependent variable, I use, in turn, three different versions of the administrative pay construct A of comparable worth analyses: the maximum, mean and minimum of the (ln of the) hourly wage rates within each job class ("max pay," "mean pay" and "min pay," respectively). All regressors are within-class means: for example, AGE_____ now denotes the *mean* age of persons within each class. (Note that the Haypoint variables—e.g., number of Hay evaluation points awarded to a class—depend exclusively on the job and are the same for all persons in the same class.) Of course, the mean of the FEMALE__ dummy variable within each class is simply its class composition—i.e., the proportion of workers in the class who are female (PCTFEMAL)—and similarly for the ethnicity dummies, so there are no sex or ethnicity dummies as such in these analyses; rather, the only sex and race variables in the class-level studies are percent variables (e.g., PCTFEMAL, the complement of the M or proportion *male* variable in the prototype comparable worth equation (3.6)). The first two rows of table 4.3 summarize unweighted analyses (the full results appear in appendix tables A4.3–4); the third and fourth rows of table 4.3 summarize analyses in which each class is weighted according to the number of persons employed in it (see appendix tables A4.5–6 for the full results).

First consider the unweighted results. Here, as in table 4.2, the most noteworthy aspect of the results is the substantial change in the class composition differential (i.e., the coefficient on PCTFEMAL, the proportion female in the class) between October 1981 and April 1986. For the specifications corresponding most closely to the one favored by comparable worth proponents—raw differentials with Haypoints, with

Table 4.3 Summary of Class-Level Pay Regressions
(dep. var. = log of class max./mean/min. pay; t in parentheses)

	Raw Differentials			Raw Diffs. With Haypoints		
Variable	Max. Pay	Mean Pay	Min. Pay	Max. Pay	Mean Pay	Min. Pay
October 1981 (unweighted):						
PCTFEMAL	−0.3381	−0.3718	−0.4002	−0.1765	−0.2028	−0.2218
	(16.133)	(17.223)	(17.299)	(10.890)	(12.464)	(12.754)
April 1986 (unweighted):						
PCTFEMAL	−0.2328	−0.2618	−0.2918	−0.0589	−0.0780	−0.0955
	(12.258)	(13.270)	(13.696)	(4.332)	(5.662)	(6.397)
October 1981 (weighted):						
PCTFEMAL	−0.3732	−0.4822	−0.4951	−0.1618	−0.2718	−0.3135
	(94.546)	(137.555)	(149.957)	(47.058)	(95.666)	(111.507)
April 1986 (weighted):						
PCTFEMAL	−0.2803	−0.3827	−0.4317	−0.0193	−0.1273	−0.2115
	(66.054)	(98.245)	(108.053)	(6.563)	(48.895)	(65.181)

	Standard Regressors			Stand. Regs. with Haypoints		
Variable	Max. Pay	Mean Pay	Min. Pay	Max. Pay	Mean Pay	Min. Pay
October 1981 (unweighted):						
PCTFEMAL	−0.2673	−0.2850	−0.3062	−0.1648	−0.1788	−0.1926
	(12.500)	(13.215)	(13.144)	(9.654)	(10.675)	(10.690)
April 1986 (unweighted):						
PCTFEMAL	−0.1558	−0.1704	−0.1941	−0.0407	−0.0509	−0.0664
	(8.139)	(8.792)	(9.234)	(2.820)	(3.585)	(4.301)
October 1981 (weighted):						
PCTFEMAL	−0.3003	−0.3646	−0.3734	−0.1562	−0.2349	−0.2674
	(59.865)	(91.359)	(93.994)	(36.437)	(76.060)	(80.129)
April 1986 (weighted):						
PCTFEMAL	−0.2979	−0.3263	−0.3829	−0.0382	−0.1114	−0.2112
	(51.323)	(69.483)	(74.966)	(9.115)	(35.487)	(48.950)

either maximum or minimum (ln of) pay as the dependent variable – the PCTFEMAL coefficient falls in absolute value during this period by over 10 percentage points in all cases.

Other aspects of the unweighted results in table 4.3 are also of interest. First, choice of dependent variable can have a considerable effect on the results. In absolute value, the smallest class composition differential (PCTFEMAL coefficient) is derived when the dependent variable is the maximum (ln of the) wage rate; using the minimum (ln) wage rate produces a differential that is larger – sometimes much larger – in absolute value; using the mean (ln) wage produces intermediate results: The variance of maximum (ln) wage rates is smaller than the variance of mean or minimum (ln) wage rates, so sex and class composition differentials with respect to the former are smaller than they are with either of the latter two measures of pay (note also that values of R^2 in the regressions for maximum (ln) wage rates are larger than they are in the regressions for the other two measures of pay). As in the individual-level analyses shown in table 4.2, controlling for Haypoints in these class-level analyses reduces the absolute magnitude of the class composition (PCTFEMAL) coefficient considerably, whereas controlling for the standard regressors (age, years of service, etc.) does so to a lesser extent.

As noted in section 3.3, class-level analyses may be viewed as grouped-data studies of the underlying microdata on individual employees, in which case – in the absence of the microdata themselves – it would seem natural to use econometric techniques derived for grouped data. Accordingly, the third and fourth rows of table 4.3 summarize analyses that are identical to those in the first two rows except in one respect: unlike those analyses, the ones summarized in the last two rows are based on regressions in which each class is weighted according to the number of persons employed in it. The main difference between the first (unweighted) and second (weighted) sets of results in table 4.3 is that the class composition (PCTFEMAL) differentials in the latter are generally higher than those in the former, except when Haypoint variables are included as regressors and the dependent variable is the maximum (ln) pay rate. (This exception may be related to the fact, noted earlier, that the variance of the maximum (ln) pay rate is smaller than the variance of either the mean or the minimum (ln) pay rate.) However, both sets of results imply a considerable reduction in the differential over time.

Individual-level vs. class-level analyses

In view of the discussion in section 3.3, differences between the class- and individual-level analyses are of particular interest. Comparison of tables 4.2 and 4.3 highlights some of the main differences; I focus on class-level analyses in which the dependent variable is the mean of the (ln of the) actual pay rates of persons in each job, since these may be regarded as grouped-data equivalents of the corresponding individual level analyses.

When the dependent variable is the mean (ln of) actual pay, the coefficients on the class composition variable, PCTFEMAL, *in the weighted class-level analyses* (last two rows, table 4.3) are all reasonably close to those obtained for PCTFEMAL in the percent version of the same specification *in the individual-level analyses* (table 4.2). For example, in the standard regressors specification, the coefficient for PCTFEMAL for 1981 (1986) in the percent individual-level results is −0.3932 (−0.2974), vs. −0.3646 (−0.3263) for the weighted results. Second, the PCTFEMAL coefficients in the class-level analyses are always higher in absolute value—sometimes substantially so, particularly in the weighted results—than the coefficients on FEMALE__ obtained in individual-level analyses using the dummies version of the same specification. For example, for the standard regressors specification, the individual-level dummies version yields a FEMALE__ coefficient for 1981 (1986) of −0.2255 (−0.1636), vs. a PCTFEMAL coefficient in the corresponding weighted class-level analysis (with mean ln of pay as the dependent variable) of −0.3646 (−0.3263).

The second of these two stylized facts is particularly noteworthy. Class-level analyses (especially weighted ones) like those in table 4.3 are grouped-data equivalents of the dummies version of individual-level analyses like those in table 4.2. Thus, *particularly* when classes are weighted according to the number of employees in them, coefficients on the class composition variable PCTFEMAL in class-level analyses should be interpreted in the same way as are coefficients on the sex indicator variable FEMALE__ in conventional individual-level analyses that otherwise use the same specification: as measures of the sex differential in pay. However, as noted in section 3.3, a key assumption implicit in conventional grouped-data estimation (that the variable determining the grouping is independent of the individual-level error term for pay) may not hold when individuals are grouped by class (i.e., job). Indeed, tables 4.2–3 indicate that, other things being equal, the grouped-data regression approach implicit in comparable worth analyses overstates the absolute magnitude of sex differences in pay relative to what is obtained in a micro-level dummies version of the same specification (e.g., standard regressors), even if weighting is not used.

These comparisons highlight the effect of aggregating by class instead of using individuals as the unit of analysis, while keeping the specification (dependent and independent variables) the same. Although this is one major difference between comparable worth and conventional economic analyses of pay, there are two others: comparable worth analyses also use an administrative pay construct instead of actual salary as the dependent variable, and use Haypoints or other measures of job characteristics instead of measures of employee characteristics as independent variables. As noted in section 3.3, the net effect of all three differences in methodology on estimated pay differentials is difficult to determine a priori. Here, too, the results in tables 4.2–3 are of interest. They indicate that using all three main components of the comparable worth approach (raw differentials with Haypoints, applied to class-level data) yields pay gap estimates that are lower, in absolute value, than those derived using the kind of conventional economic analysis (standard regressors with dummies, applied to individual-level data) that can be performed with the relatively limited set of variables (e.g., age and years of service) available in these data. For example, for 1981, the conventional estimate is −0.2255 (standard regressors with dummies, table 4.2), vs. comparable worth estimates (raw differentials with Haypoints using max pay, table 4.3) of −0.1765 (unweighted) and −0.1618 (weighted). For 1986, the estimates are −0.1636 (table 4.2) vs.

−0.0589 (table 4.3, unweighted) and −0.0193 (table 4.3, weighted), respectively.

These patterns are even clearer when one compares individual-level conventional economic analyses with class-level analyses that mimic almost exactly the procedures used by comparable worth proponents, including Minnesota's CESW. Analyses of this kind are summarized in table 4.4. The conventional economic analyses are reproduced from table 4.2; these use data on individual employees, actual (ln of) pay as the dependent variable and the standard regressors (including dummies, i.e., sex and race indicators) as independent variables. In contrast, the comparable worth analyses summarized in table 4.4 adopt the CESW's conventions (see, e.g., CESW 1982, p. 28; 1985, pp. 1, 15; 1986, p. 2): they use class-level data without weighting according to class size (i.e., number of employees in each class); the dependent variable is the maximum (ln of) pay within each class; and there are only two independent variables: HAYPOINT and PCTFEMAL. (See appendix table A4.7 for the full results.) In all cases, the class-level analyses exclude "unrated classes" (i.e., jobs with no Haypoint job evaluation score); as noted in table 4.4, some of the class-level analyses consider all classes with Haypoint scores, whereas others consider only classes that not only have Haypoint scores but also have at least ten incumbents.

The results summarized in table 4.4 are striking. Both for October 1981 and April 1986, the comparable worth analyses imply sex differentials (coefficients on PCTFEMAL) that are clearly lower in absolute value than the differentials (coefficients on FEMALE__) obtained in conventional economic analyses. Indeed, when classes with less than ten incumbents are excluded from the comparable worth analyses, the implied sex differential for April 1986 is both small, about −2.8 percent, and not statistically significant at the conventional 5 percent level (its *t*-statistic is only 1.61). In this somewhat limited sense,[16] the evidence supports CESW's claims (1985, pp. 1, 15; 1986, p. 2), quoted earlier, that Minnesota has achieved "pay equity" in state government employment.

In view of these results, it is tempting to conclude that the methodological differences between conventional economic and comparable

Table 4.4 Sex Differentials in Pay Implied by Conventional Economic and Comparable Worth Pay Regressions, October 1981 and April 1986 (*t* in parentheses)

Model	Sex Differential in Pay	
	October 1981	**April 1986**
Conventional Economic	−0.2255	−0.1636
(dep. var. = LOG_HRLY)	(74.244)	(51.292)
# of observations:	30,027	31,368
Comparable Worth (unweighted):		
(dep. var. = ln of max. hourly wage rate)		
all jobs with Haypoint rating	−0.1574	−0.0631
	(12.380)	(5.264)
# of observations:	981	1,174
all jobs with Haypoint rating and at least 10 incumbents	−0.1350	−0.0282
	(7.801)	(1.605)
# of observations:	379	403

NOTES:

Model in *conventional economic* analyses: $Y = a + Fd + Xb + e$, where Y = LOG_HRLY, F = indicator for "sex is female," X = "standard regressors," and e is an error term. Unit of analysis is the individual employee. Entries in table refer to estimates of d for the indicated date.

Model in *comparable worth* analyses: $A = k + Pp + Hh + u$, where A = maximum (ln of) pay rate in class, P = proportion of employment in class that is female, H = Haypoints for class, and u is an error term. Unit of analysis is the class (job). Entries in table refer to estimates of p for the indicated date.

worth analyses mean that, on balance, comparable worth analyses will yield estimates of the sex differential in pay that are smaller in absolute value – i.e., more conservative – than those derived using the conventional economic approach. However, it should be noted that the conventional economic analyses summarized here control for only a limited set of employee characteristics (e.g., age and years of service in state government) and, because of missing data, do not control for many other characteristics (e.g., education and total years of prior work experience). Thus, it is not possible to say whether sex differentials in pay derived from a more fully specified conventional analysis would be higher or lower than those derived from comparable worth analyses.

4.4 *Longitudinal Analyses: Changes in the Sex Differential in Pay, 1981–86*

Although the different estimators used yield rather different results, the estimates summarized in tables 4.2–4 suggest that the sex differential in pay narrowed during 1981–1986. How did this happen, and to what extent are the state's comparable worth wage adjustments responsible?

To highlight some of the issues involved, it is useful to start with a seeming paradox. On the one hand, as just noted, the comparable worth analyses in tables 4.3–4 yield estimates of the absolute *magnitude* of the sex differential in pay that are *smaller* than those obtained in the conventional economic analyses in table 4.2. On the other hand, the *change over time* in that differential is *larger* in the comparable worth analyses than it is in the conventional economic analyses. For example, the change in the FEMALE__ coefficient between October 1981 and April 1986 in the conventional economic results (standard regressors with dummies, table 4.2) is $(-0.1636)-(-0.2255)=0.0619$. In contrast, the change in the PCTFEMAL coefficient during the same period in the class-level results using the comparable worth approach (raw differentials with Haypoints with max pay, table 4.3) is between $(-0.0589)-(-0.1765)=0.1176$ (unweighted) and $(-0.0193)-(-0.1618)=0.1425$ (weighted). Similar patterns are evident in table 4.4.

This apparent paradox—smaller absolute *magnitudes* of, but larger absolute *changes* in, the sex differential in comparable worth analyses relative to conventional economic analyses—can readily be explained, however, and the explanation highlights an important point. Conventional economic analyses of cross-section pay differences by sex at different dates may be sensitive to differences in employee characteristics (particularly, ones not included in the analyses) at those different dates. Since the characteristics of state employees change over time, estimated pay differences by sex obtained in conventional economic analyses may change over time purely as a result of changes in the characteristics of state employees rather than (or in addition to) changes in the state's pay practices.

For example, sex differences in pay generally rise with age: young persons of either sex usually have relatively little prior work experience, whereas older men usually have more prior experience than do older women. Thus, even if the state's pay practices do not change at all, an influx into state employment of young women with little prior work experience could produce the appearance of a reduction in the absolute magnitude in the sex differential in pay in conventional economic analyses of successive cross-sections like the ones in this chapter that do not include an explicit measure of prior work experience because of lack of data. Likewise, suppose that sex differentials in pay widen with years of service in state employment (due, e.g., to differential rates of promotion) and that the state reduces its hiring of new employees (who, by definition, have zero years of state service and whose pay rates, by assumption, would therefore differ less by sex than would pay rates of employees with many years of service). In conventional economic analyses of successive cross-sections, this could produce the appearance of an increase in the absolute magnitude of the sex differential in pay even if the state simultaneously began to reduce the pay differential between men and women with many years of state service.

In sum, the pay differential in conventional economic analyses at a given date may be an unbiased estimate of the overall average difference in pay between men and women with given characteristics as of that date. It may not be the same, however, as the overall average pay difference between men and women with *different* given characteristics as of a *different* date, even in the absence of changes in pay practices of the employer. More generally, when the composition of state employment is changing, changes in the sex differential in pay obtained in conventional economic studies of successive cross-sections do not necessarily indicate how the sex difference in pay for a *given* set of employees – a "fixed basket of goods," so to speak – has changed.

In contrast, comparable worth analyses are concerned with classes (jobs) rather than with individual employees. As noted in chapter 3, they may fail to yield an unbiased estimate of the overall average difference in pay between men and women with given characteristics as of any given date. If the class (i.e., job) composition of state employment remains essentially the same over time, however, successive comparable worth analyses of pay may amount to analyses of the same "basket of goods," and so may yield an unbiased estimate of how the sex difference in pay for a given set of employees has changed over time.

To address this question in greater detail, I selected random samples of 1,000 white men and 1,000 white women who were present and active in state employment during the entire period (October 1981–April 1986) covered by the data. The nature of these data permits one to abstract from changes in characteristics of the state's work force over time that are an inherent feature of analyses of successive cross-sections. I then analyzed whether, holding constant (changes in) personal characteristics and other (e.g., environmental) influences, pay rose by more or less for women than for men after the state's comparable worth wage adjustments.

In these analyses, the state's comparable worth wage adjustments of July 1983, July 1984 and July 1985 are denoted by three indicator variables, AFTER783, AFTER784 and AFTER785, respectively. These variables identify observations falling after each of these dates,[17] and operationalize the notion of the "comparable worth" variable C_{it} of equation (3.7). Also, since the data refer to different dates, I attempt to abstract from cyclical and secular effects by including (in addition to variables pertaining to consumer prices) time trend terms and/or measures of private-sector wages in both Minnesota as a whole and in the Minneapolis–St.Paul MSA during the relevant quarter; these embody the environmental variables discussed in connection with equation (3.7). The time trend terms are TIMETRND and TIMETRSQ. TIMETRND is defined as the number of years (and fractions of years) elapsed as of the current date since January 1, 1960, and thus increases by one unit per year; TIMETRSQ is the square of TIMETRND (divided by 100, to facilitate formatting of the tables).[18] The private sector wage variables, LNWGMINP and LNWGMSAP, are the (ln of) private-sector monthly wage rates in the state of Minnesota and in the Minneapolis–St. Paul MSA, respectively, as of the relevant quarter. (For discussion of the basic data underlying these variables, see section 4.2.) The price variables, CPINDEX1–CPINDEX4, give the value of the Consumer Price Index for All Urban Consumers ("CPI-U") in the month immediately preceding the month referenced by the data (CPINDEX1) or three, six or nine months prior to that. (For example, for observations pertaining to October, CPINDEX1 is the September CPI-U value, and CPINDEX2–CPINDEX4 are the CPI-U values for June, March and the previous December, respectively.)

Pooled OLS estimates

The first set of analyses of this question uses pooled OLS: I simply pool observations in the random sample for each sex for all 19 quarters (making 19,000 total observations for each sex) and estimate the models described earlier (with or without percent variables, Haypoint variables and standard regressors). Since these analyses are concerned with samples of whites and are restricted to women (or men), they do not include any race or sex indicator variables.

The results are summarized in table 4.5, for women, and table 4.6, for men (the full results appear in appendix tables A4.8 and A4.9, respectively). In all three models (with time trend terms only; with private-sector wage variables only; or with both time trend and wage variables), estimated comparable worth effects as measured by the sum of the coefficients on the AFTER78*i*, i=3, 4 or 5 are about the same: roughly 9 to 12 percent for women, about −1.0 to 2.0 percent for men. The AFTER78*i* coefficients are significant at conventional test levels for women, but not for men. In models with both time trend and wage variables, (1) the wage variables usually are not themselves significant at reasonable levels; and (2) the estimated comparable worth effects are similar to those obtained in analogous models with time trend variables only.[19] In view of this, I focus on the "time trend" results (i.e., those in which the time trend but *not* the private-sector wage variables are used).

The time trend results for women in table 4.5 are essentially the same regardless of which regressors are used: relative to what would have been predicted on the basis of time trends and (changes in) their own

Table 4.5 Summary of Pooled OLS Wage Regressions for Women (dep. var. = LOG_HRLY; t in parentheses)

Variable	Raw Differentials		Raw Differentials with Haypoints		Standard Regressors		Standard Regressors with Haypoints	
	Basic	Percent	Basic	Percent	Basic	Percent	Basic	Percent
Time Trend Variables Only:								
AFTER783	0.0322	0.0338	0.0291	0.0289	0.0323	0.0337	0.0292	0.0291
	(2.216)	(2.600)	(3.925)	(3.898)	(2.370)	(2.783)	(4.246)	(4.233)
AFTER784	0.0471	0.0482	0.0482	0.0479	0.0469	0.0478	0.0482	0.0479
	(5.344)	(6.120)	(10.732)	(10.674)	(5.686)	(6.519)	(11.558)	(11.501)
AFTER785	0.0374	0.0374	0.0364	0.0360	0.0373	0.0374	0.0364	0.0361
	(3.476)	(3.895)	(6.635)	(6.570)	(3.703)	(4.181)	(7.158)	(7.103)
Sum of AFTER78i:	0.1167	0.1194	0.1137	0.1128	0.1165	0.1189	0.1138	0.1131
Private-Sector Wage Variables Only:								
AFTER783	0.0528	0.0560	0.0492	0.0489	0.0473	0.0505	0.0459	0.0457
	(6.219)	(7.378)	(11.356)	(11.308)	(5.957)	(7.142)	(11.428)	(11.384)
AFTER784	0.0341	0.0364	0.0339	0.0336	0.0312	0.0335	0.0318	0.0315
	(3.655)	(4.359)	(7.118)	(7.062)	(3.571)	(4.308)	(7.205)	(7.149)
AFTER785	0.0181	0.0193	0.0160	0.0156	0.0158	0.0173	0.0143	0.0139
	(2.693)	(3.212)	(4.673)	(4.551)	(2.509)	(3.089)	(4.485)	(4.378)
Sum of AFTER78i:	0.1050	0.1110	0.0991	0.0981	0.0943	0.1013	0.0920	0.0911
Both Time Trend and Private-Sector Wage Variables:								
AFTER783	0.0285	0.0296	0.0242	0.0240	0.0286	0.0296	0.0243	0.0242
	(1.829)	(2.126)	(3.045)	(3.018)	(1.960)	(2.279)	(3.297)	(3.285)
AFTER784	0.0438	0.0446	0.0433	0.0432	0.0436	0.0443	0.0433	0.0432
	(2.997)	(3.418)	(5.815)	(5.801)	(3.190)	(3.648)	(6.262)	(6.257)
AFTER785	0.0350	0.0349	0.0328	0.0326	0.0350	0.0350	0.0329	0.0327
	(2.391)	(2.668)	(4.392)	(4.363)	(2.550)	(2.872)	(4.738)	(4.724)
Sum of AFTER78i:	0.1073	0.1091	0.1003	0.0998	0.1072	0.1089	0.1005	0.1001

characteristics, women's pay rose by roughly 3 percentage points after July 1983 (the date of the first set of comparable worth wage adjustments), by roughly 4.7 more percentage points after July 1984 (the date of the second set), and by about 3.7 additional percentage points after July 1985 (when the third set occurred). Thus, the pooled OLS estimates in table 4.5 imply that the cumulative effect of the adjustments on pay for women was an increase of roughly 11.4 percentage points relative to what would have been expected on the basis of trends and (changes in) characteristics—such as accumulated seniority—of the women themselves. These AFTER78i effects are significant at conventional test levels.

The pooled OLS time trend estimates for men in table 4.6 are also very similar regardless of which sets of regressors are used, but are very different from those derived for women. The estimates suggest that, among men, pay (1) was essentially unchanged after the first set of adjustments, (2) rose by no more than roughly 0.5 of a percentage point after the second set and (3) rose by roughly 1.0 further percentage points after the third set, for a cumulative increase of no more than about 1.5 percentage points relative to what would have been expected on the basis of past trends and (changes in) individual characteristics. Moreover, none of the AFTER78i coefficients for men is significant at conventional test levels; in the statistical sense, the pay adjustments' effect on pay of men was negligible.

Fixed-effects estimates

Persons who were present during the entire period covered by the data may not be typical of all state employees, so inferences based on simple pooled OLS analyses of such persons may not readily generalize to the state's total employee population. To address this potential problem, I reestimated the OLS analyses allowing for person-specific fixed effects; note that all regressors that either are time-invariant or increase one-for-one with time (e.g., years since first entry date) now drop out of the analyses.

Table 4.7 summarizes these fixed-effects analyses (the full results

Table 4.6 Summary of Pooled OLS Wage Regressions for Men (dep. var. = LOG_HRLY; t in parentheses)

Variable	Raw Differentials		Raw Differentials with Haypoints		Standard Regressors		Standard Regressors with Haypoints	
	Basic	Percent	Basic	Percent	Basic	Percent	Basic	Percent
Time Trend Variables Only:								
AFTER783	0.0016	−0.0036	0.0002	−0.0008	0.0010	−0.0035	0.0001	−0.0008
	(0.093)	(0.232)	(0.028)	(0.088)	(0.064)	(0.241)	(0.011)	(0.094)
AFTER784	0.0057	0.0025	0.0050	0.0043	0.0073	0.0044	0.0057	0.0051
	(0.544)	(0.268)	(0.824)	(0.754)	(0.761)	(0.498)	(1.044)	(0.978)
AFTER785	0.0106	0.0115	0.0105	0.0108	0.0109	0.0117	0.0106	0.0109
	(0.827)	(0.989)	(1.405)	(1.523)	(0.926)	(1.076)	(1.584)	(1.688)
Sum of AFTER78i:	0.0179	0.0104	0.0157	0.0135	0.0192	0.0126	0.0164	0.0152
Private-Sector Wage Variables Only:								
AFTER783	0.0137	0.0143	0.0099	0.0106	0.0098	0.0112	0.0072	0.0081
	(1.356)	(1.561)	(1.669)	(1.895)	(1.059)	(1.306)	(1.354)	(1.595)
AFTER784	−0.0126	−0.0124	−0.0147	−0.0143	−0.0129	−0.0122	−0.0153	−0.0147
	(1.132)	(1.234)	(2.256)	(2.334)	(1.262)	(1.291)	(2.616)	(2.621)
AFTER785	−0.0133	−0.0098	−0.0144	−0.0134	−0.0145	−0.0108	−0.0152	−0.0141
	(1.661)	(1.347)	(3.052)	(3.028)	(1.975)	(1.574)	(3.597)	(3.479)
Sum of AFTER78i:	−0.0122	−0.0079	−0.0192	−0.0171	−0.0176	−0.0108	−0.0233	−0.0207
Both Time Trend and Private-Sector Wage Variables:								
AFTER783	−0.0022	−0.0072	−0.0035	−0.0046	−0.0029	−0.0072	−0.0037	−0.0047
	(0.121)	(0.429)	(0.324)	(0.452)	(0.170)	(0.457)	(0.388)	(0.504)
AFTER784	0.0019	−0.0005	0.0002	0.0002	0.0029	0.0006	0.0005	0.0006
	(0.110)	(0.036)	(0.021)	(0.027)	(0.186)	(0.045)	(0.060)	(0.073)
AFTER785	0.0079	0.0093	0.0068	0.0077	0.0076	0.0090	0.0066	0.0075
	(0.450)	(0.588)	(0.665)	(0.802)	(0.476)	(0.604)	(0.722)	(0.850)
Sum of AFTER78i:	0.0076	0.0016	0.0035	0.0033	0.0076	0.0024	0.0034	0.0034

Table 4.7 Summary of Fixed-Effects Wage Regressions for Random Samples of Whites (dep. var. = LOG_HRLY; *t* in parentheses)

	Time Trend Variables Only		Pvt.-Sector Wage Variables Only		Both Time Trend & Pvt.-Sector Wages	
Variable	Females	Males	Females	Males	Females	Males
AFTER783	0.0344	0.0023	0.0581	0.0230	0.0282	−0.0022
	(2.395)	(0.138)	(6.820)	(2.253)	(1.811)	(0.118)
AFTER784	0.0482	0.0061	0.0417	−0.0037	0.0430	0.0020
	(5.524)	(0.586)	(4.558)	(0.336)	(2.962)	(0.116)
AFTER785	0.0345	0.0096	0.0262	−0.0026	0.0328	0.0081
	(3.336)	(0.779)	(3.794)	(0.319)	(2.346)	(0.487)
AFTER78*i* Coefficients:						
Sum	0.1171	0.0180	0.1260	0.0167	0.1040	0.0079
F-M diff.	0.0991		0.1093		0.0961	

appear in appendix table A4.10). The estimates here are very similar to the pooled OLS estimates,[20] implying (for time trend models) cumulative increases up to April 1986 of slightly more than 11.7 percentage points in women's wages and of about 1.8 percentage points in men's wages. (Again, the effects for women are significant at conventional test levels, whereas the ones for men are not.) The net gain for women was thus about 9.9 percentage points. It is interesting to note that this is larger than the size of the reduction (roughly 6.2 percentage points) in the FEMALE__ coefficient in individual-level analyses with standard regressors (table 4.2), but smaller than the reductions (about 11.8 percentage points unweighted, 14.3 percentage points weighted) in the PCTFEMAL coefficient for class-level analyses using the raw differentials with Haypoints specification with max pay (table 4.3). Thus, at least as regards wage effects of comparable worth, the cross-section conventional economic and comparable worth results bracket the fixed-effects results; and the results implied by the unweighted comparable worth analyses are quite close to the fixed effects results.

In sum, the bottom-line numbers for women and men are cumulative wage gains of about 11.7 and 1.8 percentage points, respectively, after the comparable worth wage adjustments; the former effects are statistically significant, whereas the latter are not.

In this connection, it is interesting to note that both the state administration and the union representing most of the potential beneficiaries of the adjustments wanted to make "comparable worth raises . . . an addition to rather than a competitor with general salary increases, [with] no job classification [having] its salary lowered" (Evans and Nelson 1989, p. 94). Formulation and implementation of the adjustments were structured in a way that enhanced their add-on character. For example, both collective bargaining over and appropriations for the adjustments treated them as a special item, distinct from other pay changes (Evans and Nelson 1989, pp. 92–103). The evidence from the analyses of this chapter suggests that the objective of add-on adjustments was largely fulfilled: oversimplifying only slightly, one can say that the actual effect of the comparable worth wage increases was a net addition to women's pay and no change in men's pay, relative to the levels that would otherwise have prevailed.

As implied in section 3.4, however, this need not have been the case, despite the intentions of the major participants. The state ultimately determines what all jobs (and workers) will be paid, and the notion that it determines what one job (or worker) will be paid in isolation from other jobs (or workers) is implausible. Whatever it may say *explicitly*, the state might *implicitly* have chosen to finance larger wage increases for some jobs (or workers) by making smaller increases for others, by scaling down the size of cost-of-living increases, etc. Also, at least in principle, men as well as women might benefit. On the one hand, the so-called female-dominated jobs that were targeted for comparable worth wage adjustments were not all 100 percent female; rather, men as well as women were working in these jobs.[21] On the other hand, unions representing workers in predominantly male jobs might resist the narrowing of traditional pay differentials implicit in comparable worth (and, in Minnesota, actually attempted to do so: recall note 29, chapter 3). Pay increases for predominantly female *jobs* need not preclude pay increases for male *workers*, even though that was essentially the end result of the adjustments that were actually adopted.

4.5 *Longitudinal Analyses of Changes in Employment, 1981–86*

Was employment affected by the state's comparable worth wage adjustments? As noted in section 3.4, I address this question in two stages. First, I estimate the employment demand function (3.10) to obtain measures of the effect of wages on employment, other things (e.g., prices, time trend terms and variables denoting the state of the private-sector labor market) being equal. Then, I use the estimated wage elasticity of employment and estimates of the wage increase attributable to comparable worth (as derived in section 4.4) to measure the actual effect on employment.

Employment demand function estimates

The dependent variable in the employment demand analyses is always the natural logarithm of class employment. As the wage variable (the W_{it} of (3.10)), I use, in turn, either the maximum, the mean or the minimum (ln of the) within-class hourly wage rate. The sample used in estimation consists of all classes with positive employment over the entire period covered by the data.[22] Estimates are presented separately for "mixed" and predominantly female and male classes, where predominance refers to the proportion female in a class as of October 1981: classes in which under 30 percent (at least 70 percent) of the incumbents as of that date were female are called predominantly (fe)male, whereas the rest are called "mixed." The analyses control for prices, time trend terms and/or private-sector patterns, where the latter are measured by the (ln of) private-sector employment in Minnesota and the Minneapolis –St. Paul MSA (LNEMMINP and LNEMMSAP, respectively) as of the relevant quarter.[23]

The results—derived using either pooled OLS or fixed effects—are summarized in table 4.8 (see appendix table A4.11 for the complete

Table 4.8 Summary of Regressions for Class Employment Levels by Type of Class (dep. var. = ln of class employment; indep var. = maximum/ mean/minimum ln of wage rate within class; *t* in parentheses)

	Pooled OLS Estimates			Fixed-Effects Estimates		
Model, Class	Maximum	Mean	Minimum	Maximum	Mean	Minimum
Time Trend Variables Only:						
Predom. female	−2.4999	−3.1108	−3.1704	0.6963	−0.3987	−1.0536
	(31.293)	(44.816)	(55.539)	(7.779)	(3.730)	(13.016)
Mixed	−0.1730	−1.0122	−1.7845	1.6262	−1.3188	−1.8270
	(2.367)	(13.328)	(24.832)	(14.508)	(9.542)	(20.279)
Predom. male	−1.8014	−2.1028	−2.3512	0.5929	−0.6349	−1.1818
	(54.781)	(69.654)	(89.986)	(14.633)	(14.039)	(36.778)
Private-Sector Employment Variables Only:						
Predom. female	−2.4983	−3.1089	−3.1693	0.7086	−0.3713	−1.0378
	(31.277)	(44.789)	(55.515)	(7.936)	(3.492)	(12.830)
Mixed	−0.1734	−1.0119	−1.7829	1.6380	−1.2646	−1.7944
	(2.375)	(13.330)	(24.825)	(14.709)	(9.168)	(19.941)
Predom. male	−1.7999	−2.1009	−2.3492	0.5851	−0.6185	−1.1665
	(54.753)	(69.612)	(89.930)	(14.560)	(13.786)	(36.490)
Both Time Trend and Private-Sector Employment Variables:						
Predom. female	−2.5004	−3.1113	−3.1708	0.7059	−0.4131	−1.0679
	(31.289)	(44.810)	(55.530)	(7.820)	(3.816)	(13.121)
Mixed	−0.1730	−1.0123	−1.7846	1.6693	−1.3025	−1.8242
	(2.367)	(13.325)	(24.826)	(14.840)	(9.326)	(20.139)
Predom. male	−1.8014	−2.1028	−2.3512	0.6006	−0.6459	−1.1954
	(54.778)	(69.649)	(89.980)	(14.730)	(14.160)	(37.006)

results). Both in the pooled OLS and fixed-effects results, the wage elasticity for a given group is essentially the same regardless of which set of regressors is used (time trend terms only; private-sector employment variables only; or both time trend and private-sector employment variables).[24] In the interest of brevity, the following discussion focuses on the time trend results (i.e., those with time trend but *not* private-sector employment variables).

The first half of table 4.8 presents class employment function estimates obtained using pooled OLS. The coefficient on the wage variable is always significantly negative and almost always greater (often, substantially so) than unity in absolute value. These are hard to accept as estimates of demand elasticities: as noted in section 3.4, negative wage coefficients obtained using pooled OLS may reflect only the hierarchical nature of Minnesota state employment, rather than a negative effect of wage increases on employment in a *given* class.

To address this problem, I also estimated employment functions using fixed effects; these results are summarized in the second half of table 4.8. As one would expect, the wage coefficients here are lower in absolute value than those obtained using pooled OLS. Indeed, when the maximum (log-)wage rate is used as the measure of the cost of labor, the coefficient is always positive. On *a priori* grounds, the maximum (log-)wage is a less appealing measure of the cost of labor than either the mean or minimum.[25] The positive relation between the maximum (log-)wage and employment warrants further study, however.

This result apart, the fixed-effects results for equation (3.10), like the pooled OLS results, generally imply a significantly negative relation between pay and the level of employment within job classes. The time trend fixed-effects estimates (with the W_{it} of (3.10) defined as the mean ln of pay) imply elasticities of employment with respect to wages of about −0.40, −1.30 and −0.65 for predominantly female, mixed and predominantly male classes, respectively. Recall that, as noted in section 3.4, these are best regarded as output- (or budget-) constant employment elasticities, exclusive of any employment reductions attributable to the decline in the purchasing power of the state's personnel budget due to the comparable worth wage increases.

These estimates (particularly for mixed classes) are larger in absolute value than those derived in previous work on state and local government employment (see, e.g., Ehrenberg and Smith 1987a; and Ashenfelter 1977). The present research differs from prior studies in at least two potentially important respects, however. First, most prior work used either aggregate time-series data (e.g., Ashenfelter 1977) or aggregate cross-section data (e.g., Ehrenberg and Smith 1987a), whereas this research of course refers to a single governmental unit. Second, unlike the earlier analyses, this research is concerned with a setting in which there was substantial and (if the participants are to be believed) genuinely exogenous variation in wages, variation that was not dictated by market forces. This does not necessarily mean that the Minnesota experience is the equivalent of a controlled experiment, but it may mean that problems of aggregation, imprecision and simultaneity affect the present study to a lesser extent than was the case in prior work.

Estimated employment effects

Given the cumulative effects of comparable worth on wages, discussed previously, the employment elasticities just discussed imply that the cumulative effects of comparable worth on employment were about $-0.40 \times 11.7 = -4.7$ percent and $-0.65 \times 1.8 = -1.2$ percent for predominantly male and predominantly female jobs, respectively.

Thus, these estimates imply that the cumulative three-year effect of comparable worth on both women's and men's employment between July 1983 (the date of the first comparable worth pay adjustments) and April 1986 (the end of the period covered by the data) was not much different from (loss of), at most, several years of employment *growth*. "Exogenous" employment growth associated with trends (TIMETRND, TIMETRSQ) and price changes (CPINDEX1–4) between July 1983–April 1986 was about 8.0 percent for predominantly female jobs, 19.0 percent for mixed jobs and 10.1 percent for predominantly male jobs.[26] For each type of job, this exogenous employment growth is more than sufficient to offset the effects of the wage increases that actually occurred over the same period. For example, between July 1983–April 1986, the actual mean ln wage increased by about 0.178, 0.135 and 0.135 for predominantly female, mixed and predominantly male job classes, respectively. Evaluated at the appropriate wage elasticity of employment (-0.40, -1.30 and -0.65, respectively), these changes in (mean ln) wages imply *ceteris paribus* wage-induced employment reductions of about 7.1 percent, 17.6 percent and 8.8 percent, respectively – less than the employment increases implied by exogenous factors during the same period. Note that the actual changes in (mean ln) wages include the effects of the comparable worth wage adjustments; in the absence of the adjustments, then, wage changes would have been smaller and the net growth in employment would have been larger.

In sum, the wage adjustments not only did not reduce the *level* of anyone's pay; they also did not actually cause anyone to lose his or her job. Rather, they meant only that subsequent employment *growth* was smaller than would otherwise have been the case. The real losers from the wage adjustments, if any, were taxpayers and individuals – particularly women – in the private sector (or outside the workforce) seeking a state job.

4.6 *Summary and Conclusions*

The results of this chapter may now be summarized briefly. On the methodological plane, there is little to support the use of class (job) level regressions, with or without Haypoints and whether weighted or unweighted, to analyze sex differences in pay *levels*. On the one hand, the aggregation of individuals into jobs that is inherent in comparable worth analyses consistently yields estimated sex differentials in pay that are noticeably larger, in absolute value, than those obtained in otherwise-identical specifications using individual-level data. On the other hand, adopting all three main elements of comparable worth analyses simultaneously – using jobs rather than individuals as the unit of analysis, an administrative pay construct rather than actual wages as the dependent variable, and job evaluation scores instead of employee characteristics as independent variables – yields estimated sex differentials in pay that are smaller, in absolute value, than the ones obtained in conventional economic analyses of individual-level data that use the limited set of employee characteristics variables available in these data.

In contrast, comparable worth cross-section analyses – particularly unweighted ones – of pay at different dates yield estimates of the *change* in the sex differential in pay that are reasonably close to those obtained in fixed-effects analyses of individual level data.

On the substantive question of the effects of Minnesota's comparable worth wage adjustments, the evidence suggests that although the adjustments certainly did not eradicate the female/male pay gap in Minnesota state employment,[27] they did reduce it. Women clearly received wage gains, relative to what their pay would otherwise have been; although the estimates also imply that men enjoyed some wage gains as well, these are very small and statistically insignificant. Relative to what would have been observed *in the absence of the wage adjustments*, employment in female jobs fell. However, relative to *prior years*, employment in female jobs rose: that is, wage increases (and induced gross reductions in employment) for female jobs were offset by other forces, leaving a net increase in employment, on balance, relative to prior years. The effects on pay were of fairly moderate size; not surprisingly, so were the resulting effects on employment.

NOTES

[1] In 1984, the legislature required local governments to make payment on the basis of "comparable work value" a "primary consideration" in municipal employee compensation decisions. See Local Government Pay Equity Act (Minnesota Statutes, chapter 471.991, subdivision 5).

[2] Most of the following discussion is based on Council on the Economic Status of Women (1982), Evans and Nelson (1986, 1989) and Rothchild (1984a, 1984b, 1985).

[3] Hay Associates led the committees in their evaluation of the first 250 jobs; the Department of Personnel representatives then led the committees in evaluating the next 200 jobs; the remaining jobs were evaluated by the Department of Personnel representatives with input from the other committee members as needed; Hay Associates evaluated "key managerial, personnel, and particularly sensitive classes" (Minnesota Department of Finance 1979a, p. 18).

[4] For example, Committee "C" included a human resources specialist, a senior clerk-stenographer, an agricultural field inspector, a principal highway technician, the personnel director in the Department of Administration, a natural resources technician, an executive in the Department of Public Safety, and a Department of Personnel representative. See Minnesota Department of Finance (1979a, p. 17).

[5] Even before the state's comparable worth pay adjustments, pay for relatively low-level occupations in Minnesota state government exceeded that in the private sector (Minnesota Department of Finance, 1979, esp. pp I-43–I-44). For example, ". . . even before we started our pay equity program, our office and clerical workers were paid 15 percent above the prevailing wages" (Rothchild 1984b, p. 78).

[6] The task force's study was limited to state jobs that (1) had been assigned Hay point scores, (2) had at least 10 incumbents and (3) were predominantly male (i.e., jobs in which at least 70 percent of the incumbents were male) or predominantly female (i.e., at least 80 percent of the incumbents

were female). About 88 percent of nonacademic state employment was in job classifications meeting these criteria. (See Rothchild 1985, p. 108.)

[7] In Minnesota state employment, jobs are usually referred to as "classes" or "classifications."

[8] The available slice files cover October 1981, January and April 1986, and the months of January, April, July and October for each of the years 1982–1985 inclusive, making a total of 19 quarters. Each slice file contains data on about 30,000 employees; in total, the 19 slice files contain over 580,000 records.

[9] The unique identifier is the employee's scrambled Social Security number. I thank James Lee and the late Paul Roberts of the Minnesota Department of Employee Relations for preparing the slice files, and Jan Anderson, Florence Buggert and James Lee for answering queries about their contents.

[10] About 7 percent of the individuals in the slice files have state employment entry dates that change over time (usually because they leave and then re-enter state employment). I extracted both the earliest and "most recent" (as of the end of the relevant quarter) entry date for each person. Also, for some individuals, certain information (concerning, for example, birth date or sex) is missing in the initial record but is available in later records. I extracted such information and appended it to all records for each such person.

[11] As shown in table 4.1, I use a quadratic form for jobs' Haypoint scores, i.e., include both the actual Haypoint score (HAYPOINT) and its square (HAYPOISQ). This allows for the possibility that pay rises with Haypoints at a decreasing rate. In the jargon of job evaluation practitioners, this quadratic relation between pay and evaluation points – rising, but flattening out at higher evaluation point values – is a "dogleg" pattern (see, e.g., Farnquist et al. 1983, p. 362). This quadratic relation is in fact observed in Minnesota (see, e.g., appendix tables A4.1–6), in San José (see chapter 5 and Stackhouse 1980) and elsewhere (see, e.g., Willis and associates 1974, 1976).

[12] That is, the "percent female" variable varies between zero (for all-male jobs) and unity (for all-female jobs), so that the coefficient on this variable indicates the change in pay when "percent female" changes from zero to unity, other things being equal. (Similarly, the coefficient can be multiplied by 0.5 to yield the effect of changing from an all-male job to one that is 50 percent female.) Note that, in the second (percent) version, neither sex nor ethnicity is among the "other things" being held constant.

[13] Analogously, studies of union wage effects might ask (a) how pay for workers differs depending on whether they are in 100 percent or 0 percent organized firms, (b-1) how pay for workers *of given union status* differs depending on whether they are in 100 percent or 0 percent organized firms, and/or (b-2) how pay for workers *in firms that are organized to the same degree* differs depending on their union status. Addressing question (a) would entail a specification analogous to the percent version used here; addressing questions (b) would entail a specification analogous to the dumm & % version used here, with answers to (b-1) derived from the coefficient on a "percent organized" variable and answers to (b-2) derived from the coefficient on an "is a union member" dummy variable.

[14] For example, for the standard regressors specification for October 1981 (see table 4.2), $d \ln Y$ for the dumm & % version is $-0.0208+(-0.3740\times0.5832)=-0.2389$, vs. a coefficient in the dummies version of -0.2255.

[15] Controlling for Haypoints or the standard regressors reduces the class composition effect (i.e., the PCTFEMAL coefficient) substantially, but reduces the sex effect per se (i.e., the FEMALE__ coefficient) by only a small amount, in the dumm & % version relative to the percent version.

[16] Note that the analysis underlying the -2.8 percent differential excludes classes that either (1)

are unrated (do not have Haypoint values) or (2) have less than 10 incumbents. Both kinds of classes are predominantly male and generally entail rates of pay that are well above average; their exclusion clearly reduces the differential relative to what would be obtained were they not excluded.

[17] Thus, these indicators are cumulative: for example, an observation dated September 1983 will have AFTER783=1 and AFTER784=AFTER785=0, but one for September 1984 will have AFTER783=AFTER784=1 and AFTER785=0.

[18] Unemployment rates for both men and women in Minnesota and the Minneapolis–St. Paul MSA rose early in the 1980s with the onset of the 1980–81 recession but fell during the mid-1980s, so a quadratic in time seems much more appropriate than a simple linear time trend. (TIMETRSQ is generally significant at conventional test levels in both the pooled OLS analyses of tables 4.5–6 and the fixed-effects analyses of table 4.7, discussed presently.)

[19] Also, the results are not sensitive to inclusion of higher-order terms in private-sector wages (e.g., the square of LNWGMSAP) and/or terms in private-sector employment levels.

[20] In contrast with the pooled OLS results, in the fixed-effects results the private-sector wage variables are often statistically significant at conventional test levels. The fixed-effects estimates of comparable worth effects (the AFTER78i coefficients) are very similar regardless of which sets of regressors are used, however. Thus, in the interest of brevity, the discussion of fixed-effects results in the text focuses on the time trend models.

[21] As noted earlier, the state estimated that about 10 percent of the beneficiaries of the adjustments were men (see, e.g., Rothchild n.d., p. 4).

[22] Jobs with zero employment at some point are, at least at that point, inframarginal and so are not on the relevant demand function (recall section 3.4). Jobs with positive employment *throughout* the period of analysis may be atypical, but later on I address this potential problem using fixed effects.

[23] Like the private-sector wage variables, these private-sector employment variables are derived from the ES-202 file, discussed in section 4.2.

[24] Also, the results are not sensitive to inclusion of higher-order terms in private-sector employment (e.g., the square of LNENMSAP) and/or terms in private-sector wages.

[25] The maximum does not appear to be a very meaningful measure of the cost of labor: the proportion of employees actually paid the maximum wage rate for their class is never more than 31 percent in any quarter covered by the data (in most quarters, the proportion is between 22 and 29 percent). The proportion of persons actually receiving the maximum changes in a cyclical fashion because of the manner in which pay changes are implemented: between July of any given year (when new pay rates usually take effect) and the following April, the proportion receiving the maximum increases steadily, and then falls in the following July as new pay rates take effect. Also, recall from section 4.3's discussion of the class-level results for pay that the variance of maximum (ln) wage rates is smaller than the variance of mean or minimum (ln) wage rates: using maxima instead of means or minima in effect tends to overstate the similarity of jobs' pay rates.

[26] These figures are derived by multiplying the fixed-effects time trend coefficient estimates shown in the "mean" column of appendix table A4.11 for TIMETRND, TIMETRSQ and CPINDEX1–4 for each type of job by the changes in these variables between July 1983–April 1986.

[27] Contrary to the rather self-congratulatory comments of CESW (1985, pp. 1, 15; 1986, p. 2) quoted earlier in this chapter. As shown in table 4.4, even the approach that is apparently preferred by comparable worth proponents yields a sex differential in pay that is not statistically significant at the conventional 5 percent level only if one excludes all jobs that either do not have a Haypoint rating or else have fewer than ten incumbents.

Appendix Table A4.1(1) Individual Pay Regressions, October 1981 (dep. var. = LOG_HRLY; *t* in parentheses)

	Raw Differentials			Raw Diffs. with Haypoints		
	Dummies	**Percents**	**Dumm & %**	**Dummies**	**Percents**	**Dumm & %**
FEMALE__	−0.2867		−0.0151	−0.1493		−0.0152
	(92.148)		(3.531)	(64.347)		(4.781)
BLACK____	−0.0284		−0.00686	−0.0264		−0.00413
	(2.194)		(0.561)	(2.913)		(0.454)
INDIAN__	−0.0825		−0.0160	−0.0186		−0.0166
	(4.909)		(1.040)	(1.586)		(1.448)
HISPANIC	−0.0715		−0.0107	−0.0490		−0.0105
	(3.821)		(0.621)	(3.747)		(0.819)
ASIAN____	0.1319		−0.0166	−0.0111		−0.0169
	(6.205)		(0.838)	(0.751)		(1.149)
PCTFEMAL		−0.4814	−0.4663		−0.2707	−0.2555
		(131.740)	(82.759)		(88.226)	(57.774)
PCTBLACK		0.1213	0.1282		−0.0452	−0.0410
		(3.438)	(3.435)		(1.722)	(1.479)
PCTINDIA		−1.1085	−1.0924		−0.1714	−0.1548
		(18.391)	(17.562)		(3.794)	(3.322)
PCTHISPA		−0.7045	−0.6937		−0.5077	−0.4972
		(10.507)	(10.019)		(10.174)	(9.650)
PCTASIAN		1.4527	1.4692		0.1697	0.1865
		(23.367)	(22.520)		(3.599)	(3.777)
AGE______						
AGE____SQ						
SVC_FRST						
SVC_F_SQ						
SVC_MREC						
SVC_M_SQ						
AGESVC_F						
AGESVC_M						
HANDICAP						
VET_VIET						
VETOTHER						
HAY_MISS				0.6142	0.5366	0.5366
				(126.387)	(111.277)	(111.318)
HAYPOINT				0.00249	0.00210	0.00210
				(98.921)	(84.385)	(84.414)
HAYPOISQ				−0.00114	−0.00084	−0.00084
				(36.906)	(28.342)	(28.350)
Intercept	2.2344	2.3233	2.3233	1.6877	1.8108	1.8108
	(1077.741)	(1034.445)	(1034.615)	(390.069)	(387.274)	(387.417)
R^2	0.2221	0.3824	0.3827	0.6198	0.6591	0.6594

Appendix Table A4.1(2) Individual Pay Regressions, October 1981 (dep. var. = LOG_HRLY; *t* in parentheses)

	Standard Regressors			Stand. Regs. with Haypoints		
	Dummies	Percents	Dumm & %	Dummies	Percents	Dumm & %
FEMALE__	−0.2255		−0.0208	−0.1238		−0.0192
	(74.244)		(5.328)	(56.017)		(6.685)
BLACK____	0.00946		0.00132	−0.00005		0.00344
	(0.838)		(0.122)	(0.007)		(0.432)
INDIAN__	−0.0448		−0.00126	0.00356		−0.00199
	(3.068)		(0.092)	(0.348)		(0.198)
HISPANIC	−0.0237		0.00571	−0.0165		0.00510
	(1.458)		(0.375)	(1.449)		(0.455)
ASIAN____	0.1552		−0.0136	0.0307		−0.0101
	(8.389)		(0.774)	(2.374)		(0.784)
PCTFEMAL		−0.3932	−0.3740		−0.2266	−0.2088
		(109.494)	(73.447)		(78.835)	(53.408)
PCTBLACK		0.2784	0.2766		−0.0797	−0.0760
		(8.897)	(8.366)		(3.457)	(3.121)
PCTINDIA		−0.8078	−0.8058		−0.0449	−0.0423
		(15.121)	(14.627)		(1.135)	(1.037)
PCTHISPA		−0.4165	−0.4238		−0.3357	−0.3420
		(7.017)	(6.917)		(7.674)	(7.579)
PCTASIAN		1.6416	1.6524		0.4966	0.5037
		(29.802)	(28.623)		(11.957)	(11.600)
AGE______	0.0323	0.0269	0.0270	0.0165	0.0153	0.0154
	(35.249)	(32.261)	(32.355)	(25.522)	(24.751)	(24.879)
AGE____SQ	−0.3421	−0.2780	−0.2790	−0.1541	−0.1399	−0.1407
	(28.910)	(25.865)	(25.932)	(18.412)	(17.527)	(17.615)
SVC_FRST	0.0241	0.0232	0.0231	0.0241	0.0237	0.0237
	(23.010)	(24.325)	(24.232)	(32.721)	(33.790)	(33.684)
SVC_F_SQ	−0.3340	−0.2944	−0.2959	−0.3899	−0.3627	−0.3639
	(14.539)	(14.125)	(14.198)	(24.217)	(23.605)	(23.696)
SVC_MREC						
SVC_M_SQ						
AGESVC_F	−0.0848	−0.1226	−0.1209	−0.1341	−0.1535	−0.1521
	(3.189)	(5.085)	(5.014)	(7.205)	(8.650)	(8.571)
AGESVC_M						
HANDICAP	−0.0484	−0.0438	−0.0449	−0.0194	−0.0188	−0.0198
	(8.102)	(8.088)	(8.291)	(4.643)	(4.713)	(4.969)
VET_VIET	−0.00927	−0.0165	−0.0209	0.00345	−0.00070	−0.00481
	(1.745)	(3.475)	(4.348)	(0.927)	(0.201)	(1.355)
VETOTHER	−0.0232	−0.0224	−0.0268	−0.0186	−0.0180	−0.0221
	(4.997)	(5.417)	(6.366)	(5.730)	(5.914)	(7.123)
HAY_MISS				0.5568	0.4953	0.4951
				(129.615)	(115.887)	(115.900)
HAYPOINT				0.00204	0.00174	0.00174
				(90.346)	(77.915)	(77.981)
HAYPOISQ				−0.00079	−0.00057	−0.00057
				(29.025)	(21.550)	(21.570)
Intercept	1.3895	1.5841	1.5834	1.2564	1.3840	1.3835
	(84.053)	(104.175)	(104.084)	(107.319)	(121.233)	(121.177)
R^2	0.4138	0.5181	0.5186	0.7132	0.7390	0.7394

Appendix Table A4.2(1) Individual Pay Regressions, April 1986 (dep. var. = LOG_HRLY; *t* in parentheses)

	Raw Differentials			Raw Diffs. with Haypoints		
	Dummies	Percents	Dumm & %	Dummies	Percents	Dumm & %
FEMALE___	−0.2158 (67.797)		−0.0136 (3.051)	−0.0681 (33.406)		−0.0136 (4.752)
BLACK____	−0.0273 (2.142)		−0.00988 (0.783)	−0.0164 (2.128)		−0.00804 (0.997)
INDIAN___	−0.0726 (4.397)		−0.0117 (0.728)	−0.0180 (1.794)		−0.0105 (1.028)
HISPANIC	−0.0587 (3.153)		0.00085 (0.047)	−0.00216 (0.191)		0.00081 (0.070)
ASIAN____	0.0483 (2.388)		−0.00752 (0.379)	−0.0467 (3.795)		−0.00898 (0.708)
PCTFEMAL		−0.3796 (93.720)	−0.3659 (60.565)		−0.1217 (42.468)	−0.1081 (26.687)
PCTBLACK		0.0219 (0.580)	0.0318 (0.797)		−0.0378 (1.561)	−0.0298 (1.168)
PCTINDIA		−1.0592 (17.778)	−1.0474 (16.960)		−0.1878 (4.906)	−0.1772 (4.468)
PCTHISPA		−0.5778 (8.548)	−0.5787 (8.268)		0.0450 (1.039)	0.0442 (0.986)
PCTASIAN		0.7993 (12.342)	0.8069 (11.930)		−0.3781 (9.052)	−0.3691 (8.470)
AGE______						
AGE____SQ						
SVC_FRST						
SVC_F_SQ						
SVC_MREC						
SVC_M_SQ						
AGESVC_F						
AGESVC_M						
HANDICAP						
VET_VIET						
VETOTHER						
HAY_MISS				0.8104 (175.185)	0.7814 (164.422)	0.7814 (164.470)
HAYPOINT				0.00304 (135.920)	0.00291 (127.307)	0.00291 (127.347)
HAYPOISQ				−0.00164 (58.484)	−0.00154 (55.028)	−0.00154 (55.045)
Intercept	2.5001 (1144.089)	2.5832 (1013.566)	2.5832 (1013.651)	1.8466 (480.225)	1.8975 (438.806)	1.8975 (438.946)
R^2	0.1290	0.2313	0.2316	0.6785	0.6863	0.6866

Appendix Table A4.2(2) Individual Pay Regressions, April 1986 (dep. var. = LOG_HRLY; *t* in parentheses)

	Standard Regressors			Stand. Regs. with Haypoints		
	Dummies	Percents	Dumm & %	Dummies	Percents	Dumm & %
FEMALE__	−0.1636		−0.0178	−0.0438		−0.0104
	(51.292)		(4.316)	(22.310)		(4.063)
BLACK____	0.0165		0.00277	0.0122		0.00262
	(1.478)		(0.248)	(1.838)		(0.376)
INDIAN__	−0.0464		0.00021	−0.00304		0.00097
	(3.204)		(0.015)	(0.352)		(0.109)
HISPANIC	−0.0268		0.0102	0.0148		0.0100
	(1.644)		(0.637)	(1.522)		(1.002)
ASIAN____	0.0824		−0.0165	−0.00608		−0.00619
	(4.631)		(0.938)	(0.573)		(0.564)
PCTFEMAL		−0.2974	−0.2814		−0.0812	−0.0719
		(73.989)	(51.419)		(30.193)	(20.309)
PCTBLACK		0.2456	0.2424		0.1189	0.1162
		(7.275)	(6.820)		(5.652)	(5.245)
PCTINDIA		−0.8593	−0.8584		−0.1261	−0.1264
		(16.216)	(15.636)		(3.803)	(3.683)
PCTHISPA		−0.4077	−0.4174		0.0961	−0.0863
		(6.791)	(6.717)		(2.563)	(2.224)
PCTASIAN		1.1799	1.1929		0.0162	0.0206
		(20.435)	(19.807)		(0.447)	(0.543)
AGE______	0.0390	0.0353	0.0354	0.0164	0.0143	0.0143
	(37.442)	(35.605)	(35.665)	(23.272)	(22.826)	(22.878)
AGE____SQ	−0.4142	−0.3675	−0.3682	−0.1299	−0.1246	−0.1249
	(30.881)	(28.768)	(28.805)	(16.044)	(15.487)	(15.516)
SVC_FRST	0.0127	0.0147	0.0148	0.0106	0.0111	0.0112
	(3.147)	(3.845)	(3.868)	(4.420)	(4.673)	(4.696)
SVC_F_SQ	−0.0265	0.00009	−0.00313	0.2562	0.2606	0.2586
	(0.243)	(0.001)	(0.030)	(3.931)	(4.025)	(3.995)
SVC_MREC	0.00661	0.00517	0.00501	0.0120	0.0116	0.0115
	(1.663)	(1.368)	(1.327)	(5.100)	(4.960)	(4.922)
SVC_M_SQ	−0.3535	−0.3654	−0.3636	−0.6463	−0.6446	−0.6433
	(3.254)	(3.540)	(3.522)	(9.976)	(10.017)	(9.999)
AGESVC_F	−0.0983	−0.1574	−0.1581	−0.2614	−0.2754	−0.2758
	(0.985)	(1.658)	(1.666)	(4.394)	(4.660)	(4.668)
AGESVC_M	0.1460	0.1576	0.1601	0.1595	0.1631	0.1644
	(1.505)	(1.709)	(1.736)	(2.758)	(2.839)	(2.862)
HANDICAP	−0.0492	−0.0439	−0.0450	−0.00248	−0.00226	−0.00291
	(8.397)	(7.881)	(8.078)	(0.710)	(0.650)	(0.838)
VET_VIET	−0.0268	−0.0261	−0.0308	−0.00054	−0.00001	−0.00276
	(5.076)	(5.329)	(6.145)	(0.173)	(0.005)	(0.883)
VETOTHER	−0.0360	−0.0407	−0.0450	−0.00489	−0.00619	−0.00869
	(7.127)	(8.651)	(9.363)	(1.624)	(2.108)	(2.898)
HAY_MISS				0.7573	0.7374	0.7371
				(186.893)	(176.665)	(176.614)
HAYPOINT				0.00265	0.00257	0.00257
				(134.177)	(127.143)	(127.165)
HAYPOISQ				−0.00135	−0.00129	−0.00129
				(55.189)	(52.702)	(52.720)
Intercept	1.4825	1.6241	1.6239	1.4183	1.4571	1.4572
	(75.996)	(86.465)	(86.420)	(121.294)	(123.471)	(123.425)
R^2	0.3303	0.3950	0.3954	0.7624	0.7656	0.7657

Appendix Table A4.3(1) Class-Level Pay Regressions, October 1981 (unweighted; dep. var. = log of class max./mean/min. pay; *t* in parentheses)

	Raw Differentials			Raw Diffs. with Haypoints		
	Max. Pay	Mean Pay	Min. Pay	Max. Pay	Mean Pay	Min. Pay
PCTFEMAL	−0.3381	−0.3718	−0.4002	−0.1765	−0.2028	−0.2218
	(16.133)	(17.223)	(17.299)	(10.890)	(12.464)	(12.754)
PCTBLACK	0.0464	0.0558	0.0785	−0.0118	−0.00892	0.00584
	(0.735)	(0.858)	(1.127)	(0.253)	(0.190)	(0.116)
PCTINDIA	−0.0528	−0.0778	−0.0926	−0.0195	−0.0471	−0.0652
	(0.434)	(0.621)	(0.690)	(0.217)	(0.522)	(0.675)
PCTHISPA	−0.0940	−0.0958	−0.0890	−0.1212	−0.1268	−0.1248
	(0.770)	(0.761)	(0.661)	(1.341)	(1.398)	(1.287)
PCTASIAN	0.0566	−0.0452	−0.1470	0.0185	−0.0763	−0.1696
	(0.327)	(0.254)	(0.770)	(0.145)	(0.594)	(1.235)
AGE______						
AGE____SQ						
SVC_FRST						
SVC_F_SQ						
SVC_MREC						
SVC_M_SQ						
AGESVC_F						
AGESVC_M						
HANDICAP						
VET_VIET						
VETOTHER						
HAY_MISS				0.7607	0.7972	0.8440
				(28.933)	(30.209)	(29.916)
HAYPOINT				0.00203	0.00203	0.00203
				(19.487)	(19.405)	(18.194)
HAYPOISQ				−0.00083	−0.00078	−0.00073
				(9.657)	(9.086)	(7.931)
Intercept	2.5492	2.5114	2.4648	1.8485	1.7888	1.7137
	(268.126)	(256.465)	(234.867)	(70.985)	(68.430)	(61.323)
R^2	0.1354	0.1518	0.1536	0.5275	0.5597	0.5628

Appendix Table A4.3(2) Class-Level Pay Regressions, October 1981 (unweighted; dep. var. = log of class max./mean/min. pay; *t* in parentheses)

	Standard Regressors			Stand. Regs. with Haypoints		
	Max. Pay	Mean Pay	Min. Pay	Max. Pay	Mean Pay	Min. Pay
PCTFEMAL	−0.2673	−0.2850	−0.3062	−0.1648	−0.1788	−0.1926
	(12.500)	(13.215)	(13.144)	(9.654)	(10.675)	(10.690)
PCTBLACK	−0.00587	0.00317	0.0241	−0.0407	−0.0353	0.0193
	(0.103)	(0.055)	(0.390)	(0.919)	(0.813)	(0.414)
PCTINDIA	−0.0491	−0.0724	−0.0864	−0.0166	−0.0442	−0.0615
	(0.450)	(0.658)	(0.727)	(0.196)	(0.529)	(0.685)
PCTHISPA	−0.0596	−0.0501	−0.0384	−0.0998	−0.0935	−0.0866
	(0.545)	(0.454)	(0.323)	(1.170)	(1.118)	(0.962)
PCTASIAN	0.0883	−0.00059	−0.1018	0.0561	−0.0200	−0.1090
	(0.567)	(0.004)	(0.600)	(0.462)	(0.168)	(0.850)
AGE______	0.1170	0.1264	0.1322	0.0619	0.0692	0.0709
	(14.454)	(15.481)	(14.990)	(9.469)	(10.781)	(10.269)
AGE____SQ	−1.2039	−1.2959	−1.3549	−0.6058	−0.6753	−0.6908
	(12.029)	(12.837)	(12.427)	(7.551)	(8.579)	(8.160)
SVC_FRST	−0.00226	0.00026	−0.00141	0.00979	0.0134	0.0134
	(0.297)	(0.035)	(0.170)	(1.639)	(2.299)	(2.125)
SVC_F_SQ	0.2939	0.2519	0.2747	0.2036	0.1500	0.1574
	(1.949)	(1.656)	(1.672)	(1.731)	(1.299)	(1.268)
SVC_MREC						
SVC_M_SQ						
AGESVC_F	−0.1133	−0.1224	−0.1046	−0.3238	−0.3432	−0.3432
	(0.584)	(0.626)	(0.495)	(2.139)	(2.311)	(2.148)
AGESVC_M						
HANDICAP	−0.1160	−0.1136	−0.1112	−0.0865	−0.0843	−0.0811
	(2.918)	(2.835)	(2.570)	(2.790)	(2.772)	(2.479)
VET_VIET	−0.1439	−0.1425	−0.1478	−0.0997	−0.0936	−0.0925
	(4.087)	(4.012)	(3.854)	(3.625)	(3.466)	(3.184)
VETOTHER	−0.0739	−0.0761	−0.0708	−0.0396	−0.0406	−0.0329
	(2.944)	(3.008)	(2.592)	(2.022)	(2.114)	(1.592)
HAY_MISS				0.6577	0.6781	0.7216
				(25.486)	(26.785)	(26.497)
HAYPOINT				0.00170	0.00164	0.00164
				(16.896)	(16.613)	(15.389)
HAYPOISQ				−0.00066	−0.00058	−0.00053
				(8.078)	(7.300)	(6.138)
Intercept	−0.0593	−0.3378	−0.5146	0.5191	0.2785	0.1606
	(0.378)	(2.136)	(3.012)	(4.191)	(2.292)	(1.229)
R^2	0.3137	0.3544	0.3457	0.5835	0.6293	0.6274

Appendix Table A4.4(1) Class-Level Pay Regressions, April 1986 (unweighted; dep. var. = log of class max./mean/min. pay; *t* in parentheses)

	Raw Differentials			Raw Diffs. with Haypoints		
	Max. Pay	**Mean Pay**	**Min. Pay**	**Max. Pay**	**Mean Pay**	**Min. Pay**
PCTFEMAL	−0.2328	−0.2618	−0.2918	−0.0589	−0.0780	−0.0955
	(12.258)	(13.270)	(13.696)	(4.332)	(5.662)	(6.397)
PCTBLACK	0.1041	0.1035	0.1127	0.0592	0.0550	0.0584
	(1.621)	(1.551)	(1.564)	(1.342)	(1.229)	(1.206)
PCTINDIA	−0.1852	−0.1872	−0.1796	−0.1263	−0.1261	−0.1173
	(1.859)	(1.809)	(1.607)	(1.847)	(1.819)	(1.563)
PCTHISPA	−0.0642	−0.0435	−0.0222	−0.1586	−0.1442	−0.1322
	(0.611)	(0.399)	(0.189)	(2.196)	(1.969)	(1.668)
PCTASIAN	0.1054	0.0859	0.0893	0.0148	−0.00730	−0.00631
	(0.882)	(0.691)	(0.666)	(0.181)	(0.088)	(0.070)
AGE______						
AGE____SQ						
SVC_FRST						
SVC_F_SQ						
SVC_MREC						
SVC_M_SQ						
AGESVC_F						
AGESVC_M						
HANDICAP						
VET_VIET						
VETOTHER						
HAY_MISS				0.8675	0.9110	0.9682
				(37.942)	(39.300)	(38.565)
HAYPOINT				0.00241	0.00247	0.00252
				(26.893)	(27.214)	(25.555)
HAYPOISQ				−0.00117	−0.00117	−0.00113
				(15.405)	(15.143)	(13.553)
Intercept	2.8214	2.7892	2.7439	2.0260	1.9598	1.8758
	(301.324)	(286.798)	(261.248)	(90.153)	(86.023)	(76.016)
R^2	0.0791	0.0905	0.0952	0.5670	0.5925	0.5923

Appendix Table A4.4(2) Class-Level Pay Regressions, April 1986 (unweighted; dep. var. = log of class max./mean/min. pay; *t* in parentheses)

	Standard Regressors			Stand. Regs. with Haypoints		
	Max. Pay	Mean Pay	Min. Pay	Max. Pay	Mean Pay	Min. Pay
PCTFEMAL	−0.1558	−0.1704	−0.1941	−0.0407	−0.0509	−0.0664
	(8.139)	(8.792)	(9.234)	(2.820)	(3.585)	(4.301)
PCTBLACK	0.0183	0.0133	0.0153	0.0236	0.0179	0.0189
	(0.322)	(0.231)	(0.245)	(0.560)	(0.433)	(0.420)
PCTINDIA	−0.1645	−0.1580	−0.1476	−0.1155	−0.1085	−0.0970
	(1.875)	(1.779)	(1.532)	(1.783)	(1.702)	(1.400)
PCTHISPA	−0.00826	0.0261	0.0514	−0.1117	−0.0824	−0.0665
	(0.089)	(0.279)	(0.505)	(1.632)	(1.223)	(0.909)
PCTASIAN	0.1085	0.0991	0.1014	0.0327	0.0237	0.0260
	(1.032)	(0.930)	(0.878)	(0.421)	(0.310)	(0.314)
AGE______	0.1349	0.1459	0.1548	0.0620	0.0704	0.0741
	(16.607)	(17.745)	(17.352)	(9.859)	(11.364)	(11.015)
AGE____SQ	−1.3167	−1.4153	−1.4959	−0.5707	−0.6430	−0.6728
	(13.525)	(14.360)	(13.988)	(7.654)	(8.764)	(8.440)
SVC_FRST	0.0913	0.0972	0.1061	0.0554	0.0610	0.0689
	(2.212)	(2.327)	(2.340)	(1.817)	(2.033)	(2.113)
SVC_F_SQ	0.9986	0.9796	0.9958	0.7117	0.7195	0.7779
	(1.353)	(1.311)	(1.228)	(1.305)	(1.341)	(1.334)
SVC_MREC	−0.0961	−0.0974	−0.1069	−0.0452	−0.0456	−0.0529
	(2.344)	(2.348)	(2.373)	(1.492)	(1.530)	(1.631)
SVC_M_SQ	−0.7661	−0.7645	−0.7303	−0.6088	−0.6531	−0.6932
	(1.035)	(1.020)	(0.898)	(1.112)	(1.212)	(1.184)
AGESVC_F	−2.1193	−2.2097	−2.3937	−1.4062	−1.5063	−1.6970
	(2.091)	(2.153)	(2.150)	(1.877)	(2.043)	(2.118)
AGESVC_M	2.0352	2.0625	2.2211	1.1169	1.1552	1.3199
	(2.021)	(2.023)	(2.008)	(1.499)	(1.576)	(1.657)
HANDICAP	−0.1001	−0.1011	−0.1071	−0.0398	−0.0396	−0.0430
	(2.746)	(2.740)	(2.676)	(1.477)	(1.493)	(1.490)
VET_VIET	−0.0551	−0.0594	−0.0638	−0.0387	−0.0430	−0.0473
	(1.877)	(1.999)	(1.980)	(1.787)	(2.019)	(2.044)
VETOTHER	−0.0658	−0.0656	−0.0695	−0.0118	−0.00973	−0.0101
	(2.486)	(2.446)	(2.391)	(0.603)	(0.504)	(0.484)
HAY_MISS				0.7530	0.7772	0.8257
				(32.804)	(34.410)	(33.648)
HAYPOINT				0.00205	0.00204	0.00206
				(23.188)	(23.513)	(21.801)
HAYPOISQ				−0.00097	−0.00093	−0.00088
				(13.198)	(12.880)	(11.218)
Intercept	−0.3698	−0.7037	−0.9665	0.5896	0.3024	0.1258
	(2.243)	(4.215)	(5.335)	(4.746)	(2.474)	(0.947)
R^2	0.3010	0.3441	0.3414	0.6198	0.6629	0.6606

Appendix Table A4.5(1) Class-Level Pay Regressions, October 1981 (weighted; dep. var. = log of class max./mean/min. pay; *t* in parentheses)

	Raw Differentials			Raw Diffs. with Haypoints		
	Max. Pay	Mean Pay	Min. Pay	Max. Pay	Mean Pay	Min. Pay
PCTFEMAL	−0.3732	−0.4822	−0.4951	−0.1618	−0.2718	−0.3135
	(94.546)	(137.555)	(149.957)	(47.058)	(95.666)	(111.507)
PCTBLACK	0.2624	0.1193	0.2388	0.0703	−0.0471	0.0909
	(6.875)	(3.522)	(7.484)	(2.385)	(1.936)	(3.774)
PCTINDIA	−0.9720	−1.1138	−0.8922	−0.0251	−0.1741	−0.0718
	(14.918)	(19.254)	(16.375)	(0.497)	(4.159)	(1.733)
PCTHISPA	−0.3938	−0.7098	−0.5704	−0.2390	−0.5118	−0.4059
	(5.434)	(11.030)	(9.411)	(4.270)	(11.069)	(8.870)
PCTASIAN	1.7567	1.4502	1.1109	0.5413	0.1706	−0.0371
	(26.140)	(24.303)	(19.766)	(10.235)	(3.905)	(0.860)
AGE______						
AGE____SQ						
SVC_FRST						
SVC_F_SQ						
SVC_MREC						
SVC_M_SQ						
AGESVC_F						
AGESVC_M						
HANDICAP						
VET_VIET						
VETOTHER						
HAY_MISS				0.5709	0.5368	0.4360
				(105.773)	(120.393)	(98.821)
HAYPOINT				0.00196	0.00210	0.00167
				(70.034)	(90.982)	(72.937)
HAYPOISQ				−0.00066	−0.00084	−0.00045
				(19.831)	(30.524)	(16.522)
Intercept	2.3951	2.3240	2.2122	1.8941	1.8117	1.7866
	(986.892)	(1078.491)	(1089.954)	(361.235)	(418.329)	(416.857)
R^2	0.2485	0.4025	0.4382	0.5533	0.6927	0.6810

Appendix Table A4.5(2) Class-Level Pay Regressions, October 1981 (weighted; dep. var. = log of class max./mean/min. pay; *t* in parentheses)

	Standard Regressors			Stand. Regs. with Haypoints		
	Max. Pay	Mean Pay	Min. Pay	Max. Pay	Mean Pay	Min. Pay
PCTFEMAL	−0.3003	−0.3646	−0.3734	−0.1562	−0.2349	−0.2674
	(59.865)	(91.359)	(93.994)	(36.437)	(76.060)	(80.129)
PCTBLACK	0.1678	0.1577	0.2701	0.0184	0.0222	0.1472
	(5.179)	(6.118)	(10.526)	(0.701)	(1.174)	(7.177)
PCTINDIA	−0.7673	−0.7448	−0.6007	−0.1130	−0.1301	−0.0784
	(13.896)	(16.956)	(13.742)	(2.501)	(3.997)	(2.229)
PCTHISPA	−0.3465	−0.4693	−0.3496	−0.2930	−0.4108	−0.3145
	(5.664)	(9.645)	(7.220)	(5.893)	(11.470)	(8.126)
PCTASIAN	1.4002	1.2982	0.9892	0.5679	0.4583	0.2332
	(24.482)	(28.535)	(21.847)	(11.911)	(13.346)	(6.284)
AGE______	0.1873	0.1672	0.1552	0.1083	0.0920	0.0916
	(76.376)	(85.758)	(79.946)	(50.757)	(59.877)	(55.190)
AGE____SQ	−2.0254	−1.8119	−1.7420	−1.0558	−0.8871	−0.9643
	(63.455)	(71.369)	(68.938)	(38.187)	(44.544)	(44.809)
SVC_FRST	−0.0506	−0.0260	−0.0478	0.00179	0.0221	−0.00593
	(17.820)	(11.503)	(21.265)	(0.766)	(13.085)	(3.250)
SVC_F_SQ	1.2876	0.6911	0.4782	0.7852	0.2322	0.0472
	(22.782)	(15.373)	(10.687)	(17.009)	(6.984)	(1.315)
SVC_MREC						
SVC_M_SQ						
AGESVC_F	0.1396	0.1453	0.7334	−0.6937	−0.6296	0.0745
	(1.844)	(2.412)	(12.235)	(11.208)	(14.123)	(1.547)
AGESVC_M						
HANDICAP	−0.4073	−0.3672	−0.3574	−0.2226	−0.1988	−0.2219
	(23.980)	(27.178)	(26.583)	(16.003)	(19.847)	(20.496)
VET_VIET	−0.3298	−0.2577	−0.1662	−0.1304	−0.0821	−0.0187
	(20.181)	(19.826)	(12.848)	(9.732)	(8.508)	(1.799)
VETOTHER	−0.1539	−0.1619	−0.1142	−0.1029	−0.1257	−0.0892
	(13.902)	(18.396)	(13.033)	(11.338)	(19.225)	(12.626)
HAY_MISS				0.4670	0.4244	0.3313
				(90.891)	(114.673)	(82.848)
HAYPOINT				0.00137	0.00135	0.00098
				(50.311)	(69.089)	(46.490)
HAYPOISQ				−0.00024	−0.00028	−0.00005
				(7.757)	(12.709)	(2.089)
Intercept	−1.2925	−1.1050	−0.8892	−0.2904	−0.1432	−0.0539
	(30.506)	(32.789)	(26.512)	(8.139)	(5.574)	(1.941)
R^2	0.4710	0.6625	0.6456	0.6512	0.8175	0.7741

Appendix Table A4.6(1) Class-Level Pay Regressions, April 1986 (weighted; dep. var. = log of class max./mean/min. pay; *t* in parentheses)

	Raw Differentials			Raw Diffs. with Haypoints		
	Max. Pay	Mean Pay	Min. Pay	Max. Pay	Mean Pay	Min. Pay
PCTFEMAL	−0.2803	−0.3827	−0.4317	−0.0193	−0.1273	−0.2115
	(66.054)	(98.245)	(108.053)	(6.563)	(48.895)	(65.181)
PCTBLACK	−0.1097	0.00431	0.1025	−0.2373	−0.0614	0.0534
	(2.766)	(0.118)	(2.745)	(9.519)	(2.788)	(1.946)
PCTINDIA	−1.1938	−1.0788	−0.7522	−0.2837	−0.1948	0.0125
	(19.100)	(18.804)	(12.786)	(7.198)	(5.588)	(0.289)
PCTHISPA	−0.8004	−0.5876	−0.3611	−0.1445	0.0516	0.1642
	(11.283)	(9.025)	(5.409)	(3.237)	(1.308)	(3.338)
PCTASIAN	1.2809	0.7808	0.6323	0.1674	−0.3763	−0.4025
	(18.857)	(12.523)	(9.890)	(3.893)	(9.893)	(8.492)
AGE______						
AGE____SQ						
SVC_FRST						
SVC_F_SQ						
SVC_MREC						
SVC_M_SQ						
AGESVC_F						
AGESVC_M						
HANDICAP						
VET_VIET						
VETOTHER						
HAY_MISS				0.9063	0.7795	0.6191
				(187.161)	(181.994)	(116.010)
HAYPOINT				0.00280	0.00289	0.00232
				(118.892)	(139.038)	(89.505)
HAYPOISQ				−0.00149	−0.00153	−0.00097
				(51.531)	(59.952)	(30.632)
Intercept	2.6677	2.5865	2.4816	1.9841	1.9031	1.9130
	(999.391)	(1055.703)	(987.756)	(445.900)	(483.535)	(390.092)
R^2	0.1446	0.2476	0.2770	0.6637	0.7253	0.6103

Appendix Table A4.6(2) Class-Level Pay Regressions, April 1986 (weighted; dep. var. = log of class max./mean/min. pay; *t* in parentheses)

	Standard Regressors			Stand. Regs. with Haypoints		
	Max. Pay	Mean Pay	Min. Pay	Max. Pay	Mean Pay	Min. Pay
PCTFEMAL	−0.2979	−0.3263	−0.3829	−0.0382	−0.1114	−0.2112
	(51.323)	(69.483)	(74.966)	(9.115)	(35.487)	(48.950)
PCTBLACK	−0.0105	0.2386	0.3024	−0.1568	0.1271	0.2120
	(0.309)	(8.638)	(10.067)	(6.724)	(7.283)	(8.837)
PCTINDIA	−0.9412	−0.7531	−0.4799	−0.2855	−0.1601	0.0102
	(17.565)	(17.370)	(10.178)	(7.761)	(5.816)	(0.271)
PCTHISPA	−0.5426	−0.2640	−0.0938	−0.1527	0.0863	0.1737
	(8.989)	(5.406)	(1.766)	(3.696)	(2.791)	(4.086)
PCTASIAN	1.2536	1.0522	0.8451	0.3504	0.1156	0.00483
	(21.440)	(22.241)	(16.426)	(8.635)	(3.806)	(0.116)
AGE______	0.2075	0.2013	0.1791	0.0639	0.0685	0.0688
	(73.371)	(87.976)	(71.967)	(29.988)	(42.978)	(31.400)
AGE____SQ	−2.3148	−2.2102	−1.9159	−0.5554	−0.5767	−0.5598
	(61.207)	(72.231)	(57.569)	(19.718)	(27.355)	(19.321)
SVC_FRST	0.0851	0.0601	0.1267	0.1073	0.0586	−0.1199
	(4.239)	(3.705)	(7.174)	(7.816)	(5.704)	(8.494)
SVC_F_SQ	3.4941	2.5615	1.2831	6.6662	4.4602	2.4483
	(9.789)	(8.869)	(4.085)	(27.157)	(24.277)	(9.697)
SVC_MREC	−0.1768	−0.1218	−0.1855	−0.1043	−0.0361	−0.1083
	(8.902)	(7.580)	(10.614)	(7.672)	(3.548)	(7.750)
SVC_M_SQ	−3.2388	−2.6658	−1.4444	−6.3606	−4.4610	−2.5382
	(9.269)	(9.430)	(4.698)	(26.439)	(24.775)	(10.257)
AGESVC_F	−3.8686	−2.3929	−2.9781	−6.0027	−3.4598	−3.6071
	(7.964)	(6.089)	(6.967)	(18.036)	(13.889)	(10.537)
AGESVC_M	5.5059	3.7622	4.2678	5.6122	2.9723	3.3450
	(11.574)	(9.774)	(10.195)	(17.201)	(12.172)	(9.968)
HANDICAP	−0.4799	−0.3742	−0.3385	−0.0893	−0.0500	−0.0852
	(27.573)	(26.574)	(22.100)	(7.397)	(5.530)	(6.862)
VET_VIET	−0.4237	−0.3325	−0.2480	−0.1054	−0.0642	−0.0263
	(25.892)	(25.116)	(17.222)	(9.331)	(7.598)	(2.271)
VETOTHER	−0.4722	−0.4259	−0.4293	−0.1194	−0.1530	−0.2149
	(33.670)	(37.530)	(34.785)	(12.199)	(20.887)	(21.342)
HAY_MISS				0.8247	0.6700	0.5034
				(165.494)	(179.628)	(98.204)
HAYPOINT				0.00235	0.00223	0.00170
				(96.915)	(122.960)	(68.331)
HAYPOISQ				−0.00117	−0.00107	−0.00057
				(41.590)	(50.891)	(19.663)
Intercept	−1.3917	−1.5883	−1.3072	0.5927	0.2713	0.2646
	(27.944)	(39.416)	(29.828)	(16.371)	(10.013)	(7.105)
R^2	0.3854	0.5799	0.5459	0.7135	0.8324	0.7108

Appendix Table A4.7 "Comparable Worth" Pay Regressions, October 1981 and April 1986 (unweighted; dep. var. = log of class max. pay; *t* in parentheses)

	October 1981		April 1986	
Variable	Sample: A	Sample: B	Sample: A	Sample: B
PCTFEMAL	−0.1574 (12.380)	−0.1350 (7.801)	−0.0631 (5.264)	−0.0282 (1.605)
HAYPOINT	0.0010 (55.673)	0.0016 (39.634)	0.0011 (56.391)	0.0018 (40.956)
Intercept	2.0315 (203.899)	1.8861 (121.724)	2.2903 (224.511)	2.0765 (126.247)
R^2	0.8011	0.8464	0.7619	0.8261

Notes:

"Sample A" consists of all classes with a Hay evaluation point score.

"Sample B" consists of all classes with a Hay evaluation point score that also have at least ten incumbents.

Appendix Table A4.8(1) "Time Trend" Pooled OLS Wage Regressions for Random Sample of 1,000 White Women Present Continuously During October 1981–April 1986 (dep. var. = LOG_HRLY; *t* in parentheses)

	Raw Differentials		Raw Diffs. w/Haypoint	
Variable	Basic	Percent	Basic	Percent
PCTFEMAL		−0.3265		0.0052
		(52.142)		(1.324)
PCTBLACK		0.0948		0.0088
		(1.782)		(0.290)
PCTINDIA		−2.0986		0.0177
		(16.474)		(0.242)
PCTHISPA		−2.9787		0.3807
		(20.604)		(4.505)
PCTASIAN		1.7601		0.2989
		(19.021)		(5.595)
AGE_____				
AGE___SQ				
SVC_FRST				
SVC_F_SQ				
SVC_MREC				
SVC_M_SQ				
AGESVC_F				
AGESVC_M				
HANDICAP				
VET_VIET				
VETOTHER				

Appendix Table A4.8(1) (*continued*)

Variable	Raw Differentials		Raw Diffs. w/ Haypoint	
	Basic	Percent	Basic	Percent
HAY_MISS			0.7652	0.7711
			(179.680)	(161.257)
HAYPOINT			0.0030	0.0030
			(154.261)	(138.228)
HAYPOISQ			−0.0014	−0.0015
			(59.557)	(58.186)
AFTER783	0.0322	0.0338	0.0291	0.0289
	(2.216)	(2.600)	(3.925)	(3.898)
AFTER784	0.0471	0.0482	0.0482	0.0479
	(5.344)	(6.120)	(10.732)	(10.674)
AFTER785	0.0374	0.0374	0.0364	0.0360
	(3.476)	(3.895)	(6.635)	(6.570)
TIMETRND	0.4760	0.4872	0.4836	0.4838
	(2.551)	(2.922)	(5.080)	(5.090)
TIMTRSQ	−0.8860	−0.8986	−0.9040	−0.9046
	(2.647)	(3.004)	(5.293)	(5.304)
CPINDEX1	0.3217	0.2733	0.3428	0.3547
	(0.814)	(0.774)	(1.699)	(1.761)
CPINDEX2	−0.0307	−0.0891	−0.0356	−0.0315
	(0.077)	(0.251)	(0.176)	(0.156)
CPINDEX3	−0.1675	−0.1765	−0.1274	−0.1365
	(0.349)	(0.412)	(0.521)	(0.558)
CPINDEX4	0.1769	0.1441	0.0426	0.0422
	(0.589)	(0.537)	(0.278)	(0.276)
Intercept	−5.5636	−4.7973	−5.8013	−5.8457
	(3.379)	(3.261)	(6.905)	(6.969)
R^2	0.2377	0.3917	0.8012	0.8023
Sum of AFTER78*i*:	0.1167	0.1194	0.1137	0.1128

Appendix Table A4.8(1) (*continued*)

Variable	Standard Regressors		Standard Regressors with Haypoint	
	Basic	Percent	Basic	Percent
PCTFEMAL		−0.3176		−0.0066
		(54.087)		(1.801)
PCTBLACK		0.2083		0.0722
		(4.183)		(2.549)
PCTINDIA		−1.8760		0.0670
		(15.738)		(0.981)
PCTHISPA		−2.7861		0.2865
		(20.627)		(3.650)
PCTASIAN		1.7097		0.3211
		(19.781)		(6.466)
AGE_____	0.0338	0.0294	0.0055	0.0057
	(28.919)	(28.235)	(9.151)	(9.435)
AGE___SQ	−0.4355	−0.3663	−0.0542	−0.0561
	(28.605)	(26.980)	(6.890)	(7.140)
SVC_FRST	−0.0074	0.0206	0.0209	0.0204
	(0.945)	(2.921)	(5.230)	(5.097)
SVC_F_SQ	−1.0632	−0.7647	−0.4359	−0.4361
	(6.493)	(5.249)	(5.261)	(5.270)
SVC_MREC	0.0163	−0.0078	−0.0044	−0.0036
	(2.077)	(1.121)	(1.103)	(0.921)
SVC_M_SQ	0.4925	0.2436	0.1579	0.1597
	(3.021)	(1.680)	(1.915)	(1.939)
AGESVC_F	0.0007	0.0000	−0.0001	−0.0001
	(4.861)	(0.343)	(1.531)	(1.391)
AGESVC_M	−0.0004	0.0001	0.0000	0.0000
	(2.680)	(1.260)	(0.869)	(0.680)
HANDICAP	−0.0216	−0.0334	0.0046	0.0041
	(2.448)	(4.242)	(1.029)	(0.917)
VET_VIET	−0.0943	−0.0462	−0.0066	−0.0041
	(1.917)	(1.057)	(0.269)	(0.165)
VETOTHER	0.0624	0.0530	−0.0058	−0.0028
	(3.542)	(3.382)	(0.652)	(0.324)
HAY_MISS			0.7428	0.7417
			(183.819)	(163.410)

Appendix Table A4.8(1) ***(continued)***

Variable	Standard Regressors		Standard Regressors with Haypoint	
	Basic	Percent	Basic	Percent
HAYPOINT			0.0029	0.0029
			(155.667)	(137.964)
HAYPOISQ			−0.0014	−0.0014
			(59.532)	(57.241)
AFTER783	0.0323	0.0337	0.0292	0.0291
	(2.370)	(2.783)	(4.246)	(4.233)
AFTER784	0.0469	0.0478	0.0482	0.0479
	(5.686)	(6.519)	(11.558)	(11.501)
AFTER785	0.0373	0.0374	0.0364	0.0361
	(3.703)	(4.181)	(7.158)	(7.103)
TIMETRND	0.4272	0.4375	0.4580	0.4571
	(2.445)	(2.817)	(5.187)	(5.187)
TIMTRSQ	−0.8167	−0.8267	−0.8709	−0.8694
	(2.605)	(2.967)	(5.497)	(5.499)
CPINDEX1	0.3285	0.2826	0.3443	0.3551
	(0.887)	(0.859)	(1.840)	(1.902)
CPINDEX2	−0.0268	−0.0782	−0.0367	−0.0301
	(0.072)	(0.237)	(0.195)	(0.161)
CPINDEX3	−0.1651	−0.1773	−0.1272	−0.1348
	(0.368)	(0.444)	(0.560)	(0.595)
CPINDEX4	0.1821	0.1486	0.0421	0.0433
	(0.647)	(0.594)	(0.296)	(0.306)
Intercept	−5.6317	−4.8305	−5.5831	−5.6209
	(3.652)	(3.524)	(7.164)	(7.226)
R^2	0.3320	0.4724	0.8294	0.8302
Sum of AFTER78*i*:	0.1165	0.1189	0.1138	0.1131

Appendix Table A4.8(2) "Private-Sector Wages" Pooled OLS Wage Regressions for Random Sample of 1,000 White Women Present Continuously During October 1981–April 1986 (dep. var.=LOG_HRLY; *t* in parentheses)

	Raw Differentials		Raw Diffs. w/Haypoint	
Variable	Basic	Percent	Basic	Percent
PCTFEMAL		−0.3266		0.0052
		(52.138)		(1.320)
PCTBLACK		0.0948		0.0088
		(1.782)		(0.289)
PCTINDIA		−2.0963		0.0200
		(16.453)		(0.272)
PCTHISPA		−2.9784		0.3810
		(20.598)		(4.507)
PCTASIAN		1.7594		0.2983
		(19.009)		(5.580)
AGE_____				
AGE___SQ				
SVC_FRST				
SVC_F_SQ				
SVC_MREC				
SVC_M_SQ				
AGESVC_F				
AGESVC_M				
HANDICAP				
VET_VIET				
VETOTHER				

Appendix Table A4.8(2) (*continued*)

	Raw Differentials		Raw Diffs. w/ Haypoint	
Variable	**Basic**	**Percent**	**Basic**	**Percent**
HAY_MISS		0.7653		0.7712
		(179.584)		(161.174)
HAYPOINT		0.0030		0.0030
		(154.206)		(138.180)
HAYPOISQ		−0.0014		−0.0015
		(59.561)		(58.190)
		−0.5476		
		(2.397)		
AFTER783	0.0528	0.0560	0.0492	0.0489
	(6.219)	(7.378)	(11.356)	(11.308)
AFTER784	0.0341	0.0364	0.0339	0.0336
	(3.655)	(4.359)	(7.118)	(7.062)
AFTER785	0.0181	0.0193	0.0160	0.0156
	(2.693)	(3.212)	(4.673)	(4.551)
LNWGMSAP	−0.4400	−0.4298	−0.5476	−0.5505
	(0.983)	(1.075)	(2.397)	(2.413)
LNWGMINP	0.2989	0.3072	0.3945	0.3990
	(0.691)	(0.795)	(1.788)	(1.811)
CPINDEX1	0.5431	0.5298	0.5587	0.5710
	(1.546)	(1.688)	(3.116)	(3.189)
CPINDEX2	0.4587	0.4028	0.4573	0.4590
	(1.175)	(1.155)	(2.294)	(2.306)
CPINDEX3	0.2409	0.2661	0.2603	0.2484
	(0.595)	(0.735)	(1.259)	(1.203)
CPINDEX4	0.5352	0.5105	0.4372	0.4398
	(1.678)	(1.792)	(2.686)	(2.706)
Intercept	−4.9988	−4.5405	−5.1225	−5.1658
	(6.823)	(6.935)	(13.696)	(13.831)
R^2	0.2375	0.3915	0.8014	0.8021
Sum of AFTER78i:	0.1050	0.1110	0.0991	0.0981

Appendix Table A4.8(2) (*continued*)

Variable	Standard Regressors		Standard Regressors with Haypoint	
	Basic	Percent	Basic	Percent
PCTFEMAL		−0.3176		−0.0066
		(54.083)		(1.804)
PCTBLACK		0.2083		0.0723
		(4.183)		(2.550)
PCTINDIA		−1.8742		0.0689
		(15.720)		(1.009)
PCTHISPA		−2.7860		0.2865
		(20.623)		(3.648)
PCTASIAN		1.7091		0.3206
		(19.771)		(6.452)
AGE____	0.0338	0.0294	0.0055	0.0057
	(28.919)	(28.234)	(9.155)	(9.437)
AGE___SQ	−0.4355	−0.3663	−0.0542	−0.0561
	(28.603)	(26.977)	(6.891)	(7.140)
SVC_FRST	−0.0075	0.0205	0.0209	0.0203
	(0.949)	(2.914)	(5.216)	(5.084)
SVC_F_SQ	−1.0633	−0.7648	−0.4360	−0.4362
	(6.493)	(5.249)	(5.259)	(5.268)
SVC_MREC	0.0164	−0.0078	−0.0043	−0.0036
	(2.084)	(1.112)	(1.087)	(0.905)
SVC_M_SQ	0.4924	0.2434	0.1577	0.1595
	(3.019)	(1.678)	(1.911)	(1.936)
AGESVC_F	0.0007	0.0000	−0.0001	−0.0001
	(4.865)	(0.350)	(1.518)	(1.378)
AGESVC_M	−0.0004	0.0001	0.0000	0.0000
	(2.686)	(1.251)	(0.853)	(0.665)
HANDICAP	−0.0217	−0.0336	0.0045	0.0040
	(2.458)	(4.254)	(1.006)	(0.892)
VET_VIET	−0.0943	−0.0462	−0.0067	−0.0041
	(1.916)	(1.056)	(0.269)	(0.165)
VETOTHER	0.0624	0.0530	−0.0058	−0.0029
	(3.541)	(3.380)	(0.655)	(0.326)
HAY_MISS			0.7428	0.7417
			(183.714)	(163.317)

Appendix Table A4.8(2) ***(continued)***

Variable	Standard Regressors		Standard Regressors with Haypoint	
	Basic	Percent	Basic	Percent
HAYPOINT			0.0029	0.0029
			(155.605)	(137.909)
HAYPOISQ			−0.0014	−0.0014
			(59.534)	(57.242)
AFTER783	0.0473	0.0505	0.0459	0.0457
	(5.957)	(7.142)	(11.428)	(11.384)
AFTER784	0.0312	0.0335	0.0318	0.0315
	(3.571)	(4.308)	(7.205)	(7.149)
AFTER785	0.0158	0.0173	0.0143	0.0139
	(2.509)	(3.089)	(4.485)	(4.378)
LNWGMSAP	−0.5503	−0.5337	−0.6252	−0.6281
	(1.313)	(1.432)	(2.950)	(2.970)
LNWGMINP	0.3771	0.3818	0.4480	0.4528
	(0.931)	(1.061)	(2.189)	(2.216)
CPINDEX1	0.4568	0.4487	0.5009	0.5107
	(1.389)	(1.534)	(3.011)	(3.077)
CPINDEX2	0.4129	0.3622	0.4311	0.4335
	(1.129)	(1.114)	(2.332)	(2.350)
CPINDEX3	0.1078	−0.1320	0.1767	0.1640
	(0.284)	(0.391)	(0.921)	(0.856)
CPINDEX4	0.5483	0.5214	0.4460	0.4500
	(1.836)	(1.964)	(2.954)	(2.986)
Intercept	−4.3447	−3.8863	−4.4087	−4.4400
	(6.323)	(6.362)	(12.689)	(12.804)
R^2	0.3318	0.4722	0.8292	0.8300
Sum of AFTER78*i*:	0.0943	0.1013	0.0920	0.0911

Appendix Table A4.8(3) "Time Trend and Private-Sector Wages" Pooled OLS Wage Regressions for Random Sample of 1,000 White Women Present Continuously During October 1981–April 1986 (dep. var. = LOG_HRLY; *t* in parentheses)

	Raw Differentials		Raw Diffs. w/Haypoint	
Variable	Basic	Percent	Basic	Percent
PCTFEMAL		−0.3265		0.0052
		(52.139)		(1.327)
PCTBLACK		0.0946		0.0086
		(1.779)		(0.284)
PCTINDIA		−2.0983		0.0181
		(16.471)		(0.247)
PCTHISPA		−2.9791		0.3803
		(20.606)		(4.501)
PCTASIAN		1.7606		0.2994
		(19.024)		(5.604)
AGE_____				
AGE___SQ				
SVC_FRST				
SVC_F_SQ				
SVC_MREC				
SVC_M_SQ				
AGESVC_F				
AGESVC_M				
HANDICAP				
VET_VIET				
VETOTHER				

Appendix Table A4.8(3) (*continued*)

Variable	Raw Differentials Basic	Raw Differentials Percent	Raw Diffs. w/ Haypoint Basic	Raw Diffs. w/ Haypoint Percent
HAY_MISS			0.7652	0.7711
			(179.690)	(161.266)
HAYPOINT			0.0030	0.0030
			(154.265)	(138.230)
HAYPOISQ			−0.0014	−0.0015
			(59.556)	(58.185)
AFTER783	0.0285	0.0296	0.0242	0.0240
	(1.829)	(2.126)	(3.045)	(3.018)
AFTER784	0.0438	0.0446	0.0433	0.0432
	(2.997)	(3.418)	(5.815)	(5.801)
AFTER785	0.0350	0.0349	0.0328	0.0326
	(2.391)	(2.668)	(4.392)	(4.363)
TIMETRND	0.4882	0.5020	0.4963	0.4977
	(2.503)	(2.881)	(4.987)	(5.009)
TIMTRSQ	−0.8950	−0.9111	−0.9076	−0.9108
	(2.474)	(2.819)	(4.917)	(4.942)
LNWGMSAP	−0.3501	−0.3926	−0.4691	−0.4680
	(0.617)	(0.775)	(1.621)	(1.620)
LNWGMINP	0.3376	0.3817	0.4420	0.4442
	(0.697)	(0.882)	(1.788)	(1.800)
CPINDEX1	0.2862	0.2350	0.2905	0.3040
	(0.692)	(0.636)	(1.377)	(1.443)
CPINDEX2	−0.0853	−0.1544	−0.0951	−0.0952
	(0.191)	(0.387)	(0.417)	(0.418)
CPINDEX3	−0.3010	−0.3283	−0.2992	−0.3101
	(0.584)	(0.713)	(1.137)	(1.180)
CPINDEX4	0.2971	0.2804	0.1985	0.1994
	(0.861)	(0.909)	(1.128)	(1.134)
Intercept	−5.2040	−4.4141	−5.2529	−5.3195
	(2.323)	(2.205)	(4.596)	(4.661)
R^2	0.2377	0.3918	0.8016	0.8023
Sum of AFTER78*i*:	0.1073	0.1091	0.1003	0.0998

Appendix Table A4.8(3) *(continued)*

Variable	Standard Regressors		Standard Regressors with Haypoint	
	Basic	Percent	Basic	Percent
PCTFEMAL		−0.3176		−0.0066
		(54.084)		(1.798)
PCTBLACK		0.2081		0.0720
		(4.180)		(2.543)
PCTINDIA		−1.8758		0.0674
		(15.735)		(0.987)
PCTHISPA		−2.7864		0.2861
		(20.629)		(3.645)
PCTASIAN		1.7011		0.3216
		(19.786)		(6.476)
AGE_____	0.0338	0.0294	0.0055	0.0057
	(28.918)	(28.234)	(9.151)	(9.434)
AGE___SQ	−0.4355	−0.3663	−0.0541	−0.0561
	(28.604)	(26.979)	(6.890)	(7.139)
SVC_FRST	−0.0074	0.0206	0.0209	0.0204
	(0.944)	(2.921)	(5.232)	(5.100)
SVC_F_SQ	−1.0629	−0.7644	−0.4355	−0.4357
	(6.491)	(5.247)	(5.257)	(5.266)
SVC_MREC	0.0163	−0.0078	−0.0044	−0.0036
	(2.077)	(1.122)	(1.105)	(0.924)
SVC_M_SQ	0.4922	0.2433	0.1575	0.1593
	(3.019)	(1.678)	(1.910)	(1.935)
AGESVC_F	0.0007	0.0000	−0.0001	−0.0001
	(4.859)	(0.341)	(1.536)	(1.396)
AGESVC_M	−0.0004	0.0001	0.0000	0.0000
	(2.678)	(1.262)	(0.874)	(0.685)
HANDICAP	−0.0216	−0.0334	0.0046	0.0041
	(2.447)	(4.241)	(1.030)	(0.918)
VET_VIET	−0.0943	−0.0462	−0.0066	−0.0040
	(1.916)	(1.056)	(0.269)	(0.165)
VETOTHER	0.0624	0.0530	−0.0058	−0.0028
	(3.542)	(3.382)	(0.651)	(0.323)
HAY_MISS			0.7428	0.7417
			(183.832)	(163.421)

Appendix Table A4.8(3) (*continued*)

Variable	Standard Regressors: Basic	Standard Regressors: Percent	Standard Regressors with Haypoint: Basic	Standard Regressors with Haypoint: Percent
HAYPOINT			0.0029	0.0029
			(155.673)	(137.968)
HAYPOISQ			−0.0014	−0.0014
			(59.532)	(57.240)
AFTER783	0.0286	0.0296	0.0243	0.0242
	(1.960)	(2.279)	(3.297)	(3.285)
AFTER784	0.0436	0.0443	0.0433	0.0432
	(3.190)	(3.648)	(6.262)	(6.257)
AFTER785	0.0350	0.0350	0.0329	0.0327
	(2.550)	(2.872)	(4.738)	(4.724)
TIMETRND	0.4394	0.4527	0.4707	0.4711
	(2.406)	(2.788)	(5.099)	(5.114)
TIMTRSQ	−0.8258	−0.8402	−0.8744	−0.8761
	(2.437)	(2.790)	(5.107)	(5.127)
LNWGMSAP	−0.3469	−0.3871	−0.4685	−0.4655
	(0.653)	(0.820)	(1.746)	(1.738)
LNWGMINP	0.3348	0.3779	0.4413	0.4424
	(0.738)	(0.937)	(1.924)	(1.933)
CPINDEX1	0.2935	0.2455	0.2920	0.3049
	(0.758)	(0.713)	(1.492)	(1.561)
CPINDEX2	−0.0813	−0.1446	−0.0960	−0.0942
	(0.194)	(0.389)	(0.454)	(0.447)
CPINDEX3	−0.2976	−0.3280	−0.2986	−0.3079
	(0.616)	(0.764)	(1.224)	(1.264)
CPINDEX4	0.3013	0.2838	0.1978	0.1999
	(0.932)	(0.988)	(1.211)	(1.227)
Intercept	−5.2773	−4.4623	−5.0342	−5.1012
	(2.515)	(2.393)	(4.748)	(4.821)
R^2	0.3320	0.4724	0.8294	0.8302
Sum of AFTER78*i*:	0.1072	0.1089	0.1005	0.1001

Appendix Table A4.9(1) "Time Trend" Pooled OLS Wage Regressions for Random Sample of 1,000 White Men Present Continuously During October 1981–April 1986 (dep. var. = LOG_HRLY; *t* in parentheses)

	Raw Differentials		Raw Diffs. w/Haypoint	
Variable	Basic	Percent	Basic	Percent
PCTFEMAL		−0.4194		−0.2502
		(51.340)		(49.405)
PCTBLACK		0.4161		0.2090
		(6.947)		(5.731)
PCTINDIA		−3.3538		−0.0805
		(30.231)		(1.149)
PCTHISPA		−2.6597		0.3878
		(17.342)		(4.081)
PCTASIAN		1.6484		0.1123
		(12.354)		(1.357)
AGE_____				
AGE___SQ				
SVC_FRST				
SVC_F_SQ				
SVC_MREC				
SVC_M_SQ				
AGESVC_F				
AGESVC_M				
HANDICAP				
VET_VIET				
VETOTHER				

Appendix Table A4.9(1) (*continued*)

Variable	Raw Differentials		Raw Diffs. w/ Haypoint	
	Basic	Percent	Basic	Percent
HAY_MISS			0.8165	0.7843
			(150.685)	(144.869)
HAYPOINT			0.0026	0.0025
			(109.651)	(105.733)
HAYPOISQ			−0.0013	−0.0012
			(50.404)	(50.012)
AFTER783	0.0016	−0.0036	0.0002	−0.0008
	(0.093)	(0.232)	(0.028)	(0.088)
AFTER784	0.0057	0.0025	0.0050	0.0043
	(0.544)	(0.268)	(0.824)	(0.754)
AFTER785	0.0106	0.0115	0.0105	0.0108
	(0.827)	(0.989)	(1.405)	(1.523)
TIMETRND	0.4150	0.4639	0.3897	0.4070
	(1.861)	(2.297)	(2.981)	(3.311)
TIMTRSQ	−0.8095	−0.8768	−0.7725	−0.7972
	(2.023)	(2.419)	(3.293)	(3.615)
CPINDEX1	0.4715	0.4159	0.5065	0.4728
	(0.997)	(0.972)	(1.828)	(1.815)
CPINDEX2	0.1735	0.0857	0.2358	0.2206
	(0.365)	(0.199)	(0.847)	(0.843)
CPINDEX3	−0.0920	−0.2799	−0.0860	−0.1555
	(0.160)	(0.539)	(0.256)	(0.492)
CPINDEX4	0.4299	0.4196	0.4325	0.4403
	(1.196)	(1.289)	(2.053)	(2.223)
Intercept	−7.3716	−6.4883	−8.0770	−7.7770
	(3.745)	(3.640)	(7.000)	(7.169)
R^2	0.1086	0.2693	0.6938	0.7295
Sum of AFTER78*i*:	0.0179	0.0104	0.0157	0.0135

Appendix Table A4.9(1) (*continued*)

Variable	Standard Regressors		Standard Regressors with Haypoint	
	Basic	Percent	Basic	Percent
PCTFEMAL		−0.3243		−0.1905
		(40.224)		(39.476)
PCTBLACK		0.4711		0.2533
		(8.336)		(7.566)
PCTINDIA		−2.9725		0.0558
		(28.274)		(0.866)
PCTHISPA		−2.6712		0.2038
		(18.462)		(2.338)
PCTASIAN		1.7643		0.3243
		(13.969)		(4.256)
AGE_____	0.0465	0.0383	0.0154	0.0130
	(26.009)	(22.979)	(14.920)	(13.031)
AGE___SQ	−0.4764	−0.3809	−0.1031	−0.0774
	(21.563)	(18.483)	(8.064)	(6.290)
SVC_FRST	−0.0668	−0.0721	−0.0330	−0.0367
	(6.996)	(8.122)	(6.041)	(6.979)
SVC_F_SQ	−0.9030	−0.8442	−0.8303	−0.8366
	(7.737)	(7.791)	(12.397)	(12.999)
SVC_MREC	0.0754	0.0807	0.0550	0.0573
	(7.916)	(9.127)	(10.093)	(10.929)
SVC_M_SQ	0.6891	0.6548	0.5946	0.6393
	(5.910)	(6.046)	(8.894)	(9.950)
AGESVC_F	0.0024	0.0024	0.0014	0.0015
	(12.038)	(12.809)	(12.506)	(13.503)
AGESVC_M	−0.0024	−0.0024	−0.0017	−0.0017
	(11.761)	(12.903)	(14.614)	(15.866)
HANDICAP	−0.0943	−0.0835	−0.0151	−0.0137
	(13.691)	(13.039)	(3.823)	(3.611)
VET_VIET	−0.0220	−0.0328	−0.0098	−0.0173
	(4.244)	(6.776)	(3.294)	(6.023)
VETOTHER	−0.0532	−0.0486	−0.0267	−0.0251
	(10.244)	(10.064)	(8.981)	(8.766)
HAY_MISS			0.7861	0.7661
			(159.065)	(152.388)

Appendix Table A4.9(1) (*continued*)

Variable	Standard Regressors		Standard Regressors with Haypoint	
	Basic	Percent	Basic	Percent
HAYPOINT			0.0025	0.0024
			(116.266)	(112.047)
HAYPOISQ			−0.0013	−0.0012
			(54.826)	(53.948)
AFTER783	0.0010	−0.0035	0.0001	−0.0008
	(0.064)	(0.241)	(0.011)	(0.094)
AFTER784	0.0073	0.0044	0.0057	0.0051
	(0.761)	(0.498)	(1.044)	(0.978)
AFTER785	0.0109	0.0117	0.0106	0.0109
	(0.926)	(1.076)	(1.584)	(1.688)
TIMETRND	0.3861	0.4346	0.3653	0.3831
	(1.888)	(2.289)	(3.122)	(3.408)
TIMTRSQ	−0.7692	−0.8345	−0.7366	−0.7620
	(2.096)	(2.450)	(3.509)	(3.778)
CPINDEX1	0.4583	0.4148	0.4908	0.4640
	(1.057)	(1.031)	(1.980)	(1.948)
CPINDEX2	0.1144	0.0416	0.2038	0.1941
	(0.263)	(0.103)	(0.818)	(0.811)
CPINDEX3	−0.0987	−0.2542	−0.0971	−0.1505
	(0.188)	(0.521)	(0.323)	(0.521)
CPINDEX4	0.4205	0.4112	0.4279	0.4363
	(1.276)	(1.344)	(2.270)	(2.409)
Intercept	−7.6616	−6.8769	−7.9280	−7.7166
	(4.244)	(4.103)	(7.678)	(7.778)
R^2	0.2511	0.3858	0.7550	0.7740
Sum of AFTER78*i*:	0.0192	0.0126	0.0164	0.0152

Appendix Table A4.9(2) "Private-Sector Wages" Pooled OLS Wage Regressions for Random Sample of 1,000 White Men Present Continuously During October 1981–April 1986 (dep. var. = LOG_HRLY; *t* in parentheses)

	Raw Differentials		Raw Diffs. w/Haypoint	
Variable	Basic	Percent	Basic	Percent
PCTFEMAL		−0.4194		−0.2501
		(51.328)		(49.382)
PCTBLACK		0.4156		0.2085
		(6.937)		(5.714)
PCTINDIA		−3.3544		−0.0811
		(30.233)		(1.158)
PCTHISPA		−2.6577		0.3897
		(17.327)		(4.100)
PCTASIAN		1.6483		0.1120
		(12.352)		(1.353)
AGE_____				
AGE___SQ				
SVC_FRST				
SVC_F_SQ				
SVC_MREC				
SVC_M_SQ				
AGESVC_F				
AGESVC_M				
HANDICAP				
VET_VIET				
VETOTHER				

Appendix Table A4.9(2) (*continued*)

Variable	Raw Differentials		Raw Diffs. w/ Haypoint	
	Basic	Percent	Basic	Percent
HAY_MISS			0.8165	0.7843
			(150.654)	(144.838)
HAYPOINT			0.0026	0.0025
			(109.637)	(105.718)
HAYPOISQ			−0.0013	−0.0012
			(50.402)	(50.010)
AFTER783	0.0137	0.0143	0.0099	0.0106
	(1.356)	(1.561)	(1.669)	(1.895)
AFTER784	−0.0126	−0.0124	−0.0147	−0.0143
	(1.132)	(1.234)	(2.256)	(2.334)
AFTER785	−0.0133	−0.0098	−0.0144	−0.0134
	(1.661)	(1.347)	(3.052)	(3.028)
LNWGMSAP	−0.6523	−0.5106	−0.6839	−0.6546
	(1.219)	(1.054)	(2.180)	(2.219)
LNWGMINP	0.4458	0.3449	0.4498	0.4398
	(0.862)	(0.737)	(1.485)	(1.544)
CPINDEX1	0.5431	0.5880	0.5299	0.5303
	(1.293)	(1.546)	(2.152)	(2.291)
CPINDEX2	0.6060	0.5638	0.6623	0.6522
	(1.298)	(1.334)	(2.420)	(2.535)
CPINDEX3	0.1075	0.0627	0.0675	0.0328
	(0.222)	(0.143)	(0.238)	(0.123)
CPINDEX4	0.8160	0.7921	0.8010	0.8179
	(2.141)	(2.294)	(3.584)	(3.892)
Intercept	−5.5383	−5.4537	−5.8901	−5.8461
	(6.323)	(6.875)	(11.471)	(12.110)
R^2	0.1085	0.2691	0.6937	0.7293
Sum of AFTER78*i*:	−0.0122	−0.0079	−0.0192	−0.0171

Appendix Table A4.9(2) (*continued*)

Variable	Standard Regressors		Standard Regressors with Haypoint	
	Basic	Percent	Basic	Percent
PCTFEMAL		−0.3242		−0.1905
		(40.213)		(39.457)
PCTBLACK		0.4706		0.2527
		(8.326)		(7.548)
PCTINDIA		−2.9732		0.0549
		(28.278)		(0.853)
PCTHISPA		−2.6693		0.2056
		(18.447)		(2.358)
PCTASIAN		1.7642		0.3240
		(13.967)		(4.250)
AGE_____	0.0465	0.0383	0.0154	0.0130
	(26.011)	(22.980)	(14.923)	(13.033)
AGE___SQ	−0.4764	−0.3809	−0.1032	−0.0775
	(21.564)	(18.484)	(8.067)	(6.293)
SVC_FRST	−0.0668	−0.0720	−0.0330	−0.0366
	(6.986)	(8.110)	(6.026)	(6.960)
SVC_F_SQ	−0.9035	−0.8448	−0.8308	−0.8371
	(7.741)	(7.794)	(12.402)	(13.004)
SVC_MREC	0.0753	0.0806	0.0550	0.0572
	(7.908)	(9.116)	(10.079)	(10.912)
SVC_M_SQ	0.6895	0.6551	0.5949	0.6397
	(5.913)	(6.048)	(8.898)	(9.953)
AGESVC_F	0.0024	0.0024	0.0014	0.0015
	(12.031)	(12.799)	(12.494)	(13.488)
AGESVC_M	−0.0024	−0.0024	−0.0017	−0.0017
	(11.754)	(12.894)	(14.603)	(15.852)
HANDICAP	−0.0943	−0.0836	−0.0152	−0.0138
	(13.695)	(13.044)	(3.831)	(3.621)
VET_VIET	−0.0220	−0.0328	−0.0098	−0.0173
	(4.249)	(6.779)	(3.303)	(6.030)
VETOTHER	−0.0531	−0.0485	−0.0267	−0.0251
	(10.232)	(10.050)	(8.962)	(8.745)
HAY_MISS			0.7861	0.7661
			(159.027)	(152.349)

Appendix Table A4.9(2) (*continued*)

Variable	Standard Regressors: Basic	Standard Regressors: Percent	Standard Regressors with Haypoint: Basic	Standard Regressors with Haypoint: Percent
HAYPOINT			0.0025	0.0024
			(116.247)	(112.027)
HAYPOISQ			−0.0013	−0.0012
			(54.821)	(53.942)
AFTER783	0.0098	0.0112	0.0072	0.0081
	(1.059)	(1.306)	(1.354)	(1.595)
AFTER784	−0.0129	−0.0122	−0.0153	−0.0147
	(1.262)	(1.291)	(2.616)	(2.621)
AFTER785	−0.0145	−0.0108	−0.0152	−0.0141
	(1.975)	(1.574)	(3.597)	(3.479)
LNWGMSAP	−0.7199	−0.5740	−0.7346	−0.7041
	(1.467)	(1.260)	(2.617)	(2.611)
LNWGMINP	0.4867	0.3841	0.4843	0.4732
	(1.027)	(0.873)	(1.786)	(1.817)
CPINDEX1	0.4710	0.5318	0.4713	0.4801
	(1.223)	(1.488)	(2.139)	(2.268)
CPINDEX2	0.5259	0.4983	0.6088	0.6056
	(1.229)	(1.254)	(2.486)	(2.574)
CPINDEX3	0.0252	0.0172	−0.0033	−0.0190
	(0.057)	(0.042)	(0.013)	(0.078)
CPINDEX4	0.8057	0.7813	0.7965	0.8132
	(2.305)	(2.407)	(3.983)	(4.233)
Intercept	−5.3675	−5.4270	−5.4239	−5.4828
	(6.673)	(7.268)	(11.788)	(12.402)
R^2	0.2510	0.3546	0.7549	0.7738
Sum of AFTER78*i*:	−0.0176	−0.0108	−0.0233	−0.0207

Appendix Table A4.9(3) "Time Trend and Private-Sector Wages" Pooled OLS Wage Regressions for Random Sample of 1,000 White Men Present Continuously During October 1981–April 1986 (dep. var. = LOG_HRLY; *t* in parentheses)

	Raw Differentials		Raw Diffs. w/Haypoint	
Variable	Basic	Percent	Basic	Percent
PCTFEMAL		−0.4194		−0.2502
		(51.339)		(49.405)
PCTBLACK		0.4162		0.2091
		(6.947)		(5.732)
PCTINDIA		−3.3535		−0.0802
		(30.227)		(1.145)
PCTHISPA		−2.6598		0.3877
		(17.342)		(4.079)
PCTASIAN		1.6485		0.1124
		(12.354)		(1.358)
AGE_____				
AGE___SQ				
SVC_FRST				
SVC_F_SQ				
SVC_MREC				
SVC_M_SQ				
AGESVC_F				
AGESVC_M				
HANDICAP				
VET_VIET				
VETOTHER				

Appendix Table A4.9(3) (*continued*)

Variable	Raw Differentials		Raw Diffs. w/ Haypoint	
	Basic	Percent	Basic	Percent
HAY_MISS			0.8165	0.7843
			(150.680)	(144.866)
HAYPOINT			0.0026	0.0025
			(109.647)	(105.730)
HAYPOISQ			−0.0013	−0.0012
			(50.402)	(50.010)
AFTER783	−0.0022	−0.0072	−0.0035	−0.0046
	(0.121)	(0.429)	(0.324)	(0.452)
AFTER784	0.0019	−0.0005	0.0002	0.0002
	(0.110)	(0.036)	(0.021)	(0.027)
AFTER785	0.0079	0.0093	0.0068	0.0077
	(0.450)	(0.588)	(0.665)	(0.802)
TIMETRND	0.4258	0.4767	0.3922	0.4147
	(1.826)	(2.257)	(2.869)	(3.227)
TIMTRSQ	−0.8139	−0.8873	−0.7581	−0.7951
	(1.882)	(2.265)	(2.990)	(3.336)
LNWGMSAP	−0.3721	−0.3412	−0.3747	−0.3672
	(0.549)	(0.556)	(0.943)	(0.983)
LNWGMINP	0.3525	0.3313	0.3317	0.3399
	(0.608)	(0.631)	(0.977)	(1.065)
CPINDEX1	0.4308	0.3824	0.4549	0.4290
	(0.871)	(0.854)	(1.569)	(1.575)
CPINDEX2	0.1238	0.0295	0.2162	0.1820
	(0.232)	(0.061)	(0.690)	(0.618)
CPINDEX3	−0.2295	−0.4116	−0.2085	−0.2857
	(0.372)	(0.737)	(0.577)	(0.841)
CPINDEX4	0.5545	0.5379	0.5465	0.5594
	(1.344)	(1.439)	(2.259)	(2.460)
Intercept	−6.9489	−6.1526	−7.5016	−7.3082
	(2.594)	(2.537)	(4.779)	(4.952)
R^2	0.1087	0.2693	0.6939	0.7295
Sum of AFTER78*i*:	0.0076	0.0016	0.0035	0.0033

Appendix Table A4.9(3) (*continued*)

Variable	Standard Regressors		Standard Regressors with Haypoint	
	Basic	Percent	Basic	Percent
PCTFEMAL		−0.3243		−0.1905
		(40.223)		(39.476)
PCTBLACK		0.4711		0.2533
		(8.336)		(7.567)
PCTINDIA		−2.9723		0.0560
		(28.270)		(0.870)
PCTHISPA		−2.6713		0.2037
		(18.462)		(2.337)
PCTASIAN		1.7643		0.3244
		(13.969)		(4.256)
AGE_____	0.0465	0.0383	0.0154	0.0130
	(26.008)	(22.978)	(14.920)	(13.031)
AGE___SQ	−0.4764	−0.3809	−0.1031	−0.0774
	(21.562)	(18.482)	(8.064)	(6.290)
SVC_FRST	−0.0668	−0.0721	−0.0330	−0.0367
	(6.995)	(8.121)	(6.041)	(6.978)
SVC_F_SQ	−0.9032	−0.8444	−0.8305	−0.8367
	(7.738)	(7.792)	(12.400)	(13.002)
SVC_MREC	0.0754	0.0807	0.0550	0.0573
	(7.915)	(9.126)	(10.093)	(10.928)
SVC_M_SQ	0.6893	0.6550	0.5947	0.6395
	(5.911)	(6.048)	(8.896)	(9.953)
AGESVC_F	0.0024	0.0024	0.0014	0.0015
	(12.037)	(12.808)	(12.506)	(13.503)
AGESVC_M	−0.0024	−0.0024	−0.0017	−0.0017
	(11.760)	(12.902)	(14.614)	(15.865)
HANDICAP	−0.0943	−0.0835	−0.0151	−0.0137
	(13.690)	(13.037)	(3.822)	(3.610)
VET_VIET	−0.0220	−0.0328	−0.0098	−0.0173
	(4.245)	(6.776)	(3.295)	(6.024)
VETOTHER	−0.0532	−0.0486	−0.0267	−0.0251
	(10.243)	(10.064)	(8.981)	(8.766)
HAY_MISS			0.7861	0.7661
			(159.062)	(152.385)

Appendix Table A4.9(3) (*continued*)

Variable	Standard Regressors Basic	Standard Regressors Percent	Standard Regressors with Haypoint Basic	Standard Regressors with Haypoint Percent
HAYPOINT			0.0025	0.0024
			(116.263)	(112.045)
HAYPOISQ			−0.0013	−0.0012
			(54.825)	(53.947)
AFTER783	−0.0029	−0.0072	−0.0037	−0.0047
	(0.170)	(0.457)	(0.388)	(0.504)
AFTER784	0.0029	0.0006	0.0005	0.0006
	(0.186)	(0.045)	(0.060)	(0.073)
AFTER785	0.0076	0.0090	0.0066	0.0075
	(0.476)	(0.604)	(0.722)	(0.850)
TIMETRND	0.3933	0.4436	0.3661	0.3888
	(1.839)	(2.235)	(2.993)	(3.309)
TIMTRSQ	−0.7650	−0.8359	−0.7180	−0.7545
	(1.929)	(2.270)	(3.165)	(3.462)
LNWGMSAP	−0.3808	−0.3552	−0.3838	−0.3797
	(0.613)	(0.616)	(1.079)	(1.112)
LNWGMINP	0.3501	0.3330	0.3349	0.3449
	(0.659)	(0.675)	(1.102)	(1.182)
CPINDEX1	0.4118	0.3744	0.4357	0.4156
	(0.908)	(0.889)	(1.680)	(1.668)
CPINDEX2	0.0775	−0.0011	0.1900	0.1628
	(0.158)	(0.003)	(0.678)	(0.605)
CPINDEX3	−0.2322	−0.3831	−0.2193	−0.2807
	(0.411)	(0.730)	(0.678)	(0.904)
CPINDEX4	0.5428	0.5284	0.5424	0.5562
	(1.435)	(1.504)	(2.506)	(2.675)
Intercept	−7.1600	−6.4504	−7.3074	−7.1897
	(2.915)	(2.829)	(5.202)	(5.327)
R^2	0.2511	0.3548	0.7551	0.7740
Sum of AFTER78*i*:	0.0076	0.0024	0.0034	0.0034

Appendix Table A4.10 Fixed-Effects Wage Regressions for Random Samples of Whites Continuously Present During October 1981–April 1986 (dep. var. = LOG_HRLY; *t* in parentheses)

	Time Trend Only		Pvt. Wages Only		Time & Pvt. Wages	
Variable	**Females**	**Males**	**Females**	**Males**	**Females**	**Males**
AFTER783	0.0344	0.0023	0.0581	0.0230	0.0282	−0.0022
	(2.395)	(0.138)	(6.820)	(2.253)	(1.811)	(0.118)
AFTER784	0.0482	0.0061	0.0417	−0.0037	0.0430	0.0020
	(5.524)	(0.586)	(4.558)	(0.336)	(2.962)	(0.116)
AFTER785	0.0345	0.0096	0.0262	−0.0026	0.0328	0.0081
	(3.336)	(0.779)	(3.794)	(0.319)	(2.346)	(0.487)
TIMETRND	0.3940	0.3911			0.4475	0.4290
	(2.276)	(1.890)			(2.387)	(1.914)
TIMETRSQ	−0.6899	−0.7064			−0.7724	−0.7635
	(2.247)	(1.925)			(2.249)	(1.860)
LNWGMSAP			−0.2063	−0.2156	−0.4784	−0.3571
			(0.490)	(0.428)	(0.939)	(0.586)
LNWGMINP			0.1574	0.1130	0.4589	0.3382
			(0.408)	(0.245)	(1.085)	(0.668)
CPINDEX1	0.2179	0.4353	0.6640	0.7942	0.2251	0.4379
	(0.572)	(0.955)	(1.974)	(1.973)	(0.568)	(0.925)
CPINDEX2	0.0909	0.2161	0.4354	0.5864	−0.0467	0.1200
	(0.240)	(0.478)	(1.116)	(1.258)	(0.106)	(0.227)
CPINDEX3	−0.3877	−0.1685	0.3759	0.5204	−0.4478	−0.2120
	(0.912)	(0.331)	(1.410)	(1.630)	(1.043)	(0.413)
CPINDEX4	0.4748	0.5335	0.4748	0.5335	0.4748	0.5335
	(1313.348)	(1234.292)	(1313.179)	(1234.188)	(1313.390)	(1234.307)
SV_F_SQ	−0.4425	−0.1302	−0.4539	−0.1404	−0.4425	−0.1302
	(2.959)	(0.742)	(3.037)	(0.803)	(2.959)	(0.742)
AGESVC_F	−0.1975	−0.4403	−0.1827	−0.4290	−0.1975	−0.4403
	(1.705)	(2.607)	(1.591)	(2.573)	(1.705)	(2.607)
AFTER78*i* Coefficients:						
Sum	0.1171	0.0180	0.1260	0.0167	0.1040	0.0079
F-M Diff.	0.0991		0.1093		0.0961	

Appendix Table A4.11(1) Regressions for Employment Levels in Predominantly (≥70%) Female Classes (dep. var.=ln of class employment; indep. var.=maximum/mean/minimum ln of wage rate within class; *t* in parentheses)

Model, Variable	Pooled OLS Estimates			Fixed-Effects Estimates		
	Maximum	Mean	Minimum	Maximum	Mean	Minimum
Time Trend Variables Only:						
ln(wage)	−2.4999	−3.1108	−3.1704	0.6963	−0.3987	−1.0536
	(31.293)	(44.816)	(55.539)	(7.779)	(3.730)	(13.016)
TIMETRND	1.1951	1.5155	1.3235	0.0070	0.4261	0.6174
	(0.933)	(1.303)	(1.238)	(0.035)	(2.103)	(3.150)
TIMETRSQ	−2.2197	−2.7682	−2.4595	−0.0791	−0.8304	−1.1815
	(0.978)	(1.344)	(1.299)	(0.223)	(2.314)	(3.402)
CPINDEX1	3.4628	3.7743	4.0843	−0.0245	1.1242	1.8474
	(0.615)	(0.738)	(0.869)	(0.028)	(1.282)	(2.154)
CPINDEX2	−0.7146	−0.5351	−0.1628	−0.9498	−0.8516	−0.6535
	(0.128)	(0.105)	(0.035)	(1.105)	(0.985)	(0.771)
CPINDEX3	−0.2528	−0.8285	0.2423	0.7899	0.3837	0.4553
	(0.042)	(0.151)	(0.048)	(0.852)	(0.411)	(0.498)
CPINDEX4	−0.0036	0.0373	−0.6617	0.0345	0.0280	−0.2017
	(0.001)	(0.010)	(0.185)	(0.052)	(0.042)	(0.310)
Intercept	−19.2781	−22.3306	−24.4863			
	(0.848)	(1.082)	(1.291)			
R^2	0.2030	0.3431	0.4450			
Private-Sector Employment Variables Only:						
ln(wage)	−2.4983	−3.1089	−3.1693	0.7086	−0.3713	−1.0378
	(31.277)	(44.789)	(55.515)	(7.936)	(3.492)	(12.830)
LNWGMSAP	−1.6521	−2.3679	−1.9510	0.1640	−0.7026	−1.1887
	(0.253)	(0.400)	(0.359)	(0.232)	(0.986)	(1.706)
LNWGMINP	1.2017	1.9465	1.4649	−0.3459	0.8523	1.4892
	(0.185)	(0.329)	(0.270)	(0.500)	(1.221)	(2.190)
CPINDEX1	3.9383	4.8096	4.5966	0.0180	0.4754	0.8311
	(0.941)	(1.265)	(1.316)	(0.015)	(0.408)	(0.727)
CPINDEX2	−0.1160	0.1532	0.4701	−0.9437	−1.2653	−1.3063
	(0.020)	(0.029)	(0.096)	(1.065)	(1.419)	(1.494)
CPINDEX3	0.2580	−0.1733	0.7683	0.0974	1.2732	2.1196
	(0.043)	(0.032)	(0.154)	(0.084)	(1.097)	(1.864)
CPINDEX4	2.0886	2.7485	1.7130	−0.0118	0.7098	0.8126
	(0.451)	(0.654)	(0.443)	(0.013)	(0.783)	(0.917)
Intercept	−16.9059	−22.0868	−21.8242			
	(3.981)	(5.727)	(6.170)			
R^2	0.2028	0.3428	0.4448			

Appendix Table A4.11(1) *(continued)*

Model, Variable	Pooled OLS Estimates Maximum	Mean	Minimum	Fixed-Effects Estimates Maximum	Mean	Minimum
Both Time Trend and Private-Sector Employment Variables:						
ln(wage)	−2.5004	−3.1113	−3.1708	0.7059	−0.4131	−1.0679
	(31.289)	(44.810)	(55.530)	(7.820)	(3.816)	(13.121)
TIMETRND	1.3178	1.6557	1.4570	0.0349	0.4194	0.5880
	(1.001)	(1.385)	(1.327)	(0.173)	(2.046)	(2.959)
TIMETRSQ	−2.3675	−2.9312	−2.6188	−0.1460	−0.8256	−1.1304
	(1.028)	(1.401)	(1.362)	(0.401)	(2.239)	(3.160)
LNWGMSAP	−1.6589	−2.5176	−1.9537	0.5958	−0.0408	−0.3695
	(0.248)	(0.415)	(0.351)	(0.751)	(0.051)	(0.472)
LNWGMINP	0.9143	1.6705	1.1441	−0.6638	0.3233	0.8089
	(0.139)	(0.280)	(0.209)	(0.894)	(0.431)	(1.107)
CPINDEX1	2.1893	2.2147	2.6731	0.3822	0.3215	0.4769
	(0.345)	(0.385)	(0.505)	(0.309)	(0.258)	(0.391)
CPINDEX2	−0.1631	0.0216	0.4200	−0.6691	−1.0836	−1.1313
	(0.028)	(0.004)	(0.086)	(0.729)	(1.174)	(1.251)
CPINDEX3	−0.1554	−0.8532	0.3162	0.1233	0.8068	1.4177
	(0.025)	(0.150)	(0.061)	(0.104)	(0.677)	(1.214)
CPINDEX4	0.2517	0.5850	−0.3229	0.0699	0.4775	0.4190
	(0.050)	(0.127)	(0.076)	(0.076)	(0.516)	(0.462)
Intercept	−14.1001	−16.1497	−18.7862			
	(0.549)	(0.692)	(0.876)			
R^2	0.2031	0.3431	0.4451			

Appendix Table A4.11(2) Regressions for Employment Levels in Mixed (70% > % Female ≥ 30%) Classes (dep. var. = ln of class employment; indep. var. = maximum/mean/minimum ln of wage rate within class; *t* in parentheses)

Model, Variable	Pooled OLS Estimates			Fixed-Effects Estimates		
	Maximum	Mean	Minimum	Maximum	Mean	Minimum
Time Trend Variables Only:						
ln(wage)	−0.1730	−1.0122	−1.7845	1.6262	−1.3188	−1.8270
	(2.367)	(13.328)	(24.832)	(14.508)	(9.542)	(20.279)
TIMETRND	0.0020	0.1613	0.3686	−0.3761	0.2207	0.3782
	(0.002)	(0.163)	(0.393)	(1.575)	(0.909)	(1.625)
TIMETRSQ	0.0623	−0.3176	−0.7973	0.9445	−0.4584	−0.8198
	(0.035)	(0.181)	(0.480)	(2.225)	(1.061)	(1.983)
CPINDEX1	1.8671	2.2252	2.2819	0.6193	2.3694	2.2942
	(0.420)	(0.512)	(0.554)	(0.591)	(2.230)	(2.250)
CPINDEX2	−0.9983	−0.3126	−0.5233	−2.0160	−0.0751	0.5624
	(0.226)	(0.072)	(0.128)	(1.939)	(0.070)	(0.553)
CPINDEX3	1.2392	1.4758	1.5456	0.2878	1.5741	1.5541
	(0.261)	(0.317)	(0.350)	(0.257)	(1.385)	(1.424)
CPINDEX4	−2.4416	−1.8559	−1.1051	−3.1202	−1.6584	−1.0713
	(0.722)	(0.561)	(0.352)	(3.920)	(2.042)	(1.375)
Intercept	3.6546	−4.5326	−12.9114			
	(0.204)	(0.258)	(0.775)			
R^2	0.0019	0.0456	0.1414			
Private-Sector Employment Variables Only:						
ln(wage)	−0.1734	−1.0119	−1.7829	1.6380	−1.2646	−1.7944
	(2.375)	(13.330)	(24.825)	(14.709)	(9.168)	(19.941)
LNWGMSAP	−0.5139	−0.9461	−1.2417	4.5764	0.4122	−0.6388
	(0.100)	(0.188)	(0.260)	(5.312)	(0.465)	(0.759)
LNWGMINP	0.6273	1.0253	1.2945	−3.8005	−0.0205	0.8238
	(0.122)	(0.204)	(0.272)	(4.544)	(0.023)	(1.009)
CPINDEX1	2.4213	2.1475	1.5351	0.7484	0.9880	0.9254
	(0.733)	(0.665)	(0.501)	(0.536)	(0.696)	(0.678)
CPINDEX2	−0.9819	−0.5232	0.0599	−0.6091	−0.4383	−0.1205
	(0.213)	(0.116)	(0.014)	(0.570)	(0.403)	(0.115)
CPINDEX3	1.3317	1.1974	0.8764	−2.7125	1.4548	2.0555
	(0.282)	(0.259)	(0.200)	(1.946)	(1.024)	(1.513)
CPINDEX4	−2.3647	−1.1678	0.2452	−1.2660	−0.4530	−0.1857
	(0.647)	(0.327)	(0.072)	(1.171)	(0.411)	(0.175)
Intercept	−0.1265	−3.5358	−6.4837			
	(0.038)	(1.083)	(2.095)			
R^2	0.0019	0.0456	0.1414			

Appendix Table A4.11(2) (*continued*)

Model, Variable	Pooled OLS Estimates Maximum	Mean	Minimum	Fixed-Effects Estimates Maximum	Mean	Minimum
Both Time Trend and Private-Sector Employment Variables:						
ln(wage)	−0.1730	−1.0123	−1.7846	1.6693	−1.3025	−1.8242
	(2.367)	(13.325)	(24.826)	(14.840)	(9.326)	(20.139)
TIMETRND	−0.0005	0.1495	0.3441	−0.2235	0.2510	0.3833
	(0.001)	(0.147)	(0.357)	(0.924)	(1.020)	(1.623)
TIMETRSQ	0.0730	−0.2934	−0.7569	0.5385	−0.5625	−0.8550
	(0.040)	(0.165)	(0.449)	(1.234)	(1.266)	(2.008)
LNWGMSAP	−0.7477	−0.8663	−0.7928	3.7698	1.1044	0.4370
	(0.142)	(0.168)	(0.162)	(3.933)	(1.127)	(0.466)
LNWGMINP	0.7680	0.9442	0.9484	−3.1855	−0.5557	−0.0153
	(0.148)	(0.186)	(0.197)	(3.561)	(0.607)	(0.017)
CPINDEX1	1.7625	2.1758	2.3479	0.3520	1.2213	1.2618
	(0.352)	(0.445)	(0.506)	(0.236)	(0.805)	(0.866)
CPINDEX2	−1.1023	−0.4869	0.2803	−1.0422	−0.0866	0.4024
	(0.237)	(0.107)	(0.065)	(0.943)	(0.077)	(0.372)
CPINDEX3	1.0661	1.2420	1.2803	−2.5716	1.2590	1.7133
	(0.216)	(0.258)	(0.280)	(1.795)	(0.862)	(1.227)
CPINDEX4	−2.1250	−1.4584	−0.6935	−1.2631	−0.5062	−0.2809
	(0.531)	(0.372)	(0.187)	(1.141)	(0.449)	(0.259)
Intercept	3.8780	−4.5967	−13.4702			
	(0.191)	(0.232)	(0.716)			
R^2	0.0019	0.0456	0.1415			

Appendix Table A4.11(3) Regressions for Employment Levels in Predominantly Male (<30% Female) Classes (dep. var. = ln of class employment; indep. var. = maximum/mean/minimum ln of wage rate within class; *t* in parentheses)

Model, Variable	Pooled OLS Estimates			Fixed-Effects Estimates		
	Maximum	Mean	Minimum	Maximum	Mean	Minimum
Time Trend Variables Only:						
ln(wage)	−1.8014	−2.1028	−2.3512	0.5929	−0.6349	−1.1818
	(54.781)	(69.654)	(89.986)	(14.633)	(14.039)	(36.778)
TIMETRND	0.7377	0.9016	0.9983	−0.1032	0.3455	0.5540
	(1.480)	(1.892)	(2.247)	(1.266)	(4.207)	(7.043)
TIMETRSQ	−1.3980	−1.7238	−1.9312	0.2853	−0.6122	−1.0360
	(1.583)	(2.041)	(2.454)	(1.967)	(4.183)	(7.409)
CPINDEX1	1.4146	1.3833	1.3915	−0.3928	0.4558	0.7266
	(0.646)	(0.660)	(0.713)	(1.109)	(1.287)	(2.124)
CPINDEX2	0.3033	0.5081	0.7867	−0.5263	−0.0703	0.2361
	(0.139)	(0.244)	(0.406)	(1.500)	(0.200)	(0.695)
CPINDEX3	−0.0678	−0.0141	−0.1173	0.0594	0.0150	−0.0453
	(0.029)	(0.006)	(0.056)	(0.157)	(0.039)	(0.124)
CPINDEX4	−0.2357	−0.1492	0.0941	−0.7112	−0.4591	−0.2475
	(0.141)	(0.094)	(0.063)	(2.647)	(1.708)	(0.951)
Intercept	−9.9322	−12.6901	−15.2391			
	(1.122)	(1.500)	(1.933)			
R^2	0.1529	0.2258	0.3274			
Private-Sector Employment Variables Only:						
ln(wage)	−1.7999	−2.1009	−2.3492	0.5851	−0.6158	−1.1665
	(54.753)	(69.612)	(89.930)	(14.560)	(13.786)	(36.490)
LNWGMSAP	−0.0107	−0.1744	−0.3908	0.9715	−0.6615	−1.5646
	(0.004)	(0.072)	(0.173)	(3.331)	(2.252)	(5.550)
LNWGMINP	0.0081	0.1898	0.3724	−0.8464	0.6705	1.5024
	(0.003)	(0.078)	(0.165)	(2.988)	(2.352)	(5.487)
CPINDEX1	1.7132	1.6165	1.4300	0.0861	0.7918	0.9785
	(1.052)	(1.038)	(0.985)	(0.182)	(1.674)	(2.140)
CPINDEX2	0.3195	0.4439	0.6762	−0.0671	−0.1480	−0.1368
	(0.141)	(0.204)	(0.334)	(0.185)	(0.409)	(0.391)
CPINDEX3	0.0093	−0.0356	−0.2382	−0.4480	0.9704	1.6925
	(0.004)	(0.016)	(0.115)	(0.952)	(2.056)	(3.717)
CPINDEX4	0.9069	1.3626	1.8866	−0.5254	−0.3091	−0.1676
	(0.503)	(0.791)	(1.174)	(1.436)	(0.844)	(0.473)
Intercept	−7.3339	−8.7281	−9.6065			
	(4.458)	(5.551)	(5.558)			
R^2	0.1527	0.2256	0.3272			

Appendix Table A4.11(3) (*continued*)

Model, Variable	Pooled OLS Estimates			Fixed-Effects Estimates		
	Maximum	Mean	Minimum	Maximum	Mean	Minimum
Both Time Trend and Private-Sector Employment Variables:						
ln(wage)	−1.8014	−2.1028	−2.3512	0.6006	−0.6459	−1.1954
	(54.778)	(69.649)	(89.980)	(14.730)	(14.160)	(37.006)
TIMETRND	0.7508	0.9106	1.0100	−0.0811	0.3226	0.5031
	(1.466)	(1.859)	(2.213)	(0.983)	(3.883)	(6.314)
TIMETRSQ	−1.4173	−1.7373	−1.9471	0.2296	−0.5537	−0.9075
	(1.581)	(2.027)	(2.437)	(1.541)	(3.692)	(6.316)
LNWGMSAP	0.2084	0.1506	0.0353	0.5173	−0.5659	−1.1791
	(0.080)	(0.061)	(0.015)	(1.593)	(1.737)	(3.754)
LNWGMINP	−0.2897	−0.2070	−0.1072	−0.5072	0.5546	1.1458
	(0.113)	(0.085)	(0.047)	(1.674)	(1.825)	(3.910)
CPINDEX1	1.3439	1.3353	1.3029	−0.2322	0.2815	0.3848
	(0.545)	(0.566)	(0.593)	(0.459)	(0.557)	(0.788)
CPINDEX2	0.4072	0.5808	0.8619	−0.3378	−0.2748	−0.1849
	(0.178)	(0.265)	(0.422)	(0.903)	(0.734)	(0.511)
CPINDEX3	0.0266	0.0526	−0.0658	−0.4262	0.5462	1.0473
	(0.011)	(0.023)	(0.030)	(0.882)	(1.128)	(2.241)
CPINDEX4	−0.3667	−0.2425	0.0390	−0.5698	−0.6137	−0.5865
	(0.186)	(0.129)	(0.022)	(1.520)	(1.637)	(1.618)
Intercept	−9.5458	−12.4247	−14.8288			
	(0.954)	(1.299)	(1.664)			
R^2	0.1529	0.2258	0.3274			

5

Comparable Worth in San José Municipal Government Employment

In this chapter, I discuss the experience of San José, California, with comparable worth. As part of the two-year contract that settled a July 1981 municipal employees' strike, the city agreed to adjust pay for certain predominantly female city jobs along the lines suggested by a Hay Associates job evaluation. Subsequent contracts included additional adjustments. The workers' union, Local 101 of the American Federation of State, County and Municipal Employees (AFSCME), maintained that the 1981–83 contract did not provide equal pay for jobs of comparable worth in all respects (Bureau of National Affairs 1981, esp. p. 35). There do appear to have been significant changes in pay along comparable worth lines, however.

5.1 *Background*

San José, the seat of Santa Clara County, is located to the south of San Francisco. With a population of over 650,000, it is the fourth largest city in California and the fourteenth largest in the United States. San José is the unofficial capital of the "Silicon Valley," the heartland of the computer industry (San José Chamber of Commerce 1983).

San José's municipal employment runs the gamut of occupational

I am very grateful to Russell P. Strausbaugh of the San José Personnel Department for supplying me with numerous documents pertaining to San José's experience with comparable worth (including, in particular, the class listings that form the basis for the empirical studies described here); and to Shulamit Kahn for supplying additional documents and for helpful discussions. I thank Paul Decker, Ronald G. Ehrenberg, M. Anne Hill, Cordelia Reimers and participants in seminars at Indiana University, Johns Hopkins University and Princeton University for many helpful comments on previous versions of this chapter.

categories: from painter and police officer to aircraft refueler and architect; from secretary and stock clerk to senior plant mechanic and senior planner. Roughly 1500 city workers are uniformed firefighters or police; 500 are blue-collar workers represented by various craft unions and the Operating Engineers; approximately 2800 are represented by AFSCME Local 101; there are about 400 nonunion managerial employees.

Various factors led up to the 1981 strike and subsequent comparable worth pay adjustments to the city's compensation structure.[1] At the time of the strike, seven of the eleven City Council members were women, including the mayor, Janet Gray Hayes, who described San José as the "feminist capital of the world." Local 101 drew many of its leaders from workers in predominantly female jobs (e.g., the city's librarians, clerical workers and recreation specialists), who had long been concerned with women's issues, including comparable worth. In 1977, a group of female city employees, City Women for Advancement, presented a report to the City Council that advocated (among other things) paying women's jobs on the basis of an "equity standard" rather than their "normal value in the market place" (Farnquist et al. 1983, p. 359). The following year, Local 101's contract proposal included a request for a study of sex differences in pay in the city's workforce.

As collective bargaining began in 1978, however, the city government "had no desire to explore the . . . comparable worth concept" (Farnquist et al. 1983, p. 359); and in June 1978 California voters approved Proposition 13. Proposition 13, and "bail-out" legislation passed to implement it, set stringent limits on spending by California municipalities. Bargaining in San José ground to a halt. In April 1979, however, the California State Supreme Court struck down some of the key parts of the bail-out legislation. Bargaining in San José resumed, but not to the satisfaction of comparable worth proponents. Local 101 pointed out that the new city manager, James Alloway, had commissioned Hay Associates to conduct a study of management positions in order to establish an equitable management compensation system. Local 101 insisted on a similar study of nonmanagement positions. Alloway resisted, telling the City Council that "it was his professional opinion that the Hay system of job evaluation was not appropriate for setting salaries for [nonmanagement] employees, and that salaries for [such] employees should be set through the traditional collective bargaining process" (Farnquist et al. 1983, p. 360).

Local 101 was not slow to respond. In the words of Maxine Jenkins, the union's business agent at the time, in April 1979

> . . . we pulled a wildcat sickout of the women in City Hall. And I refused to sign a contract until we got the city manager to agree in writing that he would conduct an outside scientific study [of nonmanagement employees] in which we would have the right to participate. And he agreed to that, in writing. (Hutner 1986, p. 72.)

Eventually, the parties agreed that Hay Associates would be retained to perform such a study.

Agreement on *how* the study would be conducted was at least as important as agreement on whether it would be conducted; and here, too, the union ultimately prevailed on two crucial points. First, the union insisted on having a strong voice on the committee charged with actually assigning points to the jobs being evaluated. In the words of Local 101 president Mike Ferrero:

> Personnel and management resisted that with everything they had. But we fought it on a political level and the council eventually said, "If we're going to do this, this has got to be fair." And so an evaluation committee was put together with one person from personnel, who would have a vote, and the rest of the voting members were employees who were chosen jointly by management and the unions involved—there were a number of other unions, but AFSCME was much the largest. So we had a lot of input on that evaluation committee. (Hutner 1983, p. 84.)

The resulting evaluation committee consisted of one management employee and nine nonmanagement employees "chosen in a manner to maximize their representativeness across departments and employee groups" (Farnquist et al. 1983, p. 361).

Second, the union also insisted that the study be concerned only with internal pay equity, with no dollar valuation of Haypoints for jobs by relating them to the external market, and no written recommendations from the consultants (Hutner 1983, p. 84). Again, the union prevailed; each job was evaluated according to four "evaluation factors"—know-how, problem solving, accountability and working conditions—with points assigned to each. These point scores were then summed to arrive at a total "Haypoint" score, representing an "overall measure of the job's value to the organization and to allow for direct comparisons of different jobs' relative organizational worth" (Farnquist et al. 1983, p. 361); pay rates prevailing in other jurisdictions were not considered in the evaluation. In the words of the Hay Associates "Client Briefing" (Hay Associates 1981, p. 2) on the study:

> The City of San José as an employer, and the AFSCME local representing employees, each agreed to establish a "leading edge" posture on the issue of comparable worth.... The Hay Guide Chart-Profile Method of job measurement...[is] the appropriate methodology to rank jobs within the city organization without reference to the particular incumbents, external markets or how the results might be interpreted.

As soon as it was released in December 1980, the study set off a furor. According to Prudence Slaathaug, a business agent for Local 101 at the time:

> ...it was, in fact, absolute dynamite. People had it Xeroxed and routed through the city in about five minutes.... It was *the* topic of conversation. And, of course, they found the incredible inequities that had been reported all over the country. (Hutner 1983, p. 83.)

In the words of three San José personnel officials:

> Individual comparisons between specific male and female-dominated [job] classes, particularly in the media, became a popular and often emotional pastime. Should, for instance, a female dominated class like Senior Librarian...[with] 493 points and $900 [biweekly salary]...be paid the same as a mixed class like Senior Chemist (493 [points] and $1100 [biweekly salary]) with the same rating value? Or should a female-dominated Typist Clerk II (140

> points, $550 [biweekly salary]) class be paid the same as the equally valued but male-dominated Aircraft Refueler (140 points, $729 [biweekly salary]) or Automotive Equipment Inspector (140 points, $827 [biweekly salary])? (Farnquist et al. 1983, p. 363.)

Nor were these merely isolated examples. As discussed below, the study documented a pervasive pattern of "underpayment" of predominantly female jobs relative to predominantly male jobs with similar Haypoint scores. Union officials argued that this pointed to the presence of "discrimination, pure and simple," in the city's pay structure; city administrators argued that "the study did not take into account other productivity-related sex differences and sex-linked personal tastes for certain kinds of jobs" (Farnquist et al. 1983, p. 363). After several months of debate along these lines, the city administration and Local 101 began formal negotiations on the study in May 1981.

In principle, the parties could have agreed to assign pay to each job exclusively on the basis of its Haypoint score. That, however, would have entailed substantial cuts in pay for some jobs, most of them predominantly male jobs with pay rates in excess of the figure implied by the overall "trend line" linking pay and Haypoints; and neither side "considered for a minute the notion of cutting anyone's pay, since by doing so the city would have placed itself in a noncompetitive position" (Farnquist et al. 1983, p. 364). The union instead argued for raising the pay of all jobs below the trend line and preserving the pay of jobs at or above the trend line; whereas the city offered special "salary equity adjustments" for predominantly-female jobs that would have narrowed the disparities identified by the Hay study.

On June 12, 1981, the U.S. Supreme Court issued its decision in *County of Washington, Oregon, et al. v. Gunther et al.* (452 U.S. 967 (1981)). Although the Court stressed that it was not judging the merits of comparable worth, its decision appeared to open the door to comparable worth lawsuits under Title VII of the Civil Rights Act. Frustrated by what it considered to be lack of progress in their negotiations with the city, on June 18 AFSCME filed a complaint against the city with the U.S. Equal Employment Opportunity Commission (EEOC), alleging that although both the city and the union accepted the results of the Hay study, the city continued to pay "discriminatory" salaries. The city administration accused the union of bargaining in bad faith; negotiations bogged down. Finally, on July 5, the union went out on strike.

It was hardly a conventional strike. In the words of the business agent for Local 101 at the time, Bill Callahan, it was "the first strike on the issue of sex-based wage discrimination," which made it a "media event," attracting reporters from as far away as Canada and England (Hutner 1983, p. 91). Sally Reed, deputy city manager during the strike, noted that officials at the California and local chambers of commerce, business groups, and other municipalities were putting "a lot of pressure" on the city administration to resist the union (Hutner 1983, p. 90).

The major obstacle to an agreement was apparently the question of how to pay for the comparable worth pay adjustments sought by the union. According to Local 101 president Ferrero (quoted in Hutner 1986, p. 92), the city attempted to play the union's male and female members off against each other:

> They would give us comparable worth but they were going to make us pay for it out of the general salary increases of all the other members in our units. And they couldn't understand why we didn't think that was fair. You don't give pay equity on one hand and then take it away on the other, in a general wage increase.

Eventually, in time-honored fashion, the parties struck a compromise, one "that had little to do with an objective, systematic job evaluation system" (Farnquist et al. 1983, p. 365). The 1981–83 contract agreed to on July 14, 1981 provided for general salary increases of 7.5 percent during the first year of the contract and 8.0 percent during the second; and for two sets of "special equity adjustments," effective July 1981 and August 1982, for female-dominated jobs farthest below the salary-Haypoint trend line.

As part of the 1981 settlement, the city agreed to bargain over further comparable worth pay adjustments in subsequent contracts. The 1983–84 contract provided for two further adjustments, in July 1983 and January 1984; the 1984–86 contract included one additional adjustment, in July 1984.[2] Finally, the 1986–89 contract provided for two more small adjustments, effective June 1986 and June 1987.

In what follows, I consider the effects of these changes in the city's pay structure. Did they alter the relation between pay and Haypoints? Did they erase, or at least reduce, the sex differential in pay between female and male jobs with similar Haypoint values? Did they affect male and female jobs' pay differently? Did they affect employment in female or male jobs?

5.2 *Data*

This chapter's analyses of wage and employment effects of San José's experience with comparable worth are based on two kinds of data. Unfortunately, each provides only limited information and covers only a limited time period. First, the Hay study of nonmanagement jobs (Stackhouse 1980) provides data on Haypoints ("job grade points"), the maximum biweekly salary rate, working conditions ratings and sex composition of 229 full-time job classifications as of November 14, 1980. Nine "class listings"–computer printouts, prepared for internal administrative purposes, showing the maximum biweekly salary rate of each job classification–for distinct dates during 1980–88 are a second source of information. Eight of these class listings also indicate, for each job classification, the number of positions authorized and filled as of the relevant date.[3] Since all data refer to jobs ("classifications"), the analyses of this chapter are similar to the class-level analyses presented in chapter 4.

Many of the 229 jobs evaluated in the 1980 Hay study were not filled at any point during the period 1981–88. The studies in this chapter are concerned only with the 160 jobs that not only (1) were evaluated in the 1980 Hay study but also (2) had at least one incumbent throughout 1981–88.[4] One other aspect of the data on jobs worth noting at the outset is that in some cases the same job appears in the class listings in several different places; in these cases, I have combined all incumbents into one job.[5]

Tables 5.1–2 give definitions and summary statistics, respectively, for the variables derived from these sources used in the analyses of this chapter. The data do not indicate the actual proportion of employees in each classification (job) who were of either sex. Instead, each classification is categorized as either "predominantly female," "predominantly male" or "heterosexual" (i.e., neither predominantly female nor predominantly male); I refer to these as "female," "male" or "mixed." Of the 160 classifications considered in the analyses, 101 (about 63 percent) were male and 41 (about 26 percent) were female. About 39 percent of the male jobs are assessed as having relatively adverse working conditions (i.e., had WRKCON3 or WRKCON4 equal to unity), whereas none of the female jobs are. Also, the average Haypoint rating is somewhat higher for the male jobs (about 218 Haypoints) than for the female jobs (about 202 Haypoints).

The last part of table 5.2 also summarizes the seven comparable worth wage adjustments, as given in the collective bargaining agreements between the city and Local 101. The contracts express the pay adjustments made for the different jobs in terms of "salary range movements," where one salary range movement is equivalent to a pay increase of about 0.5 percent.[6] A small number of predominantly male jobs received increases in the sixth and seventh set of adjustments (none received increases in any of the first five adjustments), but, not surprisingly, most of the adjustments were made to predominantly female jobs. The first and second adjustments made relatively large changes on a relatively large scale. For example, the first set of adjustments made changes to the pay of over three-fourths of the female jobs; those receiving an adjustment were moved an average of about 9.6 salary ranges (so that, overall – including jobs that received no adjustment – pay of female jobs changed by about 7.24 salary ranges, on average). The remaining adjustments were smaller in magnitude and less widespread. For example, the final set of adjustments changed pay of about 56 percent of the female jobs by an average of about 2.8 salary ranges (entailing an overall average change, among all female jobs, of about 1.6 salary ranges).

Finally, in the longitudinal analyses discussed in sections 5.4–5 below, I have used variables pertaining to the state of the private-sector economy in the San José Metropolitan Statistical Area (MSA). These

Table 5.1 Definition of Variables Used in the Analyses

Variable	Definition
MAX_SAL	maximum biweekly salary rate of job
LMAXSAL	natural logarithm of MAX_SAL
NUMFILL	number of incumbents in job
LNUMFIL	natural logarithm of LNUMFILL
Sex Composition Dummies	
JOBMALE	indicator: job is predominantly male
JOB_FEM	indicator: job is predominantly female
JOB_MIX	indicator: job is "mixed"
JOB_UNK	indicator: sex composition of incumbents in job is unknown
Working Conditions Dummies	
WRKCON0	indicator: job's working conditions least unpleasant
WRKCON1	indicator: job's working conditions second-least unpleasant
WRKCON2	indicator: job's working conditions third-least unpleasant
WRKCON3	indicator: job's working conditions fourth-least unpleasant
WRKCON4	indicator: job's working conditions most unpleasant
Haypoint Variables	
HAY_PTS	Haypoint rating (evaluation points) of job $\times 0.01$
HAYPTSQ	square of HAY_PTS (Haypoint rating, squared, times 0.0001)
Environmental Variables	
TIMEVAR	time trend term (increases by one unit per year; =0 as of 1/1/60)
TIMEVSQ	square of TIMEVAR
LNAVWGP	ln of private-sector wages, San José MSA
LNWGPSQ	square of LNAVWGP
LN_EMPP	ln of private-sector employment, San José MSA
LNEMPSQ	square of LN_EMPP
Comparable Worth Variables	
AFTRCW1	indicator: date is on or after 7/19/81 (first comparable worth pay adjustments)
FTIMEAF	=0 if before 7/19/81; =1 if after 6/28/87 (last comparable worth pay adjustments); otherwise, =fraction of time between first and last comparable worth pay adjustments elapsed between 7/19/81 and current date
FTIMESQ	square of FTIMEAF
ADJCHG*a*	number of salary range movements given to job pursuant to *a*th comparable worth wage adjustments, $a=1-7$, through current date (dates of comparable worth wage adjustments: 7/19/81; 8/15/82; 7/3/83; 1/1/84; 7/1/84; 6/29/86; 6/28/87)
ADJ_CUM	cumulative number of salary range movements given to job through current date (sum of ADJCHG1–ADJCHG7 as of current date)

Table 5.2 Means and Standard Deviations of Variables Used in the Analyses

	All Jobs (n=160)		Female Jobs (n=41)		Male Jobs (n=101)	
Variable	**Mean**	**Std. Dev.**	**Mean**	**Std. Dev.**	**Mean**	**Std. Dev.**
Time-Invariant Variables:						
JOBMALE	0.6312	0.4839	0.0000	0.0000	1.0000	0.0000
JOB_FEM	0.2562	0.4379	1.0000	0.0000	0.0000	0.0000
JOB_MIX	0.0812	0.2740	0.0000	0.0000	0.0000	0.0000
JOB_UNK	0.0312	0.1745	0.0000	0.0000	0.0000	0.0000
WRKCON0	0.4250	0.4958	0.8292	0.3809	0.2277	0.4214
WRKCON1	0.1187	0.3245	0.1463	0.3578	0.0693	0.2552
WRKCON2	0.2000	0.4012	0.0243	0.1561	0.3069	0.4635
WRKCON3	0.1500	0.3581	0.0000	0.0000	0.2376	0.4277
WRKCON4	0.1062	0.3091	0.0000	0.0000	0.1584	0.3669
HAY_PTS	2.1941	0.8328	2.0151	0.8038	2.1771	0.8108
HAYPTSQ	5.5035	4.2562	4.6911	4.3077	5.3908	4.0485
Time-Varying Variables:						
July 25, 1980:						
NUMFILL	.	.	.	.	.	.
LNUMFIL	.	.	.	.	.	.
MAX_SAL	773.6250	197.5075	621.5024	113.6567	814.8514	172.9035
LMAXSAL	6.6202	0.2474	6.4166	0.1760	6.6804	0.2143
TIMEVAR	19.5783	0.0000	19.5783	0.0000	19.5783	0.0000
LNAVWGP	7.2189	0.0000	7.2189	0.0000	7.2189	0.0000
LN_EMPP	14.3899	0.0000	14.3899	0.0000	14.3899	0.0000
AFTRCW1	0.0000	0.0000	0.0000	0.0000	0.0000	0.0000
FTIMEAF	0.0000	0.0000	0.0000	0.0000	0.0000	0.0000
October 17, 1981:						
NUMFILL	12.1312	17.2434	16.8536	22.3187	11.7128	15.8090
LNUMFIL	1.7604	1.2205	2.1170	1.2639	1.7444	1.2166
MAX_SAL	928.3575	226.0659	771.0634	135.0299	976.9425	226.6800
LMAXSAL	6.8056	0.2344	6.6333	0.1702	6.8594	0.2223
TIMEVAR	21.7932	0.0000	21.7932	0.0000	21.7932	0.0000
LNAVWGP	7.3614	0.0000	7.3614	0.0000	7.3614	0.0000
LN_EMPP	14.4505	0.0000	14.4505	0.0000	14.4505	0.0000
AFTRCW1	1.0000	0.0000	1.0000	0.0000	1.0000	0.0000
FTIMEAF	0.0414	0.0000	0.0414	0.0000	0.0000	0.0000
October 22, 1988:						
NUMFILL	14.0625	19.4081	21.4878	27.1966	12.7524	16.0657
LNUMFIL	1.8868	1.2537	2.2416	1.4361	1.8819	1.1756
MAX_SAL	1338.5925	318.9523	1161.2000	211.0815	1388.0237	319.7562
LMAXSAL	7.1715	0.2368	7.0413	0.1799	7.2089	0.2337
TIMEVAR	28.8076	0.0000	28.8076	0.0000	28.8076	0.0000
LNAVWGP	7.7954	0.0000	7.7954	0.0000	7.7954	0.0000
LN_EMPP	14.6060	0.0000	14.6060	0.0000	14.6060	0.0000
AFTRCW1	1.0000	0.0000	1.0000	0.0000	1.0000	0.0000
FTIMEAF	1.0000	0.0000	1.0000	0.0000	1.0000	0.0000

Table 5.2 *(continued)*

Variable	All Jobs ($n=160$) Mean	All Jobs ($n=160$) Std. Dev.	Female Jobs ($n=41$) Mean	Female Jobs ($n=41$) Std. Dev.	Male Jobs ($n=101$) Mean	Male Jobs ($n=101$) Std. Dev.
Comparable Worth Pay Adjustments:						
ADJCHG1	2.0375	4.3767	7.2439	5.5622	0.0000	0.0000
ADJGOT1	0.2125	0.4103	0.7560	0.4347	0.0000	0.0000
ADJAMT1	9.5882	4.2076	9.5806	4.2565	.	.
ADJCHG2	2.0000	4.2986	7.1219	5.4872	0.0000	0.0000
ADJGOT2	0.2125	0.4103	0.7560	0.4347	0.0000	0.0000
ADJAMT2	9.4117	4.1422	9.4193	4.2172	.	.
ADJCHG3	0.3562	0.9990	1.2439	1.6090	0.0000	0.0000
ADJGOT3	0.1500	0.3581	0.5121	0.5060	0.0000	0.0000
ADJAMT3	2.3750	1.3772	2.4285	1.4687	.	.
ADJCHG4	0.4812	1.2181	1.6585	1.8249	0.0000	0.0000
ADJGOT4	0.1625	0.3700	0.5609	0.5024	0.0000	0.0000
ADJAMT4	2.9615	1.3410	2.9565	1.4295	.	.
ADJCHG5	0.7250	1.7731	2.6585	2.5749	0.0000	0.0000
ADJGOT5	0.1625	0.3700	0.5853	0.4987	0.0000	0.0000
ADJAMT5	4.4615	1.6304	4.5416	1.6145	.	.
ADJCHG6	0.5250	1.1972	1.7073	1.6769	0.1188	0.5879
ADJGOT6	0.1750	0.3811	0.5609	0.5024	0.0396	0.1959
ADJAMT6	3.0000	0.8606	3.0434	0.9282	3.0000	0.0000
ADJCHG7	0.4812	1.0987	1.5609	1.5337	0.1089	0.5459
ADJGOT7	0.1750	0.3811	0.5609	0.5024	0.0396	0.1959
ADJAMT7	2.7500	0.7993	2.7826	0.8504	2.7500	0.5000

NOTE: Means for ADJCHGa, $a=1$–7, give the mean number of salary range increments awarded to jobs (*including* jobs that received *no* increment) under the ath comparable worth pay adjustment. Means for ADJGOTa, $a=1$–7, give the proportion of jobs receiving a salary range increment under the ath adjustment. Means for ADJAMTa, $a=1$–7, give the mean number of salary range increments awarded to jobs that received an increment (*excluding* jobs that received *no* increment) under the ath adjustment.

were derived from the Bureau of Labor Statistics ES–202 data file in the same way as were the analogous variables for private-sector wages and employment used in the analyses of chapter 4 (see section 4.2 and section 3.4 for further discussion).

Since this chapter is concerned with comparable worth-induced changes in wages and employment, it is useful to begin by noting what the simple descriptive statistics in table 5.2 imply about trends in these variables for male and female jobs. In October 1981 (the first date for which employment data are available), the mean maximum biweekly salary rates in the 101 male and 41 female jobs were about $977 and $771, respectively, whereas mean employment levels per job were about 11.7 and 16.9, respectively. In contrast, as of October 1988, mean salaries were about $1388 and $1161 and mean employment levels were about 12.8 and 21.5 in the 101 male and 41 female jobs, respectively. Thus, between October 1981 and October 1988, mean pay grew by about 42.1 percent and 50.6 percent whereas employment grew by about 8.9 percent and 27.5 percent, respectively, for male and female jobs; even though women's jobs enjoyed faster wage growth, they also enjoyed faster employment growth.

5.3 *Cross-Section Analyses: Sex Differentials in Hourly Pay, 1981 and 1988*

I begin with cross-section analyses of pay using the data for July 25, 1980, and October 22, 1988. These two dates are respectively the first and last dates for which wage data are available: the first precedes the first of the strike-induced comparable worth pay adjustments, whereas the last comes after the final comparable worth adjustments, made in the 1986–89 contract. The dependent variable is the natural logarithm of a job's maximum biweekly salary rate, LMAXSAL; the independent variables refer to the sex composition of the incumbents in the job (JOB_FEM, JOB_MIX, JOB_UNK), working conditions on the job (WRKCON1–WRKCON4), and Haypoint variables for the job (see table 5.1 for further details).

The sex composition variables implicitly take male jobs as a reference; the working conditions variables implicitly use jobs with the most pleasant (least unpleasant) working conditions – those with WRKCON0 = 1 – as a reference. (In both cases, choice of the reference category is arbitrary and will not affect the results.) Finally, the analyses enter each job's Haypoints in quadratic form to allow for the possibility that pay rises with Haypoints at a decreasing rate (see note 11 in chapter 4).

The results of these analyses appear in table 5.3. The first pair of columns refers to all 160 jobs; the second, to the 101 male jobs; the third, to the 41 female jobs. The first column in each pair gives results for July 1980; the second, for October 1988. The regressions alternately exclude and then include the Haypoint variables (HAY_PTS and HAY-PTSQ); I focus on the results obtained when these variables are included.

Estimates for all jobs

First, consider the results for all jobs as of July 1980. These indicate that, in general, less pleasant working conditions (as measured by the Hay study) are associated with higher pay, although the relation is weak: only the coefficient on WRKCON3 approaches significance at conventional levels. There is a very strong relation between pay and Haypoints: other things being equal, the higher a job's Haypoint rating, the higher its pay.[7]

Also, and of particular interest here, the results indicate that as of July 1980, before San José's comparable worth pay adjustments, predominantly female jobs were paid appreciably (about 20.2 percent) and statistically significantly (t=6.65) less than predominantly male jobs with the same working conditions and Haypoint score. For "mixed" jobs, the figure is smaller but still sizeable in absolute terms (implying about 7.4 percent lower pay for such jobs, on average, relative to predominantly male jobs with the same working conditions and Haypoints) and close to significance at conventional levels (t=1.78). As noted above, the city and the Local 101 debated about whether these differences are attributable to "discrimination, pure and simple"; but there is clearly no room for argument over whether they are substantial.

The second column in table 5.3 repeats the analysis for all 160 jobs for October 22, 1988, after all of the comparable worth adjustments had taken effect. The differential between "mixed" and predominantly male jobs as of October 1988 was about −6.3 percent (t=1.71), a relatively small decline from the 1980 figure. On the other hand, by 1988, the differential between predominantly female and predominantly male jobs was only about −10.2 percent (most of the reduction had occurred by

Table 5.3 Cross-Section Wage Regressions, 1980 and 1988 (dep. var. = LMAXSAL; *t*-statistics in parentheses)

	All Jobs (*n* = 160)		Male Jobs (*n* = 101)		Female Jobs (*n* = 41)	
Variable	**07/25/80**	**10/22/88**	**07/25/80**	**10/22/88**	**07/25/80**	**10/22/88**
Without Haypoint Variables:						
JOB_FEM	−0.3444	−0.2612				
	(7.310)	(5.342)				
JOB_MIX	−0.0421	−0.0283				
	(0.624)	(0.404)				
JOB_UNK	0.2202	0.1076				
	(2.308)	(1.086)				
WRKCON1	−0.2092	−0.2453	−0.2070	−0.2564	−0.1538	−0.1718
	(3.861)	(4.356)	(2.334)	(2.701)	(2.078)	(2.252)
WRKCON2	−0.1435	−0.1510	−0.1451	−0.1687	−0.2635	−0.1521
	(2.812)	(2.847)	(2.566)	(2.789)	(1.553)	(0.869)
WRKCON3	−0.1119	−0.1504	−0.1175	−0.1686		
	(2.009)	(2.599)	(1.960)	(2.628)		
WRKCON4	−0.1871	−0.2153	−0.2120	−0.2634		
	(3.079)	(3.410)	(3.169)	(3.680)		
Intercept	6.7952	7.3421	6.8008	7.3603	6.4456	7.0702
	(180.188)	(187.369)	(158.719)	(160.542)	(224.831)	(239.204)
Adj. R^2	0.341	0.223	0.081	0.115	0.098	0.083
With Haypoint Variables:						
JOB_FEM	−0.2021	−0.1017				
	(6.654)	(3.761)				
JOB_MIX	−0.0738	−0.0632				
	(1.780)	(1.712)				
JOB_UNK	0.1239	0.0002				
	(2.112)	(0.004)				
WRKCON1	−0.0185	−0.0329	0.0237	−0.0093	−0.0331	−0.0184
	(0.524)	(1.043)	(0.445)	(0.163)	(0.667)	(0.861)
WRKCON2	0.0005	0.0107	0.0180	0.0050	−0.1693	−0.0349
	(0.017)	(0.366)	(0.494)	(0.130)	(1.628)	(0.780)
WKRCON3	0.0763	0.0608	0.0907	0.0534		
	(2.080)	(1.862)	(2.260)	(1.249)		
WRKCON4	0.0106	0.0064	0.0197	−0.0161		
	(0.268)	(0.183)	(0.448)	(0.343)		
HAY_PTS	0.5010	0.5516	0.5621	0.6085	0.3768	0.4876
	(7.873)	(9.737)	(6.660)	(6.764)	(4.140)	(12.429)
HAYPTSQ	−0.0585	−0.0637	−0.0690	−0.0753	−0.0409	−0.0548
	(4.734)	(5.784)	(3.987)	(4.082)	(2.445)	(7.612)
Intercept	5.8865	6.3347	5.7967	6.2789	5.8580	6.3194
	(72.694)	(87.868)	(59.337)	(60.298)	(51.809)	(129.672)
Adj. R^2	0.753	0.786	0.700	0.714	0.665	0.941

1983). Although this is sizable and statistically significant ($t=3.76$), it is only about half of the 1980 figure. Interestingly, the relation between Haypoint score and pay in these results for 1988 is about the same as it is in the 1980 results.[8]

Estimates for male and female jobs

The second and third pairs of columns in table 5.3 present analogous results for male and female jobs, respectively. Here the most noteworthy differences between 1980 and 1988 have to do with the regression intercepts and implied effects of (greater) Haypoints. Both intercepts rose, but the *difference* in intercepts changed very little: the male intercept rose by 0.48 (from about 5.80 to about 6.28), whereas the female intercept rose by 0.46 (from about 5.86 to about 6.32). In contrast, whereas for male jobs the pay gain associated with 10 extra Haypoints changed only slightly—from about 2.52 percent in 1980 to about 2.71 percent in 1988—the gain for female jobs rose from about 1.94 percent to about 2.42 percent between 1980 and 1988.[9] Thus, although San José's pay adjustments did not result in exactly equal pay for jobs of "comparable worth," these cross-section analyses do raise the question of whether the adjustments did at least reduce substantially the sex differentials in pay among jobs with similar Haypoint values—e.g., by raising the pay gain associated with Haypoints among female jobs to move it closer to the gain prevailing among male jobs.

Although these analyses refer to a "fixed market basket" (i.e., the same set of jobs) over time, however, simply taking the difference between the sex differentials in pay at successive dates does not necessarily disentangle comparable worth effects from other changes that went on during the same period. For example, the change in the JOB_FEM coefficient between 1980 and 1988 in table 5.3's results for all jobs is not necessarily due exclusively to San José's comparable worth pay adjustments: some of the change may have been the result of local labor market conditions, e.g., growing demand (and hence higher wages) for predominantly female jobs such as clerical positions.

5.4 *Longitudinal Analyses: Changes in the Sex Differential in Pay, 1980–88*

To analyze how pay rates changed as a result of the comparable worth pay adjustments, I now use estimates that exploit the longitudinal nature of the data. Data with information on wages are available for 10 dates (from July 14, 1980, to October 22, 1988: see section 5.2); thus the fixed effects analyses of wages have $101 \times 10 = 1010$ observations and $41 \times 10 = 410$ observations for the 101 male and 41 female jobs, respectively. Unlike the cross-section analyses of the previous section, the longitudinal analyses of wages include three other kinds of variables.

First, to embody the environmental variables discussed in connection with equation (3.7), I use price variables (CPINDX1–4), time trend terms (TIMEVAR and its square, TIMEVSQ) and/or measures of private-sector wages in the San José Metropolitan Statistical Area (MSA) as of the relevant date (LNAVWGP and its square, LNWGPSQ). As in chapter 4, the price variables give the value of the Consumer Price Index for All Urban Consumers ("CPI-U") in the month immediately preceding the month referenced by the data (CPINDX1) or three, six or nine months prior to that. Like the TIMETRND variable of chapter 4, TIMEVAR measures the number of years elapsed since January 1, 1960, and increases by one unit per year. LNAVWGP is analogous to the private-sector wage variables LNWGMSAP and LNWGMINP of chapter 4, and is derived in the same way from the ES–202 data. Second, as noted below, I include alternative specifications of the comparable worth variable C_{it} of equation (3.7).

Comparable worth variables

A review of section 5.2 indicates some of the difficulties inherent in disentangling changes in pay induced by comparable worth from changes in pay that would have occurred even in the absence of the comparable worth wage adjustments. The first problem is that, as a source of before-and-after comparisons, the data are quite limited: data are available for only ten dates during 1980–88; only two of these ten dates come before the city's first comparable worth adjustment of July 19, 1981; and only two more fall after June 28, 1987 (when the last such adjustment occurred). The second problem is that the variables in the data do not vary both cross-sectionally and over time (except those, discussed below, referring to the comparable worth pay adjustments themselves). On the one hand, as noted in table 5.2, the available information on jobs' working conditions, Haypoint ratings and (initial) sex composition is time-invariant; thus these variables drop out of a fixed-effects analysis, and in any case can shed no light on changes over time. On the other hand, the environmental variables (the time trend and private-sector wage and employment variables) vary over time but not cross-sectionally. In a setting of this kind, identifying two separate phenomena occurring over time— comparable worth effects and other effects—using data for a small number of dates will inevitably prove difficult.

These limitations dictate very simple specifications of the comparable worth variable C_{it}. As noted in chapter 3, the specifications are of two kinds: in the first, C_{it} is a function of time alone, and simply indicates whether comparable worth was "in force" as of time t and thus able to affect pay of any job i; in the second, C_{it} varies cross-sectionally as well as over time, and indicates whether (and to what extent) each job i was targeted for a comparable worth pay adjustment as of time t.[10]

C_{it} as a function of time alone. The first version of C_{it} treats the comparable worth effect on wages as a function of time alone, as embodied by two different specifications. In the first or "dummy" specification, C_{it} is a simple indicator variable AFTRCW1, equal to unity for all dates after the first set of comparable worth wage adjustments (July 19, 1981) and zero otherwise. This treats the comparable worth adjustments as equivalent to a once-and-for-all change in the level of wages.

A second or "quadratic" specification uses not only AFTRCW1 but also two continuous variables, FTIMEAF and FTIMESQ. As shown in figure 5.1 (which, for purposes of illustration, abstracts from all other factors that might affect wages, e.g., secular and cyclical effects), this provides a quadratic approximation to the pattern of comparable worth pay adjustments that occurred during July 19, 1981–June 28, 1987. Specifically, FTIMEAF is equal to zero for the two dates (July 25, 1980, and November 14, 1980) prior to the first set of wage adjustments (July 19, 1981); is equal to unity for the two dates (August 1, 1987, and October 22, 1988) after the last set of adjustments (which occurred on June 28, 1987); and, for the remaining six intermediate dates, is equal to the time elapsed between the current date and the first set of adjustments (July 19, 1981) as a fraction of the entire period of adjustments (July 19, 1981–June 28, 1987). FTIMESQ is simply the square of FTIMEAF.[11] Thus, in this quadratic specification, the coefficient on AFTRCW1 (the b_0 of figure 5.1) reflects the initial shift in pay rates that occurred with the first set of wage adjustments; whereas the coefficients on FTIMEAF and FTIMESQ (the b_1 and b_2 of figure 5.1, respectively) represent the effects of subsequent adjustments through the end of the period considered. Since both FTIMEAF and FTIMESQ equal unity as of the end of the period of pay adjustments, the final or cumulative effect of the adjustments is given by the sum of the coefficients on AFTRCW1, FTIMEAF and FTIMESQ.

C_{it} as a function of targeting. The second version of the comparable worth variable indicates the extent to which each job was targeted for a comparable worth wage increase as of time t, based on the number of salary range movements provided for each job under the comparable worth wage adjustments. Thus, this second version of the comparable worth variable varies not only over time but also cross-sectionally.

In the wage analyses described below, I use two specifications of this version of C_{it}. In the first, C_{it} for each job as of a given date is represented by seven variables, ADJCHG1–ADJCHG7, where ADJCHGa, $a=1$–7, is the number of salary range movements given to that job pursuant to the ath comparable worth wage adjustment as of the relevant date.[12] The second specification of this version of C_{it}, ADJ_CUM, denotes the cumulative number of salary range movements given to each job as of the relevant date; i.e., the sum of the ADJCHGa, $a=1$–7, as of the same date.[13]

There are obvious limitations to each of these specifications. As noted

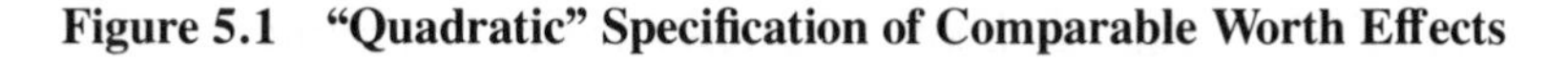

Figure 5.1 "Quadratic" Specification of Comparable Worth Effects

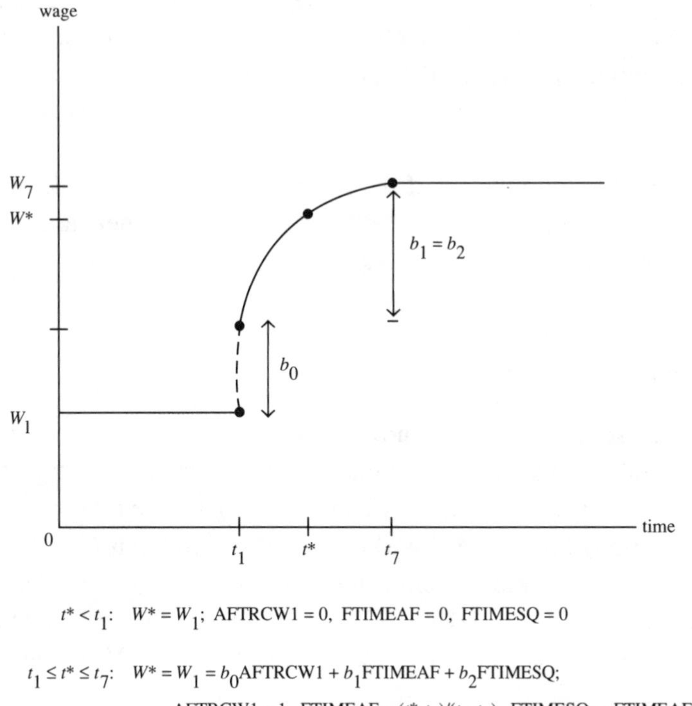

$t^* < t_1$: $W^* = W_1$; AFTRCW1 = 0, FTIMEAF = 0, FTIMESQ = 0

$t_1 \leq t^* \leq t_7$: $W^* = W_1 = b_0$AFTRCW1 + b_1FTIMEAF + b_2FTIMESQ;
AFTRCW1 = 1, FTIMEAF = $(t^*\text{-}t_1)/(t_7\text{-}t_1)$, FTIMESQ = FTIMEAF^2

$t^* > t_7$: $W^* = W_1 = b_0 + b_1 + b_2$; AFTRCW1 = 1, FTIMEAF = 1, FTIMESQ = 1

t_1 = beginning of comparable worth pay adjustments

t_7 = end of comparable worth pay adjustments

in chapter 3, specifying C_{it} as a function of targeting may entail problems of endogeneity (for example, C_{it} defined in this way may not be independent of the regression error term). Fixed-effects estimation may avoid this problem to the extent that jobs are targeted for comparable worth wage increases because they are "chronically underpaid," provided being "chronically underpaid" can reasonably be regarded as a fixed effect. However, specifying C_{it} as a function of targeting also raises a conceptual issue: even in the absence of the endogeneity problem, adopting this specification of C_{it} means that one can estimate only the effect of comparable worth on targeted jobs *relative to nontargeted jobs*.

In contrast, as noted in chapter 3, specifying C_{it} as a function of time alone permits one—at least in principle—to estimate the average effect of comparable worth on pay *relative to what pay would have been in the absence of comparable worth*. It will soon become clear, however, that, given the limited number of dates for which data are available, distinguishing comparable worth effects per se from other influences on wages using a "time alone" version of C_{it} is not feasible here.

Fixed-effects estimates

With this as background, I now discuss fixed-effects wage regressions for female and male jobs as set out in table 5.4.[14] For each type of job, the results appear in groups. Columns (1)–(3) use the first or "dummy" specification of the "time alone" version of C_{it}; columns (4)–(5) use the second or "quadratic" specification. Columns (6)–(8) use the seven-variable (ADJCHG1–ADJCHG7) specification of the targeting version of C_{it}; columns (9)–(11) use the cumulative (ADJ_CUM) specification.

C_{it} as a function of time alone. The most striking feature of the results for both female and male jobs when C_{it} is specified as a function of time alone is their extreme variation. For example, for female jobs, the dummy specification with time-trend variables (column (1)) yields an implied comparable worth wage effect of 0.0505, whereas the quadratic specification with the same time-trend variables (column (4)) yields an effect of −1.4882! Similarly, the quadratic specification with private-sector wage variables (column (5)) implies a cumulative comparable worth wage *gain* of about 7.64 percent for *men* and a comparable worth wage *loss* of about 8.13 percent for *women*! Note also (recall note 14) that, since the available data refer to only ten dates, it is not feasible to include more than nine time-varying (but cross-sectionally invariant) regressors. This means, for example, that it is not possible to include both time trend and private-sector wage variables in the quadratic

Table 5.4 Fixed-Effects Wage Regressions, 1980–88 (dep. var. = LMAXSAL; *t*-statistics in parentheses)

Variable	(1)	(2)	(3)	(4)	(5)
			Female Jobs:		
AFTRCW1	0.0505	0.0442	−0.3653	−0.0808	0.1645
	(1.804)	(1.305)	(0.488)	(2.009)	(0.829)
FTIMEAF				−2.3311	−0.5530
				(1.868)	(1.313)
FTIMESQ				0.9237	0.3072
				(2.728)	(4.627)
CPINDX1	−0.3945	0.4432	−2.6270	−3.7910	−1.5105
	(0.854)	(1.223)	(3.513)	(1.361)	(0.955)
CPINDX2	−1.3204	−1.1290	14.4221	1.7885	−2.3530
	(2.286)	(1.713)	(0.777)	(1.488)	(0.829)
CPINDX3	1.3150	0.5525	−6.1358	−2.1078	−0.0611
	(3.156)	(1.094)	(0.945)	(1.594)	(0.090)
CPINDX4	0.9978	0.8063	−9.6078	1.1751	3.0305
	(3.253)	(3.394)	(0.753)	(1.501)	(1.971)
TIMEVAR	−0.0299		2.3243	1.9886	
	(0.605)		(0.808)	(1.621)	
TIMEVSQ	0.0012		−0.0287	−0.0324	
	(1.341)		(0.731)	(1.696)	
LNAVWGP		−4.2797	260.7419		−24.0688
		(1.095)	(0.908)		(0.579)
LNWGPSQ		0.3153	−17.8642		1.7048
		(1.174)	(0.903)		(0.592)
Implied effect of comparable worth on wages:	0.0505	0.0442	−0.3653	−1.4882	−0.0813
			Male Jobs:		
AFTRCW1	0.0262	0.0333	−0.7599	−0.0758	−0.0315
	(1.454)	(1.533)	(1.525)	(2.830)	(0.238)
FTIMEAF				−0.7020	−0.0494
				(0.844)	(0.176)
FTIMESQ				0.3922	0.1573
				(1.739)	(3.555)
CPINDX1	0.6851	1.1552	−1.1294	0.3223	1.0216
	(2.301)	(4.964)	(2.267)	(0.173)	(0.969)
CPINDX2	−1.7836	−1.7911	21.2251	−0.4115	−0.5698
	(4.792)	(4.235)	(1.717)	(0.513)	(0.301)
CPINDX3	1.0298	0.5500	−8.2562	−0.4179	−0.1727
	(3.835)	(1.696)	(1.909)	(0.474)	(0.384)
CPINDX4	0.7415	0.7178	−14.9346	1.3590	1.0437
	(3.751)	(4.706)	(1.758)	(2.605)	(1.019)
TIMEVAR	0.0038		3.5142	0.5079	
	(0.120)		(1.835)	(0.621)	
TIMEVSQ	0.0003		−0.0462	−0.0089	
	(0.643)		(1.763)	(0.704)	
LNAVWGP		−4.0990	367.0802		13.2018
		(1.633)	(1.919)		(0.476)
LNWGPSQ		0.2976	−25.2220		−0.8895
		(1.726)	(1.914)		(0.463)
Implied effect of comparable worth on wages:	0.0262	0.0333	−0.7599	−0.3856	0.0764

Table 5.4 (*continued*)

Variable	(6)	(7)	(8)	(9)	(10)	(11)
			Female Jobs:			
ADJ_CUM				0.0041	0.0040	0.0041
				(19.831)	(18.894)	(23.407)
ADJCHG1	0.0055	0.0052	0.0037			
	(7.043)	(6.252)	(4.886)			
ADJCHG2	0.0022	0.0026	0.0040			
	(2.913)	(3.294)	(5.542)			
ADJCHG3	0.0085	0.0109	0.0055			
	(3.122)	(3.991)	(2.323)			
ADJCHG4	0.0039	−0.0003	0.0061			
	(1.752)	(0.174)	(3.138)			
ADJCHG5	0.0023	0.0026	0.0036			
	(2.197)	(2.401)	(3.950)			
ADJCHG6	0.0017	0.0056	0.0004			
	(0.819)	(2.408)	(0.220)			
ADJCHG7	0.0096	0.0065	0.0051			
	(3.587)	(2.174)	(1.984)			
CPINDX1	−0.0733	0.7690	−2.5421	0.3836	1.0514	−2.1292
	(0.216)	(2.494)	(6.743)	(1.514)	(4.290)	(6.339)
CPINDX2	−1.5837	−1.2642	5.4309	−1.6777	−1.3270	4.8236
	(3.613)	(2.512)	(7.373)	(4.432)	(3.248)	(7.184)
CPINDX3	1.6530	1.0771	−2.8522	1.4742	0.8663	−2.7338
	(5.556)	(2.446)	(5.789)	(5.499)	(2.438)	(6.341)
CPINDX4	0.9255	0.2702	−4.0637	0.9435	0.3502	−3.5666
	(3.493)	(1.329)	(6.988)	(4.451)	(2.052)	(7.362)
TIMEVAR	−0.1055		0.9530	−0.1260		0.8515
	(2.778)		(8.071)	(3.689)		(8.252)
TIMEVSQ	0.0023		−0.0091	0.0025		−0.0081
	(3.346)		(6.413)	(4.103)		(6.517)
LNAVWGP		−1.1133	135.7828		−0.0065	123.6500
		(0.597)	(10.423)		(0.004)	(10.801)
LNWGPSQ		0.0922	−9.2496		0.0156	−8.4160
		(0.751)	(10.394)		(0.166)	(10.774)
Implied effect of comparable worth on wages:	0.0587	0.0586	0.0561	0.0583	0.0569	0.0583
			Male Jobs:			
ADJ_CUM				0.0026	0.0028	0.0017
				(1.027)	(1.120)	(0.702)
CPINDX1				0.9551	1.2706	−0.5833
				(4.070)	(5.769)	(1.638)
CPINDX2				−1.6021	−1.4740	2.3691
				(4.584)	(4.008)	(3.328)
CPINDX3				0.8812	0.4708	−1.6821
				(3.558)	(1.470)	(3.681)
CPINDX4				0.7743	0.7197	−1.9801
				(3.940)	(4.714)	(3.854)
TIMEVAR				−0.0034		0.5941
				(0.109)		(5.433)
TIMEVSQ				0.0002		−0.0062
				(0.496)		(4.742)
LNAVWGP					−0.7465	75.4419
					(0.573)	(6.213)

Table 5.4 *(continued)*

Variable	(6)	(7)	(8)	(9)	(10)	(11)
LNWGPSQ					0.0631 (0.744)	−5.1351 (6.198)
Implied effect of comparable worth on wages:				0.0001	0.0001	0.0001

Implied effect of comparable worth on wages:

Regressions (1)–(3): coefficient on AFTRCW1.

Regressions (4)–(5): sum of coefficients on AFTRCW1, FTIMEAF and FTIMESQ.

Regressions (6)–(8): sum of products of coefficients on ADJCHG*a* and means of ADCHG*a* (*a*=1–7) (ADJCHG*a*=range increase received in *a*th comparable worth pay adjustment, including jobs receiving no increase).

Regressions (9)–(11): product of coefficient on ADJ_CUM and mean of ADJ_CUM (=sum of means of ADJCHG*a* (*a*=1–7)).

specification (AFTRCW1, FTIMEAF, FTIMESQ) of comparable worth wage effects.

It seems clear, then, that the small number of data points and the absence of variables that vary cross-sectionally as well as over time make it very difficult to distinguish, in a reliable way, between wage increases attributable to comparable worth and wage increases attributable to other (e.g., cyclical or secular) factors.

C_{it} as a function of targeting. With this in mind, consider estimates derived using the targeting version of C_{it}, shown in columns (6)–(11) of table 5.4. Rather than ask about the difference between pay in the presence of comparable worth relative to what pay would have been in the absence of comparable worth, these are concerned with a potentially more modest question: the effect of comparable worth on pay of targeted relative to other jobs. (The answers to these two questions will be the same only if comparable worth had no effects, even indirect ones, on pay of non-targeted–e.g., predominantly male–jobs.) As noted above, to the extent that jobs were targeted for comparable worth wage adjustments because they were "chronically underpaid," and to the extent that being "chronically underpaid" may be treated as a fixed effect, fixed-effects estimation avoids the endogeneity bias (due to a correlation between the regression error term e_{it} and the targeting version of the

comparable worth variable C_{it}) that may arise if OLS is used. Moreover, since the targeting version of C_{it} varies cross-sectionally as well as over time, it turns out that questions about the effect of comparable worth on pay of targeted relative to other jobs can be answered rather precisely.

Columns (6)–(8) of table 5.4 present estimates for female jobs using the seven-variable specification of the targeting version of C_{it}. (Only a few male jobs were targeted for comparable worth wage changes, and then only in the last two sets of adjustments, so no results for this specification are shown for male jobs.) Regardless of which set of "environmental variables" is used, the implied effect of the comparable worth wage adjustments on female jobs is rather stable, ranging between about 5.6 and 5.9 percent.

Columns (9)–(11) present results obtained for both female and male jobs when one collapses the seven ADJCHG*a* variables into a single cumulative variable, ADJ_CUM. Again, the implied effect of comparable worth on wages in female jobs is highly statistically significant and essentially the same (between about 5.7 and 5.8 percent) regardless of which set of environmental variables is used. In contrast, the implied effect on male jobs' wages is negligible in terms of both magnitude and statistical significance.

In sum, the city's comparable worth wage adjustments do appear to have led to genuine changes in pay for predominantly female jobs: even after one takes into account environmental forces (as measured by prices, time trend and/or private-sector wage variables) that may have affected wages over the same period, the comparable worth wage adjustments appear to have raised pay in targeted, predominantly female jobs relative to other jobs. To the extent that it is legitimate to assume that the comparable worth wage adjustments did not affect (even indirectly) pay in nontargeted jobs, the comparable worth wage effects shown for regressions (6)–(11) are also estimates of the effect of comparable worth on the cost of female jobs relative to the cost that would have prevailed in the absence of the adjustments.

Of course, in a naive view, it is not necessary to use a statistical analysis to distinguish between wage changes attributable to comparable worth and wage changes that would have occurred even in the absence of comparable worth: could it not be argued that the city's contracts with Local 101 and reports by city personnel officials document all of the pay increases awarded to jobs targeted for the special "pay equity" adjustments? The difficulty with this view is that some or even all of these pay changes might have occurred in any case (due, e.g., to changes in the cost of living or local labor market conditions): there is potentially an important difference between (1) pay changes identified by city or union officials as a consequence of comparable worth and (2) pay changes that would not have taken place, other things being equal, in the absence of comparable worth. Furthermore, neither the city nor the union has attempted to specify what, if anything, comparable worth did to pay for jobs *other than* those targeted for comparable worth pay adjustments. For example, the city may in effect have tried to finance some of the comparable worth adjustments by keeping a lid on pay for other jobs. (Indeed, as noted earlier, at one point during the 1981 strike the city threatened to do precisely this.) Alternatively, the union may have tried to increase support for the comparable worth adjustments by having male jobs (and thus, presumably, male workers) share in the gains. In either case, then, it is desirable to attempt to separate observed wage gains into components attributable to comparable worth and to other factors. Indeed, ignoring the underlying environment (as proxied by price, time trend and/or private sector wage variables) overstates the wage changes attributable to comparable worth as such: simple fixed-effects regression of LMAXSAL on ADJ_CUM *without* any environmental variables yields coefficients of 0.0164 (t=32.533) and 0.0539 (t=4.513) for female and male jobs, respectively; these are much larger than any of the coefficients on ADJ_CUM shown in columns (9)–(11) of table 5.4.

5.5 *Longitudinal Analyses: Changes in Employment, 1981–88*

I now consider the extent to which the comparable worth wage increases affected employment. As in chapter 4, the basic approach consists of two stages. First, I estimate the employment demand function (3.10) to obtain measures of the effect of wages on employment, *ceteris paribus*. Then, I use these wage elasticities and the estimates (or guesstimates?) of the wage changes attributable to comparable worth noted in section 5.4 to estimate the actual effect on employment of the "pay equity" adjustments.

Employment demand function estimates

As in chapter 4, the unit of observation in the employment demand analyses is a job (classification), and the dependent variable is always the natural logarithm of employment in the job. The wage variable (the W_{it} of (3.10)) is the (ln of the) maximum of the range of pay rates for each job (LMAXSAL).[15] Estimates are presented separately for female and male classifications. As in chapter 4, I present estimates controlling for prices, time trend terms and/or private-sector patterns, where the latter are now measured by the (ln of) private-sector employment in the San José MSA as of the relevant quarter, LN_EMPP.

As noted in sections 3.4 and 4.5, pooled OLS estimates of employment demand functions, e.g., (3.10), are implausible on *a priori* grounds: they may merely reflect the hierarchical nature of employment.[16] Accordingly, I turn directly to fixed-effects estimates for San José, which appear in tables 5.5 and 5.6 for female and male jobs, respectively. Data with information on employment are available for eight dates (from October 17, 1981, to October 22, 1988: see section 5.2); thus the fixed-effects analyses have $101 \times 8 = 808$ observations and $41 \times 8 = 328$ observations for the 101 male and 41 female jobs, respectively.

The implied wage elasticity is always at least about 0.77 (in absolute value) for female jobs; it is smaller in absolute value (at least about 0.34) for male jobs. The male wage-elasticity of employment is usually significant at reasonable levels; the female elasticity is much less precisely estimated, possibly because of the relatively low sample size for the female jobs (since fixed-effects estimation requires one degree of freedom for each cross-section unit, the effective sample sizes in the analyses for male and female jobs are $808 - 101 = 707$ and $328 - 41$

Table 5.5 Fixed-Effects Employment Regressions, Female Jobs, 1981–88 (wage variable = LMAXSAL; *t*-statistics in parentheses)

Variable	(1)	(2)	(3)	(4)
ln(wage)	−1.0536	−1.1423	−0.7662	−1.1476
	(1.107)	(1.187)	(0.890)	(1.188)
CPINDX1	−2.4428	−2.6952	0.4573	
	(0.471)	(0.518)	(0.131)	
CPINDX2	0.2405	1.5568	−0.3942	
	(0.041)	(0.254)	(0.065)	
CPINDX3	−0.5303	−1.7969	0.1751	
	(0.106)	(0.334)	(0.035)	
CPINDX4	2.1015	1.4723	1.4688	
	(0.731)	(0.484)	(0.480)	
TIMEVAR	0.0933	0.3964		
	(0.628)	(0.803)		
TIMEVSQ		−0.0052		
		(0.643)		
LN_EMPP			−0.1403	
			(0.101)	
DUMMY82				0.1699
				(1.313)
DUMMY83				0.2489
				(1.401)
DUMMY84				0.2806
				(1.515)
DUMMY85				0.3664
				(1.555)
DUMMY86				0.4857
				(1.528)
DUMMY87				0.5516
				(1.519)
DUMMY88				0.5927
				(1.483)

NOTE: DUMMY82–DUMMY88 are indicators denoting whether an observation pertains to a given date (1/22/83; 8/25/83; 3/17/84; 4/27/85; 7/7/86; 8/1/87; or 10/22/88, respectively) after the first date covered by the data (10/17/81).

Table 5.6 Fixed-Effects Employment Regressions, Male Jobs, 1981–88 (wage variable = LMAXSAL; *t*-statistics in parentheses)

Variable	(1)	(2)	(3)	(4)
ln(wage)	−0.4707	−0.5210	−0.3387	−0.5208
	(1.971)	(2.184)	(1.438)	(2.181)
CPINDX1	−1.8143	−1.9155	3.3553	
	(0.862)	(0.914)	(2.112)	
CPINDX2	−4.7577	−2.5634	−5.5300	
	(1.860)	(0.955)	(2.015)	
CPINDX3	3.5840	1.4694	4.3720	
	(1.636)	(0.631)	(2.003)	
CPINDX4	−0.3209	−1.6803	−0.7251	
	(0.290)	(1.380)	(0.600)	
TIMEVAR	0.1642	0.7043		
	(2.811)	(3.286)		
TIMEVSQ		−0.0095		
		(2.617)		
LN_EMPP			−0.3888	
			(0.655)	
DUMMY82				0.0460
				(1.300)
DUMMY83				0.0835
				(1.875)
DUMMY84				0.1285
				(2.793)
DUMMY85				0.2052
				(3.620)
DUMMY86				0.3050
				(4.352)
DUMMY87				0.3374
				(4.249)
DUMMY88				0.3195
				(3.598)

NOTE: DUMMY82–DUMMY88 are indicators denoting whether an observation pertains to a given date (1/22/83; 8/25/83; 3/17/84; 4/27/85; 7/7/86; 8/1/87; or 10/22/88, respectively) after the first date covered by the data (10/17/81).

=287, respectively). In absolute value, the lowest elasticity estimate for both male and female jobs occurs when LN_EMPP but not time trend terms is used (column (3), tables 5.5–6); however, LN_EMPP is not itself significant at reasonable test levels in either regression. Of the four estimates in these tables, the ones in column (4) are the most plausible.[17] These imply wage elasticities of employment for female and male jobs of about −1.15 and −0.52, respectively. Recall that, as noted in section 3.4, the elasticity estimates in tables 5.5–6 are most reasonably interpreted as output- (or budget-) constant employment elasticities, exclusive of any employment reductions attributable to the decline in the purchasing power of San José's personnel budget due to the comparable worth wage increases.

Thus, these estimates, like those obtained in chapter 4, are generally larger in absolute value than those obtained in previous work on state and local government employment. Again, the special nature of the situation considered here—analysis of a single employer that adopted what seem to be genuinely exogenous changes in its wage rates—may help explain why the results here differ from those in previous work.

Estimated employment effects

Given the fixed-effects wage elasticities just noted, calculation of the effect of San José's comparable worth pay adjustments on municipal employment is straightforward provided suitable estimates of the wage effects of the adjustments are available. As noted previously, the estimated wage effects indicate the impact of comparable worth on targeted relative to nontargeted jobs. If they also indicate the effect on pay relative to the levels that would have prevailed in the absence of comparable worth—which is possible, but by no means certain—then the longitudinal wage analyses of section 5.4 suggest that comparable worth may have changed wages by between about 5.7 percent and 5.8 percent for female jobs and had essentially no effect on pay for male jobs. Since the wage elasticity of employment is about −1.15 for female jobs, the wage effect for female jobs translates into a *ceteris paribus* employment effect that is between about −6.55 percent and −6.67 percent. In contrast, since the wage analyses imply that comparable worth had negligible effects on pay in male jobs, the employment effect on these jobs was likewise negligible.

Of course, *actual* employment in female jobs *rose* between October 1981 and October 1988, because other forces in addition to comparable worth wage increases were at work. In particular, the fixed-effects analyses in tables 5.5–6 imply exogenous employment growth of over 10 percent *per year* for women's jobs.[18] Thus, to say that the employment effects of comparable worth were (no more than) about −6.67 percent for female jobs is *not* to say that, due to comparable worth, employment in 1988 was lower by these amounts for these jobs than was the case in 1981. Rather, it means that, in the absence of comparable worth, employment in 1988 *would have been* about 6.67 percent higher than *it actually was*. In other words, implementation of six years of comparable worth wage adjustments in San José was roughly the equivalent of somewhat less than a year of lost growth for female jobs.

5.6 *Summary and Conclusions*

Because of the limitations inherent in the available data, conclusions about the effects on wages of San José's comparable worth wage adjustments are problematic. If they can properly be regarded as measures of the effect on wages relative to levels that would otherwise have prevailed, then the estimates indicate that San José's comparable worth pay adjustments may have raised wages by between 5.7 percent and 5.8 percent in female jobs, and had negligible effects on pay in male jobs. As a result, the six years of comparable worth wage adjustments in San José had a negligible effect on employment in male jobs, and may have reduced employment in female jobs by between 6.55 percent to 6.67 percent—roughly the equivalent of somewhat less than a year of lost employment growth.[19] In terms of employment, then, the real losers from the comparable worth pay adjustments in San José—as in Minnesota—are likely to have been persons (particularly women) in the private sector or not in the labor force who were seeking public-sector jobs.

NOTES

[1] Much of the discussion in this section is based on Flammang (1986), Hutner (1986) and Farnquist et al. (1983).

[2] According to a Personnel Department memorandum (Farnquist, 1984), the total cost of the five adjustments made during 1981–84 was approximately $6.8 million (which may be compared with a total pay and benefit cost, in 1981, of approximately $10 million). During the first two years, the special adjustments averaged about $800–$900 per employee, or about 4.5–5 percent of annual pay; subsequent adjustments were somewhat smaller.

[3] The class listings I have used are dated July 25, 1980; October 17, 1981; January 22, 1983; August 25, 1983; March 17, 1984; April 27, 1985; July 7, 1986; August 1, 1987; and October 22, 1988. The listings for October 17, 1981, and later dates include data on positions filled as of the relevant date, whereas the ones prior to October 17, 1981, do not. Other listings are available (e.g., for July 1, 1980), but the salary figures in them are the same as the ones in those just listed (e.g., for July 25, 1980). San José also maintains computerized files on the personnel histories and characteristics of individual employees. Such data, however, are not available for years prior to 1982 (recall that the first set of comparable worth pay adjustments took effect in July 1981).

[4] The results are not sensitive to this exclusion; essentially the same estimates are obtained when all 229 jobs are analyzed. (In addition, results obtained for jobs with positive numbers of incumbents when observations on a job are weighted by the number of incumbents in that job are essentially the same as when unweighted observations are used, so only the unweighted results are presented here.)

[5] For example, some incumbents in a job are designated "confidential" when they work with senior managers; and bilingual incumbents in a job sometimes have the designation "specialist" appended to their job title. In determining the total number of incumbents in such jobs, I have included persons with "confidential" or "specialist" titles.

[6] For example, Exhibit II ("Pay Equity Adjustments") of the 1981–83 contract between the city and Local 101 specifies, among other things, that job class no. 1116 (Principal Clerk) will move 13 salary ranges effective July 19, 1981, and will move a further 12 ranges effective August 15, 1982.

[7] The salary-Haypoint relation flattens out (or "doglegs") at higher Haypoint values: pay increases with Haypoints, but at a decreasing rate. Evaluated at the approximate overall average Haypoint value (219 points), an additional 10 Haypoints are associated, on average and other things being equal, with roughly 2.39 percent higher salary.

[8] Evaluated at the approximate mean value (for all jobs taken together) of 219 Haypoints, the 1988 results imply that an increase of 10 Haypoints is associated, on average and other things being equal, with an increase in pay of about 2.66 percent (vs. about 2.39 percent in the results for July 1980).

[9] In each case, these percentage figures represent the change in the natural logarithm of salary associated with an increase in Haypoints from 219 (the overall mean Haypoint value) to 229 implied by the regression coefficients for the relevant year (either 1980 or 1988).

[10] See note 26 of chapter 3 for further discussion of this distinction.

[11] For example, the value of FTIMEAF for data as of March 17, 1984, is about 0.448 (so that FTIMESQ is slightly over 0.20). To see this, note that the period of wage adjustments (1981–87) covered by the data is approximately six years long and that as of March 17, 1984, about two years and eight months had elapsed since the first adjustments of July 19, 1981.

[12] For example, a job that received a pay adjustment of five salary ranges effective as of the last of the comparable worth changes (June 28, 1987) would have ADJCHG1–ADJCHG6 equal to zero for all dates; would have ADJCHG7 equal to zero for all dates prior to June 28, 1987; and would have ADJCHG7 equal to five for all dates after June 27, 1987. Similarly, a job that never received a pay equity adjustment would have zero values for each of the ADJCHG*a* variables as of all dates. (Values shown in table 5.2 for the ADJCHG*a* are the "final" values, i.e., relevant to dates after June 27, 1987.)

[13] For example, consider a job that received an increase of five salary ranges as part of the first adjustments (July 19, 1981), a further increase of four ranges under the second adjustments (August 15, 1982), and none in any of the subsequent adjustments. Then, for this job, CUMCHCW equals zero prior to July 19, 1981; equals five for dates between July 19, 1981 and August 14, 1982; and equals nine for dates on or after August 15, 1982. The entries for ADJ_CUM in table 5.2 are the "final" values, i.e., those relevant to dates after June 27, 1987.

[14] Recall that this chapter's wage analyses refer exclusively to jobs. All of the variables—the comparable worth and environmental (i.e., time-trend and private wage) variables—included in the fixed-effects regressions of table 5.4 exhibit only time-series variation: none of them varies cross-sectionally as well as over time. (In contrast, chapter 4's analyses of wages in Minnesota were based on data for individual employees rather than jobs, and thus included variables that vary cross-sectionally as well as over time.) This has several implications for the wage analyses of this chapter. First, since the data cover only ten dates, it is feasible to include no more than nine time-varying (but cross-sectionally invariant) regressors in the fixed-effects regressions. Second, in the absence of variables that vary cross-sectionally, pooled OLS regressions with the same variables used in the fixed-effects regressions of table 5.4 yield coefficient estimates that are identical to the fixed-effects estimates; so I do not present or discuss pooled OLS results corresponding to the fixed-effects results in table 5.4.

[15] The class listings for October 1981 and later dates—i.e., for the dates considered in these analyses of employment—show the minimum as well as the maximum of the salary range for each classification; hence, to measure the cost of workers in each classification for these analyses, one can use the (ln of) minimum or maximum salary, or the (ln of the) midpoint between the maximum and the minimum. The results, however, are virtually identical regardless of which of these three wage variables is used.

[16] In a nutshell, the difference between fixed-effects and pooled OLS estimates of employment functions for San José is essentially the same as the difference for Minnesota (see particularly table 4.8): in San José as in Minnesota, pooled OLS estimates of wage elasticities of employment are considerably higher in absolute value than fixed-effects estimates derived using the same set of (time-varying) variables.

[17] The fourth column of tables 5.5–6 uses the most general possible specification of environmental variables: a set of dummies, one for each period represented in the data beyond the first, which is thus implicitly the reference category. (Note that differences between coefficients on the successive dummy variables in this fourth column measure exogenous employment growth from one date to the next.) In absolute value, the wage elasticities yielded by this specification are either about the same as or larger than those derived using any of the other variants. The general dummy variable specification is feasible in the employment analyses because the "wage" variable in these

analyses varies cross-sectionally as well as over time. In contrast, in most of the analyses of wages reported in table 5.4, there are no variables that vary cross-sectionally, and so in those analyses a fully general dummy variable specification of the kind used in tables 5.5–6 is not possible.

[18] In particular, note the results in column (4) of each table and recall the discussion in note 17, above.

[19] Note, however, that these employment effects are based on output- (budget-) constant elasticities, and so may have been magnified at least to some extent by (e.g.) expenditure cuts undertaken to help pay for the wage increases.

6

Comparable Worth in Australia

This chapter is concerned with Australia's version of comparable worth: a policy, first adopted in 1972, of "equal pay for work of equal value." Several countries have adopted pay policies that contain at least some elements of the comparable worth principle (Bellace 1980), and a number of observers have argued that Australia's implementation of "equal pay for work of equal value" has fallen far short of perfection. Nevertheless, it appears that Australia, to a greater extent than most if not all other countries, has adopted and even implemented pay-setting practices that can reasonably be characterized as akin to comparable worth. How have these policies affected wages and employment of women and men?

6.1 *Background*

To the U.S. observer, the idea that comparable worth of any kind would find a home in Australia might at first seem puzzling. Comparable worth in *Australia*, the land of Crocodile Dundee, Ned Kelly, the Outback, and Rupert Murdoch?

Perhaps the most important factor contributing to comparable worth in Australia is that "[g]overnment intervention in the labour market in Australia is almost as old as white settlement" (Deery and Plowman

I thank Jenny Acton, Patricia Apps, Sheila M. Bonnell, Clare Burton, David Card, Bruce Chapman, R. C. Duncan, Bob Gregory, Paul Miller, Martin Parkinson, Christopher Pissarides, Margaret Power, Sue Richardson, James Robinson, Stephanie Sheean, Christine Short, Margaret Thornton, Paul Volker, and participants in seminars at the Australian National University, Princeton University, the University of Melbourne, the University of New South Wales, and the University of Western Australia for many helpful discussions, letters, and comments on previous versions of this chapter.

1985, p. 107). A major result of such intervention is that wage determination is probably more centralized in Australia than in any other country in the developed capitalist world. For much of Australia's history, state intervention was consciously used to keep women out of "male jobs." Under the right circumstances, however, intervention could be used for quite different objectives. By the 1960s, an elaborate institutional structure based on state intervention in wage-setting was firmly in place. It was only a matter of time before someone would see its potential for altering sex differences in wages along lines suggested by comparable worth principles.

Government regulation of labor markets began in the late eighteenth and early nineteenth centuries, when much of the workforce consisted of convicts resettled from England. Australia's colonial governors felt it necessary to take at least some steps to regulate the terms and conditions of convict employment. The scarcity of labor led to a system of payment, even for some convict workers, and thus to additional regulations.

Between the gold rushes of the 1850s and the 1890s, government continued to intervene in labor relations, setting a "pattern of partnership between government and private institutions" (Butlin 1959, p. 38). Government itself was a major employer, concerned with building infrastructure for the young colony. In the 1890s, Australia went through a series of strikes and lockouts "of a scale and bitterness which threatened the whole fabric of the state" (Deery and Plowman 1985, p. 125), and was sharply divided on the question of tariff protection. Eventually, there developed a kind of social contract, based on tariffs and wage regulation: avoid industrial conflict by relying on government tribunals to conciliate and arbitrate disputes over wages, working conditions and the like; grant employers tariff protection against imports, but make sure they paid fair wages to their workers once they had such protection.

Accordingly, Australia began to move towards a system of conciliation and arbitration of industrial disputes.[1] In 1894, South Australia became the first state to adopt a compulsory arbitration law. The 1900 federal constitution authorized the national parliament to pass laws for "conciliation and arbitration for the prevention and settlement of industrial disputes extending beyond the limits of any one state,"[2] which led to passage of the Commonwealth Conciliation and Arbitration Act (1904). This established a Federal Court of Conciliation and Arbitration for settlement of industrial disputes. At first, the Court attracted relatively little attention, but in 1906 the Excise Tariff Act sealed the second half of Australia's budding social bargain: employers could apply for certificates of exemption that would grant them tariff protection, but granting of such certificates depended on their paying their employees a fair and reasonable wage.

Since the *Harvester* case of 1907, the Court has been a powerful force in national wage determination, and an ever-increasing fraction of the workforce has been brought into the conciliation and arbitration system. At present, almost 90 percent of employees are covered by tribunal awards of some kind. Almost 40 percent are covered by awards issued by federal as opposed to state or other awards. (This understates the true influence of federal awards, however, since state and other tribunals often follow the federal lead.)

In recent years, the Court—called the Conciliation and Arbitration Commission during 1956–89[3]—has consisted of "presidential members" (a president and 13 deputy presidents) and 28 commissioners. The president must be a lawyer; most of the deputy presidents are lawyers (although there is no requirement that they be lawyers). Of the commissioners appointed between 1956 and 1980, 43 percent were previously unionists, 33 percent came from managerial backgrounds and 20 percent were formerly in government (Dabscheck and Niland 1981, p. 243). All members are appointed by the government of the day and may serve until the age of 65.

The Commission's primary responsibility is to resolve industrial disputes by conciliation or—if attempts at conciliation fail—by binding arbitration of the claims of the parties.[4] All that is necessary for a "dispute" to exist is "that one party, usually the employer, reject some demand made by another party, usually a union" (Deery and Plowman 1985, pp. 134–5). Although other parties ("intervenors," e.g., the federal and state governments and other parties, such as advocacy groups) may participate in Commission hearings on a dispute, in general the parties consist of one or more unions, on one hand, and one or more employers, on the other.[5] Particular disputes are referred to individual commissioners; disputes regarding industries are heard by individual deputy presidents or, more usually, panels consisting of two to four members of the Commission. Disputes of national economic importance—on the standard workweek, the minimum wage, etc.—are decided by a "Full Bench" consisting of at least three members, two of whom must be presidential members.

Commission decisions, called awards, have the full force of law. Such awards cover specified employers and unions (a given award usually covers several employers or even an entire industry rather than just one firm); they tend to follow occupational (and to a lesser extent industrial) boundaries. "Roping-in" awards apply previous awards to employers newly discovered to be operating in the relevant industry.

Although the federal Commission is by far the most important tribunal with the power to affect wages and other terms of employment, individual state tribunals also issue decisions on such issues. The Commission is ultimately responsible for determining whether it or a state tribunal has jurisdiction in a given case. Federal government employees are automatically subject to federal jurisdiction, as are workers in industries that involve employers operating in more than one state; interstate unionism typically leads to federal jurisdiction. In some areas—notably, state public services (including teaching, nursing and social welfare)—workers are represented by unions within individual states; here, state tribunals typically have jurisdiction.

For present purposes, one of the most important aspects of the Commission and the state tribunals is that their pay awards determine *minimum*, rather than maximum, wage rates. Labor and management are therefore free to negotiate rates (called overaward payments) in excess of these minima. (Although rare until the late 1960s, overaward payments have become important since that time.) In determining pay awards, the Commission (or a state tribunal) is able to exercise considerable discretion. Section 40(c) of the law establishing the arbitration system specifies that the Commission is to "act according to equity, good conscience and the substantial merits of the case without regard to technicalities and legal form." The Commission may receive formal statements and documents from the contending parties, may hear sworn testimony from witnesses offered by the parties, and may conduct on-site interviews and job inspections. Use of legal counsel is not required,[6] and neither is legal formalism—although some parties, notably unionists, have complained about excessive legalism in the Commission's manner of operation.

Not surprisingly, questions about pay rates have historically been among the most contentious issues considered by the Commission (and its predecessor, the Court). Whatever may be the degree of legalism in other aspects of its operations, the Commission's wage awards do resemble court decisions in two important respects. First, if only to avoid inconsistency and charges of unfair treatment, essentially the same principles tend to be applied to claims involving different industries, in much the same way as a court would apply a given statute to different cases. Second, principles adopted in previous decisions tend to be applied to subsequent cases, in much the same way as courts follow the principle of *stare decisis* (reliance on past precedent).

The principles adopted in wage decisions have shifted over time but, in one form or another, most of them can be viewed as attempts to base wages on supply-side and/or demand-side considerations: workers' needs, employers' ability to pay, changes in the cost of living, and government policy at the micro (efficiency, equity) and macro (stabilization) levels have all played some role in the wage-setting process. The issues addressed in wage-fixing may conveniently be divided into two parts: questions about the aggregate level of wages, addressed in so-called national wage cases; and questions about wage differentials, addressed in so-called industry cases.

The aggregate level of wages

In one of the earliest cases, the 1907 Harvester Judgment (2 *Commonwealth Arbitration Reports* (hereafter, *CAR*), p. 1), Henry Bournes Higgins, president of the Court, adopted seven shillings per day (for a six-day workweek) as a fair and reasonable minimum wage for unskilled labor. Relying in part on testimony offered by a butcher, a landlord's agent and nine laborer's wives, Higgins held that this sum was in line with the budget of the average male laborer with a wife and three children, and was necessary to satisfy the "normal needs of the average employee regarded as a human being living in a civilized community."[7] The sum determined on the basis of this "needs" standard became known as the "basic wage," the wage payable for essentially unskilled labor. Higgins later introduced the concept of adjustments in the basic wage for changes in the cost of living.

The Harvester decision also recognized the need to add margins to the basic wage to allow for differentials in skill, effort, responsibility and working conditions, thereby yielding the "secondary wage." As Higgins later explained (1922, pp. 6–7, footnotes omitted):

> The secondary wage is remuneration for any exceptional gifts or qualifications, not of the individual employee, but gifts or qualifications necessary for the performance of the function, e.g., skill as a tradesman, exceptional heart and physique, as in the case of a shearer, exceptional responsibility, e.g., for human life, as in the case of winding or locomotive engine-drivers.

The job of fitter in the Metal Trades was the first classification for which a secondary wage was determined; soon, fitters—and Metal Trades awards generally—became an important benchmark for other decisions,

> . . . because fitters were employed in a wide range of industries, and because it could be extended to other classifications which required the same degree of skill and training: millers, borers, slotters, gear cutters, cutting bar drillers, lappers, precision grinders, brass finishers, turners, boiler-makers and metal moulders. In other industries the fitter's rate was applied to tradesmen such as carpenters, coopers, tailors, printing compositors, butchers, and so on. Members of the Court argued that those trades required periods of apprenticeship and training and a degree of manual skill similar to that of the fitter. The establishment of a tradesman's rate in any award in turn provided a benchmark by which the marginal relativities [i.e., differentials in "secondary wage rates"] of other classifications

> within that award could be fixed. (Deery and Plowman 1985, p. 336.)

In time, wage cases for the Metal Trades became national test cases, important both for adjustment of the basic wage and – via operation of the principle of "comparative wage justice" – for fixing the general level of the margin, i.e., the secondary wage, for the economy as a whole. "Comparative wage justice (in simple terms) requires the continuance of pre-existing relativities [i.e., wage differentials]," so as to ensure that one group does not fall behind another (Hancock 1984, p. 190). Although relative award rates can and do change, comparative wage justice tends to preserve them:

> Under the operation of the principle of comparative wage justice, the interlocking relationship between award classifications made the wage structure rigid. . . . [W]hen the Metal Trades Award varied, pressures mounted for variations to both dependent and related awards. If one award varied, related classifications in other awards would also seek a variation, on the grounds of comparative wage justice with the award already varied. Classifications within awards had then to be varied by the same proportions. Thus comparative wage justice became an important way of transmitting wage gains from one award to another. (Deery and Plowman 1985, pp. 336–7.)

In the 1930s, the Great Depression led the arbitration court to consider the demand side of the market, cutting nominal wage awards (relative to earlier levels) on the grounds that the capacity of the economy to pay high wages was severely undermined. A "workers' needs" standard gave way to an "employers' ability to pay" standard. Subsequent decisions reaffirmed the primacy of this "ability to pay" criterion and allowed, e.g., for a "prosperity loading" during periods when economic conditions were favorable. The "needs" standard was never completely abandoned, but it was certainly deemphasized. For example, although changes in the price level were still considered, they were deemed relevant not so much as indicators of changing worker "needs" but rather as a reflection of changes in employers' "ability to pay." In 1953, the court announced that it would rely on a set of macroeconomic indicators – investment, production and productivity, overseas trade and the overseas balance, retail trade indicators, etc. – in determining the national "ability to pay." There followed a number of changes and amendments to wage-setting policy that gave priority to macroeconomic concerns.

In 1967, the Court's successor, the Conciliation and Arbitration Commission, decided that it would focus on the "total wage," i.e., the sum of the basic wage and the secondary wage (Employers' Total Wage Case, 110 *CAR*, p. 196). This reflected increasing preoccupation with macroeconomic stabilization. During the 1970s and 1980s, wage decisions came to be viewed as an important tool of incomes policy, and the Commission devoted much time and attention to questions about the macroeconomic consequences of its decisions and the degree to which wage awards would be linked to inflation and productivity (Braun 1974; Deery and Plowman 1985). There was growing concern about reducing or preventing "flow-on" – the potential for awards in one industry to lead to demands, and thus wage increases, in many other industries. In 1983, the Commission decided that increases in pay rates outside the "national wage adjustment" framework (i.e., for reasons other than productivity growth or inflation adjustment) were to be strictly limited. Changes in a job's skill, effort, responsibility or working conditions could prompt wage adjustments, but only if such "work value" changes were "such a significant net addition to work requirements as to warrant the creation of a new classification." Anomalies and inequities[8] were to be brought before an Anomalies Conference, which could adjust award rates in response to inequities only if the change (1) was justified on the merits, (2) had "no likelihood of flow-on," (3) would entail "negligible" economic cost and (4) would be a "once-only matter" (National Wage Case 1983, MD Print F2900, pp. 51–2).

Wage differentials

To sum up (at the risk of further oversimplifying) the discussion thus far, Commission decisions on the total wage (or, earlier, on the basic wage and margins, i.e., the secondary wage) set the general level of wages; and comparative wage justice then passes these basic decisions through the structure of the economy, essentially preserving existing wage differentials ("relativities"). But how are wage differentials determined in the first instance?

The main concept underlying the initial determination of differentials is called "work value." Determination of work value involves "the detailed identification of job characteristics and the attachment of money values to the total package" (Hancock 1984, p. 190). One authoritative survey of awards has identified no less than 55 factors that have figured in work value assessments (Hutson 1971, pp. 163–4). For the most part, these factors may be grouped under four main headings that sound (and are) very much like those advocated by U. S. proponents of comparable worth: skill, effort, responsibility and working conditions.[9] As noted earlier, changes in these four factors are now the only circumstances that can lead to a change in work value (National Wage Case 1983, MD Print F2900, p. 50).

As Hancock (1984, p. 190) has put it, "The processes of cerebration which converted years of training or on-the-job responsibility into money have never been described." Work value determination has often been somewhat rough-and-ready. In the Marine Cooks' Case of 1906 (2 *CAR*, p. 55 ff.), Mr. Justice Higgins compared the work of marine cooks and butchers with that of butchers' assistants, whose wages had been determined by the Victoria wages board; similarly, in the Boot Trades Case of 1909 he awarded footwear industry operatives the same rate as that given to metal machinists on the grounds that "there is much general resemblance between the character of the work of such machinists and the work of factory bootmakers" (4 *CAR*, p. 1). As noted earlier, in time the Metal Trades awards were used to determine pay rates in a variety of industries; thus, for example, tin solderers in the Food Preservation industry were compared with canister makers in the Metal Trades (Food Preservers' Case, 45 *CAR*, p. 343). In general, there has been little or no use of formal job evaluations of the kind described in chapter 1; rather, work value determination in Australia has usually been relatively informal, and certainly much less systematic than (e.g.) the Hay point-factor method.[10]

Once an occupation's work value has been determined, it is reassessed from first principles only rarely, and the relativity or wage differential between a given job and others tends to be preserved via the principle of comparative wage justice: at present, changes in wage differentials are allowed only if there is a demonstration that there have been important changes in work value. The burden of proof that work value has changed, which lies squarely on the unions making the claim, can be onerous. For example, in the 1961 Professional Engineers' case (97 *CAR*, p. 233), professional engineers in the Federal Public Service argued against the historic practice of assessing their work and pay in relation to that of members of the administrative and clerical divisions of the service. Instead, they argued, their work should be compared with that of professionals in the higher reaches of the professional officer salary scale (e.g., lawyers, architects, dentists and doctors). After 180 days of proceedings spread over three and one-half years involving 26 lawyers (including 8 Queen's Counsels and the Commonwealth Crown Solicitor), during which the Commission heard about 180 witnesses, received over 600 exhibits (including several motion pictures) and conducted several on-site inspections, the Commission eventually agreed with many of the engineers' claims. Ironically, the wages of clerical and administrative officers were eventually restored to their previous relationship with those of the professional engineers (Molhuysen 1962; Deery and Plowman 1985, pp. 342–4).

Female/male differentials

Unlike other wage differentials, the arbitration system paid relatively little attention to the sex differential in pay until the 1970s. Moreover, until the 1970s, the arbitration system had effectively institutionalized a sizable differential in awards between men and women.

The Rural Workers' Case of 1912 (6 *CAR*, p. 61) was the first case to consider questions of sex differences in wages. Although the agricultural workers' unions were asking for "equal pay for equal work," Mr. Justice Higgins noted that this request was ambiguous, and that what the unions were seeking might better be described as equal pay for "work of the same character," with fruit picking, fruit pitting and fruit packing all to be treated as comparable. This Higgins was not willing to agree to. All the work was unskilled, and so it might be argued that it should all be paid at the same minimum (basic) wage. Higgins pointed out, however, that the minimum wage established in the Harvester case was the sum necessary to

> meet the normal needs of an average employee, one of his normal needs being the need for domestic life. If he has a wife and children, he is under an obligation—even a legal obligation—to maintain them. How is such a minimum applicable to the case of a woman picker? She is not, unless perhaps in very exceptional circumstances, under any such obligation. The minimum canot be based on exceptional cases. (6 *CAR*, p. 71.)

This distinction quickly hardened into precedent. In the Theatrical Case (11 *CAR*, p. 133) five years later, Mr. Justice Powers, Deputy President of the Court, established the basic terms of 50 years of subsequent decisions as follows (11 *CAR*, p. 146):

> This Court allows to men a living wage based on the assumption that the average man has to keep a wife and family of three children whatever the value of the work he does may be.
>
> The Court allows a living wage to a woman as a single woman.
>
> The single man often gets more than his work is worth, but if single men are paid less than married men the cheaper labour would be employed and they could not make the necessary provision for marriage.

There remained the question of differences in pay for occupations whose sex composition was different. In his Rural Workers decision, Higgins applied the "needs" criterion to this issue with an interesting twist. Pay for predominantly male jobs such as blacksmiths "must be such as recognises that blacksmiths are usually men" (6 *CAR*, p. 72), i.e., should be sufficient to support a family; for predominantly female jobs such as fruit packing and pitting, the wage "should be that suitable for a single woman supporting herself only" (13 *CAR*, p. 692, Clothing Trades Case 1919, summarizing Rural Workers' Case 1912). Fruit picking was a different story, for it was done by substantial numbers of both men and women (albeit with men in the majority).

> There has been observed for a long time a tendency to substitute women for men in industries, even in occupations which are more suited for men; and in such occupations it is often the result of women being paid lower wages than men. Fortunately for society, however, the greater number of bread winners still are men. . . . As a result, I come to the conclusion that in the case of the pickers, men and women, being on a substantial level, should be paid on the same level of wages; and the employer will then be at liberty freely to select whichever sex and whichever person he prefers for the work. (6 *CAR*, p. 72.)

This would have several desirable consequences, Higgins suggested. First, setting the same wage for male and female pickers would lead to "true and healthy competition – not competition as in a Dutch auction by taking lower remuneration, but competition by making oneself more useful to the employer" (6 *CAR*, p. 72.) The other benefit, implied rather than stated, was that setting the same wage regardless of sex would tend to keep women out of picking work. Accordingly, Higgins awarded adult pitters (most of whom were female) and adult female packers a wage of nine pence per hour, and awarded adult male packers and all adult pickers (men *or* women) a wage of twelve pence per hour (6 *CAR*, pp. 80–1).

In the Clothing Trades Case 1919 (13 *CAR*, p. 647), Higgins adopted the same approach but was still more explicit:

> In the case of tailoring, there is no doubt that men and women are in competition; but that the competition is weighted in favour of the women by the practice of paying women lower rates. Mr. Scovell, who appears for many employers before me, and who conducts a workshop himself, said very frankly that if he had to choose between men and women as employees in all the operations of the industry, at equal rates, other things being equal, he would always choose men. I find the lower rates habitual for women are the cause of the gradual disappearance of men from the industry in all but the most skilled

> operations, or the operations (such as pressing off) which require strength. "Women are equal to men in brains, unequal in muscle," as one employer graciously admits. I find that the lower rates for women have driven the men from the making of trousers and vests and from the making of most of the sac coats. The men are, in effect, making a last stand at body and dress coats, cutting, trimming, fitting, pressing. Is it right that this Court should aid the gentle invaders?
>
> . . . It is urged here for the employers that I should not now, by prescribing equal wages, drive the women out of employment; but it is equally serious to drive men out of employment by prescribing unequal wages. . . . [As] even the [employers] admit[,] . . . [i]f there are 1,000 jobs vacant, and 1,000 men and 1,000 women want the jobs, it is better for society – if the candidates are equally qualified – that most of the jobs should go to the men. (13 *CAR*, pp. 701–2.)

The net result was that women would be paid lower wages than men *except* in occupations in which women might displace men – in which case wages were to be equal for both women and men.

The reaction of female workers to this version of equal pay was mixed. One female tailor testified in the Clothing Trades case, "If girls got the same wages, the girls would be employed if they can do as well as the average man. . . . The girls want the same rate even at the risk of losing employment" (13 *CAR*, p. 704). Other women in similar circumstances were less sanguine:

> In Victoria, the commercial Clerks' Board on which women were not represented, deliberately fixed equal pay for women working as clerks in order to improve the chances of men clerks, and an appeal was brought by women clerks to the Industrial Appeals Court on the ground that the Determination of the Board would oust them from employment. They, therefore, asked for a lower wage to be fixed for women clerks, and the Court upheld the appeal and granted their request. (Royal Commission into Industrial Arbitration in New South Wales, 1914, quoted in Scherer 1984, p. 132.)

Such objections notwithstanding, subsequent Court decisions adopted Higgins' framework, setting a lower female wage for most occupations (except those in which women competed with men). The Clothing Trades Case had fixed the female basic wage at 35 shillings per week, 54 percent of the male basic weekly wage of 65 shillings; and it remained at roughly that ratio in subsequent cases "notwithstanding the shift from the needs to the capacity to pay approach in fixing the male basic wage" (Deery and Plowman 1985, p. 309).

During World War II, female wage rate fixing was the job of the Women's Employment Board, which made awards of between 60 and 100 percent of the relevant male rate (the largest group received 90 percent). In 1944, the Court reassumed jurisdiction over female wages. In its Basic Wage Inquiry 1949–50 (68 *CAR*, p. 698), the Court explicitly rejected union demands for equal rates for males and females as both undesirable and unsustainable, instead setting the female basic wage at 75 percent of the male figure (68 *CAR*, pp. 815–9).

The following year, the International Labour Organization adopted its Convention No. 100, calling for "equal pay for work of equal value," and Australian unionists, rebuffed by the federal Court, began pressing for equal pay – either for work of equal value, or, as a second-best, for equal work – at the state level. In 1958, the most populous and most progressive state, New South Wales, adopted relatively narrow legislation requiring equal pay for equal work; Queensland (1964), Tasmania (1966, though only for government employment), South Australia (1967) and Western Australia (1968) followed. All state governments began to implement equal pay within the state public services (although in Victoria, equal pay was confined to teachers).

Prospects for equal pay seemed to be improving. As noted earlier, in 1967 the Conciliation and Arbitration Commission (successor to the Court) had shifted from the concept of a basic wage and a secondary wage (i.e., a skill margin) to the concept of a total wage. The Commission observed that this meant that, for the time being, there would be two total wages, one for men and one for women, creating apparent anomalies.[11]

The Commission then appeared to open the door to equal pay – an equal total wage – for equal work: it awarded the same *increase* in wages to adult males and females, and noted that earlier decisions had affirmed the concept of equal *margins* for men and women doing equal work. "The extension of that concept to the total wage would involve economic and industrial sequels and calls for thorough investigation and debate in which a policy of gradual implementation could be considered," the Commission's decision said. "We invite the unions, the employers and the Commonwealth to give careful study to these questions with the knowledge that the Commission is available to assist by conciliation or arbitration in the resolution of the problems."[12]

The Equal Pay decisions. In 1968, as demonstrators marched outside, the unions, joined by women's groups, went back into the Commission to ask for equal pay for *equal* work. The Commission's decision (Equal Pay Cases 1969, 127 *CAR*, p. 1142) agreed that the concept of the "family wage" used to justify the historic male/female difference in awards "no longer has the significance, conceptual or economic, which it once had and is no real bar to a consideration of equal pay for equal work" (127 *CAR*, p. 1153). It dismissed employer predictions of economic dislocation by specifying that implementation of equal pay for equal work would be phased in over the period 1969–1972.

The Commission, however, limited the scope of equal pay in several important respects (127 *CAR*, pp. 1158–9).[13] Equal pay was to cover only jobs performed by both men and women that were "of the same or a like nature"; work "essentially or usually performed by females—in which about 80 percent of the female workforce was engaged—was specifically exempted from the decision; the Commission restricted equal pay "to work performed under the determination or award concerned," thereby prohibiting comparisons between awards, i.e., ones that would cross industry and occupational boundaries.

Perhaps not surprisingly, the unions and women's groups found this less than completely satisfactory. In 1972, they returned to the Commission seeking equal pay for work *of equal value*. The Commission's decision (National Wage and Equal Pay Cases 1972, 147 *CAR*, p. 172) opined that "broad changes of significance have occurred since 1969"—including further legislative developments within Australia, in Britain and New Zealand, and endorsement at Commission hearings of equal pay for work of equal value by the Commonwealth Government—that exemplified "a world wide trend towards equal pay for females."[14] The Commission declared (147 *CAR*, p. 177):

> In our view the concept of "equal pay for equal work" is too narrow in today's world and we think the time has come to enlarge the concept to "equal pay for work of equal value." This means that award rates for all work should be considered without regard to the sex of the employee.

In the past, work value determination had disadvantaged women:

> Differentiations between male rates in awards of the Commission have traditionally been founded on work value investigations of various occupational groups or classifications. The gap between the level of male and female rates in awards generally is greater than the gap, if any, in the comparative value of work performed by the two sexes because rates for female classifications in the same award have generally been fixed without a comparative evaluation of the work performed by males and females. (147 *CAR*, p. 179.)

The Commission now ruled, however, that henceforth "female rates [shall] be determined by work value comparisons without regard to the sex of the employees concerned."[15]

Rather than revise all work valuations and pay rates, the Commission contented itself with simply stating the new principle and leaving it up to individual commissioners to implement it through work value reviews (i.e., reevaluation of women's jobs) in individual industry cases. The Commission emphasized that work value meant value in terms of skill, effort, responsibility and working conditions—i.e., the factors traditionally used in work value reviews—rather than value to the employer (e.g., marginal productivity). "The value of the work refers to worth in terms of award wage or salary fixation, not worth to the employer."[16] As in its 1969 Equal Pay decision, the Commission's new decision provided for gradual implementation of the equal pay for work of equal value principle, with full compliance to be achieved over two and one-half years, on June 30, 1975.

In principle, then, the 1972 "equal pay for work of equal value" ("EPEV") decision had far-reaching implications; but what would it mean in practice?

Several writers have argued that the full possibilities of the decision have not been realized (Burton et al. 1987; Power et al. 1985; Short 1986; Thornton 1981). Short (1986) found only 53 Commission awards in cases brought since 1972 under the equal pay rubric – a surprisingly small number, given the potential ramifications of the 1972 decision.[17] Moreover, only one of these cases involved reassessments of work value for different job classifications.

That equal pay cases seem to represent a trickle rather than a flood may in part be due to the fact that the 1972 decision included several important caveats and qualifications (147 *CAR*, pp. 179–80). The Commission exempted existing geographic differentials from the equal value rule, and said that "pre-existing award relativities may be a relevant factor in appropriate cases." Although it cautioned that "unfamiliar issues" were likely to arise in valuing work irrespective of sex, the Commission was vague about how equal value should be determined; it suggested that "different criteria will continue to apply from case to case and may vary from one class of work to another" and that implementation of the equal value principle would require "the exercise of the broad judgment which has characterised work value inquiries." Thus, rather than adopt a set of explicit rules on work value determination that would have facilitated implementation of EPEV, the Commission retained the fuzzy and manipulable *ad hoc* approach to work value that had been used in the past.

The Commission also discouraged work value comparisons across award boundaries, thereby inhibiting consideration of whether dissimilar but arguably comparable jobs were in fact of equal value. As a rule, the Commission said, work value comparisons (and thus relative pay rates) were to be performed "where possible" by comparing "female and male classifications within the award under consideration." "Where such comparisons are unavailable or inconclusive, as may be the case where the work is performed exclusively by females," the Commission conceded that it might be necessary to compare a female job and either

(1) another female job within the same award, or (2) female jobs in other awards, or (3) male jobs in other awards; but its tone suggested that such comparisons were to be made as a last resort.

A final impediment to full implementation of EPEV derives from the centralized nature of the arbitration system. Cases are argued by employers (or groups of employers) and unions (or groups of unions). Individual workers or worker groups (e.g., a women's caucus) ordinarily are not able to put their viewpoints directly to the Commission. Interested outside parties, e.g., women's advocacy groups, may appear as intervenors, but they will inevitably have less credibility than the unions directly involved. Thus, the support of individual unions and union organizations such as the Australian Council of Trade Unions (ACTU) is important, if not essential, to implementation of EPEV.

Such support has not always been forthcoming. According to Power et al. (1985, p. 59), some unions "even went on strike to prevent equal award wages being introduced in their industry or occupation." Even if the relevant union or group of unions is not overtly hostile to EPEV, it may be unwilling to support EPEV aggressively, especially if that would entail sacrificing other objectives. Although the ACTU has long supported EPEV (Australian Council of Trade Unions, 1985), some observers have suggested that in practice it has been decidedly unenthusiastic about implementing the policy.[18]

More generally, critics of Australia's system of arbitration have often alleged that it has been dominated by a "free-wheeling free masonry of fixits called the Industrial Relations Club"—union and management officials, civil servants, lawyers and academics who have over the years acquired formidable expertise in manipulating the system, have a vested interest in continuing it in its present form, and have over the years established "a self-perpetuating, closed society making deals in its own interest, deals which, more often than not, run contrary to the national interest" (Bowers 1985).[19] In its most extreme form, this view of the Industrial Relations Club verges on a conspiracy theory. In milder versions, it resembles the well-known proposition that regulatory bodies end up being dominated by those whom they are supposed to regulate (see Stigler 1971, for a classic statement of this view). In either case, however, it suggests that, even if they are not consciously excluded by the "Ins," the "Outs" may find it hard to get the established players in the regulatory game to consider a new set of demands. In this connection, it is interesting to note that as of March 1989, only four of the Commission's 46 members were women (Thornton 1989, p. 36).

Several of the obstacles to implementation of EPEV are illustrated by Thornton's interesting case study (1981, pp. 473–7) of a failed attempt to make relatively modest comparable worth pay adjustments to the wages of typists and stenographers at the University of New South Wales. The Public Service Association (PSA), representing the workers before the Industrial Commission of New South Wales,[20] noted that the pay scales of the typist and stenographer jobs (both of which were overwhelmingly female) started lower and rose to much lower maxima than did the scale for general clerical officer (clerks) jobs, which were predominantly male. After the Commission's 1972 EPEV decision, the University adjusted the pay scales of the stenographers and typists, but the scales remained below the clerical scale. The PSA charged that this only partially implemented EPEV, and asked that the three groups' pay scales be completely integrated.

An individual commissioner rejected the PSA's case, and so did a three-judge appellate panel. Two elements of the appeal judgment[21] are of particular interest in the present context. First, the appellate panel was clearly unimpressed by the PSA's reference to other awards in which stenographer and typist scales were integrated with those of clerks ("the persuasive influence of those cases has not been sufficient for us to come to the conclusion that a complete salaries integration in regard to relevant employees at the university is justified"). The judges gave greater weight to the university's own practices prior to the 1972 EPEV decision – in particular, the fact that the university maintained separate salary schedules for (1) the typists, (2) the stenographers, and (3) two distinct groups of predominantly male clerical jobs – as indicating that there were genuine differences in work value among the different job categories.

In principle, this might have been countered by a comprehensive assessment of the work value of the three groups (typists, stenographers and clerks); but the PSA did not produce one. Rather, as Thornton notes (1981, p. 475), the PSA's evidence was mostly "individualistic and unsystematic," based on testimony from individual stenographers and typists. Indeed, the PSA devoted much of its effort to showing that some of the work performed by the stenographers and typists was *identical* to some of the work performed by the clerks; this was irrelevant to the issue of *equal value*, and—given the heterogeneity of the jobs in question—could hardly have supported a conclusion of *equal work*. Although the appeals judges suggested that "these kinds of situations might properly engage the attention of the classifications committee which exists at the university," and asked the PSA and the university to consider whether at least some pay increase for the stenographers and typists might be appropriate, they added that "we were not satisfied overall that the work value of the three groups was so similar that an integration of rates should in justice take place."

Dissatisfaction with such work value issues reached the national level in 1983, when, in the National Wage Case, several women's groups contended that implementation of the 1969 and 1972 equal pay decisions had been frustrated by the lack of "proper work value exercises" for predominantly female jobs (a failure to reassess the work value of such jobs). These groups asked the Commission to provide for such revaluations, but the Commission rejected their request. According to the Commission, "such large scale work value inquiries would clearly provide an opportunity for the development of additional tiers of wage increases, which would be inconsistent with the centralized system which we propose for the next two years and would also be inappropriate in the current state of unemployment especially among women" (National Wage Case 1983, MD Print F2900, p. 29). What the Commission seemed to have given in 1972 it seemed to have taken away eleven years later.

The 1986 Nurses Case. With dissatisfaction about implementation of EPEV growing, various unionists and women's groups eventually persuaded the ACTU to bring a comparable worth "test case," involving nurses, before the Commission. The objective was to realize (or, perhaps more accurately, expand) the full potential of the 1972 Equal Pay decision by getting the Commission squarely on record in favor of comparable worth. The Commission's decision, however, neatly side-stepped the particular issue raised by the case—comparable worth adjustments for nurses—and was unequivocally negative on the general principle of comparable worth.[22]

The Commission invoked the National Wage Case 1983, which, as noted earlier, had rejected demands from women's groups for revaluation of women's jobs. As in 1983, the Commission said it was unwilling to change wages for women's jobs if that was going to conflict with its policy of wage restraint. In language reminiscent of that used by U.S. District Judge Fred Winner in rejecting comparable worth claims of nurses in Denver,[23] the Commission declared (MD Print G2250, p. 11):

> There are . . . serious implications for flow on of any increases which might be granted as a result of these applications. Indeed the applicants and interveners supporting them made it plain that they see these proceedings as part of a wider movement to increase salaries for nurses throughout the country. The applications therefore carry great potential for undermining the current centralised wage fixing system.

Rather than accept "claims for the application of the 1972 Principle in awards in which it has not been applied," the Commission said, it would refer them to the Anomalies Conference established in the 1983 National Wage Case, where they would be evaluated subject to the strict guidelines established for wage changes (which included, *inter alia*, a requirement that there be no likelihood of flow-on).[24] This appeared to preclude large-scale reassessments of the work value of women's jobs, and to rule out any appreciable improvement in the female-male differential in award rates of pay.

Not only did the Commission materially reduce the practical potential of comparable worth to revalue women's work and raise women's wages; it also took on the general principle of comparable worth. Rather disingenuously, it asserted (MD Print G2250, p. 10) that ". . . in the United States at least, the doctrine of comparable worth refers to the value of the work in terms of its worth to the employer," and noted that this conflicted with the 1972 Equal Pay Case (which had said that equal value meant "equal in work value," *not* "of equal value to the employer").[25] In addition, the Commission asserted, valuing substantially dissimilar jobs on a common basis—as in comparable worth—would carry the doctrine of work value beyond the boundaries that were customary and appropriate for Australia (MD Print G2250, p. 9):

> At its widest, comparable worth is capable of being applied to any classification regarded as having been improperly valued, without limitation on the kind of classification to which it is applied, with no requirement that the work performed is related or similar. It is capable of being applied to work which is essentially or usually performed by males as well as to work which is essentially or usually performed by females. Such an approach would strike at the heart of long accepted methods of wage fixation in this country and would be particularly destructive of the present Wage Fixing Principles.

Further efforts by comparable worth proponents are in progress. In 1986, nurses in Victoria and South Australia sought and ultimately won wage increases in state tribunals on the grounds that the 1972 decision had not previously been applied to them. Anomalies conferences convened in response to the 1986 Nurses Case ultimately led to a 1987 "Full Bench" decision of the Commission which granted a pay increase for nurses—without, however, specifying which components of the increase were for equal pay "anomaly claims," changes in work value or other factors (Thornton 1989; Women's Bureau 1987, esp. pp. 50–51). It is also possible that litigation under the Sex Discrimination Act may eventually yield results more favorable to comparable worth than the Commission's 1986 decision (Innes 1986).[26] For the moment, however, substantial extension of the boundaries of the 1972 EPEV decision—e.g., large-scale revaluation of women's jobs, or adoption of an explicit comparable worth standard—seems unlikely.

6.2 *Effects of Equal Pay for Work of Equal Value: Previous Research*

Although Australian proponents of comparable worth feel – not without reason, as the preceding discussion indicates – that Australia's version of comparable worth has fallen well short of its potential, it should be noted that even the relatively mild "equal pay for work of equal value" (EPEV) policy may have had important effects on both wages and employment. This section is concerned with previous research on the effects of EPEV; the next section presents new results on those effects.

Comparable worth and "equal pay for work of equal value"

In view of the comments in the Commission's 1986 Nurses decision, the first order of business in analyzing the effects of EPEV is to note that, the Commission's assertions notwithstanding, EPEV, and more generally the Australian system of work valuation, is indeed a form of comparable worth. To be sure, work value determinations are generally conducted within the occupational and industrial boundaries set by awards; this diverges from the ideal of comparable worth proponents, but leaves the central principles of comparable worth essentially intact.[27] Moreover, comparisons across occupational and industrial boundaries in Australia, although not the norm, are not unheard of; for example, journalists and professional engineers have compared their work to that of professionals covered by other awards. Finally, and perhaps most important, Australian work value determinations generally *include* the same factors typically considered in most comparable worth job evaluations in the U.S. (skill, effort, responsibility and working conditions) and generally *exclude* the same factors that are usually excluded from consideration in comparable worth job evaluations in the U.S. (i.e., market considerations such as the profitability of individual employers).

Hence, as many observers have noted, the Australian system of work valuation – especially after the 1972 EPEV decision – may properly be considered a form of comparable worth. In the U.S., both proponents and opponents have regarded the Australian experience as indicative of the likely effects of introducing comparable worth in the U.S.[28] As one U.S. scholar has put it (Mitchell 1984, p. 133), the 1972 EPEV decision was indeed "roughly equivalent to the 'comparable worth' notion currently under debate in the United States" (see Aaron and Lougy 1986, pp. 40–1, for similar remarks).

Australian observers generally share this view of the similarity of EPEV and comparable worth. In the words of the ACTU (1985, pp. 30, 32), "the essential features of comparable worth or pay equity are relevant to Australia and can be applied here," for "the 1972 Equal Pay Decision embraces the concept of comparable worth or pay equity." Academic observers have generally drawn the same conclusion. For example, Thornton (1981), who argues that implementation of EPEV has been unduly restricted, notes that at least in principle it is quite similar to comparable worth as advocated in the U.S.; likewise, Gregory and Ho (1985), although disagreeing with Thornton as to the magnitude of the effects of EPEV, treat it as a form of comparable worth and argue that Australia's experience is indicative of what would happen if comparable worth were introduced in the U.S. on a large scale.

In sum, there seems to be general agreement in both countries—despite assertions to the contrary in the Commission's 1986 Nurses decision—on the similarity of EPEV and comparable worth. There is much less agreement, however, on the effect of EPEV in Australia and on what it implies about the likely consequences of widespread adoption of comparable worth in the U.S.

Effects on wages

Although EPEV has not fulfilled the expectations of its proponents, did it nevertheless have an effect on the structure of pay?

Although the female/male differential in award rates changed little during the 1960s, it fell appreciably after 1969, and especially after 1972. In 1966, female weighted average minimum (award) rates per week were 71.4 percent of the male figure, and hourly rates were 71.8

percent of the male figure; in 1969, the ratios were 72.1 and 72.7; in 1972, 77.4 and 78.2; in 1975, 91.0 and 91.9; in 1978, 93.1 and 93.9. Nor does this increase in female relative award rates seem to have been offset by a decrease in female relative overaward rates. For example, in 1973, female average hourly earnings were 76.5 percent of the male figure, growing to 82.3 percent by 1975 and 84.0 percent by 1978.[29] Thus, although neither average female award rates nor average female hourly earnings are 100 percent of the male figure, both have certainly grown substantially, relative to those of males, since 1969 or 1972.

Is EPEV responsible for some or all of these changes in women's relative pay? Based on informal inspection of simple time-series plots, several writers seem to think so (see, e.g., Gregory and Duncan 1981, p. 411; Haig 1982, p. 2; Miller 1985, p. 10; and Mitchell 1984, p. 134). This need not necessarily be the case, however; in particular, the increase in relative award rates and average hourly earnings might merely be part of a long-term trend, rather than a phenomenon attributable to EPEV as such.

There appears to be only one formal econometric analysis of wage changes induced by EPEV (Pissarides 1987). In this study, Pissarides (1987; see esp. table 1, p. 13) analyzes quarterly data on the real product wage, w^* (although not explicitly stated, the time period considered is 1966–86). This wage series, w^*, is defined as the natural logarithm of $(1+T)W/P$, where W is the ratio of (i) average weekly earnings per employed person to (ii) a "centred, [five]-period moving ave[r]age" of average weekly hours worked; P is the price of domestic value-added; and T is the rate of employment tax. In the study, w^* is regressed on several variables (the lagged value of w^*, the ratio of labor force to population of working age, the change in inflation, etc.), including an "equal pay dummy" equal to unity for quarters between 1974Q2–1975Q1 and zero otherwise.

Pissarides' results imply that EPEV raised the *general level* of *real wages* (as measured by w^*) by a statistically significant amount, but only for a relatively brief period: "the effect of the policy on the system wore off quickly after 1975 and by the end of 1976 there were no significant effects left" (Pissarides 1987, p. 26; see also table 4, p. 25).

However, the results are less than completely informative about the wage effects of EPEV. First, the "equal pay dummy" for 1974Q2–1975Q1 covers only part of the period during which EPEV was supposedly being implemented. This brief period might best be described a period not of "equal pay" but rather of "wage push," during which the government of the day hoped to raise wages generally, and to raise wages for low-wage groups (including not only women, but also other low-income workers) in particular. Second, whatever they imply about effects on the general level of pay (as measured by the w^* of the analyses), the results provide no evidence on the effect of EPEV on female/male *differentials* in pay.

Thus, although there seems to be general agreement that EPEV narrowed the female/male differential in both award rates and in earnings, this view is based primarily on simple descriptive statistics (which are not adjusted for changes that might have occurred even in the absence of EPEV) rather than on formal econometric analysis. Pissarides' results (1987) suggest that EPEV may have raised the general *level* of wages—albeit only temporarily—but provide no evidence on whether it affected the *relative* wage of women.

Effects on employment

Most analyses of EPEV have been concerned with its effects on employment (including, in particular, female/male employment differentials). These have generally *assumed* that EPEV raised pay (or award rates) of women relative to men, and then have considered the extent to which such an (assumed) increase in women's relative pay would affect their relative employment level.

In general terms, the employment effects of EPEV hinge on whether labor demand elasticities are negative and relatively large. Most analyses of the Australian labor market obtain negative elasticities, but the magnitude of the estimates varies. For example, one study (Bureau of Labor Market Research 1983, esp. pp. 141–148) considered pooled annual time-series data (for 1976–81) on employment and earnings, disaggregated by age and sex, for a cross section of 17 Australian industries. The estimated own-wage demand elasticities are negative and quite large in absolute value: they imply (e.g.) that, with other things (including output) remaining the same, an increase in the wages of adult women by 1 percent would reduce their employment by about 2.25 percent. Taken at face value, these estimates would imply that even modest EPEV-induced increases in the relative pay of women would have substantial adverse effects on women's relative employment.[30]

Bonnell (1987) used the ORANI model (Dixon et al. 1982) to simulate the employment effects of EPEV. Although ORANI provides a wealth of industrial and regional detail, it does not permit explicit disaggregation of employment by sex, so Bonnell was forced to make a number of assumptions in using ORANI to gauge the effects of EPEV on male and female employment. For most industries, her simulations imply relatively modest declines of between five and seven percent in both female and male employment, with the former falling only slightly more than the latter.

Miller's analysis (1985) is much simpler: he regressed relative employment (the ratio of female to male employment) on relative pay (the ratio of female to male wage rates) and a time trend term using annual data for 1960–80. Overall (for both public and private sectors combined), his results imply an elasticity of relative employment with respect to the relative wage that is negligible in size and not statistically significant. However, this aggregate result conceals important differences by sector. For the private sector, his results imply an elasticity of relative employment with respect to the relative wage of −0.39; for the public sector, the elasticity is *positive* and equal to about 1.00. Hence, Miller concludes, "quantity adjustment on the part of public authorities appears [to] have been responsible for the small aggregate disemployment response to the equal pay legislation."

Pissarides' more elaborate analysis (1987) of quarterly data for the aggregate economy for the period 1966–86 obtains a short-run elasticity of *total* employment (of men and women combined) with respect to the (overall) real wage of about −0.23 (t=8.05) (he does not present elasticities for each sex). Combining this estimate with his results on wages (discussed above), Pissarides calculates (1987, table 4, p. 25) that by the second quarter of 1975, EPEV had reduced total employment by about 4.3 percent, but that the effects wore off quickly: his simulations also imply that, by the fourth quarter of 1976, total employment was only 0.6 percent less than would have been the case in the absence of EPEV (or, more precisely, the "wage push" component of EPEV).

Although all of these studies suggest that employment is negatively related to wages (particularly in the private sector), none has featured prominently in discussions of EPEV. The one analysis of EPEV to have attracted attention in the U.S. suggests, as do these other studies, that EPEV reduced women's employment (relative to the levels that would have prevailed in the absence of EPEV). Ironically, however, many discussions of this analysis have generally asserted that it either (1) provided mixed evidence on EPEV or else (2) actually showed that EPEV had negligible effects on women's employment.

The research in question, by Gregory and Duncan (1981), presented two kinds of results: first, simple descriptive statistics showing the raw or unadjusted time series of women's relative employment growth rates and relative unemployment rates before and after EPEV; and, second, regression analyses aimed at isolating the effect of EPEV with other things (business cycle fluctuations and secular trends) held constant.

The simple time series show that women's employment rose (relative to male employment) both before and after EPEV, and that the female unemployment rate fell (relative to the male rate) both before and after EPEV.[31] Gregory and Duncan put heavy emphasis on these simple descriptive statistics both in their original work and in subsequent discussion of their findings. For example, discussing the employment effects of the Equal Pay Cases, Gregory and Duncan (1981) summarized their work as showing that "[s]ubstitution responses to relative wage changes appear to be very small" (p. 426); that "the level of measured female unemployment also appears to be largely unaffected by the change in relative wages [induced by the Equal Pay decisions]" (p. 426); and that, "[s]ince female employment continued to grow faster than male employment after the equal pay decisions, and since these decisions were translated into a large change in relative earnings, there have been very significant changes in income distribution in favor of working females" (p. 427).

Similarly, testifying before a U.S. Equal Employment Opportunity Commission hearing on comparable worth, Gregory summarized the implications of his research with Duncan[32] as follows (Gregory 1980, pp. 613–4):

> In response to such a change in the wages of females, relative to males, [as was induced by the Equal Pay cases,] one would expect some employment consequences. . . . In fact, our history has been, since 1969, up until the last 12 months at least, that employment of females in the market place has continued to grow faster than male employment.
>
> Furthermore, we have found that the unemployment of females relative to males has continued to fall, as it had been doing right throughout the sixties and seventies.

Likewise, in a paper prepared for a 1983 conference, Gregory et al. (1985, p. S306) asserted: "The Australian experience suggests that governments might implement equal pay provisions without serious relative employment effects for women, at least over a period of a decade or so." (See also Gregory et al. 1989; and Hutner 1986, pp. 34–41, quoting a talk given by Duncan on the Gregory-Duncan research.)

Numerous U.S. observers—both proponents of comparable worth, and researchers—apparently found these conclusions, and the simple descriptive statistics on which they were based, to be quite convincing. For example, the National Academy of Sciences/National Research Council report on comparable worth (Treiman and Hartmann, eds. 1981, p. 67, note 10) characterized the Gregory-Duncan findings as follows:

> Gregory and Duncan (1981) investigated the relevance of labor market segmentation theory to Australia's recent efforts to increase the wages of occupations filled mainly by women. They suggest that the wage increases did not negatively affect the number of women employed, in part because many employers of women were suffi-

> ciently insulated from competitive market forces to absorb the higher costs.

Similarly, Eleanor Holmes Norton, former head of the U.S. Equal Employment Opportunity Commission (who chaired the 1980 hearings at which Gregory testified), described the Australian experience in these terms (U.S. Congress, House 1983, p. 44):

> During a 5-year period beginning in 1969, Australia removed explicit differentials for pay based on sex. Using a combination of first equal pay and then comparable pay principles, Australia reduced the pay gap between full-time male and female workers from 58 percent to 77 percent.
>
> There are differences between wage setting in the U.S. and Australia, including wage minimums for all occupations in Australia. But precisely because the Australian action affected the entire economy, it should be studied to see why dislocation and other disruptive economic changes regularly predicted when this subject is discussed here, did not occur there.

(For similar remarks from another U.S. proponent of comparable worth, see Ratner 1980.) The reaction of some researchers in the U.S. was similar. For example, Mitchell (1984, p. 134) summarized the Gregory-Duncan findings[33] for a Brookings Institution survey of the Australian economy as follows:

> Economists are prone to believe that significant changes in relative prices or wages will lead to important changes in resource allocation, and they have struggled to find symptoms of such effects after the equal pay decisions. Yet the gross numbers show that the proportion of women in Australia's labor force and in total employment kept rising in the late 1970's, and that the ratio between unemployment rates for women and those for men did not rise (it fell). Researchers have had to "tease" the data to come up with any signs that the demand for women relative to men was reduced.
>
> Some have noted, for example, that the ratio of female employees to total employees rose about 1.9 percent a year from 1966 to 1970, and that if that rate had been maintained, the ratio should have

> reached a little over 40 percent by 1982. Instead it reached only 36.7 percent [footnote citing Gregory et al. (1985)]. Was the shortfall due to the relative wage effect, or was it due to other factors that slowed down the growth in employment rates for women? . . . Whatever the reasons for the slowdown [in women's relative employment] in Australia, economists no doubt were surprised (disappointed?) that it was not larger.
>
> Some attribute the employment pattern in Australia to change in industrial structure. . . . Others point to the segmented labor markets, arguing that, since men and women are not highly substitutable under current institutional arrangements, changes in their relative wage levels have little impact on their relative rates of employment [footnote citing Eccles (1980) and Gregory and Duncan (1981)]. In any case, the episode is likely to draw considerable foreign interest as word of it spreads.

Unfortunately, however, the simple descriptive evidence presented by Gregory and Duncan (1981) – on which all of these remarks are based – is essentially irrelevant to the question of whether EPEV adversely affected the employment or unemployment of women. By their nature, simple time series trends do not abstract from (rather, they *incorporate*) the host of other factors that might have affected female employment and unemployment, e.g., secular trends and business cycle fluctuations. For example, like most other developed countries, Australia has seen a substantial secular rise in female labor force participation. Thus it would hardly be surprising if female representation in the labor force and in employment continued to rise after EPEV. That this did in fact happen means only that, as a result of *all* the things that occurred during the relevant time period – not only EPEV, but everything else, including cyclical fluctuations and long-run trends – female employment was higher after 1972 than before 1972, relative to male employment. Clearly, however, such simple descriptive statistics are not meaningful evidence on the effects of EPEV per se.[34]

However, Gregory and Duncan not only presented simple descriptive statistics of this sort; they also provided a second kind of evidence on employment and unemployment effects, in the form of a set of regression analyses for the Australian economy and various sectors thereof (e.g., manufacturing). In these analyses, the effects of other factors affecting female employment and unemployment trends – business cycle fluctuations and secular trends – were explicitly taken into account. The results of these analyses present a picture that is quite different from the one suggested by the simple time series. In particular, these analyses indicate that, other things being equal, EPEV reduced women's relative employment growth and increased the female unemployment rate by sizeable amounts.

The first of the Gregory-Duncan regression analyses considered the relative growth of female employment (i.e., the difference between the rates of growth of female and male employment), abstracting from cyclical fluctuations (as proxied by the current and the one-year-lagged value of the adult male unemployment rate) and secular trends (a time trend variable) using annual data for 1948–78. This showed that, other things being equal, an increase in female (relative to male) award rates had negative, statistically significant and rather large effects on female relative employment growth.[35] Only for public authorities and community services was the effect negligible. Gregory and Duncan (1981, pp. 420–1) summarized the implications of their regression results as follows:

> We estimate that over the six years during which equal pay was introduced [i.e., 1973–78] and the average growth rate of female employment was about 3 percentage points greater than male employment, the change in relative wages reduced the growth rate of female employment compared to male employment by 1.5 percent per annum.

In other words, the regression results indicate that the increase in relative award rates associated with EPEV reduced the relative growth rate of female employment from 4.5 percent per annum to 3.0 percent per annum, i.e., by one-third of the figure that would have otherwise obtained.

Gregory and Duncan also performed a regression analysis of the female unemployment rate (1981, pp. 424–5) using quarterly data for

1964–1979. Its implications are essentially similar to those of their analyses of relative employment growth: the increase in relative award rates associated with EPEV raised the unemployment rate of women by about 0.5 of a percentage point (the actual female unemployment rate in August 1976 was 6.2 percent).

In sum, the Gregory-Duncan regression findings indicate that EPEV adversely affected both the rate of relative employment growth for women and the female unemployment rate—that, in the absence of the rise in female award rates (relative to male award rates) associated with the 1972 Equal Pay decision, women's employment would have grown faster relative to men's employment, and female unemployment would have been lower, than was actually the case. Moreover, although these effects were not cataclysmic, they were also far from trivial: a one-third reduction in the female relative employment growth rate, and a one-half of 1 percentage point increase in the female unemployment rate.[36]

A few writers (for example Ehrenberg 1989, and Killingsworth 1985, pp. 105–7) have noted that the implications of the Gregory-Duncan regression analyses are adverse. However, a surprising number of commentators have continued to misinterpret the Gregory-Duncan analyses as indicating only minimal employment consequences of EPEV. For example, Hartmann et al. (1985, p. 14) assert, ". . . some (Ratner 1980; Gregory and Duncan 1981) argue that the policy had no deleterious effects, while others (Killingsworth, [1985]) argue that institution of the policy increased unemployment and decreased job growth for women." Similarly, Dex (1986, p. 897) refers to "disagreement between authors about whether the employment effects [of the Australian experience] are negligible or significant."

A recent paper for the Brookings Institution by Aaron and Lougy (1986, pp. 40–1) exemplifies the widespread failure to interpret the Gregory-Duncan findings correctly. They first quote another Brookings author, Mitchell (1984, p. 134), who relied exclusively on Gregory and Duncan in reaching his conclusion that EPEV had only negligible effects (recall note 33). They then declare (Aaron and Lougy 1986, p. 41): "In contrast, Robert Gregory and Robert Duncan estimated that the Australian experiment with pay equalization had a perceptible impact on the growth of female employment and on the female unemployment rate."

6.3 *Effects of Equal Pay for Work of Equal Value: New Results*

I now present new estimates of the wage and employment effects of EPEV. The framework used in the analyses is similar to that used in chapters 4 (for Minnesota) and 5 (for San José): I first analyze the effect of EPEV on wages, and then consider the relation between wages and employment.

Ideally, one would proceed by considering, first, the impact of EPEV on *award rates* (since it is award rates, not actual wage rates, that the Commission affects directly); then, the relation between award rates and actual wage rates (which are affected by overaward payments as well as awards per se); and, finally, the relation between wage rates and employment. Unfortunately, the available data do not permit a three-part analysis of this kind: quarterly data on actual wage rates by sex are available only from the mid-1970s onward, i. e., after adoption of both EPEV and EPEW. Wage data by sex are available on an annual basis for a longer period, but using annual data (and moving the start of the analysis back to, e.g., the 1950s) would reduce sample sizes and raise questions (essentially unresolveable with annual data) about whether relationships prevailing in much earlier periods can reasonably be assumed to have continued through the 1970s and 1980s. Accordingly, the analyses discussed below use quarterly data, and consist of two rather than three steps: I first consider the relation between EPEV (and EPEW) and award rates, and then consider the relation between award rates and employment. In effect, the second of these is a reduced-form version of the latter two steps of the three-step analysis outlined above.

The data considered in chapters 4–5 were microeconomic panel data; in contrast, the data analyzed in this chapter consist of conventional macroeconomic time-series. Developing a formal model of the Australian macroeconomy is well beyond the scope of this chapter. Instead, I adopt the ARMA (autoregressive and moving average) approach used by many other researchers. As Ashenfelter and Card (1982, esp. pp. 761–762) note, numerous alternative models of the labor market generate ARMA representations of the data, and relatively low-order ARMA specifications seem capable of representing most of the dynamics of macroeconomic labor markets in a satisfactory but parsimonious manner.

One feature of the ARMA process is particularly important in what follows. To illustrate, consider a simple ARMA process with no moving average ("MA") component, an AR(2) or second-order autoregression:

$$y_t = b_1 y_{t-1} + b_2 y_{t-2} + e_t \tag{6.1}$$

where y is a variable of interest, the b are coefficients, e is a random term uncorrelated with the y or its own prior values ("white noise"), and t subscripts index time. Let $y_{t-1} = y_{t-2} = 1$ for $t=3$ and (to simplify) $e_t = 0$ for *all* t. Then, by (6.1), the value of y "today" ($t=3$) is $y_3 = (b_1 + b_2)$. Likewise, by (6.1) and the assumption that $e_t = 0$ for all t, *next* period's value of y, y_4, is given by

$$y_4 = b_1 y_3 + b_2 y_2 = b_1(b_1 + b_2) + b_2 \tag{6.2}$$

That is, today's value of y, y_3, becomes tomorrow's *lagged* value of y, which in part determines tomorrow's value of y, y_4.

Data

Table 6.1 summarizes the variables used in the analyses, and indicates the source for each. In brief, the analyses use quarterly data starting in August 1967 and ending in August 1982. Employment data refer to February, May, August and November of each year, and so I use award rate data for the same months. My choice of starting date is dictated by the fact that August 1967 is the first date for which monthly data for women's award rates are available. The series for award rates for both men and women were reweighted after August 1982, so that is the last date covered by the analyses.[37] It should be noted that the award rates series includes not only Commission awards as such, but also so-called "consent awards" negotiated by unions and employers to which the Commission consents at the behest of the parties.

As indicated in table 6.1, the award rates of pay used in these analyses are weekly award rates in current Australian dollars, i.e., weighted average minimum weekly rates payable for a full week's work (excluding overtime). The labor demanded at these award rates might most appropriately be measured by employment of full-time, private-sector wage and salary employees, but published data for this do not appear to be available. Instead, I consider two different series on employment: (1) total full-time employment (including government employment); and (2) private-sector (i.e., nongovernment) wage and salary employment (exclusive of employers, the self-employed and household employees, but including part-time workers).

The effect of EPEV on relative award rates

Table 6.2 presents the results on relative award rates. For present purposes, the analysis of relative award rates (LNRWAGE) is primarily concerned with whether the Commission's 1969 equal pay for equal work (EPEW) and/or 1972 equal pay for work of equal value (EPEV) decisions had an independent effect on relative award rates, over and beyond what might have been expected on the basis of secular trends, cyclical and seasonal factors, etc. In effect, the task here is to model the Commission's behavior.

As shown in table 6.2, the model of relative award rates is a simple one: LNRWAGE as of quarter t is specified as a fourth-order autoregression (AR(4)) with additional variables: a quadratic in time, seasonal dummies, and several "policy variables." In addition to equal pay variables (described presently), these policy variables include dummies for two periods: one during 1975 Q2–1980 Q4, when the Commission attempted to increase award rates in line with changes in consumer prices, WGINDEX; and the other during 1981 Q1–1982 Q4, when "all attempts to restrain wage growth were abandoned" (Pissarides 1987, p. 20), WG_FREE.

Similarly, I use dummy variables to represent the EPEW and EPEV

Table 6.1 Variables Used in the Analyses

Name	Description	Value as of 02/73	Value as of 02/79
DEQUALVA	EPEV dummy, =1 during 02/73–08/75	1	0
EQUALVAL	EPEV dummy, =1 on or after 02/73	1	1
POSTEV	EPEV dummy, =1 on or after 11/75	0	1
DEQUALPA	EPEW dummy, =1 during 11/69–02/72	0	0
EQUALPAY	EPEW dummy, =1 on or after 11/69	1	1
WGINDEX	"wage indexation" dummy, =1 during 05/75–11/80	0	0
WG_FREE	"no wage restraint" dummy, =1 during 02/81–11/82	0	0
$WAGE_s$	weighted average minimum weekly award rate payable for a full week's work (excluding overtime), all industry groups, sex group s ($s = f$ or m, for female or male), in current Australian dollars (*source:* see Note 2 below)		
	female:	52.83	149.16
	male:	68.72	160.90
LNRWAGE	log of ($WAGE_f/WAGE_m$)	−0.2630	−0.0758
$EMPL_s$	employed persons of sex s ($=f$ or m, for female or male), in thousands (*source:* see Note 4 below)		
	private wage/salary earners: female:	1251.6	1314.8
	male:	2201.9	2138.4
	all full-time workers: female:	1387.6	1426.0
	male:	3679.4	3723.4
LNREMPL	log of ($EMPL_f/EMPL_m$)		
	private wage/salary earners:	−0.5649	−0.4864
	all full-time workers:	−0.9752	−0.9598
LNQRATI	log of Tobin's q ratio (*source:* Reserve Bank of Australia 1986, table 1)	0.1989	−0.4463
LNPEXPO	log of implicit price deflator (1979–80=100) for exports of goods and services (*source:* Australian Bureau of Statistics, 1987a, table 17; 1987b, table 44)	3.7635	4.4224
LNP_GDP	log of implicit price deflator (1979–80=100) for gross domestic product (*source:* Australian Bureau of Statistics 1987a, table 17; 1987b, table 44)	3.8022	4.5120
REALGDP	gross domestic product at average 1979–80 prices (*source:* Australian Bureau of Statistics 1987a, table 7; 1987b, table 36)	24388	29704

Table 6.1 (*continued*)

Name	Description	Value as of	
		02/73	**02/79**
DEVLRGD	residual from regression of log of REALGDP on a quadratic in time, 08/66–11/84	−0.0179	−0.0148
TIMEVAR	time trend (increases by 1.0 per year: 01/70=0)	3.0833	9.0833
TIME_SQ	square of TIMEVAR	9.5067	82.5063
MONTH02	seasonal dummy: =1 if during February (reference=November)	1	1
MONTH05	seasonal dummy: =1 if during May (reference=November)	0	0
MONTH08	seasonal dummy: =1 if during August (reference=November)	0	0

NOTES:

1. Numeric suffixes for LNRWAGE, LNREMPL, LNP_GDP, LNQRATI, LNPEXPO and DEVLRGD denote lagged values of these variables (e.g., LNRWAGE3 denotes the three-quarter-lagged value of LNRWAGE).
2. Figures for $WAGE_s$, LNRWAGE, $EMPL_s$ and LNREMPL are for February, May, July, August and November of each year. Figures for LNQRATI, LNPEXPO, LNP_GDP, REALGDP and DEVLRGD are available only for March, June, September and December of each year; they are treated as figures for February, May, August and November of the same year, respectively.
3. Sources for $WAGE_s$:
   08/67–05/68: Commonwealth Bureau of Census and Statistics, *Wage Rates Indexes June 1965 to June 1968* (Ref. No. 6.21)
   08/68–05/72: Commonwealth Bureau of Census and Statistics, *Wage Rates Indexes June 1968 to June 1972* (Ref. No. 6.33)
   08/72–05/76: Australian Bureau of Statistics, *Wage Rates and Earnings June 1976* (Ref. No. 6.16)
   08/76–08/82: Australian Bureau of Statistics, *Wage Rates Australia*, monthly issues (Cat. No. 6312.0)
4. Sources for $EMPL_s$:
   private wage/salary earners: Australian Bureau of Statistics, *Civilian Employees Australia, July 1979*, Table 1 (08/67–05/79) (Cat. No. 6213.0)
   all full-time employees: Australian Bureau of Statistics, *The Labour Force Australia, Historical Summary 1966 to 1984* (08/67–08/82) (Cat. No. 6204.0)

Table 6.2 Regressions for Full-time Relative Award Rate (dep. var. = LNRWAGE; *t* in parentheses)

	(1)	(2)	(3)	(4)	(5)	(6)
DEQUALVA	0.0214	0.0167			0.0175	0.0074
	(3.425)	(2.372)			(1.853)	(0.757)
EQUALVAL			0.0205	0.0115		
			(2.219)	(1.161)		
POSTEV					−0.0090	−0.0216
					(0.554)	(1.332)
DEQUALPA	0.0023	−0.0032			0.0017	−0.0050
	(0.386)	(0.519)			(0.287)	(0.802)
EQUALPAY			−0.0073	−0.0101		
			(0.659)	(0.938)		
WGINDEX	0.0251	0.0199	0.0201	0.0146	0.0255	0.0212
	(1.936)	(1.489)	(1.529)	(1.054)	(1.944)	(1.594)
WG_FREE	0.0207	0.0255	0.0194	0.0229	0.0209	0.0274
	(1.252)	(1.529)	(1.121)	(1.314)	(1.249)	(1.657)
LNRWAGE1	0.4396	0.1921	0.4729	0.2308	0.4345	0.1409
	(3.140)	(1.121)	(3.211)	(1.287)	(3.072)	(0.809)
LNRWAGE2	0.5999	0.4085	0.5431	0.3700	0.6066	0.4003
	(3.874)	(2.358)	(3.356)	(2.082)	(3.874)	(2.332)
LNRWAGE3	0.0199	−0.0558	−0.0310	−0.0930	0.0353	−0.0149
	(0.122)	(0.344)	(0.180)	(0.553)	(0.211)	(0.092)
LNRWAGE4	−0.2857	−0.3716	−0.3307	−0.3360	−0.2701	−0.3598
	(2.114)	(2.451)	(2.308)	(2.110)	(1.942)	(2.393)
LNP_GDP1		0.1787		0.1690		0.2301
		(1.087)		(0.955)		(1.375)
LNP_GDP2		0.1238		0.1741		0.1189
		(0.626)		(0.847)		(0.607)
LNP_GDP3		0.1082		0.1491		0.0700
		(0.529)		(0.695)		(0.343)
LNP_GDP4		−0.0420		−0.1733		0.0004
		(0.268)		(1.128)		(0.003)
TIMEVAR	0.0044	−0.0003	0.0091	0.0051	0.0043	−0.0012
	(1.125)	(0.090)	(1.616)	(0.879)	(1.105)	(0.284)
TIME_SQ	−0.0001	−0.0018	−0.0004	−0.0019	−0.0001	−0.0020
	(0.601)	(2.792)	(1.322)	(2.784)	(0.564)	(3.051)
MONTH02	0.0005	0.0002	0.0005	0.0005	0.0006	0.0002
	(0.123)	(0.052)	(0.114)	(0.114)	(0.153)	(0.059)
MONTH05	−0.0007	−0.0018	−0.0004	−0.0018	−0.0008	−0.0019
	(0.173)	(0.427)	(0.096)	(0.409)	(0.185)	(0.457)
MONTH08	−0.0003	0.0005	0.0004	0.0012	−0.0005	0.0001
	(0.076)	(0.121)	(0.091)	(0.265)	(0.128)	(0.032)
Intercept	−0.0689	−1.5808	−0.1029	−1.4022	−0.0580	−1.7640
	(1.998)	(2.821)	(2.706)	(2.516)	(1.450)	(3.086)
R^2	0.9902	0.9919	0.9891	0.9911	0.9903	0.9923
D-W	2.0374	2.0921	2.0637	2.1427	1.9982	2.0240
L-B	9.01	4.39	4.24	2.35	9.76	4.98
	(0.173)	(0.624)	(0.644)	(0.885)	(0.135)	(0.547)

decisions. These dummy variables are of two kinds. One set of dummy variables, DEQUALPA and DEQUALVA, respectively, equals unity during dates when the relevant policy was *being implemented*. Thus, DEQUALPA (the dummy for EPEW) equals unity between November 1969 and February 1972, and zero otherwise; whereas DEQUALVA (the dummy for EPEV) equals unity between February 1973 and August 1975, and zero otherwise.[38] Note that these dummy variables in effect specify that the equal pay policies were shocks to the system whose *immediate* effects led directly to changes in relative award rates but whose effects at *later* dates, given the assumption of an AR(4) process, operated indirectly, through effects on *lagged* relative award rates.

The second set of dummy variables, EQUALPAY and EQUALVAL, respectively, equals unity for *all* dates *during or after* inception of the relevant policy. Thus, EQUALPAY (for EPEW) equals unity on or after November 1969 and zero otherwise; whereas EQUALVAL (for EPEV) equals unity on or after February 1973 and zero otherwise. Given the assumption of an AR(4) process for relative award rates, use of this second set of dummy variables amounts to an assumption that the equal pay policies *not only* acted as direct shocks to the system at *all* dates, *but also* operated indirectly (at dates subsequent to the policies' inception), via effects on lagged relative award rates.

By how much did EPEW and EPEV affect relative award rates? The first two columns of table 6.2 present results obtained using the first set of equal pay dummy variables, DEQUALPA and DEQUALVA.[39] Regression (1) excludes, whereas regression (2) includes, lagged variables for the price level; the price level variables are not themselves statistically significant, and so, not surprisingly, including them does not materially affect the results. (Similarly, in other regressions, not reported here, none of four lags in the "output fluctuations" variable DEVLRGD is significant when added to regressions like (2), and their inclusion does not change the coefficient on DEQUALVA.) The coefficient on DEQUALVA in regressions (1)–(2) is positive (between about 0.021 and 0.017) and statistically significant at conventional test levels. In contrast, the coefficient on DEQUALPA in regressions (1)–(2) is much smaller and is not significant at any reasonable test level. Thus, the results suggest that EPEV, though *not* EPEW, did in fact raise women's award rates of pay relative to those of men.

As noted previously, however, the coefficients for DEQUALVA tell only part of the story. They indicate the direct effect on the *current* relative award rate with *lagged* relative award rates (LNRWAG01–LNRWAG04) constant. But since today's relative award rate is tomorrow's lagged relative award rate, and since this is an AR(4) process, "turning on" EPEV also affects future relative award rates indirectly, via lagged award rates: the coefficient on DEQUALVA is only the initial effect of EPEV. To determine the long-run effect of EPEV, one must carry the calculations forward into subsequent years.

The column of table 6.3 headed DEQUALVA presents simulations for the effect of EPEV derived using the coefficients for regression (1) of table 6.2. Entries in this column are logarithmic differences (multiplied times 100 for ease of reading) in relative award rates simulated *with* and then *without* the EPEV coefficient, DEQUALVA. Since February 1973 is taken as the first date on which EPEV was operative, and since all lagged relative award rates as of that date were (by assumption) unaffected by EPEV, the entry in the DEQUALVA column of table 6.3 for February 1973 implies an initial increase in relative pay of 2.14 percent attributable to EPEV (=the coefficient on DEQUALVA in regression (1) of table 6.2, 0.0214, times 100). As just noted, however, at all subsequent dates, at least some (and eventually all) lagged relative award rates are affected by EPEV. Hence, entries in the DEQUALVA column of table 6.3 for dates after February 1973 show the logarithmic difference between (1) relative award rates *including* not only the initial EPEV effect – the coefficient on DEQUALVA – but also its longer-run effect, to the extent that it shows up in lagged relative award rates; and (2) relative award rates calculated *without* any initial or longer-run EPEV effect.

The DEQUALVA column of table 6.3 indicates that the eventual effect of EPEV on relative award rates differed from its initial effect (as given by the coefficient on DEQUALVA in regression (1), table 6.2). Between February 1973 and August 1975, EPEV raised women's award rates relative to men's by about 9.9 percentage points. However, this effect wore off rapidly: the estimates imply that, by the end of the period

Table 6.3 Simulations of Award Rate Effects of EPEV

Year	Month	DEQUALVA	EQUALVAL
73	2	2.14224	2.05505
73	5	3.08412	3.02695
73	8	4.78344	4.60276
73	11	6.13846	5.81216
74	2	7.16043	6.53021
74	5	8.18753	7.15638
74	8	8.79377	7.28384
74	11	9.30978	7.26196
75	2	9.62888	7.06396
75	5	9.79740	6.74739
75	8	9.90003	6.44865
75	11	7.76296	6.14880
76	2	6.79711	5.92004
76	5	5.04426	5.76296
76	8	3.62211	5.67252
76	11	2.53655	5.65069
77	2	1.44699	5.67177
77	5	0.78909	5.72464
77	8	0.23081	5.79168
77	11	−0.12095	5.85867
78	2	−0.31237	5.91816
78	5	−0.43075	5.96311
78	8	−0.44515	5.99242
78	11	−0.42582	6.00670
79	2	−0.37364	6.00831
79	5	−0.30557	6.00105
79	8	−0.23983	5.98835
79	11	−0.17457	5.97363
80	2	−0.11998	5.95947
80	5	−0.07497	5.94757
80	8	−0.03991	5.93890
80	11	−0.01504	5.93365
81	2	0.00223	5.93151
81	5	0.01258	5.93185
81	8	0.01797	5.93388
81	11	0.01979	5.93683
82	2	0.01910	5.94002
82	5	0.01703	5.94296
82	8	0.01421	5.94532

DEQUALVA: simulation derived from coefficients for regression (1), table 6.2.

EQUALVAL: simulation derived from coefficients for regression (3), table 6.2.

Each column shows the difference, mutliplied times 100, between (1) the predicted magnitude of LNRWAGE in the presence of EPEV (as measured by the coefficient on either DEQUALVA or EQUALVAL), and (2) its predicted magnitude without EPEV. A positive (negative) entry shows the approximate percentage amount by which EPEV raised (reduced) LNRWAGE as of the indicated date. (See text for details.)

considered (August 1982), the relative award rate was essentially what it would have been in the absence of EPEV.

Regressions (3) and (4) in table 6.2 use the second set of equal pay dummies, EQUALPAY and EQUALVAL (and either exclude or include lagged variables for the price level). Like regressions (1)–(2) in table 6.2, which use the first set of equal pay dummies, regressions (3)–(4) imply that EPEV, though *not* EPEW, did in fact raise women's award rates of pay relative to those of men. However, as shown in the EQUALVAL column of table 6.3, simulation using the coefficients for regression (3) in Table 6.2 implies that EPEV led to a *permanent* increase in the relative award rate of about 5.9 percent, relative to what would otherwise have prevailed.

The contrast between the two sets of results (for DEQUALVA, regression (1), vs. EQUALVAL, regression (3)) in table 6.3 is stark. Which describes the data better? To address this question, consider regressions (5)–(6) in table 6.2. The difference between the DEQUALVA and EQUALVAL specifications of regressions (1) and (3) in table 6.2 is that, in the latter, EPEV is assumed to have a direct effect (in addition to any indirect impact that may occur via lagged relative award rates) at *all* dates after adoption of EPEV; whereas the former specification does not entail this assumption. To test this, one may simply break up the EQUALVAL dummy (which equals unity at all dates on or after February 1973) into two parts: DEQUALVA (which equals unity during February 1973–August 1975) and POSTEV (which equals unity at all dates on or after November 1975). As indicated by the t-ratios for POSTEV in regressions (5) and (6) in table 6.2, the coefficient on POSTEV is not statistically significant at conventional levels: there is no *direct* EPEV effect on relative award rates after August 1975.

In sum, the results in tables 6.2–3 indicate that although EPEV had a sizeable *initial* effect on relative award rates—as much as 9.9 percent, by August 1975—this initial effect wore off fairly quickly. By August 1982, the relative award rate differed little from the level it would have attained in the absence of EPEV. The basic reason for this is implicit in the results for regression (5) of table 6.2: there is no indication that EPEV continued to exert an independent or direct effect on relative award rates after August 1975.[40] Beyond that date, EPEV had only an indirect effect (via lagged values of award rates); and these indirect effects ultimately died out.[41]

These results do not mean that EPEV had no effect at all: although the relative award rate eventually ended up at about the same level it would have attained in the absence of EPEV, EPEV did help it get there sooner than it otherwise would have. On the other hand, the results do not support the notion that EPEV induced a *permanent* increase in the relative award rate. Note the similarity between these results on the absence of any long-run EPEV effect on the *relative female/male award rate* and Pissarides' (1987) findings about the absence of a long-run effect of EPEV (or, more precisely, of the "wage push" segment of the longer EPEV period) on the *general level* of wages.[42]

The effect of EPEV on relative employment

I now consider EPEV's effect on relative female/male employment. Table 6.4 presents three vector autoregressions for each of the two employment series I have considered: private wage and salary earners, and all full-time workers. In the first (regressions (1) and (4)), relative employment (LNREMPL) is specified as an AR(4) process with four lags in wages (LNRWAGE) and prices (LNPEXPO). The second (regressions (2) and (5)) adds four lags in Tobin's q (LNQRATI), treated as a measure of the price of capital services. The third (regressions (3) and (6)) adds four lags in DEVLRGD, used as a measure of fluctuations in real output.

In several respects, the results for the two employment series are quite similar. As measured by the Ljung-Box statistic (see note 39), one cannot reject at any reasonable level the hypothesis that the residuals in the regressions for either series are white noise. The autoregressive component (lagged values of LNREMPL) in both regressions is significant, and there is some indication (particularly for private wage and salary workers) that employment may be less than a fourth order process. As measured by the sum of the coefficients on LNRWAGE, relative wage effects on relative employment levels are negative and

Table 6.4 Regressions for Relative Employment (dep. var. = LNREMPL; *t* in parentheses)

	Private Wage/Salary Earners			All Fulltime Workers		
	(1)	(2)	(3)	(4)	(5)	(6)
LNRWAGE1	−0.1266	−0.1990	−0.1884	−0.2132	−0.3110	−0.2818
	(0.803)	(1.078)	(0.900)	(1.625)	(2.189)	(2.262)
LNRWAGE2	0.0146	0.0779	0.0735	−0.0060	−0.0331	−0.1104
	(0.089)	(0.442)	(0.369)	(0.039)	(0.206)	(0.769)
LNRWAGE3	−0.2020	−0.2025	−0.2093	−0.0034	0.0085	−0.0330
	(1.317)	(1.248)	(1.129)	(0.024)	(0.060)	(0.263)
LNRWAGE4	0.0559	−0.0031	0.0057	−0.1904	−0.2305	−0.0855
	(0.419)	(0.022)	(0.034)	(1.580)	(1.890)	(0.753)
LNREMPL1	0.7995	0.7573	0.7909	0.4160	0.4078	0.3229
	(4.151)	(3.629)	(3.384)	(2.809)	(2.693)	(1.995)
LNREMPL2	−0.1604	−0.1437	−0.2058	−0.0879	−0.1212	0.0176
	(0.592)	(0.508)	(0.627)	(0.562)	(0.769)	(0.120)
LNREMPL3	−0.1662	−0.0988	−0.0490	−0.3274	−0.3715	−0.4544
	(0.609)	(0.348)	(0.154)	(2.020)	(2.317)	(3.256)
LNREMPL4	−0.1560	0.0246	0.0126	0.0178	0.0170	−0.0222
	(0.730)	(0.097)	(0.041)	(0.117)	(0.111)	(0.152)
LNPEXP01	−0.0878	−0.0581	−0.0710	0.0156	0.0531	0.0179
	(1.002)	(0.605)	(0.660)	(0.220)	(0.746)	(0.286)
LNPEXP02	0.2140	0.2089	0.2394	−0.0269	−0.0530	0.0308
	(1.571)	(1.487)	(1.493)	(0.236)	(0.475)	(0.309)
LNPEXP03	−0.0340	−0.0362	−0.0726	−0.0489	−0.0629	−0.1436
	(0.253)	(0.257)	(0.443)	(0.463)	(0.600)	(1.521)
LNPEXP04	0.0434	0.0739	0.0946	0.1088	0.1347	0.1783
	(0.445)	(0.685)	(0.762)	(1.394)	(1.712)	(2.566)
LNQRATI1		0.0332	0.0361		0.0227	0.0353
		(1.030)	(0.795)		(1.254)	(2.066)
LNQRATI2		0.0015	0.0075		−0.0496	−0.0388
		(0.050)	(0.173)		(1.966)	(1.306)
LNQRATI3		0.0350	0.0206		0.0043	−0.0281
		(1.034)	(0.469)		(0.165)	(1.038)
LNQRATI4		−0.0323	−0.0225		−0.0014	0.0073
		(1.091)	(0.581)		(0.069)	(0.359)
DEVLRGD1			0.0458			−0.0549
			(0.226)			(0.486)
DEVLRGD2			−0.1260			−0.1360
			(0.520)			(1.192)
DEVLRGD3			0.1300			0.3372
			(0.594)			(3.252)
DEVLRGD4			−0.0246			0.1688
			(0.110)			(1.519)
TIMEVAR	0.0062	0.0098	0.0099	0.0247	0.0265	0.0243
	(1.456)	(1.898)	(1.093)	(4.080)	(4.434)	(4.367)

Table 6.4 (*continued*)

	Private Wage/Salary Earners			All Fulltime Workers		
	(1)	(2)	(3)	(4)	(5)	(6)
TIME_SQ	−0.0005	−0.0011	−0.0011	−0.0011	−0.0012	−0.0012
	(1.105)	(1.728)	(1.176)	(2.948)	(3.384)	(3.671)
MONTH02	−0.0161	−0.0158	−0.0229	−0.0097	−0.0131	0.0193
	(2.607)	(2.299)	(0.578)	(2.156)	(2.615)	(1.007)
MONTH05	−0.0008	−0.0006	0.0088	−0.0069	−0.0091	0.0175
	(0.140)	(0.093)	(0.200)	(1.325)	(1.689)	(0.745)
MONTH08	−0.0114	−0.0138	−0.0359	−0.0102	−0.0127	−0.0440
	(1.630)	(1.765)	(0.838)	(2.059)	(2.487)	(2.004)
Intercept	−0.9446	−1.0368	−1.0324	−1.3008	−1.5098	−1.6087
	(2.484)	(2.566)	(2.286)	(4.201)	(4.631)	(5.038)
R^2	0.9470	0.9528	0.9545	0.9343	0.9440	0.9635
D-W	1.9945	1.8644	1.9635	2.0908	2.1864	2.2064
L-B	3.43	4.44	5.09	2.93	2.66	4.05
	(0.753)	(0.617)	(0.533)	(0.817)	(0.851)	(0.670)

fairly large;[43] adding variables (LNQRATI, DEVLRGD) raises the absolute magnitude of the estimated wage effects somewhat.

On the other hand, the results for the two series differ in some respects. In a nutshell, most effects seem to be "stronger" for full-time employment: wage effects (as measured by the sum of the coefficients on LNRWAGE) are larger in absolute magnitude and have higher *t*-ratios;[44] the order of the autoregressive process appears to be longer; and the relation to both cyclical fluctuations (DEVLRGD) and Tobin's *q* (LN-QRATI) seems to be stronger. Finally, and perhaps most curious, the two series appear to be related to given sets of variables in rather different ways. For example, as measured by *t*-ratios, full-time employment is relatively strongly related to the one- and four-quarter lagged relative wage, whereas private wage and salary employment is related (at best, rather weakly) to the three-quarter lagged relative wage. Similarly, for private wage and salary employment, only the one-quarter lagged value of employment is significant; whereas, for full-time employment, the one- and three-quarter lagged values of employment are significant at conventional levels but neither the two- nor the four-quarter lagged values even approach significance.

Despite these differences, the results for the two employment series have rather similar implications about the effect of EPEV on employment. This is shown in table 6.5, where I report simulations of the logarithmic difference (multiplied times 100 for ease of reading) in relative employment levels with and without EPEV. These simulations use (1) the wage effects of EPEV shown in the DEQUALVA column of table 6.3; (2) the coefficients on LNRWAGE*n*, $n=1-4$, shown for regressions (2) and (5) in table 6.4; and—because these are AR(4) processes, in which the current employment level becomes the *n*-period-lagged level *n* periods later—(3) the coefficients on LNREMPL*n*, $n=1-4$, for the same regressions.[45] As shown in table 6.5, the effects of EPEV on private wage and salary employment and on all full-time employment were quite similar: a negative (and not insubstantial) initial effect that, however, wore off fairly quickly. The declines in relative (female/male) employment induced by EPEV were greatest as of November 1975 (6.9 percent for private wage and salary workers, 5.2 percent for all full-time workers) but were negligible by the end of 1977. Note that these results on the *relative* employment effects of EPEV resemble Pissarides' (1987) results on the effect of (the "wage push" portion of) EPEV on the *level* of employment, and are about what one would expect on the basis of the findings shown in table 6.2 for EPEV's effects on relative wages.

6.4 *Summary and Conclusions*

These results on the Australian experience with equal pay for work of equal value provide something for everyone. U.S. proponents of comparable worth can take heart from the fact that EPEV had no lasting effects on female/male relative employment. Opponents can emphasize that EPEV's *initial* relative employment effect was adverse and not insubstantial. The finding that EPEV did not induce a permanent improvement in female/male relative award rates will confirm the suspicions of Australian feminists; it may also come as a relief to Australian employers (and perhaps the Commission). Had EPEV been maintained

Table 6.5 Simulations of Employment Effects of EPEV

		Employment	
Year	Month	Private Wage/Salary	All Fulltime
73	5	−0.42637	−0.66637
73	8	−0.76973	−1.30220
73	11	−1.66720	−2.02222
74	2	−2.59005	−2.95490
74	5	−3.58144	−3.58853
74	8	−4.52388	−4.21074
74	11	−5.27787	−4.57971
75	2	−5.90487	−4.84265
75	5	−6.35193	−5.03275
75	8	−6.66418	−5.15027
75	11	−6.86657	−5.23748
76	2	−6.54802	−4.60343
76	5	−6.25355	−3.96045
76	8	−5.35788	−3.20937
76	11	−4.40968	−2.23312
77	2	−3.37831	−1.56161
77	5	−2.38904	−0.90734
77	8	−1.58937	−0.51249
77	11	−0.92060	−0.22721
78	2	−0.43825	−0.01689
78	5	−0.09790	0.11685
78	8	0.12578	0.21550
78	11	0.24860	0.25410
79	2	0.30733	0.24935
79	5	0.31484	0.21866
79	8	0.29213	0.17464
79	11	0.25266	0.13611
80	2	0.20493	0.10313
80	5	0.15758	0.07590
80	8	0.11379	0.05196
80	11	0.07645	0.03011
81	2	0.04647	0.01256
81	5	0.02354	0.00021
81	8	0.00724	−0.00665
81	11	−0.00361	−0.00941
82	2	−0.01005	−0.01005
82	5	−0.01316	−0.00983
82	8	−0.01395	−0.00931

Private wage/salary employment: Simulation derived from coefficients for regression (2), table 6.4, and wage effects of EPEV in DEQUALPA column of table 6.3.

All full-time employment: Simulation derived from coefficients for regression (5), table 6.4, and wage effects of EPEV in DEQUALPA column of table 6.3.

Each column shows the difference for the indicated group, multiplied times 100, between (1) the predicted magnitude of LNREMPL in the presence of EPEV and (2) its predicted magnitude without EPEV. A positive (negative) entry shows the approximate percentage amount by which EPEV raised (reduced) LNREMPL as of the indicated date. (See text for details.)

as a permanent policy, its effects might have been quite different. In the event, however, its long-run wage effects were negligible and so, too, were its long-run employment effects.

The Australian experience also provides some ironic lessons for attempts to implement comparable worth in the U.S. As noted in chapters 4 and 5, the employment effects of comparable worth in Minnesota state employment and San José municipal employment were not particularly large, but that was primarily because its wage effects were also not very large. In long-run terms, the same general remarks apply to the Australian experience.

NOTES

[1] See Hancock (1979a, 1979b) and Perlman (1954) for discussion of the first 50 years' experience with the arbitration system.

[2] Section 51(XXXV). D'Alpuget (1977, p. 112) comments, "This paragraph [and the conciliation and arbitration system that grew out of it] has been the cause of more litigation than any other single provision in the Constitution and has provided the swimming pools and European holidays for generations of constitutional lawyers."

[3] The Conciliation and Arbitration Act has been amended numerous times since its adoption in 1904. The basic structure in effect during 1956–89 was substantially determined by amendments adopted in 1956, which divided the then Court of Conciliation and Arbitration into an Industrial Court and a Conciliation and Arbitration Commission. The Commission was responsible for preventing and settling industrial disputes about pay rates, working conditions, etc., and for issuing decisions – "awards" – on those disputes. The Industrial Court was concerned with interpretation of the Commission's awards, enforcement and control of regulations governing federally registered organizations and the like (breaches of union rules, contested union elections, etc.). This chapter focuses on the Commission and analogous bodies at the state level. For further description of the industrial relations system, see Dabscheck and Niland (1981), Deery and Plowman (1985) and Yerbury and Isaac (1971). In 1989, Parliament adopted new legislation that (among other things) created an Australian Industrial Relations Commission which took over most of the functions of the Conciliation and Arbitration Commission. Since this chapter is concerned with developments up to 1989, references to "the Commission" in the text are concerned with the Conciliation and Arbitrarion Commission rather than its successor.

[4] The Act is supposed to supplement, not supplant, bargaining between union and management (although critics of the arbitration system suggest that its modus operandi virtually ensures that many issues will go more or less directly to the Commission without first having been the subject of serious bargaining). Sections of the Act allow unions and employers to draw up their own procedures for dispute settlement. The Commission may also memorialize, by so-called consent awards and certified agreements, settlements voluntarily reached by the parties covering any and all matters previously in dispute. Finally, as noted below, the Commission only sets wage minima;

most pay rates in excess of these minima ("overaward payments") are decided by the parties, without Commission intervention.

[5] Employer associations such as the Confederation of Australian Industry and union associations such as the Australian Council of Trade Unions may also appear. (In major cases, advocates who nominally appear on behalf of relatively minor industry or union groups are in fact representing all employers, e.g., through the CAI, or all unions, e.g., through the ACTU.) Of course, state and federal government agencies are treated as "employers" in cases involving government workers.

[6] Between the late 1950s and late 1960s the main union advocate was R. J. L. (Bob) Hawke, research officer for (and later president of) the Australian Council of Trade Unions. Hawke had earned a B.Litt. in social studies as a Rhodes Scholar at the University of Oxford (he later received an LL.B., but never become a member of the bar). He is now prime minister of Australia.

[7] Seven shillings per day also turned out to be close to what "reputable" employers—municipal councils and public authorities in particular— were already paying, and had important emotional connotations: it was a "widely prevailing rate in the 1880s," abandoned during the depressed and conflict-ridden 1890s. By adopting it, Higgins could indicate to workers that he was willing to shift the balance of industrial power (Hancock 1979b, p. 131). Technically, Higgins' decision was not a wage award but a determination of whether International Harvester was paying a "fair" wage and was thus entitled to an excise tax rebate under the Excise Tariff Act. (Since Harvester was paying less than seven shillings per day, Higgins denied the rebate.) Although Australia's High Court later struck down the Excise Tariff Act (*The King v. Barger* (1908), 6 *Commonwealth Law Reports* 41), the Harvester decision nevertheless became precedent for awards under the Conciliation and Arbitration Act. Higgins was a major force behind the Constitution's provision for industrial conciliation and had a profound influence on its development; the arbitration system was truly the Eliza Doolittle of the antipodean Henry Higgins. He acquired an international reputation as social philosopher and innovator; the *Harvard Law Review* invited him to contribute several essays (reprinted in Higgins 1922), which, among other things, called for retraining programs and worker participation in industry. Like U.S. progressives such as Brandeis, Higgins was deeply interested in applying sociological and economic analyses to industrial law; for example, several of his decisions quote extensively from the works of Seebohm Rowntree and Beatrice Webb. (However, it seems unlikely that these authorities, especially Mrs. Webb, could have been entirely pleased with all of Higgins' conclusions; see "Female/male differentials," below.)

[8] Pay of some employees under state awards might exceed that of their supervisors who were subject to federal awards—an "anomaly" (Deery and Plowman 1985, p. 303). The Commission defined an inequity as a situation in which "employees performing similar work"—similar "by reference to the nature of the work, the level of skill and responsibility involved and the conditions under which the work is performed," and "truly like with like as to all relevant matters"—were "paid dissimilar rates of pay without good reason" (National Wage Case 1983, MD Print F2900, p. 51).

[9] In industry cases, the national (and, to a lesser extent, the industry's) "capacity to pay" has usually been deemed relevant. However, the Court and its successor, the Commission, have consistently refused to consider "singular profitability"—that is, the profitability of individual firms—in making pay rate awards.

[10] Burton et al. (1987) analyze the operation of the Hay system at a college in South Australia. The informal attempts at work valuation that are more typical of the Australian system have sometimes produced such an impression on commissioners that the process has quite literally come to a halt. In one case, a union representing construction workers sought to demonstrate the dangerous conditions under which its members worked by having an on-site inspection atop a

building under construction. Unknown to union officials, the commissioner conducting the inspection suffered from acrophobia. "Once up top, he [the commissioner] couldn't move," recalls an advisor to the union, "and we had to pry him off the girder he was clutching." In another case, this advisor says, a union sought to dramatize the arduous nature of its members' working conditions. One of the union's more muscular members left his usual duties, went to a stiflingly hot boiler room, stripped to the waist, covered himself with grease and began hammering away at a large anvil. In no time, recalls the advisor, "his torso was gleaming with sweat," at which point union officials led a commissioner through the room as part of an inspection tour. "When he got to the room, the commissioner was awe-struck; like the other commissioner, this one simply couldn't move. We finally had to drag him from the room before our man passed out from the unaccustomed exertion."

[11] For some members of the Commission, adoption of the total wage was less a cause than a consequence of the push for equal pay. One commissioner later said that "we needed total wage to get equal pay," even though many unionists attacked the total wage as likely to lead to greater control over wage growth (D'Alpuget 1977, p. 228).

[12] The previous year, the Commission's Cattle Station Industry (Northern Territory) Case had abolished separate rates for Aborigines, declaring, "There must be one industrial law, similarly applied, to all Australians, Aboriginal or not" (113 *CAR*, p. 669).

[13] The Commission's President, Sir Richard Kirby, had been on the bench in the 1966 case on Aborgines (see note 11) and in the 1967 National Wage Case that called upon the unions, employers and government to consider the issue of equal pay. Kirby later said he "felt really pugnacious" about the equal pay issue and "wanted to have it treated in a similar way to the Aboriginal Stockmen. . . . I was particularly keen to be on the case because I knew that my closest buddy in the commission, Mr. Justice [John] Moore, did not quite think the way I did . . . in the way he looked at the technicalities of a case. . . ." As it turned out, Kirby was unable to take part in the case for health reasons. A presidential member of the Commission later remarked that, had he been able to take part, Kirby "could have persuaded Moore to go along with him," to make a "leap in judgement . . . and go straight to the heart of the issue, disregarding technical obfuscations" (D'Alpuget 1977, pp. 230–1).

[14] That times had indeed changed is illustrated by a sidelight to the 1969 and 1972 decisions. In 1969, as lead advocate for employers in his capacity as counsel for the Meat and Allied Trades Federation, James Robinson had argued against equal pay for equal work. In 1972, as a Deputy President of the Commission, Robinson concluded with his fellow judges that the 1969 decision was too narrow and should be enlarged to require equal pay for work of equal value.

[15] In 1974, two further developments put the finishing touches on equal pay for work of equal value. First, the Commission awarded a single national minimum wage applicable to men and women alike (the first national minimum wage had been introduced in 1966 as a minimum for adult males); see National Wage Case 1974 (157 *CAR*, p. 299). Second, Australia ratified ILO Convention No. 100, advocating "equal pay for work of equal value."

[16] As we have seen, neither the distinction nor the Commission's reliance on the former, rather than the latter, concept in this first 1972 comparable worth decision was in any way novel (recall note 9). As we shall soon see, however, the Commission was to apply this language in an important 1986 comparable worth decision in a novel way.

[17] This represents all awards indexed as "equal pay cases" or "female rates cases." As Short (1986, pp. 324–325) notes, the true number of cases involving equal pay is undoubtedly larger than 53, because (1) awards that, *inter alia*, make equal pay adjustments are not always identified as such, (2) some cases that may have raised equal pay issues are still to be decided; and (3) some awards that may have made equal pay adjustments, including several cases cited in the 1972 equal

pay decision itself (!), have either not yet been published or else not been properly indexed. On the other hand, the figure of 53 equal pay awards contains an element of double counting: in several instances, the same case generated several awards (making technical corrections and the like to an initial award).

[18] This view has been expressed to me by numerous academics, civil servants and union officials. For a published example of this view, see Brereton (1986), who suggests that the ACTU may have felt that aggressive pursuit of EPEV would destroy the bargain it had struck with the government limiting aggregate pay increases.

[19] Whether the relationships between union and employer advocates and the Commission's justices are as sinister as these remarks suggest, it seems clear that they have been very close. For example, D'Alpuget (1977, pp. 194–5) describes the association between Commission president Sir Richard Kirby (note 12), union advocate Bob Hawke (note 5) and employer advocate James Robinson (note 13) in the following terms: the "intense rivalry in court [between Hawke and Robinson] was matched by an equal camaraderie outside it, which Kirby encouraged. Through a common interest in sport Kirby was able to create a friendly, often playful, atmosphere for the proceedings. Robinson shared his fancy for horseracing and all three men were devoted to cricket. During the summer, notes concealed in legal books which were passed down from the bench to the bar, apparently containing instructions for advocates, contained the latest news on the [cricket] test scores. At other times they were the names of winners at Flemington [Melbourne's racecourse]."

[20] This is the state-level equivalent, in New South Wales, of the federal Commission.

[21] Universities (Equal Pay) Case, Industrial Commission of New South Wales, *Current Review* B130 (September 1980), pp. 528–34.

[22] Barry J. Maddern, who represented the Victorian Chamber of Manufactures before the Commission in the 1972 Equal Pay Case, was Commission president and senior member of the three-judge panel that decided the 1986 Nurses case.

[23] Judge Winner said that comparable worth was "pregnant with the possibility of disrupting the entire economic system of the [U.S.]" (17 *FEP Cases* at p. 907).

[24] Thus, the Commission allowed recourse to the Anomalies Conference only in cases in which rates had not already been adjusted pursuant to the 1972 EPEV decision. Unions may, however, be able to argue that so-called EPEV increases actually awarded to their members were not, in fact, properly determined and that further adjustments are required under the 1972 decision.

[25] U.S. advocates of comparable worth often treat "of equal value to the employer" as synonymous with "of comparable worth." However, as noted in chapter 1, this has simply been a slogan rather than a definition with operational content: in all situations in the U.S. in which comparable worth wage adjustments have been attempted or implemented, "worth" has in fact been defined in terms of skill, effort, responsibility and working conditions – the same basic factors considered in Australian work value assessments.

[26] The Act was adopted in 1984; in the same year, the government issued a Green Paper on Affirmative Action, set up a pilot program on affirmative action and announced that it was considering further antidiscrimination legislation. To date, there has not been enough experience with the workings of the act to permit a meaningful assessment of it, but Deery and Plowman (1985, p. 442) suggest that it has only limited ability to tackle systemic discrimination of the kind often addressed in litigation under Title VII of the U.S. Civil Rights Act.

[27] Recall from chapter 1 that comparable worth advocates have usually urged that all jobs – clerical, managerial, blue-collar, etc. – be evaluated using a common framework. However, when this has not been possible, comparable worth has been implemented piecemeal; for example, in San

José, comparable worth was based on a Haypoint evaluation of nonmanagement jobs only (management jobs had been evaluated, and were kept, on a separate basis).

[28] Proponents who have emphasized the relevance of the Australian experience to the comparable worth debate in the U.S. include the National Academy of Sciences/National Research Council report on comparable worth (Treiman and Hartmann, eds. 1981, p. 67, note 10) and Eleanor Holmes Norton, former head of the U.S. Equal Employment Opportunity Commission (U.S. Congress, House 1983, p. 44). Opponents include Robert E. Williams and Lorence L. Kessler of the National Foundation for the Study of Equal Employment Policy, an employer group (Williams and Kessler 1984, pp. 68–70).

[29] See Short (1986, esp. pp. 320–321) for details. Wilborn (1986, p. 90) quotes Thornton (1981, p. 466) to the effect that "[i]n 1969, when the first equal pay decision was rendered, the formal ratio of female to male wages was 75 percent. In January 1981, the actual ratio was 66.5 percent." Wilborn then concludes that EPEV has "proven to be an ineffective response to the problem" of the female/male pay differential. However, these figures refer to the overall ratio of female to male *weekly earnings* (not wages), which are not adjusted for differences in hours of work. They therefore shed no light on how EPEV affected earnings *per hour of work*, and confound effects on wage rates and effects on hours of work. (However, the figures cited by Wilborn and Thornton do highlight an important discrepancy between the behavior of hourly wages and weekly earnings, which in turn suggests that EPEV may have adversely affected female employment. For further discussion of this issue, see the next section.)

[30] However, the study did not present estimates of EPEV's effects on employment, because it was concerned with changes in the labor market for youths rather than with EPEV as such.

[31] See Gregory and Duncan (1981, figure 1, p. 416, on employment; and figure 2, p. 425, on unemployment).

[32] Gregory's 1980 testimony was concerned with Gregory and Duncan (1981), which, although not published until 1981, was essentially complete by 1979.

[33] Other than Gregory and Duncan (1981), Mitchell cited only two other research studies in his discussion: Eccles (1980) and Gregory et al. (1985). However, neither of these presents any independent evidence on the employment and unemployment effects of the Equal Pay decisions; they merely cite the findings of Gregory and Duncan (1981).

[34] To put the point differently, the unemployment rate of women in Australia more than doubled while the 1972 Equal Pay decision was being implemented (it rose from 2.7 percent in 1973 to 6.2 percent in 1976). On the basis of this simple time-series trend, would it be appropriate to conclude that Equal Pay had a severely adverse effect on women? Only if it is appropriate to ignore all the other factors that might have contributed to the rise in the female unemployment rate.

[35] See Gregory and Duncan (1981, table 3, p. 418). That is, the elasticity of female relative employment growth with respect to female relative award rates (the one-year-lagged difference between the change in female and male award rates) was -0.27 ($t=1.97$) for the "other services" sector, -0.65 ($t=3.54$) for manufacturing and -0.30 ($t=2.96$) for the economy as a whole. In addition to the relative award rate variable, the regressors in each case were the current and lagged adult male unemployment rate and a time trend term. "Employment" was defined as wage and salary earners in civilian employment (and thus did not include employers or household employees).

[36] Because of data limitations, Gregory and Duncan (1981) had to analyze effects in terms of numbers of employed persons rather than in terms of person-hours. Some researchers (e.g., McGavin 1983a, 1983b; Snape 1980) have argued that this may have understated the full effect of

the 1972 Equal Pay decision on employment of women, although Gregory and Duncan (1981, p. 421–2; 1983) disagree.

[37] As indicated in table 6.1, data for private wage and salary earners are available only for August 1967–May 1979, making a total of 48 observations. Data for award rates and full-time employment are available for the entire period (August 1967–August 1982), making a total of 61 observations for each of these two series. Since the regressions in table 6.2 (for the relative award rate) and those in table 6.4 for full-time employment adopt an AR(4) specification, a total of $61-4=57$ observations is used in each of these regressions, with the first referring to August 1968 and the last to August 1982. The regressions in table 6.4 for private wage and salary earners also adopt an AR(4) specification, so here a total of $48-4=44$ observations are used, with the first referring to August 1968 and the last to May 1979.

[38] The 1969 Equal Pay Case, decided in June 1969, called for introduction of EPEW in four stages, from October 1969 to January 1972 (127 *CAR*, p. 1159). The 1972 Equal Pay Case (decided in December 1972) called for introduction of EPEV in three stages, from December 1973 to June 1975 (147 *CAR*, p. 180). Thus, construction of DEQUALPA and DEQUALVA (and their counterparts, EQUALPAY and EQUALVAL, discussed below) in effect assumes a lag of about one quarter between the issuance of each decision and the start of its implementation.

[39] In table 6.2 (and also table 6.4), entries for D-W refer to the Durbin-Watson statistic. Entries for L-B refer to the Ljung-Box (or Q) statistic, defined as $N(N+2)$ times the sum of the first K values of $\hat{p}_i^2/(N-i)$, where N is the number of observations and $\hat{p}_i$ is the ith estimated residual correlation. (See Box and Pierce 1970; Ljung and Box 1978; and Vandaele 1983, esp. pp. 106–109.) Under the hypothesis of no autocorrelation of the residuals, the Q statistic is distributed approximately as Chi-square with K degrees of freedom and provides a test for whether the data generating the autocorrelations are random (white noise). Entries for L-B in Tables 6.2 and 6.4 give the Ljung-Box statistic and, immediately underneath in parentheses, its marginal significance level for $K=6$. For $K=6$ (and also for higher values, e.g., $K=12$ or 24), the hypothesis that the residuals for the regressions in tables 6.2 and 6.4 are white noise can never be rejected at conventional test levels.

[40] The results do not, of course, indicate the *reasons* why EPEV ceased to have an independent effect on relative award rates after about 1975. There are, however, various possibilities: alleged lack of union enthusiasm for EPEV, preoccupation on the part of the Commission with other issues such as inflation control, the qualifications and constraints in the 1972 EPEV decision itself, etc. Note also that the relative award rates series analyzed in the regressions in table 6.2 includes not only awards made by the Commission on its own initiative, but also consent awards negotiated by unions and employers and simply consented to by the Commission: since the mid-1970s, unions and employers may have used consent awards to circumvent EPEV (just as it has been argued that consent awards have been used to evade the Commission's incomes policies).

[41] To see this in intuitive terms, note from the discussion of equations (6.1)–(6.2) that if the coefficients b in an autoregression are fractions (and sum to a fraction), then – in the absence of time trends, innovations such as the e of (6.1), etc. – later values of a series y will tend to be smaller than initial values. The coefficients on lagged values of the relative award rate in table 6.2 are all fractions (some are actually negative), and the results there also imply no "innovations" in relative award rates via EPEV after 1975. Hence, the initial impact of EPEV eventually wears off.

[42] In regressions not reported in table 6.2, I tested for a wage push effect during 1974Q2 –1975Q1 (the period examined by Pissarides 1987) by adding a dummy variable, DWAGPUSH, to regressions (1)–(2) and a dummy variable, WAGEPUSH, to regressions (3)–(4). DWAGPUSH was equal to unity during 1974Q2–1975Q1 and zero otherwise; WAGEPUSH was equal to unity during and after 1974Q2 and zero otherwise. In no case did either DWAGPUSH or WAGEPUSH have a *t*-

ratio in excess of unity. Hence, there is essentially no evidence of a greater effect on relative award rates during the wage push subperiod than there was during the longer EPEV period.

[43] The sum of the coefficients on LNRWAGE in table 6.4 is −0.26, −0.32, −0.31, −0.40, −0.51 and −0.51 in regressions (1)–(6), respectively.

[44] For all fulltime workers, the wage coefficients in table 6.4 for regressions (4)–(6) are jointly significant (as measured by a conventional F test) with marginal significance levels of 0.0103, 0.0071 and 0.0105, respectively. In contrast, F tests for the joint significance of the wage coefficients for regressions (1)–(3) for private wage and salary workers have marginal significance levels of only 0.4233, 0.4058 and 0.5712, respectively.

[45] The specifications underlying the regressions in table 6.4 imply that EPEV affects relative employment via *lagged* relative wages (LNRWAGEn, $n = 1-4$). Since EPEV is assumed to have been "turned on" starting in February 1973, May 1973 is therefore the first date on which EPEV affects relative employment in table 6.5.

7

Summary and Conclusions

To some analysts, comparable worth is a solution in search of a problem. In this view, observed sex differences in pay—even those obtained in careful statistical analyses that take into account sex differences in characteristics such as education and work experience—are measures not of discrimination, but rather of our ignorance. The extent of labor market discrimination is probably seriously overstated by such analyses; properly measured and analyzed, sex differences in pay may even be wholly attributable to factors other than labor market discrimination. In this view, to require equal pay for jobs of comparable worth would be to address a problem that may not exist—and, in any case, would entail serious and unwarranted interference with the workings of the marketplace.

To other analysts, comparable worth is a natural and obvious solution to a serious problem. Empirical studies of sex differences in pay lead inexorably to the conclusion that labor market discrimination accounts for a substantial part of the female/male pay gap—a conclusion that is reinforced by repeated findings that pay of jobs is lower the more "female" they are. It is both natural and appropriate to expect that, in the absence of discrimination, jobs of comparable value would pay the same wages. It is equally natural and appropriate to conclude that it is discriminatory for predominantly female jobs to receive wages that are lower than those paid for predominantly male but comparable jobs. Requiring equal pay for jobs of comparable worth is simply basic fairness. Although it may not be the whole solution to the problem of labor market discrimination, comparable worth is at least part of the answer.

This monograph challenges both views. On the one hand, as noted in chapter 3, the available evidence on sex differences in pay does indeed provide considerable support for the conclusion that discrimination by employers is a problem of substantial magnitude. Not all employers discriminate, and to a considerable extent the observed female/male pay gap is attributable to factors other than discrimination. But careful statistical analyses of the pay gap are virtually unanimous in indicating employer discrimination as a major reason (though hardly the only reason) for sex differences in pay.

In this view, the basic difficulty with comparable worth is that it is an ill-conceived solution to a serious problem. First, the rationale for comparable worth is fallacious. Second, viewed in purely pragmatic terms, comparable worth is a two-edged sword, capable of imposing costs as well as benefits on its intended beneficiaries. Third, in instances in which it has actually been implemented, comparable worth has been "the lion that squeaked": it caused less damage than its opponents feared, precisely—but only—because it did less "good" than its proponents claimed. Finally, alternative policies provide means of addressing employment discrimination that are both more effective and less likely to entail adverse side-effects.

7.1 *Conceptual Fallacies*

The fundamental premise underlying comparable worth is that, in the absence of discrimination, jobs of comparable worth (as measured by a job evaluation) would receive the same wage. As noted in chapter 2, however, this premise is false.

Implicitly or explicitly, proponents of comparable worth assert that job evaluations can determine what wages for different jobs would be (or should be). This is logically equivalent to the notion that one can determine what different fruits would (or should) sell for by performing nutritional evaluations—assessments of their caloric, mineral, vitamin, etc., content.[1]

There is a major irony here. Many proponents and many opponents share a common perception of comparable worth as a novel challenge to orthodox analyses of the way labor markets function. Yet the intellectual roots of comparable worth go directly back to that pillar of orthodoxy, Adam Smith, whose naive version of the theory of compensating wage differentials is the grandparent of comparable worth. As noted in chapter 2, the factors Smith enumerated as bases for compensating wage differentials among jobs—unpleasantness, the cost of acquiring the requisite skills, the degree of "trust which must be reposed," etc.—bear a striking resemblance to latter-day formulations of advocates of comparable worth: skill, effort, responsibility and working conditions.

Thus, Smith argued, for example, that butchering should pay relatively high wages because it is a "brutal and odious business" (or, in modern-day parlance, has undesirable working conditions). The fallacy underlying this argument (and the naive analysis of compensating wage differentials from which it is derived) is a simple one: an assumption that all individuals have identical tastes. If this is not the case—if enough individuals do not mind or even enjoy the work involved in butchering—then, as modern economists have noted, (even) in a nondiscriminatory economy it will be possible to fill all available butchers' jobs without a compensating wage differential for such work (Rees 1976, p. 340).

Just as Smith's discussion of butchers' wages suffers from a fatal flaw, the faith of comparable worth proponents in job evaluation as a tool for detecting discrimination and ensuring "equity" in wages is misplaced. In both cases, the fallacy is the same: unless everyone has the same tastes and job preferences and evaluates job attributes (e.g., skill, effort, responsibility and working conditions) in the same way, neither Adam Smith's notions about what good jobs are nor their modern-day equivalent—the results of a job evaluation—will necessarily provide any useful information about what wage differentials would be, or should be, in the absence of discrimination by employers.

Many comparable worth proponents appear to agree that "[o]nce unequal pay [for jobs of comparable worth] is understood as sex-based wage *discrimination*, even arguments that redress would be costly or might lead to some unemployment won't hold up against the basic issue of fairness and the importance of removing discrimination" (Hartmann 1986, p. 175, emphasis original). However, both the premises and the conclusions in this assertion are untenable. Unequal pay for jobs of comparable worth is not necessarily discriminatory. Requiring equal pay for jobs of comparable worth is not inherently fair, and need not remove discrimination.[2] Moreover, as shown in chapters 3–6, to the extent that comparable worth raises wages (particularly for women), it will indeed have adverse effects on employment (particularly of women) that should certainly be considered seriously.

7.2 *Costs and Benefits of Comparable Worth*

As noted in chapter 3, comparable worth is a two-edged sword. There will certainly be winners from comparable worth; but there will also be losers.

The main purpose of comparable worth is to raise the pay of persons (both women and men) in predominantly female jobs. Precisely to the extent that it suceeds in meeting this objective, however, comparable worth will also raise the cost of employing persons in such jobs. Other things being equal, then, comparable worth will reduce employment in such jobs; but it will not create new opportunities in so-called "nontraditional" jobs. Indeed, to the extent that comparable worth raises overall labor costs, it may also reduce employment in other categories, e.g., predominantly male or "integrated" jobs.

In sum, adopting comparable worth wage increases is akin to levying a tax on employment of persons in predominantly female jobs and then giving the revenues raised under the tax not to the Treasury but, rather, to those fortunate enough to keep their jobs after the tax takes effect. Some workers in predominantly female jobs stand to gain. However, other workers—both in predominantly female jobs and in other (e.g., predominantly male or "integrated") jobs—may lose. To the extent that comparable worth wage increases are not paid for by employment reductions or other wage cuts (relative to levels that would have prevailed otherwise), they will entail higher prices (in the private sector) or higher taxes and/or reductions in other programs (in the public sector).

Table 7.1 Effect of Comparable Worth on Female/Male Relative Pay

Site, Units Studied	Effect	Remarks, Source
Minnesota: actual pay for random samples of female and male employees present during Oct. 1981–April 1986	+9.9%	Cumulative effect of comparable worth adjustments during July 1983–July 1985, table 4.7 ("time trend" model)
San José: rates of pay in predominantly female and predominantly male jobs in Hay job evaluation study	+5.8%	Cumulative effect of seven waves of comparable worth adjustments, July 1981–June 1987, table 5.4, regression (11)
Australia: female and male award rates of pay		
short run (as of August 1975)	+9.9%	Table 6.3 ("DEQUALVA" model)
long run (as of August 1982)	+0.0%	Table 6.3 ("DEQUALVA" model)

7.3 *Actual Implementation*

Although theoretical analysis of the likely consequences of adopting comparable worth can be highly instructive, reviewing the effects of actual adoption of comparable worth can be invaluable. What were the consequences of the "real-life" comparable worth policies adopted in the three "test sites"–Minnesota, San José, Australia–examined in chapters 4–6?

Effects on wages

Table 7.1 summarizes wage effects of comparable worth in the three "test sites" considered. The analysis of each of these sites was concerned with the "other things being equal" effect of comparable worth on pay–that is, with the difference between what pay rates actually were (given the comparable worth adjustments actually implemented) and what pay rates *would have been* had there been no such adjustments, all else (e.g., underlying trends and cyclical fluctuations) remaining the same.

As shown in table 7.1, the results for Minnesota and San José suggest that, other things being equal, the comparable worth adjustments adopted there raised pay of women relative to men by about 9.9 and 5.8 percentage points, respectively. Equivalently, the analyses imply that, had comparable worth not been adopted but provided all else (e.g., trend and cyclical factors) had remained the same, female/male pay gaps in these two sites would be about 9.9 and 5.8 percentage points larger, respectively, than they actually are.

In one sense, these effects are clearly substantial. For example, in San José, between July 1980 and October 1988 the pay gap between predominantly female and predominantly female jobs narrowed by between about 10 and 8.3 percentage points, depending on whether one does or does not control for differences in Haypoint ratings of these jobs (see table 5.3). Thus, the 5.8 percentage point effect attributable to San José's comparable worth wage adjustments constitutes between about 58 and 70 percent of the *total* change in the sex difference in pay that took place over this period. Viewed in these terms, the effect of the Minnesota adjustments is even more striking. Between October 1981 and April 1986, the difference in pay between female and male state employees narrowed by between about 6.2 and 8.0 percentage points, depending on whether one does or does not adjust for the Haypoint ratings of the jobs held by those employees (see table 4.2, dummies and standard regressors specification, with and without Haypoint variables). Thus, the 9.9 percentage point effect attributable to Minnesota's comparable worth wage adjustments *more* than accounts for the change in the sex difference in pay that took place over this period. In other words, in the absence of the adjustments, the sex difference in pay in Minnesota would have been larger in 1986 than it was in 1981, rather than smaller, as was actually the case.

On first consideration, then, it would seem that the San José and Minnesota comparable worth pay adjustments were highly successful, at least as regards wages. However, some caveats are in order. First, the adjustments did not occur all at once. Rather, the wage effects shown in table 7.1 refer to the cumulative impact of the comparable worth adjustments, which took place over a period of years: July 1983–July 1985 in Minnesota; July 1981–June 1987 in San José.

Second, the adjustments did not eliminate all sex differences in pay. For example, in October 1988, the pay difference between female and male jobs in San José was between about 10.2 and 26.1 percent, depending on whether one does or does not adjust for differences in Haypoint ratings of these jobs (see table 5.3). Similarly, in April 1986, the pay difference between female and male employees in Minnesota was between about 4.4 and 16.4 percent, depending on whether one does or does not adjust for Haypoint ratings of the employees' jobs (see table 4.2, dummies specification with standard regressors, either with or without Haypoint variables).

Finally, neither the San José nor the Minnesota comparable worth adjustments actually resulted in "equal pay for jobs of comparable worth." At best, the adjustments made pay for jobs of comparable worth less unequal. For example, in April 1986, women state government employees in Minnesota still earned about 4.4 percent less than men who had similar characteristics (age, years of service, etc.) and were in jobs with the same Haypoint rating (see table 4.2, dummies specification for standard regressors with Haypoints); and pay in all-female jobs was 7.8 percent less than pay in all-male jobs with the same Haypoint rating (see table 4.3, "raw diffs. with Haypoints," results for mean pay). Likewise, in San José as of October 1988, pay in predominantly female jobs was 10.2 percent less than pay in predominantly male jobs with the same working conditions and Haypoint ratings (see table 5.3).

In sum, although the comparable worth pay adjustments in Minnesota and San José were not insubstantial, large sex differences in pay remained even after they were implemented. Viewed as attempts to provide equal pay for jobs of comparable worth, the adjustments were clearly less than complete.

Australia's 1972 equal pay for work of equal value decision provides the most striking example of the incomplete nature of the actual comparable worth adjustments analyzed in this work. Initially, the decision led to an increase in the award rates of women relative to men of almost

10 percentage points (by August 1975). However, after that, the impact wore off rather rapidly. By August 1986, the end of the period covered by the analyses of chapter 6, the wage effect of the 1972 decision was negligible. That is, in the long run, award rates of women relative to men were about at the level they would have been (as a result of trend and cyclical factors) in the absence of the 1972 decision.

Effects on employment

Table 7.2 summarizes employment effects of comparable worth in the three test sites considered. Like the wage analyses, the employment analyses of chapters 4–6 are concerned with the other things being equal effect of comparable worth—that is, with the difference between what employment levels actually were (given the comparable worth adjustments actually implemented) and what employment *would have been* had there been no such adjustments, all else (e.g., underlying trends and cyclical fluctuations) remaining the same. As noted in chapter 3.4, these employment effects can readily be derived by applying the appropriate wage elasticities of employment to the estimated wage effects shown in table 7.1.

As shown in table 7.2, the results for Minnesota and San José suggest that, other things being equal, the comparable worth adjustments adopted there reduced employment in predominantly female jobs relative to predominantly male jobs by about 3.5 and 6.7 percent, respectively. Equivalently, the analyses imply that, had comparable worth not been adopted but provided all else (e.g., trend and cyclical factors) had remained the same, employment in predominantly female jobs relative to predominantly male jobs in these two sites would be about 3.5 and 6.7 percent higher, respectively, than it actually is.

Although the Minnesota and San José comparable worth wage adjustments therefore had a negative effect on employment in predominantly female jobs, it is unlikely that anyone in either site actually lost his or her job as a result of the adjustment. The reason for this is simple. The wage adjustments were phased in over a period of years; their magnitudes were moderate even in cumulative terms, and were more moderate still

Table 7.2 Effect of Comparable Worth on Female/Male Relative Employment

Site, Units Studied	Effect	Remarks, Source
Minnesota: employment in predominantly female and predominantly male jobs	−3.5%	Employment elasticities shown in table 4.8 ("time trend" model for mean ln of wage rate)
San José: Employment in predominantly female and predominantly male jobs	−6.7%	Employment elasticities shown in tables 5.5 (female) and 5.6 (male) for regression model (4)
Australia: employment of women and men		
short run (as of August 1975)		
private wage/salaried workers	−6.9%	Table 6.5 ("DEQUALVA" model)
all fulltime workers	−5.2%	
long run (as of August 1982)		
private wage/salaried workers	−0.0%	Table 6.5 ("DEQUALVA" model)
all fulltime workers	−0.0%	

in any given year. In particular, the increases were small enough so that adverse effects on employment induced by them were offset by the underlying trend in employment growth.

As in the case of the wage effects, Australia provides the most striking example of small employment effects. As shown in table 7.2, the initial employment effects (as of November 1975) of Australia's 1972 equal pay for work of equal value decision were adverse to female employment and rather large, as one would expect in view of the large positive initial wage effect of the policy. However, just as the initial wage effect wore off relatively quickly, so did the employment effect. By the end of the period considered (August 1982), relative female employment was about where it would have been (based on trend and cyclical factors) in the absence of the 1972 decision.

Thus, the adverse employment effects of comparable worth in Australia, San José and Minnesota were small, but only because the effects on wages were also relatively small. Indeed, in all three settings the adverse employment effects induced by comparable worth were small enough to be offset by long-run trends. On balance, female relative employment was higher after the comparable worth adjustments than it was before they were implemented – even though in Minnesota and San José it would have been higher still in the *absence* of the adjustments.

The reverse side of this coin is that, in all three sites, the comparable worth pay adjustments did not result in "equal pay for jobs of comparable worth." The adjustments did make pay for jobs of comparable worth somewhat less unequal. Substantial sex differences in pay remained after the adjustments, however. More vigorous application of the principle of equal pay for jobs of comparable worth will certainly lead to greater increases in women's wages, greater reductions in the female/male pay gap, and greater equality of pay for jobs of comparable worth. However, the cost of these changes will be greater adverse effects on women's employment.

7.4 *Alternatives to Comparable Worth*

Even if it were necessary to choose only between comparable worth and doing nothing about labor market discrimination, the faulty conceptual premises underlying comparable worth and the adverse side effects likely to flow from it should raise serious doubt about its desirability. Yet there are numerous alternatives to comparable worth.

The main alternative is the "old-time religion": equal employment opportunity legislation as embodied in (for example) Title VII of the Civil Rights Act. Unlike comparable worth, which makes it more expensive for any employer (whether discriminatory or not) to employ persons in predominantly female jobs, equal employment opportunity laws make it more expensive for an employer to treat differently men and women who have the same qualifications and job preferences. Unlike comparable worth, which focuses only on pay of predominantly female jobs, equal employment opportunity laws can be used to attack discrimination in any aspect of an employer's practices: hiring, assignment, promotions, transfers, pay, etc.

Another alternative to comparable worth, which to date has received little attention but deserves serious consideration, is application and, if necessary, amendment of the antitrust laws to attack "deliberate underpayment of predominantly female jobs" via anticompetitive arrangements (e.g., collusive wage fixing agreements in the nursing labor market).

As comparable worth proponents quite rightly point out, neither existing antidiscrimination measures nor possible extensions (e.g., use of the antitrust laws) have achieved, or would achieve, quick results: the wheels of justice can often turn exceedingly slowly. But the tacit conclusion – that one can expect comparable worth, however misguided, to achieve results more quickly – is untenable. Some employers, primarily state and local governments, have voluntarily (and relatively quickly) adopted comparable worth wage adjustments. Others, however, have voluntarily (and with equal speed) adopted equal employment opportunity plans and other remedies for discrimination typical of the "old-time religion." Given numerous court rulings that existing law does not require employers to pay workers on the basis of a comparable worth standard, new legislation would have to be enacted before unwilling employers could be compelled to adopt such a standard; and such employers can certainly be expected to oppose such legislation (and to oppose claims made under such legislation, if adopted) with just as much vigor as employers now frequently litigate charges of discrimination brought under existing law.

All things considered, then, adopting comparable worth as a solution to problems of discrimination is akin to adopting prohibition as a solution to the nation's problems with alcohol abuse. Each is addressed to a serious problem, but the costs and difficulties of each are quite substantial – so much so as to warrant adopting other solutions instead. It is unrealistic to expect perfect solutions to the problems of an imperfect world; but however imperfect, some solutions are clearly preferable to others.

NOTES

[1] This is not entirely far-fetched. At congressional hearings some years ago, Nancy D. Perlman of the National Committee on Pay Equity stressed the equivalence of comparable worth and nutritional evaluations of fruit (U.S. Congress, House, 1983, p. 69). It nevertheless seems unlikely that orange-growers would be able to persuade Congress to peg the price of oranges to the price of apples even if these two fruits were found equivalent in a nutritional evaluation.

[2] In a bizarre (but perhaps not entirely unexpected) twist, the city of St. Paul, Minnesota, granted substantial comparable worth wage increases to its police after the state adopted legislation requiring comparable worth in local government. (See Evans and Nelson 1989, esp. p. 156.) Once they learn how to "play the system," other workers in jobs not normally regarded as either underpaid or predominantly female may follow the lead of the St. Paul police.

References

Henry Aaron and Cameran Lougy (1986), *The Comparable Worth Controversy*, Washington, DC: The Brookings Institution.

Mark Aldrich and Robert Buchele (1986), *The Economics of Comparable Worth*, Cambridge, MA: Ballinger.

Orley C. Ashenfelter (1977), "Demand and Supply Functions for State and Local Government Employment: The Effect of Federal Grants on Nonfederal Governmental Wages and Employment," pp. 1–16 in Orley C. Ashenfelter and Wallace E. Oates, eds., *Essays in Labor Market Analysis*, New York: Wiley.

Orley C. Ashenfelter and David Card (1982), "Time Series Representations of Economic Variables and Alternative Models of the Labour Market," *Review of Economic Studies* 49: 761–782.

Orley C. Ashenfelter and John Pencavel (1976), "Estimating the Effects on Cost and Price of the Elimination of Sex Discrimination: The Case of Telephone Rates," pp. 111–124 in Phyllis A. Wallace, ed., *Equal Employment Opportunity and the AT&T Case*, Cambridge, MA: MIT Press.

Australian Bureau of Statistics (1987a), *Historical Series of Estimates of National Income and Expenditure, Australia, September Quarter 1959 to June Quarter 1980 (Supplement to December Quarter 1987 Issue of 5206.0)*, Cat. No. 5207.0, Canberra: Australian Bureau of Statistics.

Australian Bureau of Statistics (1987b), *Quarterly Estimates of National Income and Expenditure, Australia, December Quarter 1987*, Cat. No. 5206.0, Canberra: Australian Bureau of Statistics.

Australian Council of Trade Unions (1985), *Working Women's Charter Implementation Manual No. 2: Equal Pay*. Melbourne: Australian Council of Trade Unions, February 1985.

Jonathan B. Baker and Timothy F. Bresnahan (1985), "The Gains From Merger or Collusion in Product-Differentiated Industries," *Journal of Industrial Economics* 33: 427–444.

James N. Baron and Andrew E. Newman (1989), "Pay the Man: Effects of Demographic Composition on Prescribed Wage Rates in the California Civil Service," Chapter 5 (pp. 107–130) in Michael, Hartmann and O'Farrell, eds.

Richard W. Beatty and James R. Beatty (1984), "Some Problems with Contemporary Job Evaluation Systems," Chapter 4 (pp. 59–79) in Remick, ed.

Gary S. Becker (1964), *Human Capital*, New York: Columbia University Press.

Mary E. Becker (1984), "Comparable Worth in Antidiscrimination Legislation: A Reply to Freed and Polsby [1984]," *University of Chicago Law Review* 51: 1112–1134.

Mary E. Becker (1986), "Barriers Facing Women in the Wage-Labor Market and the Need for Additional Remedies: A Reply to Fischel and Lazear [1986a]," *University of Chicago Law Review* 53: 934–949.

Perry C. Beider, B. Douglas Bernheim, Victor R. Fuchs and John B. Shoven (1988), "Comparable Worth in a General Equilibrium Model of the U.S. Economy," pp. 1–52 in Ronald G. Ehrenberg, ed., *Research in Labor Economics*, Volume 9, Greenwich, CT: JAI Press, Inc.

Jan Bellace (1980), "A Foreign Perspective," pp. 137–172 in Livernash, ed.

Eugene Benge (1946), *Job Evaluation and Merit Rating*, New York: National Foremen's Institute.

Barbara Bergmann (1971), "The Effect on White Incomes of Discrimination in Employment," *Journal of Political Economy* 79: 294–313.

Barbara Bergmann (1985), "The Economic Case for Comparable Worth," pp. 71–85 in Hartmann, ed.

Barbara Bergmann (1988), *The Economic Emergence of Women*, New York: Basic Books.

Barbara Bergmann and Mary Gray (1984), "Economic Models as a Means of Calculating Legal Compensation Claims," Chapter 10 (pp. 155–173) in Remick, ed.

David E. Bloom and Mark R. Killingsworth (1982), "Pay Discrimination and Litigation: The Use of Regression," *Industrial Relations* 21: 318–339.

Ruth G. Blumrosen (1979), "Wage Discrimination, Job Segregation, and Title VII of the Civil Rights Act of 1964," *University of Michigan Journal of Law Reform* 12: 399–502.

Ruth G. Blumrosen (1986), "Remedies for Wage Discrimination," *University of Michigan Journal of Law Reform* 20: 99–161.

Sheila M. Bonnell (1987), "The Effect of Equal Pay for Females on the Composition of Employment in Australia," *Economic Record* 63: 340–351.

Peter Bowers (1985), "The Club: Centre for the Fixes and the Fixers," *The Sydney Morning Herald*, May 25, p. 25.

G. E. P. Box and D. A. Pierce (1970), "Distribution of Residual Autocorrelations in Autoregressive-Integrated Moving Average Time Series Models," *Journal of the American Statistical Association* 65: 1509–1526.

Anne R. Braun (1974), "Compulsory Arbitration as a Form of Incomes Policy: The Australian Case," *International Monetary Fund Staff Papers* 21: 170–216.

David Brereton (1986), "Comparable Worth Concept Rejected," *Legal Service Bulletin* (April): 87–89.

Charles Brown (1982), "The Federal Attack on Labor Market Discrimination: The Mouse That Roared?" pp. 33–68 in Ronald G. Ehrenberg, ed., *Research in Labor Economics*, Vol. 5, Greenwich, CT: JAI Press.

Bureau of Labour Market Research (1983), *Youth Wages, Employment and the Labour Force*, Research Report No. 3, Canberra: Australian Government Publishing Service.

Bureau of National Affairs (1981), *The Comparable Worth Issue*, Washington, DC: Bureau of National Affairs.

Clare Burton, Raven Hag and Gay Thompson (1987), *Women's Worth: Pay Equity and Job Evaluation in Australia*, Canberra: Australian Government Publishing Service.

N. G. Butlin (1959), "Colonial Socialism in Australia," Chapter 2 (pp. 26–78) in H. G. J. Aitken, ed., *The State and Economic Growth*, New York: Social Science Research Council.

Glen G. Cain (1986), "The Economic Analysis of Labor Market Discrimination: A Survey," Chapter 13 (pp. 693–785) in Orley C. Ashenfelter and Richard Layard, eds., *Handbook of Labor Economics*, Volume 1, New York and Amsterdam: North-Holland.

Carin A. Clauss (1986), "Comparable Worth – The Theory, Its Legal Foundation, and the Feasibility of Implementation," *University of Michigan Journal of Law Reform* 20: 7–97.

Commission on the Economic Status of Women, State of Minnesota (1985), *Pay Equity: The Minnesota Experience*, St. Paul, MN: Commission on the Economic Status of Women.

Commission on the Economic Status of Women, State of Minnesota (1986), *Newsletter #104*, St. Paul, MN: Commission on the Economic Status of Women.

Alice Cook (1984), "Developments in Selected States," Chapter 15 (pp. 267–283) in Remick, ed. (1984).

Commission on the Status of Women, State of Illinois (1983), *Pilot Project: A Study of Job Classifications Currently Used by the State of Illinois to Determine if Sex Discrimination Exists in the Classification System*, Springfield, IL: Commission on the Status of Women, State of Illinois (mimeo).

Council on the Economic Status of Women, State of Minnesota (1982), *Pay*

Equity & Public Employment, St. Paul, MN: Council on the Economic Status of Women.

Braham Dabscheck and John Niland (1981), *Industrial Relations in Australia*, Sydney: George Allen & Unwin.

Blanche D'Alpuget (1977), *Mediator: A Biography of Sir Richard Kirby*, Melbourne: Melbourne University Press.

Virginia Dean, Patti Roberts, and Carroll Boone (1984), "Comparable Worth Under Various Federal and State Laws," Chapter 14 (pp. 238–266) in Remick, ed. (1984).

Stephen J. Deery and David H. Plowman (1985), *Australian Industrial Relations* (second ed.), Sydney: McGraw-Hill Book Co.

Department of Finance, State of Minnesota (1979a), *Recommended Job Content Evaluation and Salary Plan for the State of Minnesota*, St. Paul, MN: Department of Finance, State of Minnesota.

Department of Finance, State of Minnesota (1979b), *Public Employment Study: Final Report*, St. Paul, MN: Department of Finance, State of Minnesota.

Eugene J. Devine (1969), "Manpower Shortages in Local Government Employment," *American Economic Review* 59(2): 538–545.

Shirley Dex (1986), review of Hartmann, ed. (1985), *Economic Journal* 96: 897.

Peter B. Dixon, B. R. Parmenter, John Sutton and D. P. Vincent (1982), *ORANI: A Multisectoral Model of the Australian Economy*, Amsterdam and New York: North-Holland.

Sandra Eccles (1980), "Female Employment: Real and Apparent Gains," *Australian Bulletin of Labour* 6: 172–85.

Francis Y. Edgeworth (1922), "Equal Pay to Men and Women for Equal Work," *Economic Journal* 32: 431–457.

Ronald G. Ehrenberg (1989), "Workers' Rights: Rethinking Protective Labor Legislation," Chapter 6 (pp. 137–172) in D. Lee Bawden and Felicity Skidmore, eds., *Rethinking Employment Policy*, Washington, DC: Urban Institute Press, 1989.

Ronald G. Ehrenberg (1989), "The Effects of Comparable Worth: What Have We Learned?" pp. 90–106 in Mark R. Killingsworth and M. Anne Hill, eds., *Comparable Worth: Analyses and Evidence*, Ithaca, NY: ILR Press.

Ronald G. Ehrenberg and Robert S. Smith (1982), *Modern Labor Economics*, Glenview, IL: Scott, Foresman and Company.

Ronald G. Ehrenberg and Robert S. Smith (1987a), "Comparable-Worth Wage Adjustments and Female Employment in the State and Local Sector," *Journal of Labor Economics* 5: 43–62.

Ronald G. Ehrenberg and Robert S. Smith (1987b), "Comparable Worth in the Public Sector," Chapter 10 (pp. 243–288) in David A. Wise, ed., *Public Sector Payrolls*, Chicago: University of Chicago Press.

Paula England and Bahar Norris (1985), "Comparable Worth: A New Doctrine of Sex Discrimination," *Social Science Quarterly* 66: 629–643.

Sara M. Evans and Barbara J. Nelson (1986), "Initiating a Comparable Worth Wage Policy in Minnesota: Notes from the Field," *Policy Studies Review* 5: 849–862.

Sara M. Evans and Barbara J. Nelson (1989), *Wage Justice*, Chicago: University of Chicago Press.

Robert L. Farnquist (1984), "Impact of Pay Equity Adjustments" (memorandum to Mayor and City Council of San José), mimeographed, San José, California: Director of Personnel, City of San José, California.

Robert L. Farnquist, David R. Armstrong and Russell P. Strausbaugh (1983), "Pandora's Worth: The San José Experience," *Public Personnel Management* 12: 358–368.

Marianne A. Ferber (1986), "What Is the Worth of 'Comparable Worth'?" *Journal of Economic Education* 17: 267–282.

Daniel R. Fischel and Edward P. Lazear (1986a), "Comparable Worth and Discrimination in Labor Markets," *University of Chicago Law Review* 53: 891–918.

Daniel R. Fischel and Edward P. Lazear (1986b), "Comparable Worth: A Rejoinder [to Holzhauer 1986 and Becker 1986]," *University of Chicago Law Review* 53: 950–952.

Franklin M. Fisher (1980), "Multiple Regression in Legal Proceedings," *Columbia Law Review* 80: 702–736.

Janet A. Flammang (1986), "Effective Implementation: The Case of Comparable Worth in San José," *Policy Studies Review* 5: 815–37.

Mayer G. Freed and Daniel D. Polsby (1984), "Comparable Worth in the Equal Pay Act," *University of Chicago Law Review* 51: 1078–1111.

Michael E. Gold (1983), *A Dialogue on Comparable Worth*, Ithaca, NY: ILR Press.

R. G. Gregory (1980), testimony before the U.S. Equal Employment Opportunity Commission, pp. 611–25 in U.S. Equal Employment Opportunity Commission, *Hearings Before the United States Equal Employment Opportunity Commission on Job Segregation and Wage Discrimination*, Washington, DC: U.S. Equal Employment Opportunity Commission.

R. G. Gregory, R. Anstie, A. Daly and V. Ho (1989), "Women's Pay in Australia, Great Britain, and the United States: The Role of Laws, Regulations, and Human Capital," Chapter 10 (pp. 222–242) in Michael, Hartmann and O'Farrell, eds.

R. G. Gregory and R. C. Duncan (1981), "Segmented Labor Market Theories and the Australian Experience of Equal Pay for Women," *Journal of Post Keynesian Economics* 3: 403–28.

R. G. Gregory, P. McMahon and B. Whittingham (1985), "Women in the Australian Labor Force: Trends, Causes, and Consequences," *Journal of Labor Economics* 3 (Supplement): S293-S309.

Morley Gunderson and W. Craig Riddell (1988), *Labour Market Economics: Theory, Evidence and Policy in Canada*, second ed., Toronto: McGraw-Hill Ryerson Ltd.

B. D. Haig (1982), "Sex Discrimination in the Reward for Skills and Experience in the Australian Labour Force," *Economic Record* 58: 1–17.

K. J. Hancock (1979a), "The First Half-Century of Australian Wage Policy –Part I," *Journal of Industrial Relations* 21: 1–19.

K. J. Hancock (1979b), "The First Half-Century of Australian Wage Policy –Part II, " *Journal of Industrial Relations* 21: 129–60.

K. J. Hancock (1984), "The Arbitration Tribunals and the Labour Market," Chapter 9 (pp. 182–199) in Richard Blandy and Owen Covick, eds., *Understanding Labour Markets*, Sydney: George Allen & Unwin.

Heidi I. Hartmann (1986), "Pay Equity for Women: Wage Discrimination and the Comparable Worth Controversy," Chapter 14 (pp. 167–186) in Robert K. Fullinwider and Claudia Mills, eds., *The Moral Foundations of Civil Rights*, Totowa, NJ: Rowman & Littlefield.

Heidi I. Hartmann, Patricia A. Roos and Donald J. Treiman (1980), "Strategies for Assessing and Correcting Pay Discrimination: An Empirical Exercise," unpublished staff paper, Committee on Occupational Classification and Analysis, Assembly of Behavioral and Social Sciences, National Research Council, Washington, DC [Published as Donald J. Treiman, Heidi I. Hartmann and Patricia A. Roos, "Assessing Pay Discrimination Using National Data," Chapter 9 (pp. 137–154) in Remick, ed. 1984.]

Heidi Hartmann, Patricia A. Roos and Donald J. Treiman (1985), "An Agenda for Basic Research on Comparable Worth," pp. 3–36 in Hartmann, ed.

Heidi I. Hartmann, ed. (1985), *Comparable Worth: New Directions for Research*, Washington, DC: National Academy Press.

Edward N. Hay and Dale Purves (1951), "The Profile Method of High-Level Job Evaluation," *Personnel*, September, 162–170.

Edward N. Hay and Dale Purves (1954), "A New Method of Job Evaluation: The Guide Chart-Profile Method," *Personnel*, July, 72–80.

Hay Associates (1981), "Client Briefing from the Reward Management Division of Hay Associates on the San Jose, Calif. Strike and the Comparable Worth Issue," Philadelphia: Hay Associates, mimeographed. [Reprinted in Bureau of National Affairs, 1981, pp. 124–7.]

James J. Heckman (1979), "Sample Selection Bias as a Specification Error," *Econometrica* 47: 153–162.

James J. Heckman and Richard Robb (1985), "Alternative Methods for Evaluating the Impact of Interventions," Chapter 4 (pp. 156–246) in James J. Heckman and Burton Singer, eds., *Longitudinal Analysis of Labor Market Data*, Cambridge: Cambridge University Press.

James J. Heckman and Jose Scheinkman (1987), "The Importance of Bundling in a Gorman-Lancaster Model of Earnings," *Review of Economic Studies* 54: 243–256.

Mary Heen (1984), "A Review of Federal Court Decisions Under Title VII of the Civil Rights Act of 1964," Chapter 12 (pp. 197–219) in Remick, ed. (1984).

Richard I. Henderson and Kitty Lewis Clarke (1981), *Job Pay for Job Worth*, Atlanta, GA: College of Business Administration, Georgia State University.

Henry Bournes Higgins (1922), *A New Province for Law and Order*, London: Constable & Co., Ltd.

James D. Holzhauer (1986), "The Economic Possibilities of Comparable Worth," *University of Chicago Law Review* 53: 919–933.

Frances C. Hutner (1986), *Equal Pay for Comparable Worth*, New York: Praeger.

John Hutson (1971), *Six Wage Concepts*, Sydney: Amalgamated Engineering Union.

Jane Innes (1986), "The ACTU's Comparable Worth Test Case," *Legal Services Bulletin* (April): 86–7.

IRRC News for Investors (1988), "Shareholder Activity: Votes Are Strong for Ending Non-equity SA Ties," Vol. 15 (June): 118–126.

IRRC News for Investors (1989a), "Shareholder Activity: New Issues Highlight 1989 Proxy Season," Vol. 16 (February): 22–39.

IRRC News for Investors (1989b), "Shareholder Activity: Support for South Africa Proposals Hits All-Time High," Vol. 16 (June): 110–119.

Eliot Jaques (1964), *Time-span Handbook*, London: Heinemann.

George Johnson and Gary Solon (1986), "Estimates of the Direct Effects of Comparable Worth Policy," *American Economic Review* 76: 117–125.

Rita Mae Kelly and Jane Bayes, eds. (1988), *Comparable Worth, Pay Equity, and Public Policy*, New York and Westport, CT: Greenwood Press.

Clark Kerr and Lloyd H. Fisher (1950), "Effect of Environment and Administration on Job Evaluation," *Harvard Business Review* 28(3): 77–96.

Mark R. Killingsworth (1985), "The Economics of Comparable Worth: Analytical, Empirical, and Policy Questions," pp. 86–115 in Hartmann, ed.

Mark R. Killingsworth (1987), "Heterogeneous Preferences, Compensating

Wage Differentials and Comparable Worth," *Quarterly Journal of Economics* 102: 727–742.

Jan Kmenta (1971), *Elements of Econometrics*, New York: Macmillan.

Cotton M. Lindsay (1980), *Equal Pay for Comparable Work: An Economic Analysis of a New Antidiscrimination Doctrine*, Coral Gables, FL: Law and Economics Center, University of Miami.

E. Robert Livernash, ed. (1984), *Comparable Worth: Issues and Alternatives*, Washington, DC: Equal Employment Advisory Council.

G. M. Ljung and G. E. P. Box (1978), "On a Measure of Lack of Fit in Time Series Models," *Biometrika* 65: 297–303.

Merrill R. Lott (1926), *Wage Scales and Job Evaluation*, New York: Ronald Press.

Burton Malkiel and Judith Malkiel (1973), "Male-Female Pay Differentials in Professional Employment," *American Economic Review* 63: 693–705.

Leslie Zebrowitz McArthur (1985), "Social Judgment Biases in Comparable Worth Analysis," pp. 53–70 in Hartmann, ed.

E. J. McCormick (1979), *Job Analysis: Methods and Applications*, New York: American Management Associations.

E. J. McCormick, P. R. Jeanneret and R. C. Mecham (1972), "A Study of Job Characteristics and Job Dimensions as Based on the Position Analysis Questionnaire (PAQ)," *Journal of Applied Psychology* 56: 347–368.

Robert T. Michael, Heidi I. Hartmann, and Brigid O'Farrell, eds. (1989), *Pay Equity: Empirical Inquiries*, Washington, DC: National Academy Press.

Ann R. Miller, Donald J. Treiman, Pamela S. Cain and Patricia A. Roos, eds. (1980), *Work, Jobs and Occupations: A Critical Review of the Dictionary of Occupational Titles*, Washington, DC: National Academy Press.

Paul Miller (1985), "Female Labour Supply and the Consequences of Equal Pay for Females in Australia: Another Look at the Evidence," unpublished manuscript, Department of Economics, University of Western Ontario, Waterloo, Ontario.

Jacob Mincer (1974), *Schooling, Experience and Earnings*, New York: Columbia University Press.

Daniel J. B. Mitchell (1984), "The Australian Labor Market," pp. 127–94 in Richard E. Caves and Lawrence B. Krause, eds., *The Australian Economy: A View from the North*, Washington, DC: Brookings Institution.

P.C. Molhuysen (1962), "The Professional Engineers' Case," *Australian Economic Papers* 1: 57–78.

Bruce A. Nelson, Edward M. Opton and Thomas E. Wilson (1980), "Wage Discrimination and the 'Comparable Worth' Theory in Perspective," *University of Michigan Journal of Law Reform* 13: 231–301.

New York Times (1984), "Speakes Criticizes Pay Equity Plan," p. 9, October 20.

New York Times (1985a), "U.S. Panel on Civil Rights Rejects Pay Equity Theory," p. A–12, April 12.

New York Times (1985b), "Equal Pay is Not Needed for Jobs of Comparable Worth, U.S. Says," p. A–12, June 18.

New York Times (1986), "Washington State Settles Dispute Over Pay Equity," p. A–15, January 2.

New York Times (1987), "Business and the Law: States Leading on Pay Equity," p. D–2, June 22.

New York Times (1988a), "Excerpts from Jackson's Speech: Pushing Party to Find Common Ground," p. A–18, July 20.

New York Times (1988b), "Excerpts from the Democratic Platform: A 'Revival of Hope,'" p. A–20, July 20.

New York Times (1989a), "A New Ontario Law Matches Women's Wages With Men's," p. A–1, July 27.

New York Times (1989b), "Pay Equity for Women's Jobs Finds Success Outside the Courts," p. 1, October 7.

Winn Newman (1976), "Presentation III," pp. 265–272 in Martha Blaxall and Barbara Reagan, eds., *Women and the Workplace*, Chicago: University of Chicago Press.

Winn Newman and Jeanne M. Vonhof (1981), "'Separate but Equal'–Job Segregation and Pay Equity in the Wake of *Gunther*," *University of Illinois Law Review* 1981: 269–331.

Ronald Oaxaca (1973), "Male-Female Wage Differentials in Urban Labor Markets," *International Economic Review* 14: 693–709.

Walter Y. Oi (1986), "Neglected Women and Other Implications of Comparable Worth," *Contemporary Policy Issues* 4: 21–32.

June O'Neill (1984a), "The Comparable Worth Trap," *The Wall Street Journal*, Op-Ed Page, January 20.

June O'Neill (1984b), "Additional Prepared Statement of June O'Neill," pp. 262–264 in U.S. Congress, House of Representatives, *Federal Pay Equity Act of 1984*, Part 1, Hearings before the Subcommittee on Compensation and Employee Benefits, Committee on Post Office and Civil Service, Serial No. 98–29, Washington, DC: U.S. Government Printing Office.

June O'Neill, Michael Brien and James Cunningham (1989), "Effects of Comparable Worth Policy: Evidence from Washington State," *American Economic Review* 79 (Supplement, May): 305–309.

Peter F. Orazem and J. Peter Mattila (1989), "Comparable Worth and the

Structure of Earnings: The Iowa Case," Chapter 8 (pp. 179–199) in Michael, Hartmann and O'Farrell, eds.

Toby Parcel (1989), "Comparable Worth, Occupational Labor Markets, and Occupational Earnings: Results from the 1980 Census," Chapter 6 (pp. 134–152) in Michael, Hartmann and O'Farrell, eds.

T. T. Paterson and T. M. Husband (1970), "Decision-Making Responsibility: Yardstick for Job Evaluation," *Compensation Review*, Second Quarter, 21–31.

Mark Perlman (1954), *Judges in Industry: A Study of Labour Arbitration in Australia*, Melbourne: Melbourne University Press.

Suzanne M. Perrin (1985), *Comparable Worth and Public Policy: The Case of Pennsylvania*, Labor Relations and Public Policy Series No. 29, Philadelphia: Industrial Research Unit, The Wharton School, University of Pennsylvania.

David Pierson, Karen Shallcross Koziara and Russell Johannesson (1984), "A Policy-Capturing Application in a Union Setting," Chapter 8 (pp. 118–137) in Remick, ed.

Christopher Pissarides (1987), "Real Wages and Unemployment in Australia," Discussion Paper No. 286, Centre for Labour Economics, London School of Economics.

Margaret Power, Christine Wallace, Sue Outhwaite and Stuart Rosewarne (1985), "Women, Work and Labour Market Programs," prepared for Committee of Inquiry into Labour Market Programs, Department of Economics, University of Sydney, Sydney, New South Wales.

John Raisian, Michael Ward and Finis Welch (1985), *Comparable Worth: Issues, Evidence, and Impacts*, Los Angeles, CA: Welch Associates.

John Raisian, Michael Ward and Finis Welch (1988), "Implementing Comparable Worth: Conceptual Issues and Impacts," Chapter 8 (pp. 183–200) in Garth Mangum and Peter Philips, eds., *Three Worlds of Labor Economics*, Armonk, NY: M. E. Sharpe, Inc.

Ronnie Ratner (1980), "Research: Wage Discrimination and Pay Equity," in Nancy D. Perlman and Bruce J. Ennis, eds., *Preliminary Memorandum on Pay Equity: Achieving Equal Pay for Work of Comparable Value*, Center for Women in Government, State University of New York at Albany, Albany, New York.

Albert Rees (1976), "Compensating Wage Differentials," pp. 336–349 in Andrew Skinner and Thomas Wilson, eds., *Essays on Adam Smith*, Oxford: Oxford University Press.

Helen Remick (1984), "Major Issues in *a priori* Applications," Chapter 7 (pp. 99–117) in Remick, ed.

Helen Remick (1988), "Comparable Worth in Washington State," Chapter 14 (pp. 223–236) in Kelly and Bayes, eds.

Helen Remick, ed. (1984), *Comparable Worth and Wage Discrimination*, Philadelphia: Temple University Press.

Reserve Bank of Australia (1986), "Research Report: 'Tobin's q'—Some Updated Data," *Reserve Bank of Australia Bulletin*, pp. B6–B11, June.

John Riley (1974), "Testing the Educational Screening Hypothesis," *Journal of Political Economy* 87 (Supplement): S227–S251.

Jennifer Roback (1986), *A Matter of Choice: A Critique of Comparable Worth by a Skeptical Feminist*, New York: Priority Press Publications.

Patricia Roos (1981), "Sex Stratification in the Workplace: Male-Female Differences in Economic Returns to Occupation," *Social Science Research* 10: 195–224.

Sherwin Rosen (1983), "A Note on Aggregation of Skills and Labor Quality," *Journal of Human Resources* 18: 425–431.

Nina Rothchild (n.d.), "Pay Equity: The Minnesota Experience," mimeographed press release, Department of Employee Relations, State of Minnesota.

Nina Rothchild (1984a), "Overview of Pay Initiatives, 1974–1984," pp. 119–128 in U.S. Commission on Civil Rights, Vol. 1.

Nina Rothchild (1984b), testimony at Consultation on Comparable Worth, pp. 73–86 in U.S. Commission on Civil Rights, Vol. 2.

Nina Rothchild (1985), testimony at hearings, pp. 103–49 in U.S. Congress, House, *Options for Conducting a Pay Equity Study of Federal Pay and Classification Systems*, Serial No. 99–13, Subcommittee on Compensation and Employee Benefits of the Committee on Post Office and Civil Service, Washington, DC: U.S. Government Printing Office.

San José Chamber of Commerce (1983), *Economic Fact Book—1982–1983*, San José, California: San José Chamber of Commerce.

Peter Scherer (1984), "Comment," pp. 131–5 in Mavis Hoy, ed., *Women in the Labour Force: The Proceedings of a Conference*, Canberra: Australian Government Publishing Service.

Donald Schwab (1980), "Job Evaluation and Pay Setting: Concepts and Practices," pp. 49–77 in Livernash, ed.

Donald Schwab (1985), "Job Evaluation Research and Research Needs," pp. 37–52 in Hartmann, ed.

Christine Short (1986), "Equal Pay—What Happened?" *Journal of Industrial Relations* 28: 315–335.

Adam Smith (1776), *The Wealth of Nations* (republished, Edwin Cannan, ed., New York: Modern Library, 1937).

James P. Smith and Michael P. Ward (1984), "Women's Wages and Work in the Twentieth Century," Report R-3119-NICHD, Santa Monica, CA: The Rand Corporation.

Sharon Smith (1977), *Equal Pay in the Public Sector: Fact or Fantasy*, Princeton, NJ: Industrial Relations Section.

Elaine Sorensen (1986), "Implementing Comparable Worth: A Survey of Recent Job Evaluation Studies," *American Economic Review* 76 (Supplement, May): 364–367.

Cynthia Stackhouse (1980), *City of San José: Study of Non-Management Classes*, Philadelphia: Hay Associates (mimeo).

Ronnie Steinberg (1986), "The Debate on Comparable Worth," *New Politics* 1(1): 108–126.

George J. Stigler (1971), "The Theory of Regulation," *Bell Journal of Economics and Management Science* 2: 3–21.

Diana Stone (1985), "Comparable Worth in the Wake of *AFSCME v. State of Washington*," *Berkeley Women's Law Journal* 1: 78–114.

Diana Stone, ed. (1987), *Pay Equity Sourcebook*, San Francisco: Equal Rights Advocates and National Committee on Pay Equity.

The Vice President, Office of the Press Secretary (1988), "Excerpts of Remarks by Vice President George Bush, Annual Convention of the National Fed. of Business and Professional Women's Clubs, Albuquerque, New Mexico, Sunday, July 24, 1988," Office of the Vice President, Washington, DC: mimeographed.

Margaret Thornton (1981), "(Un)equal Pay for Work of Equal Value," *Journal of Industrial Relations* 23: 466–81.

Margaret Thornton (1989), "Pay Equity: An Australian Perspective," unpublished manuscript, School of Law, Macquarie University.

Donald J. Treiman (1979), *Job Evaluation: An Analytic Review*, Washington, DC: National Academy of Sciences.

Donald Treiman and Heidi I. Hartmann, eds. (1981), *Women, Work and Wages: Equal Pay for Jobs of Equal Value*, Washington, DC: National Academy Press.

Urban Research Center, New York University (1987), "Wage Discrimination & Occupational Segregation in New York City's Municipal Work Force: Time for a Change," New York: Urban Research Center, New York University, mimeo.

U.S. Bureau of Labor Statistics (n.d.), "Employment and Wages Public User Files—Draft," Washington, DC: U.S. Bureau of Labor Statistics, mimeo.

U.S. Civil Service Commission (1977), *Instructions for the Factor Evaluation System*, Washington, DC: U.S. Government Printing Office.

U.S. Commission on Civil Rights (1984), *Comparable Worth: Issue for the 80's*, Volumes 1–2, Washington, DC: U.S. Government Printing Office.

U.S. Commission on Civil Rights (1985), *Comparable Worth: An Analysis and Recommendations*, Washington, DC: U.S. Government Printing Office.

U.S. Congress, House (1983), *Pay Equity: Equal Pay for Work of Comparable Value*, Parts I and II, Serial No. 97–53, Committee on Post Office and Civil Service, Subcommittees on Human Resources, Civil Service and Compensation and Employee Benefits, Washington, DC: U.S. Government Printing Office.

U.S. Congress, House (1988), "Federal Equitable Pay Practices Act of 1988," Report 100–914, Committee on Post Office and Civil Service, Washington, DC: U.S. Government Printing Office.

Walter Vandaele (1983), *Applied Time Series and Box-Jenkins Models*, New York: Academic Press.

Wall Street Journal (1985a), "Labor Letter," p. 1, April 16.

Wall Street Journal (1985b), "In Minnesota, 'Pay Equity' Passes Test, but Foes See Trouble Ahead," p. 27, May 10.

Wall Street Journal (1988a), "Labor Letter," p. A–1, June 7.

Wall Street Journal (1988b), "Pay Equity Gets a Tryout in Canada – and U.S. Firms are Watching Closely," p. B–1, December 28.

Washington Post (1985), "Comparable Worth Meeting Resistance," p. A–6, June 11.

Paul Weiler (1986), "The Wages of Sex: The Uses and Limits of Comparable Worth," *Harvard Law Review* 99: 1728–1807.

Finis Welch (1969), "Linear Synthesis of Skill Distributions," *Journal of Human Resources* 4: 311–325.

Finis Welch (1988), "The Comparable Worth Pay Regression," unpublished discussion paper, Los Angeles: Unicon Research Corporation.

Doris M. Werwie (1987), *Sex and Pay in the Federal Government*, New York: Greenwood Press.

Steven L. Willborn (1986), *A Comparable Worth Primer*, Lexington, MA: Lexington Books.

Steven L. Willborn (1989), *A Secretary and a Cook: Challenging Women's Wages in the Courts of the United States and Great Britain*, Ithaca, NY: ILR Press.

Robert E. Williams and Lorence L. Kessler (1984), *A Closer Look at Comparable Worth: A Study of the Basic Questions to be Addressed in Approaching Pay Equity*, Washington, DC: National Foundation for the Study of Equal Employment Policy.

Norman D. Willis and associates (1974), *State of Washington Comparable*

Worth Study, Seattle, WA: Norman D. Willis and associates (reprinted in U.S. Congress, House, 1983).

Norman D. Willis and associates (1976), *State of Washington Comparable Worth Study Phase II*, Seattle, WA: Norman D. Willis and associates (reprinted in U.S. Congress, House, 1983).

Norman D. Willis and associates (1980), *State of Connecticut Objective Job Evaluation Pilot Study*, Seattle, WA: Norman D. Willis and associates.

Women's Bureau, Department of Employment, Education and Training (1987), *Pay Equity: A Survey of 7 OECD Countries*, Information Paper No. 5, Canberra: Australian Government Publishing Service.

Yale Law Journal (1981), "Equal Pay, Comparable Work and Job Evaluation," *Yale Law Journal* 90: 657–680.

Dianne Yerbury and Joseph E. Isaac (1971), "Recent Trends in Collective Bargaining in Australia," *International Labour Review* 103: 421–52.

Arthur Young & Co. (1984), *Study to Establish an Evaluation System for State of Iowa Merit Employment System Classifications on the Basis of Comparable Worth*, Des Moines, IA: mimeo.

Arthur Young & Co. (n.d.), *A Comparable Worth Study of the State of Michigan Job Classifications*, Lansing, MI: mimeo.

INDEX